Childcraft

THE HOW AND WHY LIBRARY

VOLUME 15

Guide to Childcraft

World Book, Inc.

a Scott Fetzer company

Chicago   London   Sydney   Toronto

Childcraft—The How and Why Library
(Reg. U.S. Pat. Off.)

World Book, Inc.
525 West Monroe
Chicago, IL 60606

© 1990, 1989, 1987, 1986, 1985 by World Book, Inc. © 1982, 1981, 1980, 1979 U.S.A. by World Book-Childcraft International, Inc. © 1976, 1974, 1973, 1971, 1970, 1969, 1968, 1965, 1964 U.S.A. by Field Enterprises Educational Corporation.
International Copyright © 1987, 1986, 1985 by World Book, Inc.
International Copyright © 1982, 1981, 1980, 1979 by World Book-Childcraft International, Inc.
International Copyright © 1976, 1974, 1973, 1971, 1970, 1969, 1968, 1965, 1964 by Field Enterprises Educational Corporation.

ISBN 0-7166-0191-5
Library of Congress Catalog Card Number 90-70178
Printed in the United States of America
A/IA

Acknowledgments

The publishers of Childcraft gratefully acknowledge the following artists, photographers, publishers, agencies, and corporations for illustrations in this volume. Page numbers refer to two-page spreads. The words "(left)," "(center)," "(top)," "(bottom)," and "(right)" indicate position on the spread. All illustrations are the exclusive property of the publishers of Childcraft unless names are marked with an asterisk (*).

1: (top left to right) Victoria Beller-Smith, Lawrence Migdale; (bottom left to right) Lawrence Migdale, © Victoria Beller-Smith *
12-13: Phoebe Dunn
14-15: © Lynn Sechler, Healthwise from Custom Medical *
16-17: Susan Perl
18-19: Phoebe Dunn
20-21: Susan Perl
22-24: Phoebe Dunn *
26-27: (left) Victoria Beller-Smith, (right) Phoebe Dunn *
30-35: Phoebe Dunn *
36-37: © Victoria Beller-Smith *
38-39: Phoebe Dunn
40-41: (left) © Peter W. Gonzalez *; © Jim L. Steere, Nawrocki Stock Photo *; (right) Phoebe Dunn *
46-49: Phoebe Dunn
50-51: (left) Phoebe Dunn; (right) Susan Perl
52-55: Phoebe Dunn
58-59: (left) Susan Perl; (right) Phoebe Dunn *
60-61: © Steve Parke, Medichrome *
62-63: Phoebe Dunn
64-65: Victoria Beller-Smith
66-67: © David R. Frazier Photolibrary *
68-69: (left) © Lawrence Migdale *; (right) Phoebe Dunn
70-71: Susan Perl
72-73: (left) Lawrence Migdale; (right) Susan Perl
74-76: Phoebe Dunn
78-79: (left) Lawrence Migdale; (right) Phoebe Dunn
80-85: Phoebe Dunn
86-87: (left) Susan Perl; (right) Phoebe Dunn *
88-94: Phoebe Dunn *
96-97: (left) David Falconer, David R. Frazier Photolibrary *; (right) Susan Perl

98-100: Phoebe Dunn
102-105: Charles Moser
114-115: Larry Frederick
134-137: Data from the National Center for Health Statistics
149-154: Charles Moser
170-171: Julius E. Ginsberg, M.D. *
176-177: Childcraft photo; diagram, Mary Ann Olson
180-181: (left) Lewis Shapiro, M.D. *; (right) Childcraft photo
182-183: photo, Rick White; diagram, Mary Ann Olson
184-185: D.C. Lowe, Medichrome *
186-187: Children's Memorial Hospital, Chicago *
188-189: (top, left to right) Division of Dermatology, University of Arkansas Medical School *, John H. Gerard, NAS *; (center, left to right) William B. Allen, Jr., NAS *, Woodrow Goodpaster, NAS *; (bottom, left to right) Charles Mohr, NAS *, John E. Stonitch, NAS *
190-191: Anthony Ravielli
192-193: (left) Eric V. Gravé *; (right) Shriners' Hospital for Crippled Children *
194-195: (left) Childcraft photo courtesy Bailey N. Jacobson, D.D.S., M.S., and Sheldon W. Rosenstein, D.D.S., M.S.D.; (right) Childcraft photo
196-197: Anthony Ravielli
198-199: (left) Anthony Ravielli; (right) Charles Kallick, M.D.
200-201: Charles Kallick, M.D. *
202-203: Greg King; Kinuko Craft
204-205: John Curtin, M.D. *
206-207: (left) Richard L. Jacobs, M.D.; (right) © Michael Fisher, Custom Medical *
212-213: Charles Kallick, M.D. *
214-215: Victoria Beller-Smith
216-217: Kinuko Craft
218-219: (top) Anthony Ravielli; (bottom) Childcraft photos
220-221: Lowell Stumpf
222-223: © Ray Stott, The Image Works *
224-225: Beltone Electronics *
228-229: Childcraft photo; diagram, Mary Ann Olson
230-231: (left) Lewis Shapiro, M.D. *; (right) Anthony Ravielli
232-233: (left) Larry Mulvehill/Science Source/Photo Researchers *; (right) diagram, Mary Ann Olson
236-237: Victoria Beller-Smith
238-239: Anthony Ravielli
240-241: (left) Charles Kallick, M.D. *; (right) diagram, Mary Ann Olson
242-243: Childcraft photo
244-245: (left) Private medical collection *; (right) Lester V. Bergman & Associates *
246-247: (left) © David R. Frazier Photolibrary *; (right) Eric V. Gravé *
248-249: (left) Lawrence Migdale; (right) Anthony Ravielli
250-251: Childcraft photo
252-253: photo, Rick White; diagram, Mary Ann Olson
258-259: (left) Charles Kallick, M.D. *; (right) Kenrad Nelson, M.D. *
260-261: Lewis Shapiro, M.D. *
262-264: Charles Kallick, M.D. *
266-267: (left) Mary Ann Olson; (right) Lewis Shapiro, M.D. *
268-269: (left) Stuart Markson; (right) Anthony Ravielli
270-272: Childcraft photos
276-277: Hugh Spencer, NAS *
278-279: (top, left to right) Nick Drahos *, Nick Drahos *; (center) John H. Gerard *; (bottom, left to right) John H. Gerard *, Walter Chandoha *
282-283: (left) Childcraft photos; (right) Charles Kallick, M.D. *
286-287: (left) Lewis Shapiro, M.D. *; Private medical collection *; Shriners' Hospital for Crippled Children *
288-289: (left) Kinuko Craft; (right) Childcraft photo
290-291: (left) Childcraft photo; diagram, Mary Ann Olson; (right) Childcraft photo
292-293: © Custom Medical *
294-295: Childcraft photos
296-297: Anthony Ravielli
298-299: Private medical collection *
300-301: (left) Presbyterian—St. Luke's Hospital *; (right) Childcraft photos; diagrams, Mary Ann Olson
302-303: (left) Childcraft photos; diagrams, Mary Ann Olson; (right) Anthony Ravielli
304-305: Lewis Shapiro, M.D. *
306-307: (left) Childcraft photo; diagram, Mary Ann Olson; (right) Charles Kallick, M.D. *
310-311: Lewis Shapiro, M.D. *

Cover: Beverly Pardee

Preface

This volume of *Childcraft* is designed to help you meet the challenge of parenthood. It is divided into four sections: (1) Growth and Development; (2) For Special Consideration; (3) a Medical Guide; and (4) Learning with *Childcraft*.

Growth and Development describes how children develop from birth through the preteen years. This description helps you understand your child and provides guidelines for solving some of the problems that arise at each stage of development.

For Special Consideration deals with subjects that may affect you or your child at any stage in the child's life—choosing a baby sitter, moving, growth, the working mother. It deals with problems of a special nature that, fortunately, touch the lives of only some parents—such as mental retardation, physical handicaps, and drug addiction. Also included are two helpful lists. The first catalogs agencies and organizations that you may want to contact for additional or special help. The other is a collection of books for further reading.

The Medical Guide contains more than 200 articles dealing with a child's health, safety, and well-being. The articles are alphabetically arranged for quick and efficient use. Cross references are included to help you locate information you may have difficulty finding. *See also* entries appear at the end of many articles to lead you to related topics for additional information.

The last section contains suggestions for using *Childcraft* at home and in the classroom.

Obviously, no one person is qualified to give expert advice on all the subjects presented in this volume. For this reason, the editors sought the assistance of more than 40 physicians, psychiatrists, educators, and dentists. The result of their work is a body of information that we feel will give you a good understanding of your child's behavior, and confidence in your abilities to guide your child through the crucial years leading to adulthood.

Volume 15

Guide to *Childcraft*

Contents

Contents

Contributors

A person whose name appears in front of an article either wrote it originally or became responsible for its accuracy by critically reviewing the work of another. In the Medical Guide, articles are followed by the initials of the responsible contributor. A contributor who reviewed and revised or added substantially to an existing article is listed as a consulting editor. This list also includes contributors of photographs to the Medical Guide.

All material in the first three sections of the *Guide to Childcraft* were revised and updated under the direction of Dr. Steven Waskerwitz, Associate Professor of Pediatrics, The Medical College of Pennsylvania; and Director, General Pediatrics, Allegheny General Hospital, Pittsburgh, Pennsylvania.

Section One: Growth and Development

Berson, Minnie P., B.A., M.A., Ed.D.
Professor of Elementary Education and Director,
  Early Childhood Programs
Illinois State University

Blaine, Graham B., Jr., A.B., M.D.
Assistant in Psychiatry, Adolescent Unit
The Children's Hospital Medical Center (Boston)

Diamond, Eugene F., M.D.
Clinical Professor of Pediatrics
Loyola University (Chicago)

Hymes, James L., Jr., A.B., M.A., Ed.D.
Specialist in Early Childhood Education

Kovel, Arthur, M.D.
Director, Section of Adolescent
  Medicine
Allegheny General Hospital (Pittsburgh)

Puczynski, Mark S., M.D.
Associate Professor of Pediatrics
The Medical College of Pennsylvania
Director, Pediatrics
Allegheny General Hospital (Pittsburgh)

Redl, Fritz, Ph.D.
Professor Emeritus, Wayne State University

Salsburey, Donna, M.D.
Assistant Professor of Pediatrics
The Medical College of Pennsylvania (Pittsburgh)

Shaffer, Diane, M. Ed.
Child Development Specialist
Allegheny General Hospital (Pittsburgh)

Sheldon, Steven H., D.O., FAAP
Professor of Pediatrics and Physiology
Chairman, Department of Pediatrics
Chicago College of Osteopathic Medicine

Smith, Lendon H., B.A., M.D.
Author, *The Encyclopedia of Baby & Child Care*

Weinberger, Howard L., M.D.
Professor, Department of Pediatrics
State University of New York
Health Science Center at Syracuse, N.Y.

Section Two: For Special Consideration

Bayley, Nancy, B.S., M.S., Ph.D.
Consulting Psychologist
University of California (Berkeley)

Chess, Stella, M.D.
Professor of Child Psychiatry
New York University School of Medicine

Cone, Thomas E., Jr., B.A., M.D.
Senior Associate of Clinical Genetics
The Children's Hospital Medical Center (Boston);
Clinical Professor of Pediatrics, Harvard Medical
  School

Dittmann, Laura L., B.S., M.A., Ph.D.
Professor, Institute for Child Study
University of Maryland

Freyer, David R., D.O.
Assistant Professor of Pediatrics
Wayne State University College of Medicine

Fosarelli, Patricia, M.D.
Assistant Professor of Pediatrics
Johns Hopkins University

Giesy, Julie, R.N., M.S.N.
Clinical Supervisor, Inpatient Pediatrics
Allegheny General Hospital (Pittsburgh)

Jenkins, Gladys Gardner, B.A., M.A.
Lecturer Emeritus, Department of Home
  Economics
University of Iowa

LeShan, Eda, B.S., M.A.
Contributing Editor, *Woman's Day*
Author, *The Conspiracy Against Childhood; Sex
  and Your Teenager*

Lis, Edward F., B.S., M.D.
Professor, Department of Pediatrics
University of Illinois College of Medicine
Director, Center for Handicapped Children
University of Illinois Hospital

Myklebust, Helmer R., B.A., M.A., Ed.D.
Adjunct Professor of Education
University of Illinois (Chicago)

Prior, Michele, R.N., M.S.N.
Pediatric Clinical Specialist
Allegheny General Hospital (Pittsburgh)

Rotenstein, Deborah, M.D.
Assistant Professor of Pediatrics
The Medical College of Pennsylvania (Pittsburgh)

Schulman, Jerome L., B.A., M.D.
Head, Division of Child Psychiatry
Children's Memorial Hospital (Chicago)

Torrance, E. Paul, A.B., M.A., Ph.D.
Head, Department of Educational Psychology and
    Alumni Foundation Distinguished Professor
University of Georgia

Walters, James, B.A., M.A., Ph.D.
Professor, Child and Family Development
University of Georgia

Walters, Lynda, B.C.E., M.S., Ph.D.
Assistant to the Editor,
    The Family Coordinator

Section Three: Medical Guide

The planning and editing of all articles in the
Medical Guide was supervised by Dr. Don M.
Hoffman, Practicing Pediatrician, Elmhurst Clinic,
Elmhurst, Illinois.

(L.D.) Dalal, Leena, M.D.
Attending Pediatrician
Allegheny General Hospital (Pittsburgh)

(C.F.F.) Ferguson, Charles F., A.B., M.D., FACS
Senior Otolaryngologist (retired)
The Children's Hospital Medical Center (Boston)

(S.G.) Galli, Sharon, M.D.
Assistant Professor of Pediatrics
The Medical College of Pennsylvania (Pittsburgh)

(J.J.G.) Gartland, John J., A.B., M.D.
James Edwards Professor of Orthopaedic
    Surgery and Chairman of the Department
Jefferson Medical College of Thomas Jefferson
    University

(M.G.) Green, Morris, A.B., M.D.
Perry W. Lesh Professor and Chairman,
    Department of Pediatrics
Indiana University School of Medicine;
Physician-in-Chief, James Whitcomb Riley
    Memorial Hospital for Children

(T.M.H.) Holder, Thomas M., M.D.
Chief, Section of Cardiothoracic Surgery,
    Department of Surgery
The Children's Mercy Hospital (Kansas City)

(J.S.H.) Hyde, John S., M.D.
Professor of Pediatrics and Immunology
Rush-Presbyterian-St. Luke's Medical Center

(S.L.K.) Katz, Samuel L., M.D.
Professor and Chairman,
    Department of Pediatrics
Duke University Medical Center

(A.M.M.) Margileth, Andrew M., B.S., B.A., M.D.
Professor and Vice Chairman,
    Department of Pediatrics
Uniformed Services University of the Health
    Sciences
F. Edward Hébert School of Medicine

(F.O.) Oski, Frank, B.A., M.D.
Professor and Chairman of the Department of
    Pediatrics
Johns Hopkins University School of Medicine

(H.D.R., Jr.) Riley, Harris D., Jr., B.A., M.D.
Professor of Pediatrics, Department Head
University of Oklahoma Health Sciences Center;
Medical Director of Children's Memorial Hospital
    (Oklahoma City)

(R.O.S.) Scholz, Roy O., B.S., M.D.
Assistant Professor of Ophthalmology
Johns Hopkins University

(A.G.S.) Swanson, August G., B.A., M.D.
Director of Academic Affairs
Association of American Medical Colleges
Washington, D.C.

Photo Contributors to the Medical Guide

Curtin, John W., M.D.
Professor of Surgery and Chief of the
    Departments of Plastic Surgery
University of Illinois College of Medicine and
    Rush-Presbyterian-St. Luke's Medical Center

Ginsberg, Julius E., S.B., M.D.
Professor Emeritus
Northwestern University Medical School

Jacobs, Richard L., B.A., M.S., M.D.
Associate Professor of Orthopedic Surgery
University of Illinois College of Medicine

Jacobson, Bailey N., D.D.S., M.S.
Assistant Professor of Orthodontics
Northwestern University Dental School

Kallick, Charles A., M.D., FAAP
Chief, Section of Infectious Diseases
Cook County Hospital (Chicago)

Nelson, Kenrad E., A.B., M.D.
Associate Professor
Department of Preventive Medicine and
    Community Health
University of Illinois College of Medicine

Rosenstein, Sheldon W., D.D.S., M.S.D.
Associate Professor of Orthodontics
Northwestern University Dental School

Shapiro, Lewis, M.D.
Clinical Professor of Dermatology
College of Physicians and Surgeons
Columbia University

Spaeth, Ralph, M.D.
Clinical Professor of Pediatrics
University of Illinois College of Medicine

Section One

Growth and Development

The New Baby: Birth to 18 months

A baby is such a small thing to make such a big difference in your life. Soft and cuddly, the new baby is something to be proud of. But the little one also means 2 A.M. feedings, rashes and drooling, and diapers that always are wet. First tooth, first fever, first step, first fall—they are all part of your new baby. But they are also part of a very special challenge that you as a parent accept—the challenge of guiding and helping your child become a strong and independent human being who will someday also want to accept a real challenge.

By Howard L. Weinberger, M.D.
Donna Salsburey, M.D.,
Consulting Editor

Portrait of the baby

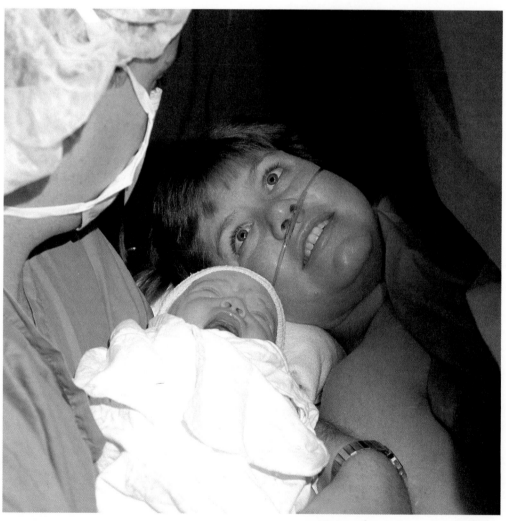

The long months of waiting and wondering are over—the baby is born.

Suggestions for baby supplies and equipment

Clothing

Booties or socks, 2 or 3 pairs
Bunting, or coat and hood
Diapers: 3 to 6 dozen cloth diapers or a
    weekly supply of disposable diapers
Diaper pins
Gowns, kimonos, or sleepers, 6
Undershirts, 6
Sweater and cap, 1 or 2
Waterproof pants, 4 to 6

Bed

Bassinet, crib, or cradle
Crib blankets, 2 lightweight and 1
    winterweight
Crib bumpers, 1 set
Crib sheets, 3 or 4 (or pillow slips, if
    you use a basket or bassinet)
Mattress, firm
Waterproof mattress pad, 2

Nursery items

Chest of drawers
Cool-mist vaporizer
Diaper pail
Laundry hamper
Dressing (changing) table
Rectal thermometer
Rocking chair for parent
Swing

Bath

A & D ointment or petroleum jelly
Bath towels and washcloths, 3 or 4
Cotton swabs and cotton balls
Mild baby soap and lotion (non-perfumed)
Nail scissors with blunt ends
Receiving blankets, 3 or 4
Tub, plastic or inflatable

Feeding supplies

Bibs, 3 or 4
Breast feeding: bottles with nipples and
    caps, 3 or 4
Bottle feeding: bottles with nipples and
    caps, 8
Bottle and nipple brush
Extra nipples and caps
Funnel
Measuring cup

Outing supplies

Car seat
Carriage or stroller
Carriage robe or blanket
Diaper bag

The first time you see your baby will be shortly after he or she is born. The baby may be quiet and sleepy or crying lustily. The baby's head may appear pushed out of shape because the skull bones are soft and pliable. Skin may be beet-red and coated with a white cheesy substance that will wash off.

Some newborns have almost no hair. Others are born with long, soft hair that rubs off during the first few weeks of life and is replaced by their normal hair. Their eyes may be puffy, especially after the eye drops that doctors use to prevent infection. Newborns' hands and feet are probably wrinkled and may be blue or mottled.

All in all, newborns hardly look like the bundles of joy parents have been picturing for several months. Were the magazines wrong? Where are the healthy skin, the bright blue eyes, the ribbons in the hair? And where was the smile of recognition when the nurse put the baby in Mother's arms?

Be patient. This is the baby's first day in the world, and he or she is not quite groomed for an official reception. Give your baby time. And give yourself time. The joys, and hard work, of parenthood are just beginning.

Caring for the baby

Almost all new parents handle their babies as though they are water-filled balloons—ready to burst. These parents are usually overconcerned about care of the baby's navel and nails, the soft spot in the baby's skull, and (if the child is a boy) the circumcised penis.

The navel usually requires minimal care. Immediately after birth, the doctor clamps the umbilical cord, then carefully cuts it off close to the baby's body. The small piece of cord still attached to the baby is called the umbilical stump. It dries up and falls off in one to three weeks, leaving the navel to heal. Occasionally, a drop of blood will appear on the stump or around the navel when the cord falls off. Dab this away with sterile cotton, and report it to your doctor if more than a few drops are present. Keep the area around the stump dry and clean. Do not cover the cord with the diaper. Your doctor may recommend that you wipe the area around the stump with alcohol until it is completely healed. Until the stump falls off, and until the navel is healed, your doctor may recommend sponge baths for the baby. Occasionally, the stump may become irritated and cause redness around the navel. If this happens, an infection may be present. Call your doctor.

Newborns' nails are often very sharp, and a baby may get many scratches if the nails are not clipped. For the first week or two, the hands may be covered with "mittens" (socks or underwear sleeves) to protect the baby. After the first week, the nails should be cut straight across using nail scissors with blunt ends. It is easiest to trim the nails while the baby is asleep.

The soft spots are areas in the baby's skull where the bones have not yet come together. A very tough membrane covers and protects these areas. Ordinary handling and washing of the baby's head and scalp will do no harm.

The circumcision will appear red and may be swollen for several days. Apply Vaseline, petrolatum, or A & D ointment to the penis each time the baby's diaper is changed until the penis has healed. After a few days you can wash the penis with sterile cotton and a mild soap. Do not apply alcohol because it may sting. Talcum powder may also be irritating. Report any signs of bleeding or infection to your doctor.

Sleeping

During the first few weeks, your baby will probably sleep from feeding to feeding. But as the baby gets older, sleep time diminishes. At first the baby is awake more during one part of the day. Then the baby sleeps less during other times of day. By the time the baby is a year old, he or she will probably take only two naps a day—one in the morning and one in the afternoon.

Neither phone nor doorbell nor barking dog should distract you when bathing your baby.

Most newborns are not disturbed by lights or by some noise and activity around them, but if it is possible, you should provide a separate room for the baby.

It has become popular among some parents to keep the young infant in the same room as the parents—even in the parents' bed. This can facilitate breast feeding and is thought to enhance "bonding." It is, however, a mixed blessing. There is some evidence that these infants develop more sleep problems later in the first year. Some parents have a difficult time moving the infant out of their room once this pattern has begun. When space is limited, the baby can still be somewhat separated from the rest of the room by a room divider or a screen. The new baby will be most comfortable in a bassinet or a small crib. When the baby is older, a high-sided crib is a necessity.

Bathing

You do not have to bathe your baby every day (three times a week is fine), and bath time does not have to come at the same time every day. But whenever you do bathe your baby, remember safety. To avoid falls, never leave the baby on a high place. And never leave the baby alone in a tub of water. Place everything you need for the baby's bath and dressing within easy reach ahead of time so that you will not have to turn your back to find anything.

Either an ordinary, small plastic tub or an inflatable plastic tub placed on the kitchen table lets you bathe the baby while you are standing. This position is more comfortable and safer than bending over a full-sized tub.

Line the tub with a diaper or towel to keep the baby from sliding around. There are also spongelike fitted devices available that fit into the sink or tub to aid in bathing the young infant. Use only a small amount of water until you get used to handling the baby. The water should be about body temperature, or 98° F. (37° C), which will seem neither hot nor cold when you test it on your wrist or inner elbow. With one hand under the baby's head, and the other under the buttocks or grasping both legs, lower the baby into the tub. Let the baby sit in the tub, leaning back a little. To support the

baby's head, hold your arm behind the baby's neck and grip the baby's arm under the armpit. First, wash the baby's face without soap. Then, with soap, wash the scalp and the rest of the body. When you are finished, lay the baby on a towel and pat the baby dry. Do not rub the baby's tender skin with a rough towel. Take special care to keep baby powder with talc away from the baby's head so that the baby does not inhale the powder. Inhalation of powder can lead to a serious breathing problem.

At each bath, wash the scalp with a mild soap, then comb the scalp with a fine-tooth comb. This helps prevent cradle cap (a crust that forms on the baby's scalp).

Whenever you bathe a baby girl, gently clean between the folds of the labia where a cheesy substance accumulates. When bathing an uncircumcised boy, never forcibly retract the foreskin. The foreskin will have loosened enough to be retracted over the head of the penis by the time the baby is two years old. At that time it is important to cleanse under the foreskin at each bath.

Diapers

Many families automatically decide to use disposable diapers for their newborns. These diapers come in a variety of sizes and absorbencies. Diaper companies advertise that disposable diapers keep moisture away from the baby's skin and, therefore, help decrease diaper rash. Cloth diapers also have a number of advantages. They are generally less expensive to use and eliminate the concern about environmental contamination from plastic waste. A diaper service will deliver clean, fresh diapers and pick up soiled diapers each week, and eliminate the need for daily soaking, washing, and drying. Babies need 6 to 8 dozen diapers per week for the first several weeks.

At changing time, never put an open safety pin near the baby. Always close the pin immediately after you remove it from the baby's diaper. The baby may pick up the pin and swallow it. Closed safety pins may pass easily through the baby's bowels. An open safety pin is more likely to get stuck.

Each time you change your baby's diaper, wash the diaper area, using cotton balls dipped in lukewarm water, or premoistened wipes. (Do not use alcohol unless your doctor advises it. Alcohol may irritate the skin.) This cleansing of the diaper area is particularly important after each bowel movement. Generally, do not use rubber or plastic pants until the baby is a few weeks old. The pants retain moisture and heat, which may cause diaper rash. If your baby seems to wet a great deal, use two diapers, especially at night.

Feeding the baby

Many mothers are now choosing to breast-feed their new babies. This pattern has been encouraged by physicians and nurses because of the recognized benefits of breast-feeding to the infant—and the mother. The newborn infant receives valuable protection against infection in the first few days of life from colostrum—the clear fluid which precedes the production of milk.

To get a big, healthy burp, gently pat or rub the baby's back.

In many parts of the world, breast milk is the safest pattern of feeding, since it is not dependent on the availability of pure water and/or refrigeration.

Many people advocate breast-feeding as the optimum way to foster the mother-child relationship. It should be pointed out, however, that bottle-fed babies are held in essentially the same position for feeding and that most infants and mothers "bond" independent of the method of feeding or the feeding pattern.

Fathers of breast-fed babies should be encouraged to be involved in the early care of the infant in many ways. Some mothers will pump their breasts to allow the infant to feed from a bottle once a day (or night). This allows the father to participate actively in feeding.

If you choose breast-feeding, your doctor will probably recommend that the baby be given vitamins with fluoride daily. (Most infant formulas are supplemented with vitamins.)

Whether you breast-feed or bottle-feed, doctors usually recommend following a modified demand feeding schedule during the baby's first few weeks. The baby usually takes two to three ounces (60 to 90 milliliters) of milk or formula at each feeding. Then, after sleeping for 2 to 3 hours, the baby awakens for the next feeding. As the baby grows, the stomach capacity increases. At 8 to 12 weeks, the baby will take four to six ounces (120 to 180 milliliters) at each feeding and require only five or six feedings every 24 hours.

Babies sometimes spit up their feeding, usually just a few minutes after they have finished. This may be just a dribble of several drops of milk. If spitting up happens more than one-half hour after the feeding, it will probably be a cheesy material that smells sour because the stomach juices have already started to curdle the milk for digestion. Do not be alarmed. These babies usually weigh enough for their age. The spitting up probably is caused by an overflow from a full stomach.

In some cases, the baby spits up early during a feeding. When this happens, the baby's stomach may be filled with air from crying or from improper feeding techniques.

If this seems to be the case, burp the baby before and several times during feeding. After the baby has been fed, hold the baby upright on your lap or over your shoulder (with a diaper or cloth to protect your clothing) and pat or rub the baby's back until you hear a burp. You can also prop the baby up against a cushion for 15 to 20 minutes after the feeding. Never feed the baby by propping a bottle in the crib. By doing this you and the baby miss the mutual pleasure of feeding, and the baby might choke on the milk.

Breast milk and infant formulas provide an adequate source of iron and are recommended for the first year. Cow's milk is a poor source of iron for infants.

Weaning

Wean your baby gradually from the breast or the bottle, allowing plenty of time for the baby to get used to a new way of eating. The baby will decide when the time is right. All you have to do is follow the baby's lead. At about 5 or 6 months, provide an empty cup as a plaything. Then, one day, offer a few sips of milk from the cup. Gradually, over the next several weeks, the baby may learn to enjoy drinking from the cup. At each feeding, give the baby as much milk as he or she will take from a cup. Then allow the baby to nurse or offer a bottle. After a while, omit the daily breast- or bottle-feeding that the baby is least interested in. This is usually the breakfast or lunch feeding. Offer only a cup of milk at this time. After a week, omit another breast- or bottle-feeding, if the baby is willing. Then, in another week, omit the last of the feedings by breast or bottle. Some mothers, however, wish to continue to breast-feed through the baby's first year. Infants of these mothers may need additional sources of iron in the second 6 months of the first year. (See Solid foods.)

Babies' willingness to be weaned may vary. Teething babies or ill babies may revert to the bottle. Babies may be entirely weaned at one year old, or they may cling to an evening bottle for a longer time. It may be comforting to note that it is rare to see a child entering school with a bottle in a lunch box.

This table can be used as a guideline for introducing your baby to solid foods.

Age	Food
4 months	Cereals: Rice, oatmeal, barley, wheat, mixed cereals
5-6 months	Fruits: Applesauce, pears, bananas
6-7 months	Vegetables: Carrots, squash, peas, sweet potatoes, spinach, beans
7-8 months	Meats: Lamb, chicken, beef, liver, veal
After 9 months	Egg yolks, finger foods, table foods

Solid foods

Many mothers regard the introduction of solid foods as the surest sign that their babies are growing up. Some feel that solid foods make babies sleep better and longer at night. But feeding of solids may be started too early. In some cases, when a spoon touches the front part of the baby's tongue, the tongue rapidly attempts to push the spoon out. Too early attempts are also generally frustrating and messy, since most of what does get into the child dribbles right back out again. The frustration involved in overcoming the baby's efforts to fend off food can set up a poor eating pattern. Mealtimes should be pleasant experiences, not battles between opposing forces.

Most pediatricians recommend waiting until a baby is 4 months old before introducing foods by spoon. At this time, start strained foods in small amounts, increasing the amounts as the baby's capacity and interest increase. The first foods introduced should be cooked, strained cereals with iron added to them. A teaspoon of rice cereal mixed with enough of the baby's formula to give it a smooth consistency is an excellent first food. Although the rice may be tasteless to you, it offers a new and important experience for your baby. The baby's tongue feels a new consistency. Cereal should not

"They're off and running!" is the starting cry of many a meal when baby learns to walk.

be added to the milk in the baby's bottle because this deprives the baby of a pleasurable learning experience. Rice cereal is good to start with since it is unlikely to cause allergic or other reactions (such as diarrhea). After a few days, oatmeal, barley, wheat, and last of all, mixed cereals can be introduced one at a time.

After cereals, introduce other strained foods, one food at a time. Then, if any reaction occurs—such as a rash or diarrhea— you can easily identify the offending food.

Some parents prefer to prepare their own strained foods for their baby. This has the advantage of ensuring that there are no chemical additives in the foods. Be sure not to flavor the foods to suit your taste. Especially, do not add unnecessary salt or sugar to the prepared foods. A variety of devices are available to grind and purée foods. Some of these are very expensive, but others, such as a blender or foley mill, can be purchased at more modest prices and are perfectly adequate.

Introduce junior foods (still mostly strained, but with some chunks of food) when the child has one or two primary teeth (6 months old or later). Some babies prefer to skip junior foods and go directly to mashed potatoes, cottage cheese, eggs, ham-

burger, and other table foods. Most babies at this age also enjoy hard cookies and toast. By the time they are a year old, most children enjoy sucking and gnawing at a chicken leg or lamb chop.

Mealtimes

At about one year, your child may appear to eat less, even though he or she is becoming more active. A mother who complains that her child is not eating may be surprised to discover that the child is gaining weight. At this age, the tremendous growth rate which has taken place during the baby's first year tapers off. The child moves around more and spends relatively less time eating. Often a considerable amount of ingenuity is required to prevent mealtime from deteriorating into a chase or a battleground.

The 1-year-old should be eating about three times a day and learning the meaning of mealtime. Feed the child at the table at about the same time as the rest of the family. To avoid too much disruption, you may feed meat and vegetables first, and then let the child eat dessert while the family eats dinner. Offer small portions that the child can finish. If the portions are not enough, offer second helpings. This technique avoids the situation in which the 1-year-old is faced with a seemingly overwhelming amount and choice of foods, a situation that will force a small child to either surrender and be stuffed full, or to rebel and not eat at all.

Encourage self-feeding by cutting the food into bite-sized portions that are easy to handle. Do not expect a 1-year-old to be adept with a spoon and fork. Expect a fairly messy high chair, clothing, and baby after each meal. However, some limits must be set. Do not let the child throw food around. This can be especially embarrassing when visiting friends or relatives. On such visits, you may want to bring along a plastic garbage can liner to place under the high chair or feeding table. This allows for quick cleanups and saves carpet cleaning and bad feelings among friends. If the child does not eat enough at mealtimes, do not allow between-meal snacking. This will lead to more difficulty at the next meal.

Sometimes a 1-year-old begins to drink more and more milk at the expense of meats, vegetables, and other foods. This may follow an illness, or it may be because the child is teething. But often it is a result of mealtime conflicts. The bottle seems a simple solution to getting what an adult feels are adequate calories into the child. But, milk lacks iron. If this "simple solution" continues beyond a few weeks, the child may suffer serious iron deficiency leading to anemia. As a rule of thumb, it is best to limit milk intake at one year to 24 to 32 ounces (70 to 95 milliliters) at most per day.

Growth and development

Every child is an individual. He or she grows and develops at his or her own rate. Two children in the same family are no exception. One may walk at 9 months, but the other may not walk until the first birthday. Generally, however, growth and development can be fairly well predicted. For more information, see GROWTH in the section For Special Consideration.

The first month

The average newborn weighs from 6½ to 8 pounds (3 to 3.5 kilograms) and is anywhere from 18 to 22 inches (45 to 55 centimeters) long. In the first three to five days,

the infant may lose up to 10 per cent of birth weight. This occurs because more fluids are lost than are gained through feeding. There is no need to worry. The baby's weight is usually back up to birth weight in one or two weeks.

The first few weeks of your baby's life are taken up mostly by eating and sleeping, and crying when hungry, wet, or otherwise uncomfortable. The newborn's breathing is erratic during sleep—at times very noisy and fast, at times very quiet. All newborns breathe through their noses and find mouth breathing almost impossible. This makes it possible for them to feed and breathe at the same time, without ever having the bottle or breast removed from their mouths.

Newborns keep their hands tightly clenched most of the time and hold them close to their faces. When they are picked up, their arms and legs may stiffen or make jerky movements. Their hands and chins may tremble at times. These movements gradually disappear after the first few weeks.

At times young infants move about the crib and go from one end to the other. While lying on their backs they may kick, and when held erect, may make stepping motions.

We now know that even newborn infants are responsive to their environment. They can hear and they can look at objects—especially the human face and bright lights. They let you know when they are hungry or wet and are comforted by being fed and changed—as well as by the sound of their parents' voices. Babies are born with certain reflex actions. A noise or movement can set off flailing of the arms and legs, quivering of the chin, and loud crying. In the first month, the ringing of a bell can make babies stop what they are doing. If an object is put against an infant's palm, the baby will grip the object and then drop it. A soft touch of the finger or the nipple of the mother's breast is enough to make an infant turn in that direction and start sucking.

When prone, a newborn baby can raise the head and move it from side to side. But in general, during the first month of life, the baby has little control of the head. The head lags when you lift the baby to a sitting posi-

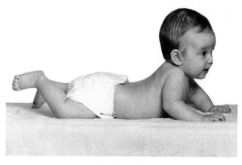

3-4 months: usually lifts chest

tion. For this reason, you should keep a hand behind the infant's head when you lift your baby.

Age 1 to 4 months

Between 1 and 2 months of age, infants are able to raise their heads up above a flat surface. As babies grow, they can hold their heads up for longer periods of time. Also between 1 and 2 months, most babies can briefly follow a bright object or light.

By 2 months, babies usually stop crying on hearing their mothers speak, even though wet, hungry, or uncomfortable. At about four to six weeks, babies smile for the first time, generally in response to mother's voice. In the next few weeks, babies will begin smiling at all pleasant voices, then familiar faces, and make cooing sounds in response to familiar voices. This is the beginning of language.

At 3 months, babies' heads still bob when they sit, but they have much more consistent head control. When lying on their stomachs, babies 3 to 4 months old can raise their heads and chests well above the mattress while supporting their weight on their forearms.

Three-month-old babies may spend long periods of time looking at their hands and watching their fingers move. Babies play with their hands as toys. Near 4 months, babies can bring their hands together in front of them, and before long they may actively suck their thumbs.

Although at about 3 months babies still cannot reach out and grasp objects, their arm and hand movements do increase. The hands are no longer tight little fists. Babies hold objects that are placed in their hands.

By 4 months, babies can hold and shake a small, toy rattle.

By the second or third month, most babies are able to focus and follow faces and objects more consistently. They can also focus on objects they are holding. Their eyes may cross, particularly if they stare at objects for a long time. Do not let this concern you unless your baby's eyes persistently remain crossed.

When babies are about 4 or 5 months old, they will probably roll over for the first time, usually from the belly to the back. Before very long, they may roll over on the stomach.

At about 4 months, babies may start to laugh aloud, with a deep belly laugh. At first the sounds of their laughter may surprise and scare them into short periods of crying. But soon, the infants laugh in response to almost any pleasant sound or smiling face.

At this age, babies will begin to anticipate feeding time. As soon as they recognize the bottle, they may wave their arms and legs excitedly and make sucking movements.

At 5 months, babies are able to pull up to a sitting position when they are lifted by the hands, and they can sit alone for about half an hour if they are propped up. Some more placid infants, particularly if they are plump, do not sit alone with support until the seventh month or so.

7-8 months: usually sits without support

By 7 months, most babies can get up on their hands and knees. By 8 or 9 months, most babies can pull themselves upright to a full standing position. A baby of this age should never be left in a crib with the sides down.

During these months, babies are busy exploring their own bodies and all things around them. Everything seems to go into the mouth—not only the thumb and hand, but also toys, toes, and even the ribbons on nightshirts. As can be expected, babies also drool a lot.

13-15 months: usually walks alone

9-10 months: usually creeps

One of the biggest enjoyments of watching your baby grow is seeing the first tooth come in. Preceded by weeks of drooling, and followed by more of the same, the first tooth produces pride that is a forerunner of what you will feel when baby takes that first step.

The first tooth generally breaks through the gums when the baby is 6 or 7 months old. But if it does not come until several months later, do not be concerned. As you will be told over and over again, every child is an individual. (For more information about the teeth, see TEETH AND TEETHING in the Medical Guide.)

At some time in this period, usually at 6 months, babies may develop a fear of strangers. In all likelihood, this represents an increasing ability to tell familiar faces from unfamiliar ones. Stranger anxiety is less likely to occur in babies who have multiple caretakers.

Major milestones of motor development

Age in months	Activity
1-2	Lifts head when lying on stomach
3-4	Lifts chest when lying on stomach
4-5	Reaches out and grasps objects; Rolls over
5-6	Sits up if propped
6-7	Transfers objects hand to hand
7-8	Sits without support
8-9	Grasps small objects with thumb and index finger
9-10	Crawls; Creeps on hands and knees; Stands with support
11-12	Walks with support of one hand
13-15	Walks alone; Climbs onto furniture; Turns the pages of a book
16-18	Runs stiffly; Feeds self

Usually, the skills of motor development come one after another in orderly fashion. In some instances, the achievement of one skill depends on successful achievement of a previous one—for example, a baby learns to take hold of an object voluntarily before learning how to pass it from one hand to the other. Sometimes, however, children skip milestones. For example, although most infants crawl and then creep before walking, others may skip the crawling and creeping stages completely. Every child is different. No two infants, even in the same family, develop at exactly the same rate.

Babies love the shine, noise, and texture of pots and pans.

At 6 to 7 months of age, babies develop the ability to pass objects from one hand to the other. Infants can grasp an object, move it over to the opposite hand, and take hold of it with that hand.

By about 8 or 9 months of age, babies usually begin to use the thumb and index finger for grasping small objects. And they use both hands simultaneously—feeding themselves cookies with one hand while banging a cup or plate with a toy held in the other hand.

Age 9 to 12 months

At this age, babies reach out into their environment, not just with the hands but with the whole body. They can sit, lie on the back, and then sit again. By 9 or 10 months, infants can crawl on the stomach and creep on hands and knees. They can support their weight by holding onto the sides of the crib or playpen.

Most babies of this age can pull themselves up to a standing position without any help. A mother might put her baby down in the crib or playpen, only to find the child standing by the time she turns around. In the beginning, however, babies may not know how to sit down again. About this time, cruising from one piece of furniture to another becomes an exciting event. By the end of the first year, most babies can walk with one hand supported, and some can walk without any support at all.

By the age of 1 year, babies can "sing" to music and play pat-a-cake, and they may enjoy looking at picture books. They can also understand simple commands.

During this period, babies learn to do many things with their hands and fingers— poke, point, touch, lift, twist, squeeze, pick up, and drop. Simple items such as spoons, pots, and pans can keep children busy for hours. Babies become quite adept at repeatedly dropping toys, utensils, or food from high chairs and over the sides of playpens. This can be quite upsetting, especially when cereal hits the kitchen floor or dropped glasses shatter. Console yourself with the fact that this is all part of babies' normal development. They are learning that if they drop something, it will fall. They are also learning a new way of getting attention.

Babies use spoons more at mealtime—but less to feed themselves than to splash the spoons in their food. They can drink from cups by the end of the first year, although this is usually pretty messy. To save on breakage, and for safety, you may want to use plastic cups. Remember not to put a 1-year-old to bed with a bottle filled with milk or any sugared drink or juice. It could lead to a severe form of caries affecting the upper front teeth.

Age 13 to 15 months

During this period your baby will probably begin to walk alone, gaining new independence and leading to considerable exploring.

They will climb onto and off furniture. Since babies don't know the difference between dangerous and safe situations, you should set limits on this activity.

Children of 15 months get joy from dumping items out of bottles and boxes, and may practice this skill by emptying wastebaskets and pouring liquids out of bottles. Be certain that medicines, household cleaners, and other poisons are out of reach. A simple chain lock keeps kitchen closets closed, and locks for cabinet doors are also available. If one cabinet can be filled with pots, pans, plastic jars, and other favorite toys, let your baby open that one and play with its contents. This should divert the baby's attention from the locked doors. Also be certain that there are no house plants anywhere within your baby's reach.

Although they are very active, babies will sit still for long periods of time, turning the pages of magazines or picture books, or playing with blocks and toys. They will also assist in dressing and undressing themselves, although this "help" may lengthen the process.

At this age, children still babble as they develop a vocabulary of 10 to 20 words. However, some children of this age virtually quit using words so that they can spend more time learning other skills. It is as though they can concentrate on the development of only one major skill at a time.

At about this time children also understand a number of verbal commands, particularly "no." Children at this age understand "no" so well that they start using it for their own purposes. They push toys or food that they don't want away from them. They may not want to give up toys or stop enjoyable games just when parents want them to. It becomes increasingly hard to substitute one activity for another.

Age 16 to 18 months

At this age, children's motor activity is reaching such a fine level of control that they start to run instead of walk. In fact, it may seem that they are on the run constantly, going from room to room with frustrating speed. And they are now able to walk up and down stairs while holding on to someone's hand.

A baby about a year and a half old can walk up and down stairs with help.

Feeding time for children at this age is somewhat neater because they have better control of the spoon. They can now scribble with crayons on paper and—when unsupervised—on the wall or floor. They enjoy building towers of two or three blocks and then knocking them down. They begin to play with push and pull toys, and often try to push or pull them through the furniture. You may be able to determine whether your child will be left-handed or right-handed at around 18 months, but this trait is seldom demonstrated before the end of the second year. Any earlier consistent preference for one hand over another should be brought to your doctor's attention. It could be a sign of weakness of the opposite arm or hand.

By the time children are 18 months old, they should know the names of many household items. They may not be able to call them by name, but they understand what the items are and can associate the names with pictures, as well as with the objects themselves.

Children at 16 to 18 months are a conflict between dependence and independence. They set out on their own to explore the environment—climbing, walking, opening doors, trying to dress themselves, and helping to feed themselves. But they still must be helped down from the steps they have climbed, given the proper food, protected from accidents, and cuddled and cooed over when they scrape their knees.

Health and safety

One of the best ways to keep your infant healthy is to take the baby to a physician who can regularly check the child's development and give immunizations against many infectious diseases. The doctor may help prevent problems from occurring, or may catch a minor problem early and deal with it before it worsens. The doctor may also discover any medical quirks the baby has, such as an allergy to a specific medicine.

Since infants grow at such a rapid rate and are continually developing new skills, they should be seen by the doctor on a regular basis. The currently recommended schedule of visits to the doctor in the first two years is: prenatal visits; examination in the

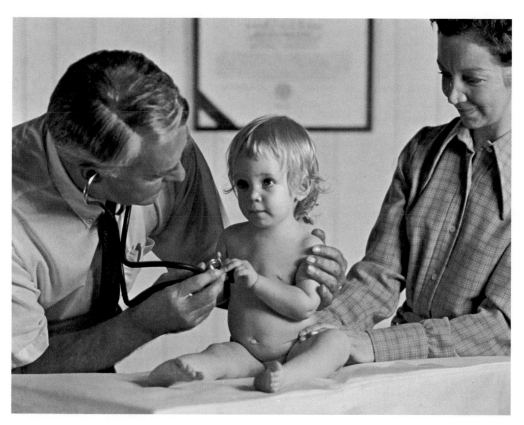

A doctor tries to ease a child's fears by his friendly, interested manner. Regular visits help build a trusting relationship between the doctor and child.

nursery after birth (once or twice); at 2 weeks; and then at 2, 4, 6, 9, 12, 15, and 18 months; and again at 2 years of age.

Shots

Your baby should be immunized against diphtheria, tetanus, whooping cough (pertussis), polio, measles, rubella (German measles), mumps, and Hemophilus influenza type B. Except for oral polio vaccine, which is given by drops, the other vaccines are given by injection. The MMR vaccines—measles, mumps, and rubella—usually require only a single shot to give adequate protection. The DPT vaccines—diphtheria, tetanus, and whooping cough—are also usually given in a single shot, but at three different times. Oral polio vaccine is usually given at the same time as the DPT shots. The third dose of oral polio vaccine is now optional in most parts of the United States. The H.i.B. vaccine is recommended at 18 months.

Babies should be immunized as early as possible, because most of the infectious diseases can be contracted then, and some (such as whooping cough) are more severe in young children than in older ones. Also, the younger the children are when they get shots, the less likely they are to remember them as unpleasant experiences.

(For more information on immunization, see the following articles in the Medical Guide: DIPHTHERIA, GERMAN MEASLES, IMMUNIZATION, MEASLES, POLIOMYELITIS, SHOTS, WHOOPING COUGH, and TETANUS.)

Common illnesses and conditions

In the first years of life, the stomach and intestines may be very sensitive to any change in children's health. Some infants vomit or have diarrhea with almost every illness—colds, earaches, intestinal infections, or more serious illnesses. The younger the infant, the more serious vomiting and diarrhea may be. Rapid losses of body fluids by vomiting and diarrhea can cause dehydration, which, if severe enough, may require hospitalization and intravenous feedings to restore fluids.

Most infants have between 3 and 8 small bowel movements a day of soft, pasty stool.

This is not diarrhea. Diarrhea is an intestinal disorder marked by frequent, loose, watery bowel movements. Sometimes diarrhea develops from too much sugar, too much liquid, or too concentrated a formula. Too little sugar, too dilute a formula, or too little liquid can cause dry, hard stools (constipation). If you breast-feed, be cautious of your diet. Foods that cause diarrhea or gas in the mother are likely to have the same effect on the baby.

If diarrhea occurs without vomiting, follow these measures.

Do not feed the baby any fruits, meats, or vegetables.

If you are breast-feeding, try to find out what food in your diet is causing the diarrhea, and stop eating that food.

If you are bottle-feeding, your doctor may recommend using a ready-made preparation of water with electrolytes that may be needed to replenish those lost in the diarrheal stool.

Some physicians recommend that you continue feeding the baby "through the diarrhea"; others will recommend eliminating

Here are a few of the common illnesses and conditions you may encounter during your baby's first 18 months. Each illness or condition is discussed in detail in a separate article in the Medical Guide.

Illness	Symptoms
Colds	Trouble eating, stuffy nose
Colic	Crying; hard, flat, or distended abdomen; gas
Cradle cap	Whitish scales on the scalp; yellow, greasy crust on the scalp
Diaper rash	Red pimples and irritation in the diaper area
Earache	Fever, irritability, pulling or rubbing at ears, crying when moved, turning head from side to side
Eczema	Itching rash, usually on the cheeks, inside of elbows, and back of knees
Hernia	A bulge in groin
Prickly heat	Pink rash, most noticeable in the folds of the skin
Roseola infantum	Fever, faint rash

milk and milk products for several days to weeks after an episode of diarrhea.

Give the baby diluted weak tea, broth or clear soups, liquid gelatin, flat ginger ale, or other clear fluids alternately with the special milk feedings. If your baby is still hungry, give him or her rice cereal, mashed bananas, and applesauce.

If vomiting occurs alone or complicates the diarrhea, limit feedings to less than an ounce at a time. If vomiting or diarrhea lasts beyond 6 to 12 hours, call your doctor.

(For more information, see the separate articles on Diarrhea, Vomiting, and Dehydration in the Medical Guide.)

Accidents

In the United States alone, about 20,000 children under the age of 15 die each year because of accidents. That is more than the next three leading causes of death combined.

One of your biggest jobs as a parent is to be alert to dangers of which your child cannot possibly be aware. It is important to check all aspects of the home for safety. Cribs, playpens, and gates should conform to safety standards. Take extra care to keep baby walkers away from stairwells. Cover all electric outlets with plastic caps. Never leave a young child alone in a bathtub. A small child can drown in very shallow water or turn on the hot water and be severely scalded. Burns in the kitchen can occur from boiling hot water, hot plates, and the oven itself. The crawling baby can pull up to a standing position, pull a pot off the stove, and be scalded by the spilling contents. Use gates to prevent falls down a flight of stairs. Take precautions to prevent the young child from accidentally drowning in a backyard swimming pool.

Medicines are the most common poisonous substances accidentally taken by children. House plants are now a very common source of ingestions. Following this comes a whole series of cleaners and sanitizing agents (most often found in the bathroom); cosmetics (generally in or on nightstands in the bedroom); paint and furniture polishes; and insecticides, gasoline, and charcoal lighter fluids.

Here are some ways to "poison-proof" your home.

Look at your home through the eyes of a curious, mobile toddler.

Find out which of your common household items are poisonous.

Keep all drugs, poisons, and household chemicals out of a child's reach.

Put medicines back in their usual storage place immediately after using them.

Discard medicines after you have recovered from the illness for which they were prescribed, as well as outdated medicines, by flushing them down the toilet.

Never store poisonous or inflammable substances in food or beverage containers. They may be mistakenly consumed.

Keep syrup of ipecac on hand, but never use it until checking with your doctor or the nearest poison control center.

Toys

Since anything babies play with is bound to be put into the mouth, toys should have smooth surfaces, and they should be easy to wash. There should be no sharp edges or detachable parts such as glass eyes, buttons, pompons, and bells.

Even though loving relatives and friends shower your baby with elaborate rattles, and gadgets to be suspended over carriages or crib, you have to select and offer the baby only those playthings that are safe and appropriate for your baby's age. If you ever decide to repaint one of your baby's toys, never use a lead-base paint, because it can cause lead poisoning.

Simple toys are best, especially for babies: rattles that cannot be broken or chewed into small pieces; teething rings; dolls and animals made of cloth, plastic, or rubber; spoons and cups; spools strung together; cereal boxes; and, of course, something that floats in the bathtub such as a sponge whale or a soft rubber duck.

Common concerns

Spoiling

Young infants cannot be spoiled by too much love and attention. From the parents' response to their needs, they learn to feel secure and develop good relationships with their parents. The notion that it is good for a baby to cry just for the sake of crying is not a sound one.

It is natural for new babies to be the center of attention in their families. During the first two years, they are dependent on their parents. They are held, carried, fed, bathed, changed, and dressed. As they grow, this physical dependence tapers off. Throughout the first year, babies are carried or pushed in a stroller. At one year, they begin to walk, but they are still carried or pushed much of the time. But when they are 18 months or 2 years, they don't want to be carried at all. This progression is repeated over and over with feeding, bathing, and dressing.

Parents who really are spoiling their children have a hard time "letting go." They are not willing to let the children do things for themselves, even though the children are ready to do so.

Setting limits

Setting limits means setting up guidelines, which all children need. As a parent, it is your responsibility to set reasonable limits. Often a child's negativism is merely a way of testing you to see if you are being consistent.

Certain limits parents set are obvious. Do not let children crawl or walk onto the street. Do not let them pound on a glass door or window. Do not let children near a hot stove. These limits protect children.

Other limits are less easy to set, but just as important. Parents should establish a bedtime hour—not too early while babies are still playing and alert, and not too late when they are irritable and overtired. Parents should not be overrigid about the time. If children have had longer naps than usual, they may not be ready for sleep at the regular hour.

If successful, the guidelines parents set can serve as a basis for children's behavior throughout childhood.

Toilet training

Many parents want to know how early they can begin toilet training. There is a natural desire to want a child "out of diapers." However, attempts at training too early can do more harm than good. They merely set the stage for confrontations between parents and children, and for mutual frustrations and anxieties.

In general, parents should wait until children have mastered walking before attempting training. This usually occurs after 18 months. Bowel control most often is attained before bladder control. Daytime bladder control is generally attained before nighttime control. Girls are usually toilet-trained earlier than boys. Since each child is different, no single schedule should be expected to hold for any two children.

You will find further information on toilet training in THE TODDLER section.

You and your baby

The coming of a baby into a home is bound to cause a certain amount of conflict. From time to time, mixed feelings are aroused in parents as well as in brothers and sisters.

Most fathers of first babies have their moments of wondering if their wives will be as considerate and understanding as they were before the baby's arrival. New mothers have their bad times, too, when they feel resentful or depressed about being so "tied down"—or about what seems to them lack of consideration from their husbands. When you are tired, everything is harder to do, especially taking care of the new baby. So try to get as much rest as possible. Take advantage of the baby's nap-time to take care of yourself. Fathers who help with night feedings can make the first few months more tolerable for everyone. And if

the new baby is not a first one, the children in the family will inevitably feel, on occasion, that life was better before the baby came. These feelings are universal. They are nothing to be ashamed of.

The relationship between father, mother, and the baby is very important. The baby learns and develops skills, to a considerable degree, in response to the stimulation and love provided by you, his or her parents. You in turn, become sensitive to your baby's needs—both physical and emotional. Only then can you respond to them appropriately.

Every baby develops a different relationship with his parents, different from any other set of parents and child. Even children in the same family react differently to their parents, because no two babies enter the same family. Each child should be viewed as an individual. It often is necessary to modify an approach which has been successful in dealing with one child in the family, when the same situation comes up with another child. Certainly, what works for a neighbor may not be appropriate for you.

Magazines, television programs, and books are full of general advice for parents. What is more important is the development of confidence in *your* abilities to deal with *your* child. Despite all the advice and pressures, you are still the one responsible and the one best able to solve day-to-day problems. Try to anticipate the needs of your children. Meet the needs with love, not overprotection. And help provide the environment for each child to grow and develop to his or her full potential.

Bedtime should be a happy time—a time for lullabies and talking.

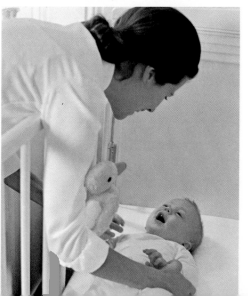

The Toddler: 18 months to 3 years

For months you have been saying, "I can't wait until my baby can walk." "I can't wait until my baby can talk." And suddenly—your baby can! Suddenly, your baby is a toddler—a walking, talking, jumping, grabbing, pot-bellied, knock-kneed toddler, who always seems to have a runny nose. What a difference from the baby you brought home from the hospital! Now the toddler stands, and has a new outlook. How sure, how cocky, how independent! Every object seen is a new challenge. And yet, the toddler is still very dependent on you— for love, for physical needs, for the setting of limits on aggressive behavior, for praise when it is earned. The toddler is a paradox, loudly proclaiming independence one minute; then seeking to be hugged and cuddled the next.

By Lendon H. Smith, M.D.,
Diane Shaffer, M.Ed.,
and Steven Waskerwitz, M.D.,
Consulting Editors

Portrait of the toddler

Toddlers "toddle" for only a few weeks. By the time they are 18 months old, they are running, dashing, plummeting headlong into their environment—testing, tasting, clawing, groping, eyeballing, listening, poking, probing, stamping. They act as if they must analyze the entire world and have only one day to do it.

At times during this period the child seems determined to conquer or even to destroy the environment. Actually, the toddler is trying out big muscles used for running, jumping, climbing, pounding, and hitting. The child's nervous system and attention span are not developed well enough to settle down to quiet work. You are doomed to fail if you try to force silent, stationary activity. A certain amount of time and energy must be channeled into big-muscle activity before the toddler can go to the next level.

Motor abilities and development

Keep in mind that no child can perform a task until the part of the nervous system responsible for its performance is sufficiently developed. Pushing children beyond their physical and mental capacities only frustrates both parents and children. Every new activity toddlers perform indicates that nerves and muscles have developed sufficiently to allow them to perform it. They must acquire the ability for task A before going to task B. Toddlers sit before they stand. They stand before they walk. They walk before they run.

The age at which children are able to perform specific tasks is largely determined by heredity. But it is also influenced by such variables as environmental encouragement, nutrition, sickness, availability of toys, and the time to practice.

Yet even though each child is different, children master abilities at fairly predictable times and in a fairly predictable order. Average 18-month-old toddlers generally can eat without help, drink from a cup, use a spoon, use 15 to 25 words accurately, walk well, stack a few blocks, and pretend to do housework. At 2, toddlers run well, throw a ball, jump in place, scribble, turn pages, combine a few words, listen to stories, and know their first name. Toilet training may begin. (For more information, see TOILET TRAINING in Common Concerns.) At 3, toddlers walk up stairs alternating feet, ride a tricycle, copy a circle and a cross, and know their age and full name.

Growth

A toddler grows more slowly than a new baby. Most girls at 18 months have acquired about half of their adult height. Boys at age 2 are about halfway there. Body length increases in the second year by 3 to 4 inches (7.5 to 10 centimeters), and in the third year by 2 to 3 inches (5 to 7.5 centimeters). (See GROWTH, page 132.)

Toddlers' appetites usually diminish. At 2 years, children eat to live. At 2 months old, the infants were living only to eat. This appetite loss upsets most parents. They feel

The average 18-month-old toddler can eat
with a spoon and drink from a cup.

By about 18 months, a toddler can
usually build a tower of two or three blocks.

By the age of 2, most toddlers can throw
a ball and are able to run well.

A 2-year-old toddler may become fascinat
with copying a circle that you draw.

that their toddlers must be sick if they do not eat. The real reason for the toddlers' loss of appetite is that they are so busy exploring that food becomes less important. By the time children are 18 to 24 months old, motor skills have developed enough to allow them to feed themselves as much as they need.

Parent vs. toddler

Toddlers constantly play games in which they test the physical properties of their environment. They confirm the law of gravity, the stickiness of juice, the wetness of water, and the heat of flame. They also discover their parents' distress when they have gone too far. Toddlers learn by exploring— by looking, doing, and touching. They can now use their eyes and hands to satisfy their curiosity and now that they are walking, they can decide what to look at, touch, and feel.

It is important for toddlers to touch things in order to learn. But they have no idea what is unsafe to touch or eat. Toddler-proof your home by putting things you don't want the toddler to have out of reach. This will decrease the number of times each day you hear yourself saying "no-no."

Toddlers are also beginning to develop a sense of worth or self-esteem. As they begin to feel confident, they will sense your support as you encourage learning. If toddlers are stopped from exploring with a lot of "no-no's," they may begin to feel sad and confused. They need love and encouragement to explore and learn.

Of course, rules must be introduced and enforced. Toddlers must be given consistent messages to help them develop self-control. Toddlers need their parents to provide rules that will help them explore, learn, and satisfy their curiosity safely in a large and sometimes frightening new world. Parents should teach their toddlers, by example and loving discipline, respect for living things and dangerous objects.

Typical day

Most toddlers seem to be early risers. It may be because of wet diapers, a full blad-der, hunger, or just because they want to get on with the joyful business of living.

Most children are very good at undressing themselves at 2, but dressing themselves is another story. Since it is difficult for them to balance on one foot or to stand up with the face covered by a shirt, they should sit on the floor while dressing or undressing.

Parents can help by sitting on the floor behind the toddlers to help them practice putting on and taking off clothing, using some of the same movements the toddler should use. As toddlers become more skillful, the amount of help should decrease. Parents should allow toddlers to choose their clothing whenever possible. Toddlers will probably be more interested in dressing themselves if they choose what they wear.

Most toddlers adapt to three meals a day, but some prefer several light meals. These children can be offered small amounts of fresh fruits and vegetables, cheese, and peanut butter—all good, nutritional foods.

Outdoors, a toddler has the chance to run and shout and use up tremendous energy.

Breakfast

Breakfast for toddlers should include fresh fruit or juice and an egg or other food high in protein, along with some whole-grain cereal or bread.

After breakfast, the toddler is ready for action. Try a walk through the neighborhood or a stroll in the park. This will give the toddler a chance to see, feel, and hear new things, as well as to run and shout.

Back home again, let the toddler listen to music or watch a carefully selected television program. This will give you both a breather before lunch.

Lunch

For lunch, you might offer your toddler a peanut-butter sandwich and a glass of milk or vegetable juice. This could be alternated with bean or lentil soup, cheese, or some lean meat. Skip luncheon meats with nitrates, or soups and canned pasta with MSG (monosodium glutamate). Nitrates and MSG are both unnecessary salts.

For dessert, offer fruit or a cookie made with honey rather than sugar.

Nap

After lunch is a good time for a nap. Naps are often a quiet time for parents, too. The nap should be long enough to be a real break for both mother and toddler, but not so long that the child will not go to bed at a reasonable time at night.

Some self-winding children cannot relax and sleep. They suspect that when mother wants them to nap, something big is going to happen that they will miss. They know shutting their eyes and relaxing leads to sleep. To avoid this pitfall, they sing, talk, toss, pick their noses, pace the floor, gaze out the window—anything to keep busy and prevent sleep. After two hours, when nap time is just about over, they fall asleep and—if not awakened—will sleep until 8 P.M. and then not sleep again until 1 A.M.

Even if toddlers do not sleep during nap time, a quiet period has some value. Mothers and toddlers can meet each other afterward with a fresh approach. When toddlers get up from a nap, a whole-grain snack and some juice might provide just enough energy to hold them until supper.

Dinner

The ideal meal should be a relaxed, happy time that the whole family—father, mother, toddler—can enjoy together. However, what often happens is far from ideal.

Commuting problems and the toddler's early bedtime often make it impractical to hold dinner until both parents get home. In such cases, the toddler should eat dinner early with the parent who is home and then have dessert with the other parent. The ideal family dinners can be saved for less hectic weekends.

Evening time

A pleasant evening routine is the best way to establish a successful bedtime. Parents can establish a calm evening routine for their toddlers: a warm bath, pajamas, a light healthy snack, and several quiet stories lead to being tucked in for the night.

Let your child know that you will be there if needed, but that it is time to go to sleep. Be firm. You can tell the child that sleep is needed for a wonderful day tomorrow. If your child gets out of bed, be consistent and don't change the rules. Take the child back to bed. Some children want to sleep with a favorite blanket or stuffed toy. Avoid stimulating toys in the crib or bed. Some toddlers will sleep better if there is a night light in their room. Shut the door to keep out household noises—but don't lock it.

Most children need and want rules. They like to break them, but that is no reason for not having them. A reasonable bedtime should gently be insisted upon. Parents should back each other up on a mutually agreed-upon time.

If both parents work outside the home, it can be difficult to go home from work, prepare dinner, do dishes, give your child a bath, and get the child into bed in a tranquil manner. You may feel as if you have no quality time with your child because your evening schedule revolves around chores. Try to have your child nap longer during the day so that a little later bedtime can be arranged. Try to keep the evening activities quiet, so that the transition to bedtime and sleep goes smoothly.

For more information, see SLEEP in the Medical Guide.

The toddler's education

The role of play

Toddlers at play are really at work coping with their environment. They think they have complete control, but they learn that many things are immovable (walks, trees, cement). They also learn that some things are taboo (hurting pets, hurting other children) and that some things are painful (a hot stove, falling).

When they are with other children their own age, they usually try to dominate. But, depending on their sex and their genetic and neurological makeup, they may sit quietly as passive observers or tearfully withdraw to thumb-sucking. Or, they may ignore playmates for a ball, blocks, or a stuffed animal. Children rarely play together until they are close to 3 years old.

Because human beings want and need love from other human beings, children learn to control impulsive, aggressive, domineering attitudes when their onslaughts bring tears, withdrawal, or counterattacks from playmates. Parents usually act as referees when toddlers are romping together. It is not fair to expect toddlers to behave like perfect ladies and gentlemen. This is a period when they just have to run roughshod over their environment. A hellion at home may be an angel at nursery school. This is a good sign that the toddler has some ability at self-control. By age 3, the child should be able to play with another child sometimes, or at least play alongside another child.

Toys

When toddlers play, they imitate things they have experienced themselves and things they see adults doing. Toddlers cuddle and feed dolls and stuffed animals. They follow parents around and "help" with chores. They enjoy clambering under tables and chairs to dust furniture legs. Using toy carpet sweepers or toy lawn mowers, they clean rugs and cut grass. They probably won't stay with jobs very long, but they get a sense of belonging and develop manual skills while walking, crawling in and out of small places, and pushing their toy tools.

"Playing" with mother is not merely play. It is an important way the toddler learns.

Toddlers are talkers. And although they are not very good at first, they improve day by day. The best thing you can do is be a good listener.

Educational toys for toddlers have simple parts that fit together. Some of these toys have big bolts and locks, gears and wheels. Some come apart in several pieces and require dexterity to reassemble—dexterity children gain only through practice.

Here are some other playthings toddlers will enjoy:

Toys with handles that they can push and pull along the floor

Large balls they can throw and chase

Objects that they can load and unload in a toy truck

Boxes that fit together, and into which they can put things

Baby dolls and stuffed animals

A sandbox or dirt pile for digging in

A bathtub or small pool for splashing and kicking in, with sponges to squeeze, boats or animals that float, and a plastic pitcher to fill up and empty

A broom or other housekeeping toy to "help" with

Learning to talk

Speech is one indication that we are intelligent beings. It is also a more effective way to communicate than kicking and shoving. When toddlers begin to talk, they are more able to get their points across without frustration. Temper tantrums begin to decrease. Toddlers spend so much of their time imitating others that their speech and vocabulary, in general, will reflect the verbal skills of those around them. Avoid baby talk. State sentences and messages to a toddler directly and clearly. Offer choices, but make sure both options are ones you can live with. To encourage toddlers to go to bed, say, "Do you want to say your prayers now or after you get into bed?" To get them to eat some peas, say, "Do you want six peas or seven peas?"

Parents need to listen when their toddlers speak. Smiles and nods will encourage children's speech attempts. If toddlers have trouble remembering the right words, th

Toddlers like to imitate their parents and often enjoy helping with some of the work around the house, such as baking pies and mowing the lawn.

should be asked to try to tell the same thing in a different way. Stammering at age 3 is a normal stage in speech development. Thoughts seem to be going faster than the ability to say the words. Overzealous attempts to correct toddlers' speech may make them self-conscious and frustrated. For more information, see STUTTERING in the Medical Guide.

Storytelling

Educators know that children who come from homes where reading and books are valued are more likely to succeed academically than those from homes without this interest. Toddlers can be encouraged to read and listen and enjoy literature if their parents read to them from books that were written with the appropriate age and attention span in mind.

Story time can be a rich twenty minutes for parents and children and long cherished by both. It may be the only time during the day that nagging and whining are absent. It brings new thoughts and feelings to the participants. As a result, a toddler will often break in with a question or an observation. When this happens, stop reading for a moment. Your toddler probably wants to learn something or share something with you.

Sometimes, a child wants to hear the same story every night. A word or two cannot be skipped without loud protest: "You didn't say *rabbit!*" It is difficult to say why some children want or need to have one favorite story read over and over again. Do not be concerned about it. This stage, too, will pass.

Learning by imitation

A wise philosopher once stated that children force parents to become more mature. Parents sense the responsibility they have in civilizing the animal inside every child and raising the child to become a responsible adult. Parents who love their children will feed love into, and provide limits for, their children. Then these children, when they become parents themselves, will be able to imitate these methods. Some of the most disorganized young adults become the most efficient housekeepers when away from their mothers and confronted with the challenge of their own children.

Sometimes it is difficult, but parents should let their children know the joys and rewards of being parents and responsible adults. Toddlers need to experiment with these roles by imitating them. They also need to feel the variety and range of human emotions—love, fear, anger, grief—and learn when these are appropriately expressed. For example, a toddler should not be sheltered from the fact of a loved one's death, but be allowed to experience the sorrow of the loss.

Health and safety

Accidents

One function of parents is to prevent their children from hurting themselves in a dangerous world. A toddler's all-embracing habit of getting into everything needs its rightful outlets, but it also calls for strong checks and a defining of limits. Toddlers are surrounded by many dangers, and so they must necessarily be surrounded by many safeguards.

Toddlers need to be both hemmed in and kept out. Closed doors are not enough, because toddlers soon learn to turn knobs. Locked doors keep toddlers out of poten-

tially dangerous places. Safety gates also provide restraints in dangerous places, such as the top or bottom of stairs.

Bathrooms especially need to be safe. The contents of medicine cabinets fascinate toddlers. The shapes and colors of bottles draw children to this cabinet. As toddlers become adept at unscrewing or removing bottle tops, they are more likely to sample the contents.

To protect your child, buy medicines and drugs with child-resistant caps. Even so, keep medicines locked up. Be sure to return them to the cabinet after use. If the pretty

Gates at the top and bottom of stairs can prevent many toddler accidents. These safeguards may make your toddler unhappy, but they are necessary.

pills are out of sight, your toddler will not be tempted to taste or eat them. The major cause of child poisonings is aspirin and aspirin substitutes, so buy them in small amounts and keep them in a safe place.

Added hazards arise as toddlers learn to climb. They don't confine themselves to the usual climbing, like stairs. They are all too often after things that are out of reach. They quickly learn where the cookies are kept, and they will most likely have a special interest in climbing on top of radiators or furniture to get to window ledges.

Toddlers also have a great desire to poke and pry, which often leads to probing electric outlets with hairpins or bobby pins. You can buy covers for your electric outlets from a hardware store.

To further accident-proof your home, kneel down on the floor and pretend you are a toddler bent on exploring everything within reach. Is the cord for the coffeemaker still plugged into the wall? Is a purse with pills in it within reach? Does the coffee table have sharp edges? Are ant paste, paints, cleansers, and soaps within reach? Look at your stove. Have you left any pot handles pointing into the room? Be sure to have one or more smoke detectors in your home, and check them once a month to be sure they are working properly.

Teach your toddler to buckle up immediately on getting into a car. Don't start the car until everyone is buckled up in a seat belt.

Common conditions and infectious diseases

A healthy toddler frequently develops minor infections. A parent can expect a child in this age group to have 5 to 6 colds per year, 2 episodes of gastroenteritis (diarrhea), and 1 to 2 episodes of otitis media (ear infections). Day care is a minor risk factor which will increase these frequencies. Older children who have been in day care seem to have fewer common illnesses later because their resistance has been built up. One or more smokers in the household greatly increases the number of cold-like illnesses a child will have. Fever may also be common at this time. It may be the first sign of a serious infection. For a temperature of over 101° F. (38.2° C), consult your pediatrician. In most cases, toddlers are resilient and bounce back quickly to normal activity once illness peaks.

The frequency of previously common contagious diseases such as measles, German measles, diphtheria, whooping cough, mumps, and polio has been drastically reduced because of current immunization procedures. Chicken pox remains a common contagious disease that toddlers easily catch if exposed to it. If children are healthy, they may be miserable with the disease for a few days, but in most cases complications do not occur. In this age group aspirin is not advised for the treatment of fever because of its association with Reye's syndrome. It is particularly important that children with chicken pox not be given aspirin.

Noninfectious conditions also are common during this age period. A number of these result from confusion regarding diet. Parents often become concerned because their toddlers are "picky eaters" or have "poor appetites." Usually if toddlers are offered a variety of foods and balanced diets, even the picky eaters will balance their diets over time. Parents should be assured that if the children's height, weight, and physical exams are normal and if the age-appropriate screening tests (see below) are normal, their children's diets are probably satisfactory. Making mealtime or food an issue can lead to future problems.

Constipation is common among toddlers because parents often urge them to consume too much milk and other dairy products. Consequently, the children do not eat enough meat, fruit, and vegetables, which have more fiber than milk and bread.

Anemia, because of iron deficiency, is common for the same reason as constipation. Parents encourage toddlers to eat large quantities of dairy products at the expense of other foods, such as meat and green vegetables. Iron deficiency results because white foods contain relatively little iron.

A final condition that can be a problem for toddlers is lead poisoning. It usually occurs in areas polluted with lead (air, water, and so on) and in areas where houses have lead-base paint. Children may have high levels of lead without symptoms, but high levels of lead can lead to serious, acute illness or long-term effects. Parents concerned about childhood lead poisoning should consult the pediatrician.

Preventive Health Care

Two or three visits to the pediatrician for preventive health care are recommended for the child between the ages of 18 and 36 months. At the beginning of the visit, the pediatrician observes the child and discusses any concerns the parents might have. The doctor will also ask about the child's behavior, development, and diet. A thorough physical examination follows. With information obtained from these procedures, the pediatrician will counsel the parents regarding any condition identified, expectations for the child's behavior, and the child's expected development in the near future. Pertinent safety issues will also be discussed. At the conclusion of the visit, age-appropriate preventive measures are ordered by the pediatrician. These measures usually include immunizations and screening tests.

When the child reaches 18 months, most physicians will give the child the DPT shot—diphtheria, pertussis (whooping cough), and tetanus (lockjaw)—and the OPV (oral polio vaccine). These are boosters for the primary series of immunizations given to the child in infancy. At this same age, it is also recommended that the toddler also receive the HIB shot (H influenza B). This vaccine is effective in preventing H influenza B, meningitis, and epiglottitis (bacterial croup).

During the office visit, the pediatrician may also take blood samples from the toddler for screening tests for iron deficiency anemia and lead poisoning. Screening tests are a major cornerstone of preventive care. These tests are performed at ages when children are prone to a disease or a condition, but before the child has symptoms. Identifying such conditions early and beginning treatment can prevent more serious illnesses.

Finally, by 18 months, the child will be screened for tuberculosis. If an exposure has occurred since the screening, the physician will test the child again for tuberculosis.

For more information, see the following articles in the Medical Guide: CHICKEN POX, DIPHTHERIA, IMMUNIZATION, TETANUS, TUBERCULOSIS, and WHOOPING COUGH.

Teeth, feet, eyes, and ears

"Toothbrush at 2, the dentist at 3" is a rule that encourages good dental habits. When toddlers near 2, they probably watch with fascination while their parents brush their teeth. Because of their passion to imitate things other people do, they will probably want to brush their teeth, too. This is a great time to hand toddlers their own toothbrushes and let them try. They will not brush well at first, but with a little help they will catch on. The best time to have toddlers brush is after each meal. This means three times a day, which in most homes is nearly impossible. The most important brushing time is after supper. This brushing cleans teeth for the long night ahead. If brushing three times a day fails, aim for two times—after breakfast and after supper.

A fluoride is a compound that helps make teeth strong and reduces tooth decay. In many areas children receive fluoride from the water they drink. If fluoride is not available in the water, they should receive it as a supplement prescribed by their doctor or dentist.

If your toddler walks with the toes of both feet pointing inward and the heels pointing outward, the child is pigeon-toed. This condition is common before walking is well established. Corrective measures are taken only under extreme circumstances.

The lazy eye begins in this age group. The muscles of the lazy eye are weak and, if they are untreated, they may cause the eye to cross. Usually, a doctor puts a patch over the child's good eye so that the lazy eye has to work harder.

If your child has not imitated any words by the age of 2, he or she may have a hearing loss. Consult your pediatrician. The doctor will probably suggest that you take the child to a specialist in hearing problems, so that the child's hearing can be evaluated. For more information, see DEAFNESS in the Medical Guide.

Common concerns

Toilet training

Successful potty training is probably the most significant and potentially stressful task facing a toddler. Knowing exactly what your toddler must learn will increase your understanding of the process of potty training.

Learning to use the potty is a very gradual process. A child must have physical control and be able to understand what is expected. Most children do not have reliable daytime control of their muscles until they are 2½ to 3 years old. Nighttime control may not be gained until 3 or 4 years. Boys usually take longer to train than girls.

In order to successfully use the potty, the child must:
- Understand what you want;
- Realize what is about to happen—and tighten the appropriate muscles;
- Get to the bathroom;
- Undress;
- Get safely on the potty (often trying this with pants down around the ankles);
- Relax the muscles; and
- Get off the potty, pull up the pants, and complete all the hygiene tasks.

With all of this in mind, do yourself and your toddler a favor. Wait until your child is ready. Starting too early is very frustrating for everyone concerned.

Before beginning on the potty training, help your child to understand what this is all about: what urine and feces are; where they come from and where you want them to go.

Children learn by imitating. Give your toddler the vocabulary a child needs to talk about going to the bathroom, and help your

child learn to use those words at the appropriate times. Keep all references to the potty and body functions positive. Avoid acting like body products are dirty or messy. You want your child to tell you when he or she has to go.

Toddlers want to be able to do things for themselves, so dress your child in elastic-waisted pants sized big enough to pull down independently. Avoid snaps, zippers, and overalls. Use disposable diapers for a while so your child can unfasten the tapes. Introduce "big kid" training pants.

Finally, introduce your child to the potty chair. The type that sits on the floor allows your child to feel more secure because the feet are firmly on the ground.

There are two basic readiness signals to look for before beginning potty training. First, there is physical readiness, indicated by having dry pants for longer periods of time. Second, there is cognitive readiness, indicated when your child begins to use the words you've taught in order to tell you what is happening when he or she begins to urinate or have a bowel movement in the diaper or pants.

Now is the time to suggest that your child sit on the potty several times a day. Both boys and girls should sit on the potty, because standing to urinate is difficult for little boys to manage. They are still too short to aim over the edge of the potty. Choose likely times—after meals or snacks, first thing in the morning, while the bath water runs, or any time your toddler's diaper has been dry for a long time.

Make your toddler's time on the potty pleasant, and let your child get up as soon as he or she is ready to do so. Each time your child uses the potty, give praise. There is no need for bribes of candy or toys.

Accidents will happen. Be patient. Never scold or punish your child for having an accident. React casually and say that next time you'd like your child to try to use the potty so the pants will stay dry.

If no progress has been made after a week or so, go back to diapers and try again in several weeks.

Remember, you will need to be patient and loving and supportive of your toddler. Accidents will happen after you think potty training has been completed.

Temper tantrums

Being independent can be terribly frustrating for toddlers. They have the desire to do things beyond their abilities. They try very hard and fail, or perhaps your rules or limits do not allow room to try something your toddler is very anxious to do.

Because toddlers become frustrated so often and don't have the vocabulary to explain themselves or put up a reasonable argument, temper tantrums abound.

Temper tantrums are emotionally and physically exhausting for both you and your toddler. Avoiding them is not easy. Toddlers experience frustration as they learn to dress, to feed themselves, to build things, and to play successfully. They are not able to judge or protect their tolerance levels in order to avoid emotional explosions.

Most toddlers have tantrums—some more than others. But as their skills develop and they become less frustrated, temper tantrums decrease. As their language skills improve, toddlers are able to talk about their feelings instead of kicking and hitting.

Preventing tantrums or defusing one that has started is not easy. Your goal should be to keep a tantrum from starting. Although this demands a great deal of patience and creativity, it is often less taxing than coping with a kicking and screaming toddler.

Try to keep your toddler out of situations that are too overwhelming, including toys and activities geared toward older children

with higher levels of small- or large-muscle coordination. In general, make sure that the toys available are appropriate for your toddler and that your toddler can play with them independently with success. If there are not enough interesting toys around, your bored but curious toddler will head for things that are off limits to touch.

As something becomes frustrating, help your toddler in a way that lets a young child successfully complete the task. Your toddler will feel good, and you will have avoided a tantrum. Another option is to redirect your child. For instance, saying "Those blocks are having trouble staying on top of each other, so let's try building another way instead" gives your child another more appropriate way to play with the blocks.

All parents worry that if they don't stop a tantrum toddlers will hurt themselves, but children rarely hurt themselves during temper tantrums. You will not be able to eliminate temper tantrums, but you should make every effort to control them.

There are two approaches to controlling tantrums: (1) to ignore them; (2) to hold and comfort your child during a tantrum.

You can ignore a tantrum by standing near your toddler until it subsides, or you can leave the room or carry your child to a special place to calm down away from the rest of the family. By successfully ignoring your tantrumy toddler, you will avoid feeling bad and giving in to the tantrum.

In dealing with your toddler, acknowledge those hard-to-handle feelings: "I can see you're very angry because the blocks keep falling down, but I'm going to leave until you calm down. When you're ready to talk to me, let me know."

You can also reduce your toddler's frustration by giving in a little yourself. Allow your toddler to wear that striped shirt with the plaid pants if it's really important. Think carefully before you automatically say "no." But if you wait until the tantrum has started and then say "yes," you will reinforce the temper tantrum.

This does not mean that you will always do what your toddler asks, but that you will say "no" only when the answer really is "no." Stick with your decision, tantrum or no tantrum.

As a tantrum subsides, you can help your child regain control. Cuddle your child; say you're sorry the child was so upset and you're glad he or she is feeling better.

Public tantrums will upset you more than tantrums at home. Do not have a battle with your child because you are embarrassed. Look for a quiet place where you can help your child cool down. It may be the end of a grocery store aisle or in your car. If you are visiting, ask your host if there is a room that you might use.

"No! No! No!"

A toddler's first word may be "Mamma" and the second may be "Daddy." Or the first may be "Daddy" and the second "Mamma." Here the language controversy usually ends, because it is almost universally accepted that a toddler's third word will be "No." Why? Because toddlers hear the word so much from their parents.

At 18 to 24 months, toddlers who are developing normally will shake their heads, say "No," and look at their parents while touching "taboo" objects like a hot stove, television knobs, or the garbage. They are learning self-control, but someone has to teach it to them. And parents are the ones who have to do it. Toddlers who are doing dangerous things have to be disciplined— there will be time for the social niceties later on. At this stage in a toddler's life, the parents' main responsibility is to keep the child whole.

In dealing with your toddler, don't frustrate yourself by setting up occasions for discipline. Remove valuable and dangerous things from view. Keep your favorite bric-a-brac out of reach for a few months. Do not offer a toddler a large, fat, slippery glass of juice. The child will most likely spill it and you will find yourself saying "No! No! No!"

There should, of course, be a good number of "Yes" situations about—some places where toddlers can make a mess with clay or blocks, pull-apart toys, and some paper that can be ripped up. Children who hear "No" too often may develop a poor self-image. They may go through life thinking that they cannot do anything right.

Jealousy toward a new baby

No matter what a child is told about the joys of having a brother or a sister, the older child nonetheless feels jealous of the new baby. A toddler is no exception. The toddler feels dethroned from the central and exclusive position formerly enjoyed in the affection of his or her parents. Even though the parents try to reassure the toddler of their continuing love, the child sees that love is now no longer his or her monopoly but obviously shared with the baby. Because the toddler depends on this love, the baby appears as a rival who threatens his or her status.

Jealousy assumes many forms. Each of these has a double purpose: to express hostility and to attract greater amounts of parental attention, though not necessarily love. Some youngsters come right out with their resentment. "I hate my brother! You don't love me any more!" What is called for is patient reassurance that feeling angry because of the baby is understandable—that the lot of an older child is indeed difficult at times. Also point out that there are compensations, too. Given this kind of sympathy, your youngster will usually return to his or her former good disposition. This might also be a good time to step up compensation—to give the older child special privileges, such as staying up later at night, being read to more, and having more outings with one or both parents.

Other children show their distress in a more roundabout fashion. They may pretend that the baby belongs to another family and has only come to visit. Or they may hug the baby too strenuously. Frequently, they regress to other ways of coping with the world: thumb-sucking, clinging to mother, insisting on having a bottle just like their new brother or sister. Children who have been toilet-trained for some time may begin to wet the bed at night or have daytime accidents. Deal with these toddlers' anxieties by reassuring them rather than reprimanding them. They should be given a bottle if they request it. Parents should devote more time to them and give them age- and status-appropriate activities that make them feel that being more grown up is fun.

You and your toddler

Parents of toddlers must act as the grand marshals of a parade. Noisy exhibitions of exuberant fury must somehow be channeled and controlled. Toddlers need rules to follow, just as marching bands in a parade need a routine and a cadence to follow. Toddlers are more secure if they know their limits, and they frequently need to be told when they have stretched those limits too far.

Toddlers need:

Freedom to explore in a safe environment;

Consistent limits set on their aggressive acts, especially hurting others;

Recognition of their accomplishments by love and praise;

Expectations based on their developing muscular abilities;

Security that their parents will be consistent and help them regain their self-control;

More "yeses" than "noes."

With an impulsive toddler about the house, there is little time or need for a "significant dialogue." Do what you have to do at the time when it is needed. The toddler's behavior may make you scream at times. But if you loved your child as a newborn, and if you adored your infant when he or she smiled at you at 4 months of age, you will somehow keep the toddler intact until you can get your breath again at age 3.

Ideally, you should be equipped with:

A sense of humor;

Energy;

A sympathetic spouse, in-laws, and doctor;

The ability to nap;

The conviction that you are winning more often than you are losing.

Many toddlers like to arrange their toys before they are ready to go to sleep.

The Preschooler: 3 to 5 years

At about 3, youngsters enter the pre-school years— truly formative years, marked by intellectual growth, rapidly developing motor skills, much greater social maturity, and emotional richness.

Most 3-year-olds are beginning to use words well. During the next two years, they will more than double their vocabularies. And they will want to know more and more.

At 3, most children are beginning to be able to ride a tricycle but are still learning to use their hands. But at 5, these youngsters will be able walkers, runners, and climbers who can handle things with dexterity.

These children are ready and eager to learn. It is up to parents to keep this sense of curiosity and wonder alive.

By James L. Hymes, Jr., Ed.D.
"Health and safety" section
by Eugene F. Diamond, M.D.
Diane Shaffer, M. Ed., and Steven
Waskerwitz, M.D., Consulting Editors

Portrait of the preschooler

The way children use tricycles says a lot about how their motor skills are developing during this age span. When children are 3, they are almost surely beginners on trikes. At first, they may be content merely to sit on the seat. Then they start to experiment with the pedals, but, in the beginning, don't quite get the hang of them. Sometimes they want to move forward, but the trike goes backward. Then for a while, they ride along rather deliberately, proud of their movement and steering. Soon, they discover how fast they can go. They don't slow down for turns. They ride as close to people as they

Even though preschoolers may be together, they may not always play together. Two may make sand cakes, while a third plays alone.

can. If they have to stop, they wait until the very last second and then put on the brakes hard. Every bit of this hard pumping, daring turning, smart steering, and skilled stopping is accompanied by noises—motor noises of "brr-brr" and horn noises "honk, honk."

Parents can also see progress in motor development as the preschoolers gradually acquire greater skill in dressing themselves. By the time they are 3, children can unbutton the front and side buttons of clothes, but they have a hard time buttoning them. They cannot tell the back of their clothes from the front, and so they often put pants on backward. They may still need some help in putting on shirts, sweaters, and other articles of clothing.

When they are 4, preschoolers dress themselves with little help, but the process may seem to take forever. They can now button and unbutton side and front buttons on their clothes. They are also able to distinguish between the front and the back of their clothes and put them on correctly.

Social development

The way two preschoolers play together on their trikes shows changes in social growth as well as motor development. Two 3-year-olds may simply like to be near each other on their trikes. They may bump each other experimentally with little, testing, hardly touching bumps. A little laughter, a little giggling often go along with the bumps and touches, but there is seldom any great flow of words. One of the youngsters may decide to head off somewhere; to some near destination, because at this age children do not yet go far afield. The other will probably follow, but not always right away. A little thought has to go on first. The social response is not yet quick, sure, and certain.

As they near their fifth birthday, these same two youngsters are very different. There is almost no "just sitting." They are sure to be on the go. There are almost no quiet times.

The 3-year-old business of one child's going off on some venture while the other tentatively follows is out. Now they play together. They have plans and they talk about them, sometimes with a few spats and brief fallings-out. Once they cook up an idea, each one is likely to carry it out with modifications that make the plan his or her own. These older preschoolers have grown into social creatures who get thrills from being with each other.

The pleasure of each other's company, the excitement of what they are doing together sometimes becomes so overwhelming that toilet-trained children occasionally "forget" and come home wet. In their own list of priorities, these preschoolers have put first things first. Being with a friend, playing with a friend—now that is something new.

Language development

Intermingled closely with social development is another major advance of preschool years—the development of language. By the time children are about 4, they become chatterboxes who never shut up.

Preschoolers do not simply chatter, however. Their talking involves all the parts of speech, gradually longer sentences, and a greater clarity. Language development and social development aid one another. Most

It takes time, but preschoolers eventually learn how to dress themselves—shoes and all.

Preschoolers, both boys and girls, like to work along with their parents on such jobs as washing the family car. Imitation is one way a preschooler learns.

preschool children still fight at times, of course. If they are greatly provoked, they may even bite and kick. But they gradually learn to use words to settle their differences and their disputes.

The great growth in a preschooler's speech can trouble adults. Preschoolers seem to talk too much. They frequently interrupt because what they have to say is still the most important thing in the world to them. They often talk too loudly. Commonly, around the age of 4, they go on a spree of name-calling and experimenting with nonsensical singsongs.

One other occasionally annoying characteristic of the preschooler is a never-ending stream of questions. Inquiries increase and become more complex from about 3 years on. The questions *Why?* and *How come?* are asked more often, as well as questions such as, "Where do babies come from?" Preschoolers are trying hard to understand what objects and relationships are, how things work and what things are for.

The preschooler's education

Preschoolers' constant questions reflect another side of development in these years—their intense curiosity and their thirst for knowledge. One of the most outstanding characteristics of preschoolers is that they are so completely ready to learn—about the world around them, about themselves as part of that world, about other children, and about adults. Preschoolers are curious, open, and responsive. Their eyes go out to all that is around them. Their ears pick up what is around them. Their hands are tools for fascinated exploration.

One of the most important tasks for parents is to keep this burning curiosity and charmed sense of wonder alive. Children will go far with curiosity and wonder. Without them, now and in the years ahead, children will have to be pushed or pulled or lured.

Most parents appreciate curiosity. Sometimes, however, without meaning to, they discourage it. Curious children may trouble and frighten parents. Parents worry about safety. When parents' irritations or their worries mount, the danger is that children will hear *No* and *Don't* and *Be careful* and *Watch out* too often. Parents must take precautions, of course. But at the same time, they should make sure that the world does not seem like a "bad" or "dangerous" or "not nice" place to the child. Curiosity cannot stand a never-ending stream of discouragement.

Parents must also be careful not to let their children's curiosity wither from lack of stimulation. Children desperately want to know more and to understand their world.

Trips

Trips are one of the best ways of bringing new, stimulating, mind-stretching experiences to young children. Preschoolers are basically uninformed—they simply do not know much yet because they have not lived long enough, or experienced enough. No one can really tell children at this age about the world. The children do not yet have the background or knowledge to understand the meaning of the words. They have to see things first. They need firsthand experiences. Later, words can build on these experiences. Trips, now, are a perfect solution to learning for preschoolers.

Trips for preschoolers should be short. Young children tire easily, and a tired, fussy

Trips to a fire station or other nearby places are treats for a preschooler.

child learns little. The destination does not have to be spectacular, either. To a young child, the filling station, the supermarket, the florist shop, the post office, the barn, the stream, the airport, and other everyday locations are a treat.

Time transforms an everyday "trip to mail a letter" or "trip to get a quart of milk" into an educational experience. A good trip for a child has a slow, relaxed pace with time for talking en route, both coming and going. There ought to be time, too, for several short stops along the way. Unexpected side explorations can sometimes be better than the main trip itself. And at any stop, en route or at your destination, your pre-schooler needs time to stand and watch, time to touch, time to explore. Preschoolers cannot take in all they want to know at a glance. On trips, there are countless opportunities to point out sights your child might otherwise miss. And there are countless opportunities to ask provocative questions that might not otherwise occur to the child.

Stories

Good storybooks, like good trips, stimulate children. Stories bring a part of the world closer to them so that they can take a closer

Story time is a time for companionship and conversation. Try to make it a daily event.

look at it and come to understand it more fully. Stories may be make-believe or about real people and events. They may involve animals that seem almost human. They may include more adventure than most people have in their everyday lives. But fiction or nonfiction, children's books help preschoolers get a better handle on the people, the events, the objects in the real life that exists around them.

The trick in reading a story well to your child is the same trick as in taking the child on a successful trip. Take your time. Do not rush to the end of the story. Let your child interrupt to ask a question, even if it takes you both off on a tangent. Story time should be a daily event, and often an evening event—a time for companionship and conversation between you and your preschool child.

Enriching the preschooler's play

Language and social development, increased knowledge, longer attention span, and vastly improved physical coordination all combine to produce the most distinctive characteristic of preschool children. They are highly imaginative and have the special capacity to make believe. They can take on any roles that suit their fancy. There should be no fixed roles for boys and for girls. The children themselves can become anything they want to be—baby, cowboy, wild animal. A chair can become a horse or a plane or an animal cage. To adults looking on, preschoolers seem to spend all of their time "just playing." The play of preschool children is far from a waste of time, however. It is highly significant activity that teaches important emotional, intellectual, and social lessons.

Children at play draw on what they know. They very often play house, for example, mostly because life at home is what they know best. The play is imaginative, but it is firmly grounded in reality. The more children know—the more places they have been, the more things they have seen—the richer their play will be.

Preschoolers need toys and materials, too, with which to carry out their play. The same toys are for all to use. They are not ear-

Boxes are toys that stretch a child's imagination. They can be whatever the child wants them to be—a car, a rocket, a grocery store, a house.

marked "this is for boys" and "this is for girls." Good preschool toys set up rough outlines and give the child's fertile mind freedom to fill in the details. A tricycle, for example, is obviously some kind of moving vehicle, but the child decides whether it is a horse, ambulance, police car, ship, rocket, plane, bus, truck, fire engine, or tank. Among the best playthings are boards, boxes, blankets, sand, cartons, wagons, chairs, dolls, simple cars and boats, and other materials that can be used in various ways. They let the richness come from a child's own flow of images.

One kind of imaginative activity is special to this age—creating an imaginary playmate. Youngsters without many real age mates, and youngsters who have no brothers or sisters, are most apt to make up an imaginary friend. But even youngsters with many real-life pals may add one more: their own, personal, not-seen-by-adults child. The imaginary playmate can be someone to boss or someone who gives support and comfort. This unseen friend is important to a child. Try to make the few short-term adjustments needed to fit this new member into your home.

Television and the preschooler

The fascination television holds for preschoolers is an indication of their thirst for stimulation. TV's fast-moving pictures and continuous sound lure many young children into watching contentedly for hours. For better or for worse, television is a teacher. Television viewing affects children's language and their awareness of the world around them.

Television also provides relaxation and entertainment. However, viewing presents many hazards. There is reason to worry about the impact of TV's violence on the feelings and morals of youngsters, to be concerned about the impact of commercials on their taste and the effect of long hours of passive watching on their personality. One must also be concerned because too much television viewing can rob a family of time for talk and shared activities, and can also deprive children of creative play with their age mates. The television set should not become a "baby sitter."

Some families react to these concerns by having no TV set. When TV is available, it is important for parents to make thoughtful decisions about what programs to view and how long children may watch. Involving preschoolers in these decisions will offer them learning experiences about choices and responsibilities.

It is also wise to watch television often enough with your children so that you can discuss with them the ideas, feelings, and values the programs may generate. You may also wish to consider becoming involved with groups working to improve television for preschoolers. If good programs are available, and if viewing hours are wisely regulated, television can be a positive educational force. For further information see CHILDREN AND TELEVISION in For Special Consideration.

Schools for the preschooler

Many 3- and 4-year-olds go to school. Some are in nursery school, usually for half a day, because the parents want to supplement the stimulation and companionship they can offer at home. And some 4-year-olds go to public kindergartens. Other children of this age are in a group situation all day because both parents work or because they come from a single-parent family. These children usually go to a day-care or child-care center.

It may be hard for some adults to imagine a "school" for children only 3 or 4 years old. "School" to these adults means a teacher in front of the classroom, the children seated at desks, books as the major tool for teaching, and the children hushed and quiet with no moving about. Obviously, this is not the style of 3- and 4-year-olds.

The ways of schools for 3- and 4-year-olds fit the children who come. The schoolroom is more like a workshop than a lecture hall. The youngsters move about. They spend most of their time in small groups of two or three or four. They begin to learn to live, work, and play together. They learn to take turns, to settle disputes fairly, and to cooperate. The program is also planned to let children use their bodies well. A good school for children this age has both indoor and outdoor facilities and gives ample time for climbing, balancing, swinging, and other activities that build muscle coordination in preschoolers.

The children hear stories and music. They sing songs and take many short, educational trips. They are surrounded by informative and challenging pictures and exhibits. There is ample time for them to ask many questions of their teacher and of their friends. Their knowledge, their language, and their awareness of the world around them are always growing.

The children also have the opportunity to express themselves through block play, sand play, artwork of many kinds, and working with carpentry tools and wood. Outdoors, they use such equipment as boards, boxes, big blocks, tricycles, climbing apparatus, and wagons. They are almost constantly involved in make-believe play—play that gives them the chance to use their initiative, to think, to plan, to develop their attention span, and to build their capacity for problem solving. (For additional information, see DAY CARE in For Special Consideration.)

Common concerns

The preschool period can be a happy time in family life, free from overwhelming problems. One reason for this is that preschool children can do so much more for themselves. They can be independent in feeding themselves, in dressing, and in using the toilet. They are no longer the physical drain on their parents that they were as infants. Another great help is their delight in the world and in the people around them. Their eagerness, openness, and good feelings about being alive can be quite contagious. No age, however, is completely angelic. There are always some rough spots.

Dawdling

The conflict between a young child's time schedule and that of parents is often a trouble area. Most adults have watches on their wrists. They are going somewhere and know exactly how many minutes they need to get there. Young children loaf along and dream along, undriven and unpressured. Adults call this pace "dawdling." Children, of course, have no special name for what they do. This slower pace is the way they act. It can take a child what seems like ages to finish eating, to get dressed, or to "come along." The child tends to stop and fascinatedly watch the world go by. This special pace is a part of being a 3-year-old or a 4-year-old. It is a part of the newness of being able to do things for one's self—a part of the wonder at the world.

The best approach for coping with dawdling is to make some minor adjustments.

For example, with eating and dressing, allow as much time as possible so that your child has leeway for dreaming. But if something pressing lies ahead, pitch in with a helping hand to speed up the eating or dressing process. Do not nag or pester. Angry words seldom produce a speed-up. There will be times when reality demands that the meal be ended—the available time has simply run out. There is no great harm in a child's experiencing this. The harm comes only when—as the food is taken away—adult anger, nagging, and complaining come to take its place.

It may help you to keep your balance if you remember that this slow pace does not go on forever. The time is not far distant when you may worry more because your child bolts food and jumps into whatever clothes are left around.

Fears

Some problems arise, too, because it is so easy to forget that the 3-year-olds in particular, but also the 4-year-olds, are still little, dependent children. They have grown so much. They can do so much more for themselves. But they have many moments when they feel like the "little babies" that they, in part, still are. When parents forget this, they often are harsher than they should be. This is especially true when these children get frightened. And a wide, unpredictable range of events and sounds and sights can scare them. Preschoolers are still new to this world. And every day, their greater mobility opens up more and more of the world. The loud, the unexpected, the new, the big, the fast-moving, the dark—it is hard to know what will take their breath away next, but a great many events can.

The quick, easy response is the pep talk: "You're not afraid of a little thing like that, are you?" Parents are not afraid, but parents are old-timers. The preschooler's only reply, which is often screamed with the whole body, is to say in effect, "I certainly am afraid . . . that's what this fuss is all about."

Worse than the pep talk is unsympathetic scoffing and shaming: "Don't be a little baby . . . Don't be a scaredy cat . . . You're supposed to be a big (boy or girl)." When children are afraid of dogs, of thunder and lightning, or of the dark, it hardly helps to have the added fear of losing their parents' love and respect.

A much more effective way to deal with fright is to accept the fact that your child is frightened. Give support and comfort so that the child feels strong enough to face the frightening event. Sometimes just moving over to stand by the preschooler's side is all the support that is needed. Sometimes this,

Accept the fact that your child has fears. Then give the support and comfort needed.

plus a comforting word or two, does the trick. Youngsters who are deeply upset have to be held and patted and comforted. The goal is to give enough support so that they feel better, without doing so much that they feel pushed back into babyhood.

Then, when your child has calmed down a bit, try to teach the youngster how to cope with the experience the next time it happens. The more competence the child has, the fewer fears there will be. Explain the cause of thunder and lightning, or why it gets dark. Teach the preschooler where to pat a dog, how to hold the hamster, so that the child can manage the situation the next time it arises.

The most upsetting fear of all, of course, occurs when children think their parents do not love them. Any one of a wide variety of happenings can start this unhappy train of thought. Being left alone in a strange new setting like a hospital, a doctor's office, Sunday school, or nursery school can start it. The hazard is separation. Young children easily translate "Separation . . . they are leaving me" into "Separation . . . they don't love me." Harshness, coldness, and busyness can have the same effect. The child feels alone and unprotected.

Sometimes the events parents think ought to make a child feel big have the opposite effect. A new baby in the family and starting school are two examples. The wise approach is the same as with all fears. Give support and be understanding until the child is able to cope with the problem.

Toilet-talk

Some troubles come along in these years because preschoolers are still young children. But other difficulties pop up because these are such "big-feeling" children. Much of the time these youngsters want to feel big, and much of the time parents are glad about this feeling. But there are moments when almost every parent wants to say, "Slow down . . . Not THAT big!"

Because of their increased control of language, preschoolers do not have to use gross, physical displays to prove their bigness—as they did when they were only 2. Tantrums are rarities, almost nonexistent.

Reasoning is the best approach to discipline. But it is a slow method requiring patience.

But the more refined ways can be as irritating and as troubling as the grosser ways.

Three-year-olds, and especially 4-year-olds, are apt to use toilet-talk because they sense it is "shocking language" and a means of seeming big, tough, and clearly independent. Words like "do-do" and "grunt-grunt" and "wee-wee" become, for a while, standard adjectives to describe anything. Some families simply live with these sounds. The "shocking" noises run down after a while as children find other, more "improved" and "mature" ways of making the same point. Some families let the noises go for a period and then, when they think the children have made their point, say "That's enough of that." Or they give them some funny-sounding substitute word.

Discipline

Developing good discipline in children is one of the most important jobs of parenthood. But this vital task takes time, patience, and understanding.

Many parents believe that discipline and punishment are the same thing. But punishment is only one of several ways to teach discipline. It is not the only way, nor is it the best. It is, in fact, the most difficult to use wisely, and often produces the very opposite of the result parents want.

Many parents also believe that children resent discipline. These parents not only hesitate to punish their children, but seldom use any of the better methods to build discipline. They want to be good to their children and end up by being too lenient. Undisciplined children are almost always unhappy children. They never know what the limits are, and this is unsettling. They need someone to teach them what is right and what is wrong, and why.

Wise parents do not shrink from disciplining their children. But instead of using one method all the time, they seek, instead, to puzzle out why their children misbehave, and then to take whatever action best fits the situation. For example, young children often misbehave because *they simply do not know any better.* When this is the problem, one appropriate method of discipline is to patiently explain what the rules are and why rules are important. You try to teach so that your child will understand.

Teaching is effective only if parents believe in what they are saying. Their way of talking must convey that the lesson is important. And the process must never be one of "talking to the wind"—to a child who pays no attention, or listens with only half an ear. When you say, "Stop," and tell the child why, the action must stop—at least for that moment.

For example, if your child is beating on a window with a stick, say very firmly:

"Stop that. Windows are made of glass, and glass breaks easily. So don't hit the window with your stick. The window may break."

Take the stick away, and move the child away from the window.

Reasoning is a slow method. You cannot expect a child to learn because you talk over an incident just once. But in the long run, reasoning is a good method because it helps children learn values that they can act on when they are on their own. It is also a method that respects the child's growing independence.

Besides explaining and giving reasons, you should praise your children when they act well. Praise, especially when it directly follows good behavior, is a booster to learning. For example, if your child comes to the ta-

ble with clean hands, or acts in a way you expect, offer immediate praise. You might say, "That's good!" or "I like to see that!" or whatever honest words of praise fit the situation. Your welcome approval reinforces the child's good behavior, making it more apt to be repeated.

"Not knowing any better" is only one reason for misbehavior, just as reasoning is only one method for teaching discipline. At times, children do the wrong thing because of the *setting* they are in. When this seems to be the case, the way to discipline is not by talking, but by action. Change the setting to make it easier for the child to be good. This approach is especially useful with children too young to really understand words, but it also works with older children. For example, things that a toddler should not touch should be put out of reach. Older children who have to sit for a long time on a car ride or while waiting in a doctor's or dentist's office will behave much better if you give them a book to read or color, or a game to play.

Another reason for misbehavior lies in children's *feelings*. Children have to feel right to act right. Some boys and girls are driven to bad behavior because they desperately need more love, or more attention, or a feeling of importance. They do things they know they should not do. A jealous child, for example, may hurt a baby sister or brother. Of course the baby must be protected, and the behavior must of course be stopped. The temptation is to punish children driven by upset feelings, but the surest way to help them is to give them the love, or attention, or importance their behavior shows they need.

Parents have to be thoughtful in choosing an approach to discipline, one that fits the child and the situation. This sensitive process of deciding what action to take itself contributes to discipline. It is an expression of love, and the foundation of all good behavior is a child's sense of being loved. Children unconsciously identify with parents who show their love. Slowly but steadily, they will take on the attitudes and values of their parents. What is learned through this process of identification does not show up immediately, but the lessons are instilled in the child. Good behavior will evolve in time.

Health and safety

For information on growth in height and weight during these years, see GROWTH in For Special Consideration.

Dental care

During the preschool period, your child should visit the dentist. Arrange with your dentist to take your preschooler with you on one of your routine visits. Then, your child can sit in the dentist's chair, examine some of the dentist's instruments, and become acquainted with the dentist. This helps prepare for the child's own first visit. (See TEETH AND TEETHING in the Medical Guide.)

Accidents

Parents should be keenly aware that preschoolers are at great risk for injuries. Specifically, accidental trauma is the leading cause of death in preschool children. Motor vehicle accidents account for the greatest number of these deaths, followed by drowning, fires, poisonings, and gunshot wounds. A significant reduction in childhood injuries would do more for the overall health of the preschool population than finding a cure for all childhood cancer.

Parents have the vital role in preventing childhood injuries. Parents must develop a thorough understanding of normal preschool development to make the environment safe, and to change high-risk behavior in their children.

Normal preschoolers have a lot of energy. They are developing new skills such as throwing balls, climbing trees, riding tricycles, and running. They often lack sufficient coordination. Simultaneously, their personalities are egocentric—they view the world through their own eyes. They believe things won't change unless they will it. Make-believe and television become reality to preschoolers.

The best way to prevent injury to preschoolers is to provide a safe environment. And the most effective means to do this is for parents to identify what will make their children's environment safe. Parents should:

Buy and install smoke alarms and frequently check to ensure that they are in working order;

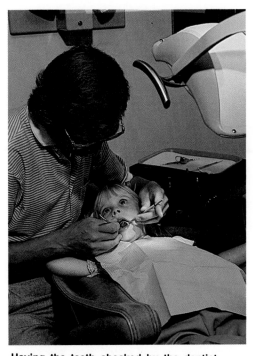

Having the teeth checked by the dentist should be routine by the age of 3.

Turn the water heater down to 120° to 130° F.;

Insist upon the use of automobile safety belts;

Lock up all poisons, have syrup of ipecac (used to induce vomiting after poisoning) in the house, and post the poison control numbers near the phone;

Lock all dangerous areas;

Make sure play surfaces are safe. (The safest surface for playground equipment is sand, 10 inches deep. Packed earth is safer than asphalt.)

Modification of the child's behavior can further reduce childhood injuries. Teach your child how to recognize and react to dangerous situations and how to develop sound safety habits. It is imperative that parents be good role models, that they practice good safety habits, and that they be aware that preschoolers need constant supervision, because children at this age don't understand danger.

To change the preschooler's behavior, parents must establish restraints and enforce them. (These rules can be modified as the child matures.) Here are some suggestions for safety for preschoolers.

As situations arise, parents should teach preschoolers about street and traffic safety, "stranger danger," animal safety, water safety, fire safety, and playground safety.

Similarly, viewing television with preschoolers is an excellent way for parents to teach safety to preschoolers by identifying and discussing hazardous and unrealistic situations with them. Age-appropriate books about safety are widely available and should be read to preschoolers. Children can also be taken to safety programs that are sponsored by community agencies such as the local police department, fire department, or Red Cross.

Making preschoolers active members in "safety surveillance" will also contribute to their learning about safety and reduce the risk of injury. For example, children should be required to pick up toys after play and store them in safe places. Children should accompany their parents on periodic safety checks of the home so that they can observe how smoke alarms work, how the house is made safer for younger brothers and sisters, how play areas are checked for safety, and so on. Preschoolers should also take part in family fire drills and be encouraged to ask questions about things they don't understand. Preschool children can be given the responsibility for reminding others to "buckle up" when they are in cars and for checking the street for cars before others are allowed to cross.

Parents' primary responsibility for the safety of preschoolers is supervision. Parents should thoroughly investigate preschools and day-care centers and then choose those that are safe and have reputable care providers. (For additional information about day care, see DAY CARE in For Special Consideration.)

Preschoolers should learn to float and swim. Teach them yourself or put them into a swimming class run by professional instructors.

You and your preschooler

The preschool years can be a delightful time for families. The children are now beyond the age when their physical care was a wearisome chore. And they have not yet reached the age when they will be so wrapped up in school demands and friends that parents feel squeezed out of their children's lives. Parents are lucky—and obviously the children are lucky—when whole families can find time to enjoy these years together.

These years are a time for companionship—a time for walks together and for short trips. They are a time for shared experiences at home. Youngsters have their moments of wanting to work along with parents, helping in their own way with cooking, cleaning, and other interesting household and yard chores.

These years are a time for words, for stories, and for music. They are the years for listening to children and for talking with children. Children's questions ask all about the ins and outs of our world and give parents the most magnificent teaching time for explaining and interpreting for children. The preschooler's behavior gives parents many opportunities to talk about values and about discipline.

These years are a time for the shared awe and delight in the charming, never-ending variety of our world of bugs and nuts and bolts, of clamshells and cars, snakeskins, leaves, the birth of baby kittens, and the hot, smoky smell of a truck engine.

Parents who work outside the home must make careful plans to find the time to share all this with their children. The special effort it takes proves very rewarding to parents and children alike.

Lucky parents and lucky preschoolers enjoy many times together. But wise parents know that even at this early age children need more than their parents. These are wonderful years for youngsters to come to know well their wider family of grandparents, uncles, aunts, and cousins. These are the years when parents can help their children find friends in the family doctor and dentist. It is also the time for them to discover the librarian in the public library.

Equally important, children need friends their own age in these years. Accommodating children's increasingly strong social drives is one of the values of a good child-care center for children whose parents both work, or who are from one-parent homes, and it's one of the reasons for nursery schools. Parents can also satisfy their children's yearning for companionship through informal play groups, taking turns with friends and neighbors in providing supervision while two or three children play together. Some invite their children's friends for lunch or to join the family on a short trip, or simply to come to the house to play.

Preschoolers are in an in-between age, not totally dependent, not totally independent—a mixture of both, sometimes all in a few minutes. It is easy to overestimate what these children can do and to expect too much. It is also easy to underestimate them and to open up too little physical challenge and too little social and intellectual stimulation. Parents' best safeguard and guide is to keep a watchful eye on their children, to judge from their behavior how they are feeling at the moment—big and brave and bold, or like little babies—and to enjoy the children just the way they are.

The School-Age Child: 5 to 8 years

Children between 5 and 8 years old tell you exactly what they feel and think. They inform you readily if they are sick, happy, or miserable. They flaunt their skills proudly and proclaim their thrills and horrors loudly.

School-age children are high-spirited. They laugh easily. They are full of ideas and questions. Yet, they will withdraw into themselves and reflect.

In school, most 5- to 8-year-olds are wide-awake mentally and uncomplicated emotionally. These are crucial years for children—probably the most important years of their education. Adults at home and school must make sure that children get the best possible start in their school careers.

By Minnie P. Berson, Ed.D.
"Health and safety" section by
Eugene F. Diamond, M.D.
Mark S. Puczynski, M.D.,
Consulting Editor

Portrait of the school-age child

It is extremely easy to see how much 8-year-olds have changed since they were 5. It is not so easy, looking at them when they are 5, to realize how much they will have changed by the time they are 8. It is, however, important that parents of children entering school be able to look ahead. Parents should be aware of the many changes that will occur in their children during the early school years. They should also understand their children's physical, mental, emotional, and social needs so that they will be better able to meet those needs.

Social development

At this age, for the most part, boys play with boys and girls play with girls. When

Between the ages of 5 and 8, girls usually play only with other girls, and boys with other boys. A favorite game of school-age girls is jumping rope.

friends of the same sex are not available in the neighborhood, a child usually finds playmates in school and invites them home to play, eat, or stay overnight.

Children between 5 and 8 years old have lots of initiative. They are interested in accomplishments and want to do things well. They need encouragement and respect.

School-age children like the feeling of responsibility—of doing something needed to make the home operate smoothly. Parents may have difficulty finding things for children to do. Convenience foods make helping with meals less important. Automatic dishwashers may eliminate the need to wash and dry dishes. Power lawn mowers are too dangerous for school-age children to use, and so children may not be able to cut the grass. However, it is extremely important for school-age children to have some responsibilities. These tasks, of course, should be ones children of this age are capable of handling—such as making their own beds, cleaning their rooms, setting the table, or putting groceries away.

When children start school, an important person enters their lives—their teacher. The teacher is often the first adult friend children make on their own. If they like their teacher, they want their parents to feel the same way. Most children are aware of every detail of their teacher's appearance and respond to every smile or frown.

Imitation

During these years, it is only natural for girls to imitate and want to be like their mothers, other women, and older girls. Similarly, boys imitate and want to be like their fathers, other men, and older boys.

At one time, little girls were expected to be interested only in activities labeled as feminine, such as playing with dolls and jumping rope. Little boys were expected to be interested only in activities labeled as masculine, such as playing baseball and football.

Today, girls and boys, as well as their parents, are comparatively free of the stereotype roles that society once demanded of them. Now the choice is up to the individual. Games and other activities no longer bear sexist labels. This can be noted in ev-

erything from the advertising and packaging of games, toys, and play materials to the clothes children wear.

A factor contributing to the diminishing of sexism, especially in the United States, is that more than 50 per cent of mothers of school-age children work outside the home. Children in these families see both parents go off to work. And at home, children see them share household duties as well as the responsibilities for their youngsters. The increase in households with a single parent has also added to the changes in the duties and responsibilities of parents.

Inevitably, little girls become women and little boys become men. Meanwhile, children are being increasingly encouraged to make highly personal choices, without sexist labels. These choices will help children develop interests and competencies that will lead to fuller, more satisfying lives.

Fathers and school-age children

The quality of the relationship between a father and his school-age child is important. It is possible that both boys and girls will have almost all their important dealings with women until they reach the secondary schools. This predominantly female world is not good for boys. Boys need as many experiences with men as possible. They need men, especially a father whom they admire, to set a pattern for them. Boys grow into manhood in part through their physiological maturing, but also through seeing how men act and talk and work and plan, how they react to each other, and how they interact with women. The companionship of men, of a good father in particular, is an essential ingredient in a boy's growth to manhood.

Girls, too, need the companionship of their fathers. A predominantly female world is not good for them either. Fathers help girls know what men are like and how men respond to different situations.

Visits away from home

Through visits away from home, school-age children gradually develop social graces and independence. They try out new foods and become accustomed to unfamiliar routines. They learn new skills by sharing family chores in other households. They make friends with children in other communities. Children also test and develop skills in relating to people away from home. They learn that all mothers are not alike, nor are all fathers, big brothers, or little sisters. Visits to homes of friends for playing, eating a meal, or spending the night all add to social development.

Before allowing a visit away from home, parents should consider their child's and the hosts' needs. Do the hosts like and want the child? Is the host family reasonable and flexible? Will they be patient as the child tries to fit into their situation? Have they been told of the child's special needs? If the child is on special medication, are they willing to supervise the dosage? Is the child a bed-wetter—a condition that would be acceptable in some households and rejected in others? Does the child have occasional nightmares? Is the child allergic to certain foods or materials? Prospective hosts should be told about any unusual characteristics, so

that they have a chance to reconsider if the child's needs seem too great for them to meet.

Making choices

During the school-age years, a child learns to make choices—within limits. For example, a child may have pronounced preferences in food. Some children eat vegetables only when they are raw. Some children prefer fruit juice rather than fresh fruit. So long as it is reasonably convenient and the child is eating nutritionally balanced meals, allow these choices. The experience adds to personal development.

Clothing presents more opportunities to learn how to make intelligent choices—within limits. At bedtime, for example, allow the child to decide what to wear the next day. You may also want to let the child pick out some new clothes at the store. At this age, the child may start to be caught up in fads. Sometimes, gym shoes are the impor-

Visits away from home—for a day or overnight—help the school-age child develop socially. First visits are often with a grandparent or other relative.

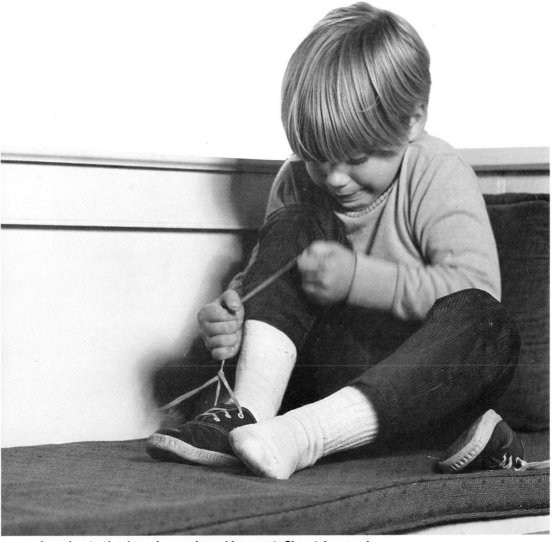

Learning to tie shoes is a major achievement. Shoe tying requires small muscle control and good eye-hand coordination.

tant symbol, and the brand name or label may be as important as the style. For girls, "hair things"—bows, barrettes, or combs—may be the "in" symbol. Again, respect the child's choice, within reason.

Allowances

Giving a regular allowance may be a worthwhile educational experience for a child. An allowance gives a child a realistic, firsthand experience in planning how to spend money and how to get full value for it. An allowance also provides the child with a natural opportunity to learn arithmetic and to begin to develop a sense of logic.

The child may buy unwisely at first, or may spend all the money immediately, forgetting that no more will be forthcoming for several days. But this may help the child learn to choose wisely and spend carefully, because an allowance also involves making choices.

You may wish to start your child with a small weekly allowance and give the same sum on the same day of each week. As your child learns the possibilities and limitations of the allowance, and as your child's needs multiply, increase the amount. Your child will become ready to take on the additional responsibility of managing the money needed for school expenses—bus fare, school supplies, or milk money. As you increase the amount of the allowance, you may want to discuss ways of budgeting the allowance with your child. Help the child figure out how much must be spent each week on essential expenses. You may also want to talk about ways of spending any extra money.

An allowance should be considered a child's share of the family income, and therefore should be no more than the family can afford. An allowance should be considered the child's own money. Do not control your child's buying. Let the child make mistakes and learn from those mistakes. Do not *insist* that a young child save part of the allowance. A savings program will take on importance when the child has something to save for. Never withhold an allowance because of disobedience, poor grades, or unwise spending. An allowance is not a bargaining tool to guarantee a child's good behavior, nor should it be considered a bribe.

Primary-grade classrooms can often be identified by rows of toothless smiles.

Motor development

"Slow but steady" characterizes the development of motor skills during the school-age years. For example, a 5-year-old is usually not ready for writing. The small muscles that control fingers and hands are not developed well enough. Writing also requires that the eye and hand work together. This eye-hand coordination is not well developed in a 5-year-old. Even 6-year-olds still find writing difficult.

Seven-year-olds usually concentrate hard when writing. They grip the pencil tightly and usually hold it close to the point. Their letters are uneven in size. By the time they are 8 years old, their eye-hand coordination and the small muscles in their hands and fingers are much better developed. As a result, they can write more evenly and easily. Physical maturation and the ability to concentrate on a purpose also aid children's writing.

Children's large muscles are also still developing. Girls at this stage are better coordinated than boys. Both boys and girls are physically active—they run, climb, skip, hop, and jump, and they like to be on the go at all times. Too long a time assigned to a chair and desk without a break can lead to restlessness and boredom.

Other physical characteristics

Growth in height and weight during the years from age 5 to age 8 is also slow but steady. The average child adds 2 to 2.4 inches (5 to 6 centimeters) in height and 5 or 6 pounds (2 or 3 kilograms) in weight each year. For more information, see GROWTH in For Special Consideration.

A distinguishing characteristic of the school-age child is a big smile—and the wide-open spaces that show where the primary teeth have fallen out to make room for the permanent teeth. Six-year molars are breaking through, and permanent incisors are beginning to appear. For more information, see TEETH AND TEETHING in the Medical Guide.

School days

Starting School

Starting school is a major adventure and a dramatic change from past living. Most children can hardly wait to start school. They take this challenge in stride, because their normal growth—in language, attention span, social interests, curiosity, and independence—enables them to welcome school without strain. There are, however, a few ways parents can make it even easier for their children to move into school life without emotional upsets.

Adjusting to school will be easier if children have had the experience of being away from home without their parents. Children who have often gone to the store with a neighbor, eaten lunch at a friend's house, or visited nearby relatives, or who have attended nursery school, usually have no problem in leaving home to move into a classroom environment.

School adjustment will also be easier for children who have experienced accepting people other than their parents as authorities. Children who have been in the care of good baby sitters, for example, will probably have less trouble accepting a teacher. Children who have played with their friends in a neighborhood backyard or a house down the street, responding to whatever mother was in charge of the play, have a foundation for working with a teacher.

Most children beginning kindergarten or first grade know other youngsters in their neighborhood who will be their classmates. Seeing familiar faces helps a child adjust. If a child has no friends in school, invite one or two future classmates to your house to play, or for lunch, so that your child can begin school knowing some of the children.

Most schools set aside one or more days in May or June for the registration of children who will enter kindergarten the following fall. At registration, the mother may have to present the child's birth or baptismal certificate. At a typical registration, children visit their prospective classroom for a short time to meet their future classmates. A few typical activities may be carried out, to let children sample what kindergarten will be like.

Learning in the kindergarten-primary grades

Some school-age children approach learning (and life) in a systematic manner. They proceed in logical, methodical ways. Others are cautious. They move forward only when they are sure of themselves. Still others dive in and then look around. Both parents and schools must recognize, understand, and accommodate the child's unique way of learning.

Practically speaking, the child in the kindergarten-primary grades is taught to read, write, and work with numbers. The curriculum includes language arts, social sciences, mathematics, science, music, and art. These subjects generally are not taught as separate courses, though. They are integrated into a total experience for the child.

A child learns best through firsthand experiences—seeing, hearing, touching, smelling, and above all, doing. Children need

Hesitation, anxiety, anticipation, and fear are all a normal part of a child's behavior on the first day of school.

But there is time, too, for laughing and playing—for making new friends in an environment completely unlike home.

Then the learning process begins. Numbers must be mastered and objects identified. Letters must be drawn and words formed.

At the end of the school day, children are happy to share with their parents the work done and the many things learned.

these firsthand experiences before they can learn to read. Some children arrive at school able to print, to identify letters, or even to read a little. Others are almost totally illiterate—no great tragedy at age 5. By the end of the second grade, most children are reading—anywhere from preprimer to fourth-grade level. Most understand the basics of phonics. They are learning to associate the sounds in words with written letters, and they are able to spell many words by applying some simple phonetic rules.

Social studies, in these early school years, generally means learning about people and the world about them. A group of kindergarten children studying their town may take trips to some of the important places in the town. They may lay out a model of the town, using various sizes of boxes for houses, stores, post offices, and schools. Trucks, cars, and buses are placed on roads. People are made with modeling materials. And there is much, much talk from the children—discussing observations, asking questions, and checking impressions. Actually, what started out as a study of "our community" moves into geography, economics, consumer education, ecology, science, safety, history, mapmaking, and map reading.

Science is experienced firsthand, too. For example, a child may prove that a magnet will only attract things made of iron by conducting experiments with a magnet and nails, paper clips, erasers, paper, and fabric. Then the child may make magnets—a simple one from an ordinary needle or even an electromagnet from a nail, a piece of wire, and a battery. Next, the child may make a compass or a buzzer to discover how magnets are used in different objects. By making these items, the child understands better how they work.

School-age children enjoy music and art. Most of them love to sing, and some even make up their own songs. They use rhythm instruments—drums, cymbals, tambourines—alone or to accompany a song or a record. They like moving, dancing, and dramatizing or marching to music. Most school-age children like to paint, to work with clay, and to draw with crayons and pencils.

School-age children also like stories and poetry. They enjoy being read to. When given the opportunity to use their imagination, they compose delightful stories and often write interesting poems.

The monthly calendar, displayed in jumbo size in many kindergarten classrooms, is also

Imaginative children can create a city of their own with sand and cardboard boxes.

A calendar is an aid for teaching a child about many things—time, holidays, seasons.

a learning device. At first, the calendar does not mean too much to the children. But as days go by, the children begin to learn the days of the week, dates in sequence, weekdays and weekend days, and the meaning of time and its components. The children have experiences with words, letters, numbers, holidays, seasons, and changes in the outdoors.

The parent and the school

During these years, the basis for the home-school relationship is formed. Conferences during the early years should serve both the teacher and the parents by identifying and discussing the unique needs and interests of the child.

Parents should try to meet their child's teacher before the child starts to school. At this meeting, parents should talk openly about their child. Then, when school starts, the teacher will already know something about the child and will be able to help the child develop.

Most schools provide time for parent-teacher conferences. At these conferences, teachers can give parents samples of their children's work; describe the children's behavior with other students and teachers; and discuss their habits, attitudes, capabilities, strengths, and weaknesses. Conferences give parents a chance to raise questions that cannot be answered adequately by report cards, and they give the teachers an opportunity to learn more about the child's life outside school. Conferences help parents and teachers work together to help children reach their potential.

Parents should also meet the parents of other children in their child's classroom. These meetings can be informal—a coffee hour or an evening meeting that includes both fathers and mothers. Or the teacher, children, and parents may get together after a class play or other special school function.

Inquisitive school-age children learn best when they can study things firsthand.

Health and safety

It is important that children have a physical examination before entering school. Many school systems require children to have boosters for diphtheria, tetanus, pertussis, polio, and tuberculin skin tests. Eye, ear, and teeth examinations are encouraged at this time. Children whose problems are found and corrected before they enter school will live and learn with greater zest than the children with eye, ear, or teeth defects.

Safety

Getting to school is one of the most important events of the day for school-age children. Before children start to school, parents or older children should walk with them from home to school so that the children can learn the route and what entrance of the school to use. The parents or older children should emphasize the correct way of crossing streets—crossing only at corners, obeying school patrols and crossing guards, observing traffic signals, and watching for traffic.

Parents should teach their children to go directly to and from school without stops or side trips. They should also teach their children never to accept rides from strangers and never even to stop to talk with strangers. Parents should not, however, give these instructions in a frightening manner, but should give them matter-of-factly—as part of the children's learning about their new role and their new responsibilities. Five-year-old children should know their full name and street address before they go to school, in case they get lost.

Some parents prefer to walk with their children during the first days of kindergarten, to make certain that they know the way. Some children are fortunate to have classmates and walking companions on the same block. But even if two reliable 5-year-olds go together, it is reassuring to send them with an older child as an escort.

Even then, there can be complications. An older child who is escorting a younger one may regard the younger as a burden and make the journey an unhappy one. An older brother or sister may look on the younger child as a special possession and become so bossy that the younger child protests bitterly. Check carefully on any such arrangement rather than taking for granted that all is the way you want it to be.

In some communities, children in kindergarten and the primary grades regularly ride to school on the school bus. Generally, children are picked up by these buses at designated corners along the route. Check to see that someone on board is responsible for helping the younger children board and exit. It is also important to know whether the school vehicle is in good condition, whether the driver is reputable and qualified, and whether the roads traveled are safe from unusual hazards. If you have any doubts, talk them over with a school official.

Children of this age are particularly in danger from traffic when it is dark outside. They do not realize as they walk along dimly lit roadways that motorists have difficulty seeing them. You can purchase retroreflective materials that make the child easier to

Safety rules for walking to school include learning how to cross streets.

see. Such materials reflect the headlights of approaching automobiles. Retroreflective materials come as tape or tags that can be attached to clothing or bicycles.

Common illnesses and conditions

Communicable diseases are quite common during the school-age years. Some of these illnesses can be avoided by vaccination, but parents of school-age children must learn to take in stride the usual run of colds, sore throats, and coughs.

If your child has been exposed to a communicable disease, the teacher or school nurse will probably send a note home informing you of the fact and telling you what symptoms to look for. If your child develops the symptoms, keep the child home from school and call the doctor.

Here are some common illnesses you may encounter with your school-age child. Each illness is discussed in a separate article in the Medical Guide.

Illness	Symptoms
Chicken pox	Fever; blistering rash; cold symptoms
German measles	Fever; rose-colored rash; cold symptoms
Impetigo	Blisterlike sores that form a crust
Measles	Five to seven days of high fever, cough, runny nose, and watery eyes; rash
Mumps	Swelling of glands on top of jawbone and in front of earlobe
Scarlet fever	Rash with a rough "goose-bump" feel; scarlet flush over face and trunk
Strep throat	Sore throat; fever

Common concerns

During the early school years, children are presented with a new social environment and social challenges unlike any they have had before. At home they were usually in an atmosphere in which it was taken for granted that they belonged and were accepted. This gave them a natural security. Certainly at home, children have had to adapt to parents and brothers and sisters. But the home atmosphere is unlike the challenge and interaction provided by contact with 25 or 30 classmates. Because of these new conditions, differences related to sex and age may become apparent and certain problems may appear in the children's lives.

Sex differences

Girls, when they start school, appear more mature than boys—and they are, because they have a more rapid maturation rate than boys do during these years. Physically and emotionally, girls are more apt to become organized and ready to work with symbolic and abstract tasks sooner than boys.

Patty can print her name correctly when she enters kindergarten, while Peter, who is the same age, may only recognize the first letter of his name. This does not mean that Patty is the brighter of the two. It may mean merely that someone took the time to teach her what she knows and that she may have been eager to learn this. Peter, on the other hand, may already know about many other things. Having classmates who can print their names and a teacher who can be helpful may encourage him to learn. It may

also encourage him to share his knowledge with others.

Boys do indeed have much intellectual curiosity, but they more often focus their curiosity on physical, biological, and mechanical areas. They like to take things apart—like flashlights, old clocks, old radios—to find out what the component parts are and how they work. They discover and explore things by poking around. They are liable to walk in the kitchen with wet feet and ask the question, "Where does the water go after it goes down the sewer?"

This is not to say girls do not show these interests. Many do. And many go on to become scientists.

Age differences

No matter how bright children may be, it may make an immense difference whether they have lived less than five years or almost six years when they enter kindergarten. Younger children are less mature than their classmates and less experienced. They are often—though not always—at a disadvantage.

Suppose September 1 is the cutoff date for kindergarten entrance in a school district. This means that a child who became 5 years old on September 2 of the previous school year is in the same class with the child who will be 5 on September 1 of the current year. The child entering kindergarten at nearly six years has a decided advantage over a classmate at five years. The older child is better coordinated, more able to

Age differences may lead to problems in social adjustment as well as learning problems.

control impulses, and more able to concentrate on a learning task. If the younger child is a boy, he may find it doubly hard to compete with his classmates.

Regardless of intellectual ability, many kindergarten children cannot bridge the age-maturity gap between themselves and their older, more mature classmates. They may also have difficulty conforming to the arbitrary learning timetable of many schools. The real test comes in first grade, when most schools require children to begin reading. As one boy sadly commented, "I always get a stomachache before I go to school. I go anyhow and I feel sicker because I don't catch on. And everybody knows I don't catch on. It's no fun."

The younger kindergarten child should be closely observed for the development of social and other school-related readiness skills. A delay in the acquisition of these skills may be due to immaturity, and a developmental evaluation should be considered.

Masculinity, femininity

This is the age when a problem with sex identification may become evident in a child. The child, especially a boy, may be ridiculed by his classmates. The child may also appear to be confused and pained among classmates, even at the kindergarten or first-grade level.

Do not leap to the conclusion that a child has a problem in sex identification because of a few surface traits or activities—merely because a girl is skilled in athletics, for example, or because a boy helps his mother dust furniture. However, if a girl deeply resents being a girl or if a boy deeply resents being a boy, a problem may exist.

School-age children enjoy all kinds of boisterous, bustling activities.

If a problem in sex identification is handled during these kindergarten-primary years, chances of improvement are far greater than if parents wait. When the child's problem is viewed as something that will be "outgrown," difficulties multiply and eventually the child becomes enmeshed in the web of added preadolescent and adolescent problems. The original problem is then submerged, and the child's life may become increasingly bewildering and lonely. If parents believe that their child has a problem in sex identification, they should seek professional help from a psychologist or child psychiatrist. The child's doctor or teacher may be able to provide the names of agencies and specialists who can help the child and parents.

Some boys meet with academic failure in the primary grades because they are more interested in such things as dismantling a radio or taking apart a flashlight.

School problems

School is such an important part of a child's life that all youngsters face some problems in the many years that they spend there. Therefore, parents and teachers must stay in close communication.

Problems that have their origin in school may show up only at home. For example, a youngster who operates under tension all day long at school may seem like an earnest, conscientious child to the teacher. The parents may be the only ones to see the outbursts that reflect the strain the child is feeling. Similarly, a youngster may appear at home to be working smoothly. The teacher, watching the child in a different setting and in comparison with other children the same age, may be the one who first becomes aware that a problem exists. The parents and the teacher must have some means of sharing their insights, so that any problems can be spotted before they become too severe, and solutions can be developed.

Unwillingness to go to school

The first sign of a school problem may be a child's unwillingness to go to school. Some kindergarten and first-grade children show their fear of school openly. They cry, say that they hate school, and are unwilling to leave home. Sometimes unwillingness to go to school shows in disguised form through frequent complaints of illness or through prolonged dawdling and other delaying tactics. A fear or dislike of school can be a troubling problem. All the "legal" arguments parents are apt to use carry little weight in a young child's mind.

There are, of course, no pat solutions to this or any other problem. The causes can be many, and they vary from child to child. The only good solution is the one that gets to the root of the difficulty with individual children. Some youngsters may hesitate because they have not had sufficient experience in being away from home; others because the group at school is too large for them to cope with; others because they have specific fears, such as the school toilet or the bus ride. This unwillingness can also be a sign that a child is experiencing learning difficulties.

When parents and teachers begin to talk together and pool their information, they usually can uncover the difficulties and make plans that help children identify the problems, cope with them, and possibly solve them. The parents' attitudes are important while this search is going on. On the one hand, they must feel sympathetic to children who have problems. Life can be uncomfortable when something is going wrong. On the other hand, parents must have a broad, basic confidence that problems can be solved, and must communicate it. The steady sureness that solutions will be found and that life can go on is often one of the most helpful ways of building self-confidence and security in children.

Problems related to success and failure

As children move further into their school careers, more difficulties are apt to stem from their successes and failures in academic work, and from relationships with classmates and teacher. Children are like the rest of us. They cannot go through day after day of failure, of not liking their assigned tasks, and of not enjoying people with whom they associate, without feeling some dissatisfaction. Adults change their jobs when they feel this way. Children cannot leave school physically. Their only alternative is to leave mentally—to daydream, to give up in despair, to become rebellious.

Again, there is no single answer to every child's trouble. A patient, mutual search by parents and teacher is the only wise procedure. A physical difficulty, with vision or hearing in particular, may be the cause in some cases. Academic work puts the first great strain on hearing and vision. A complete physical examination is often a wise first step in seeking solutions.

Children, of course, vary greatly in their ability to do schoolwork. They vary in their native intelligence, in their growth rate, and in their ability to handle specific kinds of subject matter. There is always the possibility that, without meaning to, either parents at home or teachers at school may be asking more of the children than they are able to do. When goals and expectations are set too high, children almost always do not succeed as well as they could. The school administration's solution is sometimes to readjust its program, aiming more realistically at goals that youngsters can achieve. Sometimes parents must make the adjustment in their expectations at home so that their children feel that they are good human beings and not constant failures.

Some youngsters face a problem because they are "underachievers." They have considerably more ability than they use. They glide through their days, operating on only a small part of their ability. On the face of it, this may seem not like a problem but a joy. However, youngsters are much more contented when they work up to their ability. Unchallenged, these children can move quite easily into various forms of misbehavior that reflect their discontent.

It is easier to overlook children who are underachieving than the child who daily meets failure. Failing children quickly call themselves to adult attention. Underachievers can slide by unnoticed. Parents and teachers need not search for problems that do not exist, but it is important for both to talk together so that real problems are not ignored. A parent's account, for example, of a child's unusual persistence and success with a hobby or an out-of-school activity may be the tipoff to a teacher that the youngster has more ability than the school has tapped.

Family problems and school

The demands of schoolwork sometimes uncover tension youngsters are feeling in their out-of-school lives. Children who worry about their place in the family, or about their relations with their brothers and sisters, cannot concentrate and meet the rigors of academic work. These difficulties may well have gone unnoticed during the children's simpler, less demanding years before school. Many school systems have psychologists who are trained to spot and treat such problems. Many communities have child guidance centers or family service societies that can help with these problems.

Social problems

School, of course, is not all academic work. A school is a social center, too. Conflicts and achievements in getting along with classmates take place daily. A child's social acceptance or rejection is important in itself and often has repercussions on how well the child learns. The lonely child frequently adds academic difficulties to other miseries.

Problems in a child's social life are perhaps the hardest of all for adults to solve. Adults cannot force one child to like another. But they can sometimes help a child to be more likable. Teaching the isolated child some skills that other youngsters value is one useful approach. Inviting classmates home after school is another way. Teachers can use seating arrangements or school activities to help bring together children who may learn to like each other.

Solutions to school problems

Parents and teachers both must realize that it takes time, patience, and wisdom to solve all human problems. It is so easy to believe that there are quick solutions—the teacher should assign more work in school; the parents should take away privileges until a child's work improves. In individual instances these may be useful approaches, but they are not cures in every case. In some instances, a final cure may take a long time to achieve. Some of the factors that can be involved—for example, large class size, a teacher's long-established way of teaching, or a home's way of treating a child—do not lend themselves to modification overnight.

Parents and teachers both must feel good will and be patient in working together if answers are to be found. No one wants a child to face a problem needlessly. Everyone wants the best for a child. But school and family life both center around humans, and humans change slowly. It is important to recognize, too, that there are some problems children have to solve themselves. There are other problems that have no solutions, but children can be taught to live with them and even gain strength from the experience.

You and your school-age child

Between the ages of 5 and 8, most children are open, energetic, and easy to get along with. Perhaps that is why some parents and teachers tend to coast along with them. Some mothers and fathers—frustrated and exasperated with older children in the family—take refuge in these easy-to-manage children. They can easily lose sight of the fact that the early school years can serve as a foundation for good preteen and teen-age behavior. Here are some suggestions for making the most of the early school years.

Tailor your expectations to fit children's abilities. Then the children will be encouraged to go on learning. They will not become discouraged because they cannot meet unrealistic goals.

Emphasize the positive, stressing the things children can do and not overemphasizing achievement, especially in school. Children should not be told that they have to *be* the best. Instead, they should be told to try to *do* their best.

Children should not be given rewards for grades. This makes them believe they must always be compensated for doing well. If you think your children can do better work in school, discuss the problem with the teachers. Teachers can help you determine gentle ways to help a child.

School-age children like stories and enjoy being read to, so you should continue to read to your child. Reading by parents builds up relationships that help make communication easier as the child grows older.

Remember, also, that good communication requires that you be a good listener. If your child has something to say, take the time to listen, even if what the child has to say seems of little importance at the time.

Help your child develop a sense of responsibility. Assign some chores—drying dishes, taking the garbage out, making the bed, keeping a clean room. Also, recognize and encourage responsible behavior by praise. Remember that responsible behavior also includes such everyday events as getting up and going to school and coming home promptly after school.

Give the child choices in hobbies or extra activities. Do not force such things as taking dancing or music lessons solely because other children the same age are taking them. Respect the uniqueness and individuality of your child.

Children need help that allows them to develop their own abilities. Too much help may lead to overdependency. Too little help may result in feelings of inadequacy or frustration. Give your child the right kind of help. For example, if your child writes a letter and asks you for help in spelling certain words, give the child help with only those words. Do not rewrite, correct, or criticize the letter.

The most important way to help school-age children be sucessful is to accept them as they are and inspire them to become what they want to be. And what do most children want? They want to be liked, to have interesting work to do, and to be respected. This is human and universal, and highly possible if the home and the school work together to achieve this end.

The Preteen: 8 to 13 years

The preteen is a volatile, changing individual who is beginning to be free of dominant adults. Preteens are now extremely interested in and influenced by their circle of friends and acquaintances, or peers. Preteens have a code to follow and secrets to keep. This gang phase and other preteen behavior may be hard on you. However, it is just as important that your child go through these phases as it was to go through the crawling, creeping, and toddling phases. You can deal with the preteen period if you try to understand what is going on, and if you remind yourself that a child's growing up usually costs a lot in adult comfort.

By Fritz Redl, Ph.D.
"The Preteen's Health" section
by Eugene F. Diamond, M.D.
Arthur Kovel, M.D.,
Consulting Editor

Portrait of the preteen

Preteens are not quite the children they were. And yet, they are not quite the teenagers they will become. They are in a transitional period—a period of preparation. Something new is going to be added, and for this reason they are changing. They are something like a department store that is undergoing renovation while still conducting business.

Preteen changes and preparations may shake children's personalities. These children used to be fairly easy to get along with and eager to please. Suddenly they become reluctant and defiant. Boys who used to pride themselves on keeping a neat room drop their clothes on the floor as they make their way to the bathroom for the nightly shower. Girls who depend on parents for the choice of their clothes suddenly break down in tears when an adult makes the slightest comment on their appearance. Reluctance, defiance, and tears—all are characteristics of preteens.

When children were younger, they usually relied on their parents' judgment. They felt safe and secure and had pleasant personalities. But during the preteen years, they pick up new ideas. They make more of their own judgments, and they are not always confident that their judgments are correct. They become less secure, and as a result their personalities may become a little less likable. Every preteen goes through this to a certain extent. It is part of loosening up the childish personality to make room for the independent adolescent personality. A child's adolescence may, in fact, actually "begin" during this preteen period.

The body itself—especially a girl's—is preparing for the changes and additions brought on by puberty. And, of course, the preteen is preparing to move away from family ties—a move that will be the child's major task during the teen-age years.

This time of preparation and change begins around the end of the fifth or sixth grade and usually lasts into the seventh or the beginning of eighth grade. As in all de-

Preteens often avoid shows of affection.

velopmental stages, exact ages cannot be given. Individual differences in physical, intellectual, and emotional growth are as varied as are the circumstances under which youngsters go through such a phase. Also, not every child gets hit by this change in the same way, nor in all areas of life at the same time.

Restlessness

If your preteen reaches for gadgets on your desk while you are having a serious talk, don't think the child is being disrespectful. Fiddling with everything in sight while supposedly doing homework does not mean the child wants to play instead of work. The preteen literally cannot help it. Any gadget in sight must be handled. This "manipulative restlessness" is enormous. Workbooks look as though they had been fished from last year's trash can. Pencil tops are chewed up long before the writing parts are even slightly used. And if no gadgets are around, then body parts are acceptable substitutes. The child may pull at one earlobe or the other, drum fingers on the desk or table, scratch at elbows, or twist locks of hair.

The preteen's restlessness also shows up in a short activity span. Most preteens cannot stick to anything for long, even if it is something they enjoy—an experience for which they have been longing.

Parents should try to allow for their preteens' restlessness, and when they have to interfere, they should do so in a reasonable and friendly way, without showing indignation or excitement. They should try to provide opportunities for children to rid themselves of restlessness with as little disturbance to others as possible. For instance, periods of quiet work can be broken up with some activity—giving preteens a chance to move around, stretch, sing, talk, and yell. Preteens just cannot be forced to spend most of the day sitting and writing, reading, or listening. If parents or teachers can suggest ways for preteens to satisfy the need for activity and manipulation, the children will probably find it easier to remain quiet when they must study or do other things that require sitting still.

The restless preteen is almost always in motion.

Even when seriously at work, a preteen may be biting a lip or chewing a pencil end.

Talking, laughing, shifting in a chair—the preteen finds it hard to do "nothing."

Almost every preteen indulges in daydreams—fantasies that help the child deal with new feelings or feelings that are not easily expressed.

Also, remember that children cannot easily change preteen habits and behavior patterns. They have to go through this stage. They do not purposely do these things to annoy adults. Parents should avoid constant nagging and reminders that make preteens embarrassed and self-conscious.

Forgetfulness

Preteens forget. And, there seems to be no excuse—especially since they can remember things their parents wish they would forget. For example, a teacher assigns homework on Friday to be turned in Monday. The teacher writes the assignment on the board and makes half the class repeat it. Yet on Monday, when the assignment is due, a third of the class has forgotten all about it.

Obviously, children sometimes use forgetting as an alibi. The amazing thing is that half of those who said they forgot were tell-

ing the truth. They *really* forgot. Preteens block out things that interfere with their pursuit of happiness. These memory blocks save them from unpleasant guilt feelings. A person who really forgets obviously cannot help it. Remind your preteen of obligations, but try to do so without nagging.

Daydreaming

Otherwise alert preteens may stare into space in the middle of a class, even when the subject is one they are good at and interested in. Youngsters of other ages can tell you what they daydream about. However, if you ask preteens what they were thinking about they usually answer, "Nothing." This may not be an evasion. Preteens have an extraordinary ability to think of nothing—or at least nothing that they can describe or name. Frequently, their daydreams are not organized at all. One picture after another flits through their minds. You might compare this to your own thoughts just before falling asleep.

When there is content in the daydreams, this varies as widely as do preteens themselves. However, two basic kinds of daydreams dominate preteen fantasies.

One is a "technological" daydream. Many technically inventive and gifted children spend a lot of time looking at such things as a speck on the wall or a piece of string or wire. In their minds, such spots of color or pieces of metal or wood combine in the widest range of possibilities; they see "gadgets." Children may come out of such technical daydreams with imaginative, demonstrable products.

The other trend in daydreams concerns extreme power, cruel victory, destruction, fear of destruction, rebellion, mourning, and so on. They include the whole range of emotional relationships the preteen lives through, moves away from, or contemplates moving into. Many people worry that comic books and television create these daydreams. Indeed, such things may at one time or another be the cause. But if comic books and television were not available, children would still daydream about unpleasant things.

Daydreams fill a need of youngsters who are leaving one world (childhood) and wondering about entering another (the teen-age years). They must deal with puzzling and unpredictable themes, but cannot deal with some of them directly because they would be punished by shame, guilt, terror, panic, fury, or rage. So they daydream.

For example, if a boy dreams of cruelly killing a wild monster, it may not mean that he has such wild needs troubling his soul. It may simply mean that he was terribly embarrassed the day before when his father scolded him in front of his buddies. The child cannot consciously direct rage against his father, because he loves his father and knows his father was right. However, the shame still burns. How can he deal with it? He does so in the same way he deals with otherwise unmentionable pain—he projects it into the future or the past. He makes familiar people into strange ogres or powerful enemies. He destroys with vehemence something that obviously cannot have anything to do with his real life. Only then can he let out the total force of his anger or panic or guilt or shame or rage.

Success and praise

For young children, rewards that are "deserved" are especially gratifying. Things received only by "chance," while pleasant, are not a source of pride. Not doing a job or assignment is shameful, while "working hard at it" is something to be proud of.

During the preteens, this view of success and failure may suddenly reverse, at least in part. Preteens are especially proud of what they get away with. The fact that they worked hard on an assignment may be embarrassing, and they may even try to hide what they did from their group. To get something undeservedly ("This stupid teacher doesn't even know I haven't done any work at all!") seems to be the height of glory. Argument against this attitude is not effective. Actually, many youngsters pretend this attitude, though they do not mean it. But the group code demands that preteens make light of their virtues, brag about shrewd evasion of the consequences of their actions, and glory in the luck or skill that brought them ill-gotten and undeserved gain.

It is easy to see, then, why youngsters of this age often react irrationally when praised. For preteens, open praise makes them think they are being treated like babies or teachers' pets. Praise may be more painful to them than the praising adult can imagine. If a preteen is told that he has acted like a "little gentleman," or that she has acted like a "little lady," chances are that the child will be insulted rather than complimented.

Even the type of argument used with preteens needs examination. A boy may well accept the fact that you want him to come to dinner with clean fingernails. But arguing that a "nice little boy" would not want to appear with dirty fingernails is like throwing gasoline on a burning fire. Anything that makes preteens feel that you are treating them "like little kids" hits the youngsters the wrong way. This does not mean that parents should not interfere. But, they should try to treat their children as the maturing young people they are.

The preteen and "the gang"

Ever since children entered school, they have been learning that the group is something to be reckoned with. Always, part of their concern was to be accepted according to the group standards set by the neighborhood play group or their schoolmates. In the preteen period, however, what was perhaps a marginal problem suddenly becomes an essential adjustment.

The most important part of the world used to be the family. Suddenly, the "kid

During the preteen period, the gang may become more important than the family.

culture" of the neighborhood takes over. Now the important thing in the children's lives is to be in line with the code of their peers, even at the cost of considerable open conflict with their families. Characteristics of group leaders take on extra significance in the lives of preteens.

Parents become "The Adults"

Many parents report that what hurts most during the preteen period is the peculiar way in which preteens cut off whatever relationships have existed between them and their parents by suddenly making their parents "The Adults." You know that they know better, that they love you, but—especially in public—they treat even your fair demands as angry insults from an enemy. In fact, once your child has shifted you from the role of parent to the role of "The Adult," nothing personal may remain. You may become two power agents in battle.

You may happily suggest to your daughter that she have some of her friends over for a party. Her comment: "Where will you be?" You stammer something about being somewhere in the house and assure your offspring that you will not intrude on her fun. You get the rejoinder, "But we don't want any *Adults* around." It is hard to accept the fact that to your own child you are suddenly an archenemy. Of course, you should take consolation in the fact that not all preteens react so dramatically.

Your child's attitude is normal. In fact, the more youngsters are "attached" to a

Experimenting with lipstick is normal for a preteen girl but may cause conflict with parents.

parent, the heavier is their need to defend against the parent—or the attachment to the parent. It is often the very loving and beloved parent, the very cordial teacher, who bears the brunt of this puzzling behavior. And although it is easier to understand than to bear, it should not be taken personally. The battle stance between the preteens and parents or teachers as "the authorities to be challenged" does not mean that the relationships deteriorate permanently. It only means that, in certain moments of their lives, children perceive themselves as members of the preteens. And that leaves parents and teachers in the role of "The Adults."

Most preteens experience such moments frequently. There is no reason for concern unless the experiences become so all-inclusive that no personal relationship remains between parent and child.

Secrecy

Another way the preteen may try to cut you out of things is to have secrets. Girls, especially, may tease you by mentioning something somebody said or did, and then clam up if you want details. The youngster who previously ran to you with every little concern now cuts you off. Inquiries about what happened at school are met with a curt "Nothing."

This secrecy has reasons, though, and is part of the normal preteen trend. Partly, it is the preteen's need to have a domain safe from adult invasion. The content of a secret may be irrelevant. It is the fact of having one that counts.

Even some of the preteens' need to collect things and keep the things in their pockets or dresser drawers is part of that need to have their own domain. For example, if parents try to get the preteen's stamp or coin collection transformed into a well-organized enterprise, parents may find that the child loses interest in the hobby. The hobby has become family domain instead of something for the child alone to deal with.

Related to the need for secrets is the fact that at this age communication often comes easier with other adults than with parents. This does not mean that your child has lost confidence in you. It is simply typical.

Picking up the dare

During the preteens and teens, even the most wonderful youngster may become extremely vulnerable to the compelling illogic of a dare. Under certain conditions a preteen must pick up a dare, no matter how silly, dangerous, disgusting, or obnoxious it is. A child who does not pick up a dare loses honor in the eyes of the group.

Picking up the dare is seen most clearly in the older teen-ager. In the preteen years, the kind of dare children are exposed to is not so easy to recognize, but plays as heavy a role. A preteen may, for example, accept a dare to put thumbtacks on the teacher's chair, talk dirty in public, thumb the nose at an adult, or talk back to an adult.

Dare situations may develop even when the gang is not around. Psychologically, preteens may feel that the gang is looking over their shoulders. If the way parents scold preteens or demand compliance seems to constitute an unwritten dare, the youngster may suddenly become silly, stubborn, fresh, or defiant. They then become actors in a show put on for the benefit of the absent group. They have to accept the dare or

Preteens must pick up a dare. If they do not, they lose honor in the eyes of the gang.

they will violate the code that governs their actions.

In dealing with a dare, avoid "extraneous reasoning." Do not resort to, "Your cousin Janice doesn't wear lipstick," or "When I was your age, I never would have done that."

Fortunately, only a few situations at a time become loaded with this dare-vulnerability. In all other areas the child remains as reasonable, or at least as easy to influence, as before. For one youngster, being asked to wear warm underwear or put on boots and mittens may be an unbearable demand; for another, an anxious admonition not to climb a tree or talk back to a teacher is an unbearable challenge. For another, a parent's concern about lipstick, table manners, or language may be it. And what is "it" changes from time to time.

These dares, although changeable, are fairly easy to identify. A more important concern, and one that is not easy to satisfy, is just what constitutes a dare when your preteen is alone with the gang. If the child shows signs of disturbing behavior, or is having unusual trouble at school, you will want to know if it is in response to a dare or if a basic problem is involved. Your child's teacher or school counselor may help you answer this difficult question.

If your youngster is heavily dependent on what you consider the bad standards of the group, the worst thing you can do is preach against them. This is considered an additional dare for the child to show loyalty to those friends, in spite of knowing better and being sure that you are right. Strengthening your child's own judgment and awareness is the only safe way to help, but this is a long-time job. Remember that success is not achieved overnight.

Face-saving

Many minor issues of daily life, such as schedules or parents' suggestions about what clothing to wear, may put children into a situation in which they are afraid of surrendering too openly to adult demands. Immediate and easy acceptance of adult orders somehow reminds preteens too much of early childhood years. Even though they realize that their parents' demands are perfectly reasonable, they still have to fight before surrendering. It is honorable to surrender after battle, but simply giving in is cowardly and childish. This has nothing to do with the question of children's love for their parents and their respect for parents' values. They need to maintain pride in their own decision-making powers.

In fact, just to have the proud feeling of doing the right thing, children may do what parents suggested "on their own." They can only achieve this feat if they first refuse to do something, and then do what their parents want because they themselves "decided" to do it.

Any mother who has ever sponsored a Cub Scout meeting may remember that her own child behaved the most poorly. The reason for the bad behavior was simply that obeying mother in public can be construed by others in the gang as childish. The only way to show that the child is no longer hanging onto mother's apron strings is to defy her openly. Stop your child's behavior or tolerate it—but do not discuss it in front of other children.

The need to show up well in the group does not end with the preteen period. The preteens have only begun practicing it. In many cases it will be with them, and you, all through the teen-age years. And, sorry to say, it is likely to get worse.

Toughness

Young children, when having problems, seek refuge in a friendly adult apron. If serious problems hit teen-agers, they long for the friendly shoulder of an understanding adult. Most preteens want neither—or if they do, they would rather be "caught dead" than admit it.

The informal preteen group code views any friendly talk with an adult as childish, sissyish, and cowardly. Also, according to preteen philosophy, trouble is a source of pride, not shame. You do not have problems as a preteen. You cause problems for others. Then they cause problems for you, so you fight back or take it. It may be hard to handle, but it is better to go under in glory than to ask for help or advice.

When preteens gather, they may not want "The Adults" intruding at their parties.

Preteen love

Love in the preteen years is like a game. And it is a game that almost every preteen in the group plays. Preteen girls spend much time trying to get a "boyfriend," and many preteen boys are busy trying to find a "girlfriend." But these friendships seldom blossom into love.

Most preteen boys and girls do not see the person of the other sex as a love object in the way that will become apparent in adolescence. There are, however, many exceptions to this, and a semblance of being in love may become apparent from time to time. But preteen boys generally consider girls merely as members of the other sex. Girls are acceptable, or not, primarily on the basis of the same criteria by which anybody else is acceptable to the group. Girls operate in the same way, but they quickly tire of boys their own age and develop "crushes" on older boys in higher grades.

During these years, boys and girls still consider each other "closed groups." The importance of getting a girlfriend or a boyfriend is in winning the game. Then a girl can tell her less fortunate girlfriends that she has a steady, that she is in love. And the boy can go bragging to his buddies. Probably all they do is walk home from school, go to the library, or go skating— accompanied by the group. Left alone they might well have a hard time carrying on a five-minute conversation.

Organized groups and school

Most preteens want to be as far away from the family as possible. It may mean only the basement—where somehow family rules and regulations do not apply so strongly. Or it may be a tree house, a shack, or even wandering the neighborhood.

Organized groups

Many preteens join organized group activities—the Boy Scouts, the Girl Scouts, the Camp Fire Girls, church groups, camping groups, cycling groups. These groups give preteens a chance to satisfy two of their great needs—being out of the house and doing something. Because of these two needs, you should take care when looking at preteen clubs or organizations. No organization should use as bait the child's yearning to belong to a group, while hiding actual motives. Some organizations use the time simply to stress table manners, obedience, fingernail cleanup, language mouthwash, and such other things as lofty ideals of character and education.

This does not, of course, mean that these characteristics cannot be part of the preteen curriculum. But the main thing is that preteens need a place where they can be what they are—rambunctious, out of step with what you may think is best for them—free to express the feelings and the thoughts of being a preteen.

Outside the home, the preteen is on the way to becoming his or her own person. See that any organization your child joins is flexible enough to make room for preteen devel-

opment. Be sure that the atmosphere a preteen needs to grow in does not get lost among more marketable demands.

The preteen and school

Teachers find that many students who have been models for getting things done on time suddenly become fidgety and unreliable when they become preteens. This is a passing thing, and teachers usually allow for it. But what are *parents* to do when their preteen seems to lose interest in school, neglects homework, and receives grades that are lower than what they know is possible?

Attitude toward school

Most preteens gripe about school. "This teacher hates me." "They give us too much homework." Griping about school is common among preteens and usually can be ignored. It is much like the eternal griping about boarding school food or being in the army.

But be careful not to add to your child's seeming negativeness. What you say about schools in general may easily affect the child's attitude toward school. Preteens are always ready for an argument to hide behind, something that will get them "off the hook." If you criticize collectively the schools and the educational system of your neighborhood, your preteen may find it easy to develop a stereotyped concept of school.

Homework

Preteens generally consider homework an undesirable thing. Unfortunately, many

Group activities are important because they give preteens a chance to be out of their homes and doing something—both basic needs of the preteen.

adults figure that things that are undesirable but necessary should be done first, before pleasurable activities are pursued. They consider the pleasurable activity to be something to look forward to. For this reason, parents often say, "Complete your homework first; then go skating." The trouble with this reasoning is that preteens seldom study hard when they are thinking of somebody else already skating. A better plan might be to suggest that your preteen do 20 minutes of homework first, go skating for 45 minutes, and then come back home to finish. This allows for the child's short attention span by breaking up the work into two periods. It also reduces the number of unavoidable confrontations between parent and child.

Be sure that homework gets done, but be flexible enough to make allowances for preteen behavior that affects the way in which it gets done.

Report cards

Most parents worry when their children bring home grades that are lower than the children's normal abilities indicate they should be. Low marks usually call for more supervision to ensure that homework is being done and that the children are properly motivated.

Children who have persistent problems in school may need tutoring. Tutors can give children the individual attention they need to stick to schoolwork. Good tutors can interest children in subjects which have previously bored them.

Your child's teacher can help you decide if a tutor is needed, and for how long. The time will vary according to your child's needs. The important thing to remember is that using a tutor when your child is a preteen may help set up better study habits for the important adolescent years.

The preteen's health

Height and weight

Usually during the period from 8 to 13, major physical changes start to occur in a child's body. The most obvious change is a rapid increase in height and weight. In girls, this growth spurt usually begins between the ages of 11 and 14. Girls may continue growing until they are 17 or 18 years old. Boys start their rapid increase in height and weight somewhat later, usually between 12 and 16 years of age. Since their growth spurt is usually greater, and since it contin-

ues until their early 20's, most of them catch up and pass the girls in size by the end of high school. For more information, see GROWTH in For Special Consideration.

Other signs of maturity

Other signs of maturation usually accompany the increase in height and weight. There are changes in body contours and development of secondary sex characteristics. In girls, the leggy, straight-up-and-down appearance changes to a more rounded figure. This change in body contour is due to the settling of body fat over the hips, thighs, and chest; widening of the pelvis; and development of the breasts.

The changes in the body contour of a boy are due to an increase in muscle strength in his arms and legs, broadening of his shoulders, and an increase in the size and structure of his skeleton.

Sex development in girls

Secondary sex development in girls usually begins with the development of the breasts, starting with an enlarging of the nipples and then a gradual increase in the size of the breasts. At this time your daughter may become interested in brassieres—because "everyone else is wearing one." If your daughter is an early developer, or if she is a late developer, the best rule of thumb to follow in this matter is, "Are her girlfriends wearing them?" If they are and she is not, she will most likely feel left out.

Girls hit their growth spurt earlier than boys, a fact that shows up at school dances.

Soft, downy pubic hair—which later darkens and coarsens—is the next stage of sex development. Growth of hair under the arms follows the growth of pubic hair.

The first menstrual period usually occurs about the time of underarm hair growth. This may be preceded by several months of vaginal discharge, which may be blood-tinged. For the first year or two, periods may be irregular because the development of the ovum (egg) and ovulation (the release of eggs) occur irregularly. Almost all girls have their first period between ages 11 and 15.

Menstruation occurs because of interaction between the ovaries and the pituitary gland. When menstrual bleeding stops, the ovaries release hormones called estrogen into the bloodstream. Estrogen causes rapid growth of the inner lining of the uterus. When estrogen is released, the pituitary gland releases a hormone called FSH.

FSH increases the production of estrogen and also causes an egg to begin ripening in an ovary. As the egg ripens, the ovaries secrete other hormones called progesterone, which also help build the lining of the uterus. When progesterone is released, the pituitary gland releases a hormone called LH. When the ratio of FSH to LH reaches a certain point, the egg is released. If the egg is not fertilized, the ovaries stop making estrogen and progesterone. Without these hormones, the lining of the uterus breaks down, causing menstrual bleeding. (For more information, see MENSTRUATION and VAGINAL DISCHARGE in the Medical Guide.)

Sex development in boys

Secondary sex development in boys begins with an increase in the size of the penis and testicles, accompanied by a growth of pubic hair. Hair appears next under the arms, and then on the face. About the time hair starts to grow under the boy's arms, there is a change in the tone of his voice. First the voice may break, alternating between high and low tones. Then it gradually deepens.

When the pubic hair becomes coarse and curly, the boy usually begins to produce sperm. Sperm are produced continuously in the testicles. Sometimes, the accumulated sperm and other secretions are discharged in

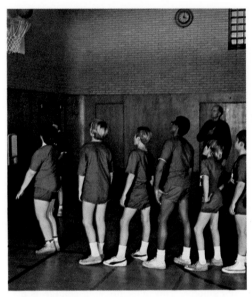

The unpredictable growth spurt of the preteens results in children of many sizes and shapes.

a nocturnal emission (a wet dream). Explain to a boy that this may happen. Otherwise its occurrence may frighten him, or—since it is usually accompanied by sexual fantasies during sleep—it may leave him with undeserved guilt feelings.

Dental care

Primary-grade children were conspicuous when they smiled because of the spaces in their mouths where their primary teeth had fallen out. Many preteens who smile are conspicuous because of the braces they wear to help straighten their permanent teeth.

After the six-year molars have fully erupted, your dentist should examine your child's teeth for irregularities. Some irregularities—protruding front teeth, too much space between teeth—cannot be corrected without braces. Your dentist will probably suggest an orthodontist (a dentist who specializes in correcting irregularities of the teeth) to apply this treatment.

Although many children dislike wearing braces, the results are well worth the inconvenience and possible embarrassment to them—and the cost to you. (For more on this subject, see BRACES, DENTAL, and MALOCCLUSION in the Medical Guide.)

Common concerns

When preteens are about 8 or 9 years old, they are no special worry. Sure, they are noisy, forgetful, and restless; but they are also frank, loyal, and friendly.

Then, around 10 or 11, the problems start. Body image and personal appearance become matters of concern for many preteens. Some boys become sensitive about being shorter than girls their own age. And, just as often, those girls who have hit their spurt in height early may feel embarrassed about being taller than their classmates and walk hunched over to appear shorter.

Both boys and girls may take pride in looking sloppy. Sweat shirts, oversize shirts with the tails hanging out, and bleached-out jeans may be just the thing. Hair may be very long or very short. Corners of bedrooms accumulate dirty clothes daily.

Do not be dismayed. This is a stage preteens outgrow. Just keep the lines of communication between you and the child open. And do not nag.

Problems such as acne, overweight, and underweight arise. (See separate articles on each of these subjects in the Medical Guide.) The whole movement away from the influence of family, and toward that of friends, increases. Everything, it seems, is a "special problem." One potential problem deserves extra attention.

Preteens want to know more about sex than they did previously. And it is important that they know as much as the other members of their group. Children who are much less informed than their playmates run the risk of being ridiculed. They may be-

come afraid to say anything when sex is mentioned. Or they may exaggerate the importance of sex knowledge they do not possess to such a degree that the whole matter is unduly emphasized.

Preteens should already know the basic facts about where babies come from. Now they start to ask for more specific facts concerning human reproduction. This is not wrong. Ideally, children should feel free to go to their parents first for this kind of information. Answer the questions accurately. Do not talk about sex in general terms. Do not give vague ideas about how babies begin and where they grow.

Talk about your child's body, how it functions, and what is going to happen to it in the next few years. This is important even though the developments may actually be a year or so off. It is important that the child be prepared emotionally for what is happening and is going to happen before entering adolescence, so that fear, anxiety, or abnormal curiosity can be resolved.

It is especially important that children be put at ease about new body sensations and observations of growth in their own body organs. Preteen girls should know about menstruation long before it occurs. Boys, also, should know something about this process. (For information on how to explain this process, see MENSTRUATION in the Medical Guide.)

One subject worries parents needlessly— masturbation. Most developing boys and girls masturbate. Do not be concerned about it. Masturbation is entirely normal.

You and your preteen

During their preteen years, boys and girls go through so many changes, both physical and emotional, that growth seems to disorganize them rather than improve them. The preteen period is one in which children grow "away from" more than they grow "into." They lose most of the characteristics with which you were familiar when they were children. Yet they neither look nor act as they will when they are teen-agers.

Perhaps no other period of childhood development offers so many chances for parents to lose their tempers or become alarmed, sensitive, or indignant. But parents should try to figure out the best approach to each problem as it arises and to separate their own emotional attitudes from the problem. They should try to be the voice of authority without becoming authoritarians.

Some parents correct their child continuously and in the child's weakest moments. They give a moralistic speech each time their preteen daughter is five minutes late for dinner. They tell their preteen son that he will never amount to anything because he shows such irresponsible behavior at school.

Paying so much attention to surface behavior is unwise. If you feel there is an issue in which you should interfere, plan your strategy wisely. Do not start a campaign of daily scolding and nagging. Let the misbehavior crystallize itself into definite incidents that can be well demonstrated and interpreted. Accompany this interpretation with a happy and secure personal relationship, and follow it up with a period of special interest in and companionship with your child. You may win more of your child's trust and cooperation in the end if you do not insist on coming out on top in each little situation along the way.

Remember, few children show all the problems of the preteen period, and few of them go through all the difficulties at the same time. Life with your child from 8 to 13 should be fun. The basic test is not whether you have problems with your preteen, but whether you can enjoy your preteen child in spite of whatever problems may arise, and help your rapidly maturing youngster through a period that is as difficult for the child as it is for parents.

Keep lines of communication open between you and your changing preteen.

Adoption

By Eda LeShan, B.S., M.A.

A couple considering adoption should be as clear as possible about why they're doing it. Many childless couples feel they have failed as men and women. In addition to feeling frustrated and disappointed, they may even feel guilty or angry. Sometimes they feel their marriage is threatened or become ashamed, afraid they are "losing face" with friends and relatives. Some couples think adopting a child will help them fulfill their own unrealized ambitions. None of these are good reasons for adopting a child.

A couple should adopt a child primarily because they want the joys and challenge of being parents—not because the child may be the means of correcting an unsuccessful marriage, or of giving them status with friends and relatives. A couple is ready to adopt a child only when they respect themselves as human beings worthy and ready to offer love and understanding, and when they can accept what every parent must accept—the fact that there is no way of knowing exactly what a child will be like.

Social agencies can help

Because motives and feelings are so important when adopting, it is wise to consult legally recognized social agencies about adoption. Carefully trained, experienced workers can help a couple explore their motivations, give them advice and guidance, and explain the importance of legal protection. A couple that adopts a child through sources that are neither recognized nor licensed cannot always be sure that the child is legally available for adoption. There is always the possibility that the biological parents may change their minds and want

the child returned to them. Also, independent sources are usually unable to provide the kind of information and advice that agencies can provide through the experienced study that is done to make the adoption most satisfying for the child and the adopting parents.

A social agency is the best source for ensuring maximum help and continued assistance. Information about recognized public and private agencies is available through state welfare authorities such as the state department of public welfare, the department of public assistance, or the state department of social welfare.

Because of advances in child psychology, as well as changing circumstances, many

Parents should adopt a child only through a licensed agency.

agencies now have more flexible adoption rules and regulations. Factors such as race, religion, age, and background are not as restrictive as they used to be. In general, there is increasing awareness of the importance of family experience in every child's life. However, fewer babies are available for adoption than ever before. Many people use some form of birth control, and more unmarried mothers keep their babies. But older children, and those with special problems, are available. Many couples thinking of adoption consider one of these children.

How it feels to be the parents of an adopted child

Parents of an adopted child experience all the joys and satisfactions of natural parents. They also experience all the normal problems, challenges, and stresses. But having an adopted child is not exactly the same as having a child of your own—mainly because parents who adopt tend to be too hard on themselves.

All parents sometimes wonder whether they are doing a good job when their child is unhappy, naughty, angry, fearful, shy, bossy, or jealous. But parents who adopt are likely to be extrasensitive to such behavior. When their child misbehaves, they often jump to the conclusion that somehow they are inadequate as parents.

If parents employ love, support, and guidance as the basic ingredients for helping the child grow, and if they can anticipate the unfolding of their child's unique qualities with interest and joy, they need have no fear about their ability to be good parents.

Talking to the adopted child

Children should be told that they are adopted. Sooner or later they will find out anyway. Some parents find the easiest way to introduce the word "adoption" is to tell children about themselves as tiny babies. All children love to hear stories about their babyhood. Sometimes the opportunity may come through looking at pictures in an album, or telling or reading a story about an adopted child. It is wise to postpone any detailed discussion until the child is 6 or 7

years old. Before then, when the child asks for details about the adoption, it is possible for you to say with complete honesty, "There are things you cannot understand until you are older. I will tell you then."

Usually, it is a good idea to explain to close friends and relatives how you are handling the subject of adoption with the child. If the groundwork has been properly prepared, it will not matter if someone says something to the child that represents a different point of view.

The child's questions about adoption will change as the child grows older. At first, the child will be interested only in the circumstances that brought him or her to you. At 7 or 8, the child may begin to ask questions about the birth parents. When answering such questions, try to keep the lines of communication open so that the child will feel free to ask you questions whenever confused or troubled. If questions are brushed aside, the child might find it difficult to share important feelings with you. The information the child asks for is secondary to the sharing of feelings.

Do not sentimentalize or romanticize the facts of the adoption. You can tell the child that there were good reasons for the adoption, that the biological parents were concerned for their child's welfare, and that giving the child up was an act of responsibility and caring.

Yet, no matter how good the reasons for adoption are, some children may feel that their birth parents gave them away because they were defective in some way. Even when the adoptive parents tell the children that they were adorable, beautiful children, and show baby pictures to prove it, the children may still have feelings of rejection. To a young child, it is incredible that parents would give away their baby unless there was something wrong with the baby. Such feelings of rejection may leave an emotional scar, especially in a child who is particularly sensitive. But this is true of many life experiences. It is true of the child who is lame, or sickly, or slower to learn than other children the same age. Every child has some feelings of being different. But, in general, children are strong enough to face almost any reality if it is shared with loving parents.

Some special problems

Even though all parents face similar problems with their children, adoptive parents may encounter special problems that arise because of the fact that they have adopted. Here are three of them.

Brothers and sisters

In any family, children will at times resent or be jealous of each other. They will quarrel, bully each other, and fight. But they will also enjoy each other's companionship, fight for each other when threatened by outsiders, and on occasion even team up against their parents.

In families made up of both biological and adopted children, parents sometimes create problems by singling out the adopted children for special attention. Often this is done in the mistaken belief that the adopted children will feel more secure. Usually the result is just the opposite. The adopted children are made aware that somehow they really are different from the others. They may even think they are being given favored treatment because they are not as capable as the other children in the family. At the same time, the biological children may feel a growing resentment against the adopted ones because the biological children feel cheated. Parents must take care to make it quite clear that each of their children—biological or adopted—is loved.

Adopting an older child

Adopting older children may involve other kinds of problems. Older children may remember their biological families, or they may have had trouble adjusting in other settings—such as orphanages or foster homes. An older child's adjustment to an adoptive family will be made easier if the child is helped to share memories and feelings with the new family. An older child needs a bridge between the past and the present to face the future. Adopting parents may have to face the fact that children who have been deprived of love and acceptance will constantly test their adoptive parents to see if indeed the parents will love them and keep them, even when they misbehave. During such an adjustment, which is hard on both parents and child, an adoption agency can play an important part in guiding the

When a family has an adopted child and natural child, a parent must make it clear that each of the children is loved.

Adopting an older child may present special problems as well as pleasures. Contact the adoption agency if you have any problems.

family toward a solution. Patience, compassion, and the readiness to ask for expert help are some of the basics necessary for the successful adoption of an older child.

The search

Instances of extreme curiosity about the biological parents rarely occur in the adopted child. Usually, the child feels so close to the adoptive parents, that the idea of once being part of another family seems unreal. But should the child raise the question of a search for the biological parents, the adoptive parents should understand the child's curiosity without letting it lead to any action. Usually, the child is not truly concerned in searching for the biological parents. In raising the question of a search, the child may just be testing the adoptive parents and may be saying, "Prove that you are more my parents than those who brought me into the world." If the child persists in the search, it should be pointed out that the natural parents' decision to give up their child must be respected; that whatever the circumstances, it was a difficult decision for them to make and it must have been necessary for the child's well-being.

According to adoption laws, search for parents is not desirable. Most states have laws requiring that a court order be obtained before adoption records can be seen,

and the order is issued only under the most unusual and special circumstances.

Many young adults who are adopted seek out their biological parents, with varied results. Occasionally, there is disappointment when the biological parents are found. Many abandon the search and strengthen the bond with the adoptive parents.

Adoption and the law

Usually, an adoption decree ends all rights and duties between the child and the biological parents, and makes the child the legal child of the adoptive parents. The adopting parents become responsible for the child's education, care, and support. Each state and territory has its own adoption laws. When adopting parents and the child they seek to adopt live in different states, the adoption is governed by the law of the state where the adoption proceedings are brought, and the adopting parents must comply with the law of that state if the adoption is to be legally binding.

Almost all states issue a new birth certificate for the adopted child. This bears no information about the biological parents. It does not indicate in any way that the child is adopted. The new birth certificate carries the child's new name and the names of the adopting parents. Also, most states have laws or statutes making all proceedings in an adoption secret. The old birth certificate is sealed and filed. It may be obtained only under court order.

In matters of inheritance, the adopted child is entitled to inherit property from the adoptive parents except when a will states that inheritance is restricted to "heirs of the body." Some states bar an adopted child from inheriting property from the biological parents or other blood relatives. But other states prohibit the adopted child from "being debarred from inheriting" from biological parents or other blood relatives.

Laws pertaining to inheritance by adopted children vary from state to state. Information about inheritance, as well as any laws governing adoption, may be obtained from the state welfare authority in your state or from the social agency that handled your child's adoption.

Behavioral disorders in children

By Jerome L. Schulman, M.D.

At times, all children behave in ways that puzzle or worry their parents. Many children may even show what seem to be symptoms of a behavioral disorder. Symptoms such as extreme aggressiveness, fears, and compulsions indicate a behavioral disorder only when they are severe or occur frequently. Be careful not to let your concern about your child's behavior exaggerate the significance of a symptom. Fortunately, most children are mentally healthy.

Behavioral disorders and mental retardation are different from one another, but sometimes it is hard to tell them apart. Emotional problems may make learning so difficult that even a normally bright child may appear developmentally delayed. (See THE MENTALLY RETARDED CHILD in For Special Consideration.)

The importance of physical health

Before concluding that a behavior problem is the result of emotional disturbance, you should be certain that your child does not have some physical illness. Many symptoms of behavioral disorder can be created or made worse by a physical illness. Regular medical checkups are important. They become even more important if your child is having an emotional problem.

Where emotional problems can occur

A child may be thought of as living in four worlds and being expected to behave in

certain ways in each of these worlds. If the child's behavior is frequently very different from what is thought of as normal, there may be a behavioral disorder.

Family and home—the first world

A child's first world is the family and the home. One's attitude toward oneself, toward other people, and toward life in general begins here. In a normal situation, there is a bond of affection between the parents, and between the child and each parent. They enjoy each other's company, but each has other interests. Gradually, the child moves from almost total dependence in infancy to almost total independence toward the end of adolescence. Throughout these years, the child is expected to pay a reasonable amount of attention to family rules and to perform tasks that are reasonable in terms of age and ability.

A child may have a behavioral disorder if there is not a good relationship with parents, if independence proceeds too slowly or too rapidly, or if family rules and tasks are ignored. Attitudes toward other children in the family are hard to classify because quarreling and jealousy are a normal part of the brother-sister relationship. They seldom indicate a behavioral disorder.

School—the second world

A child lives in this second world about 1,000 hours a year during childhood. A child's tasks in school are, within reasonable limits, to perform well and to conform socially, to be interested in studies, to see learning as an opportunity for a full and productive life, and to become interested and involved in extracurricular activity.

All parents have ambitions for their children. A problem may occur if the child's ability does not match the parents' expectations. The child's attitude toward school may become bad, or achievement may fall below ability. Also, if behavior at school makes frequent discipline necessary, it may indicate a behavioral disorder for which help is needed.

Friendships—the third world

As children move from infancy into childhood, they encounter a third world—the world of friendships. This world becomes increasingly important as children grow older. Childhood associations are extremely important. Children begin to learn social customs and patterns of behavior by imitating adults and by influencing and being influenced by other children. Much of the ability to be good at adult relationships grows gradually out of a good childhood beginning. Normally, the child should want to be with friends and should feel wanted by them. They should enjoy being together.

Parents should be concerned about the child who is always alone, the child who tries to buy friendship with bribes, the child who either acts the fool to get other children to laugh at him or her or who is aggressive toward other children, and the child who always prefers to play with much younger or much older children. And certainly parents should be concerned about the older child whose friendships lead to antisocial behavior such as vandalism or stealing.

The inner world—the fourth world

The child's inner world is in some ways the most important and the most difficult to understand. It is the world of thoughts, fears, hopes, attitudes, and ambitions. Children see themselves in many ways. They may think of themselves as smart or stupid, lovable or unlovable, ugly or good-looking, good or bad. Together, these self-evaluations make up what is known as the self-image. When a child has a strong and continuous feeling of not measuring up to other children, it is reasonable to assume that there is an emotional problem.

Everyone has to face problems of one kind or another throughout life. In spite of this, the well-adjusted person continues to find life a source of satisfaction. Such a person is usually optimistic about the future. If this feeling of optimism never occurs, then there is an emotional problem.

Specific symptoms

The most serious symptoms of behavioral disorder may be referred to as thinking disorders. They may occur singly or in combination. A child who is unable to respond to people or surroundings or is completely without a sense of time has a thinking disorder. The child may hear voices or see things that do not exist. This should not be confused with the behavior of the normal child, who may sometimes play with and talk to an invisible friend.

Obsessions are thoughts that occur repeatedly until they interfere with normal thought processes. At times a normal child may have an experience similar to an obsession, such as a tune that keeps running through the mind. This is short-lived and does not interfere much with normal thought processes.

Compulsions are urges to repeat certain acts over and over even though there is no reason to do so, such as the uncontrollable urge to repeatedly wash the hands. This is not the same as a child's urge to avoid stepping on cracks in a sidewalk, which is more a game than a compulsion.

A phobia is a fear so terrifying that it prevents the child from carrying on normal activities. It is one symptom of a behavioral disorder that gives parents much concern. This is not to be confused with the normal child's dislike of school at certain times, or with a young child's fear on first entering school.

Anxiety is a nameless dread not related to anything specific. Anxiety is harder to understand than a phobia because the cause of the child's fear is hard to pinpoint.

Extreme aggressiveness, such as a compulsion to hurt other children or to be cruel to animals, must also be considered a symptom of a serious behavioral disorder if it is frequent.

Some symptoms of behavioral disorders interfere with the normal body functions. Among these are tics, hysteria, enuresis (regular bed-wetting), and encopresis (the constant inability of the child to control bowel movements).

Tics, or habit spasms, are sudden repeated movements of muscle groups. Generally these occur in the muscles of the face, but they may involve any muscle group. The child has no control over a tic.

Hysteria is best described as the loss of a physical or sense function because of emotion. Hysteria may cause blindness or the loss of the sense of touch. It may also cause paralysis of arms or legs.

Enuresis and encopresis may be considered symptoms of a behavioral disorder if they occur in a child who has previously been bowel and bladder trained.

What to do about behavioral disorders

If your child frequently shows symptoms of a behavior disorder, do not ignore the symptoms and hope they will disappear in time. Your child is too important for you to rely on chance.

Parents should discuss the problem together. It is extremely important that the discussion take place during a time of calm and good feeling rather than when parents are upset and angry because the child has behaved badly.

During the discussion, parents must decide how the family as a group, and each member, behaves differently from the average. Do not hesitate to admit that your own behavior may be different. In a variety of ways, everyone is likely to be on one side or the other of the average.

Also, you must be able to admit that while the ways you do things may work well with some children, and may even be necessary, they have not been successful with the disturbed child. This admission calls for a willingness to accept the fact that your behavior is related to your child's difficulty, and that a change in your approach to the child may be a solution to the problem.

Parents may have problems

The *perfectionist parent* believes there is a place for everything and that everything must be in its place at all times. As a result, demands on the child are often unreasonable. The child's room is never kept neat enough to please the perfectionist parent. If the child gets a "B" on an otherwise straight "A" report card, the child is criticized and made to feel inadequate. The child is constantly compared to others, but no matter how hard the child tries, the perfectionist parent is never quite pleased. Emotional problems of the child can often be related to this abnormal demand for perfection. The perfectionist parent should try to be less rigid about rules and to look for behavior that can be praised.

The *inconsistent parent* creates an uncertain environment by changing rules so often that the child cannot know what is expected. Most parents are inconsistent at times, but when they constantly change rules relating to the child's behavior, it is damaging to the child and should be corrected.

The *overprotective parent* shields the child excessively, either because the parent cannot bear the thought that the child is growing up, or because of undue concern for dangers in the world outside the home. This attitude may inhibit the development of independent skills. The parent who recognizes that overprotection is a problem can find a reasonable guideline for correcting it by studying the behavior of parents with well-adjusted children.

The *indulgent parent* buys the child's affection by never setting any limits. This may also be the source of the child's behavioral disorder. Children are much more comfortable when they have rules to follow. Rules prepare a child to face the many situations where individual desires must be put aside in favor of group needs.

Quarreling parents may also contribute to a child's problems, if the quarreling is constant. The obvious solution is to avoid quarreling in the child's presence and to compromise their differences.

The *uninvolved parent* has little to do with the child. Such a parent will be unable to convince the child of his or her love, interest, and concern. Children need models after which they can pattern their own behavior. To be effective models, parents must be available and interested in the child.

The *punishing parent* tends to deal with problems by thinking up new and unusual punishments. Although punishment may be essential on some occasions, it should not be excessive, and there should be sufficient praise to counterbalance it. If a child shows symptoms of a behavioral disorder, and has been punished a great deal, it is reasonable to assume that more punishment will only tend to aggravate the condition.

Changing tactics

When parents recognize that previous methods of handling their child have been unsuccessful, and even harmful, they should plan a new program. If the child is old enough to reason with, the process will be made easier by a frank discussion when all are feeling friendly. The parents should tell the child how concerned they are and how much they want to help. They should indicate to the child how they plan to change their behavior, and they should agree to meet on a regular basis to discuss progress. The child should be allowed to speak freely during the discussions, and nothing the child says should be held against him or her.

If the child's behavior has become a problem at school, it is important that parents discuss the problem with the child's teacher and other staff, such as the principal, the school psychologist, a social worker, or the school nurse. These people are interested in the child and can offer advice and guidance. This may be extremely valuable in helping parents understand why their child is behaving badly.

When to seek professional help

Usually, it is difficult for parents to admit, even to themselves, that their child may need psychological support. And it is reasonable for parents to assume that they can work on some of their child's problems without outside help. If there is any improvement, they should continue. But if in a reasonable time, there is no improvement, it is time to seek professional help.

If the child's problem is in the category discussed under "Specific symptoms," parents should consult their pediatrician or the family doctor. If necessary, the parents will be referred to a psychiatrist, a clinical psychologist, or to the local mental health clinic. Often it is easier for an outsider, especially one with specialized training, to approach the problem with greater objectivity or from a different point of view.

When parents seek help for their child, they must be prepared to accept the fact that they may be partly responsible for their child's emotional problem. Parents should be willing to learn how they have contributed to the problem and to work with the doctor to produce good results.

Children with behavioral disorders tend to respond favorably to treatment, especially when all members of the family are trying to help. The treatment of an emotionally disturbed child often requires a great deal of time and patience on the part of parents and child guidance specialists.

For one thing, a disturbed child is, as a rule, completely unaware that anything is the matter. For another, disturbed children seldom want to change their ways. The professional working with the child may need time to bring the child to the point where the child wants to do something about the behavioral disorder.

Parents should not be discouraged if psychiatric treatment or treatment in a child guidance clinic fails to produce immediate results. Diagnosis and treatment take time, and the results may be slow in coming. A severe behavioral disorder usually takes a long time to develop. It follows that as long a time may be required to correct it.

Fortunately, many of the emotional illnesses of children can now be treated successfully. Ongoing research in the important field of mental health should offer even more help in the future.

Mark S. Puczynski, M.D.
Consulting Editor

Children and television

By Patricia Fosarelli, M.D.

In the last 30 years, television has become a pervasive part of our lives. Children, especially, are attracted by its magic. Children in the United States watch an average of two to three hours of TV per weekday and an average of four to six hours on weekend days, and even more during summer vacations and school holidays. By the time many children become high school seniors, they will have spent more hours watching TV than sitting in a classroom. School-age children who watch more hours of TV per day tend to be poorer students than those who watch fewer hours per day.

Since so many programs have violent or sexual overtones, the average child is exposed to much that is undesirable. This exposure is heightened if a home has cable TV through which children can be exposed to "adult" programs. In addition to violence and sex, children are also exposed to blatant commercialism, which imparts a sense of greed to many affluent children and a sense of deprivation to many children of modest means.

How do children learn?

Young children learn by observing. They mimic both positive and negative behaviors that they see around them. An example is the young child who utters an obscenity, just as he or she has heard an adult do, after being frustrated in some task.

Young children who watch many television programs will try out some of the behaviors they see. If they see a pro-social act (helping or comforting someone in need), they are likely to mimic it. If they see a hostile act (hitting or screaming at another person), they might also mimic it. The likelihood that hostile behaviors will be mimicked is higher if the children live in an environment that is already hostile, such as a household in which parents and children constantly bicker.

What programs do children prefer?

Young children prefer programs with lively music, animated figures, female characters, babies of either sex, and a happy tone. They also prefer short programs, because their attention span is so limited. Studies have shown that young children cannot follow the story line of a moderately complicated plot. For example, many 3- and 4-year-olds cannot order the sequences properly in familiar fairy tales. These children remember violent sequences but cannot consistently remember the events leading to a violent act or the consequences of the act.

If this inability to understand cause and effect is typically at work in normal 3- and 4-year-olds for familiar stories, it is even more likely for unfamiliar, long, or complicated stories. Add the effect of "seeing" such a story, especially if highly violent acts are shown, and it is easy to understand why children are especially likely to selectively remember the violent episodes.

Specific effects of TV on children
Violence

Numerous studies have demonstrated that children are influenced, at least on a short-term basis, by what they see on TV. When preschoolers watched pro-social programs, they tended to be more cooperative, tolerant, and helpful to others. When they watched programs with violent overtones, they tended to behave more aggressively and in a more intolerant fashion. These findings were consistent whether the program seemed real or was an animation (cartoon) and whether it was a brief clip (5 minutes) of violent action or a longer segment. Children who watched aggressive programs tended to act aggressively toward *both* animate and inanimate objects.

Most of these studies examined only short-term effects of TV violence on children—the effects seen for up to three hours after watching the program. However, at least two studies have suggested that elementary-school children who watched more than three hours of TV per day and who preferred violent programs were more likely, ten years later, to do poorly in school and to be rated as "difficult" by peers.

The effect of repeatedly watching violent TV programs may be intensified if the child lives in an aggressive, hostile environment. In such cases, children are getting a double dose, real and fantasy, of violence in their lives. For these children the violence on the screen might be very believable, since they see the same behavior in their homes or neighborhoods. It is not difficult to see how such children might easily take a violent view of life.

The effect of watching violent TV programs may be somewhat diluted if parents actively watch with their children. Active TV viewing with one's child can be beneficial because it is individualized education, and it can help dilute the effect of seeing violence on TV.

Active TV viewing means that parents take the opportunity to teach children about what they see. For example, a parent can say, "Did you see what happened to that one guy? Why do you think he got beaten up? Is it practical to beat someone up just because the person disagrees with you? If you and your friend disagreed, how would you settle it? How do you think I should settle it if I disagreed with my friend? Do you think this show is real, or is it pretend? Why?"

An even better strategy, of course, is to limit the amount of violent adult-type TV programming a child sees. Preschoolers and most younger elementary school-age children cannot readily follow the plots of adult dramas. If a TV character is shot, these children might not recall (or even know) the motive for the shooting or understand the consequences of the act.

Sexuality

Young children do not understand the intricacies of sexual relations. Permitting young children to watch "adult" programs, especially those with blatant sex, will confuse and frighten them. This is especially true if the children live in homes in which they have observed a range of adult sexual behavior, including sexual intercourse or nude sexual play, violent or aggressive sexual behavior, bickering about infidelities, or a parent's "stay-over" boyfriends or girlfriends.

Many "adult" TV programs also make great use of sexual stereotypes: handsome, strong men who are rarely shown as weak; gorgeous women who frequently are portrayed as somewhat helpless.

The best strategy is to prevent children from watching programs with blatant sexuality. If your child accidentally walks in during a sex scene on TV or if a program suddenly shifts gears with an escalation of sexual activity, don't think, "My child won't understand it anyway." Don't ignore the situation, and don't shoo the child out of the room (which will only heighten curiosity). Instead, ask what the child saw and what he or she thinks it means. Discuss these impressions with your child.

Prejudice and role stereotypes

Many programs portray the elderly, the poor, certain ethnic groups, or people in low-status occupations stereotypically. For example, the elderly might be portrayed as foolish or forgetful, the poor as shiftless, certain ethnic groups as lazy or dishonest, and people in low-status positions as stupid. Studies have shown that children are likely to believe such TV stereotypes if they have no direct contact with the type of person portrayed.

A great injustice is wreaked upon members of the group adversely portrayed, because their self-esteem is diminished. This is even more tragic for children, who might become ashamed of their parents' jobs or ethnic backgrounds.

Active TV viewing is very helpful in these situations. If you and your child see a TV portrayal that is unfavorable, especially needlessly so, ask "What do you think of that person? Do you like him or her? Why or why not? Do you know anybody like that? How would you feel if people didn't like (your dad, mom) because (he/she) has a certain job or skin of a certain color? Would you think that is unfair? How should we decide whether we like someone?" Remind your child that the program is not real.

Not all stereotypes are totally negative. TV programs depict, with few exceptions, mothers as attractive, all-wise, and all-patient, and fathers as strong but sensitive, attractive people with no glaring defects. In fact, most TV parents are nice people who (especially the fathers) are a little confused by their too-cute, too-smart offspring; sometimes, the parents look a little foolish. In real life, most parents are not fashion models; they do not have limitless patience; they might be weak or have defects. Children who believe too strongly in the television models of parents and family might be disappointed in their own very real (but otherwise wonderful) parents.

Active TV viewing with your child helps in these situations. Remember, don't become defensive, no matter what your child says! For example, upon seeing an idyllic family scene to which your child murmurs, "I wish this house was like that," you could say, "Yes, wouldn't it be great if no one got upset? If kids did all their chores and if parents always had a lot of time for fun things? If brothers and sisters and parents never argued? That would be great. But remember, this is just a TV show; it's not real. Who would watch it if all it showed was yelling? No one. When programs are written, they're done in such a way that people will find them nice to watch. Do you know any real families like the one we're watching? Who? Do you think our family could be the stars of a TV show? Why or why not?"

Commercials

Commercials confuse young children. They find it difficult to separate them from the rest of the program. In one young child's mind, a man was chased by police because he was speeding to get some chewing gum! Young children do not understand that many commercials are hyperbole, or overblown language—and they do not understand the special effects that make inanimate objects talk, walk, or seem larger than they really are. They may be disappointed when they see the actual product.

Young children are very influenced by ads for products on TV. Studies have demonstrated that children prefer highly advertised products in toy stores and supermarkets. In one study, a group of preschoolers was prevented from watching Saturday morning TV programs for 4 weeks before Christmas. Compared with a group of preschoolers who watched Saturday TV as usual, they made fewer demands for products and were less disruptive in stores.

Although some countries ban or severely limit commercials during children's TV programs, this is not the case in the United States. Commercials for toys, candy, or sugar-coated cereals are prominent on Saturday morning children's programs, especially before Christmas.

Commercials lend themselves to active TV viewing by parent and child. When you see a ludicrous commercial, say to your child, "Look at that! Have you ever seen a book talk? I haven't. How do you think they did that?" When you see an obvious visual exaggeration of a product, say, "Did you see that doll? I've seen that doll in a store, and it's not nearly that big. How do you think they did that? And you know how it moves? With batteries, but they didn't mention that. Without batteries, it wouldn't move at all!" This kind of education can make children wiser consumers.

When you see an ad for sugar-coated cereal or candy, say, "Have you ever tasted that? Was it good? Why did you like it? Was it sweet? Sweet means there's a lot of sugar in it. Too much sugar can cause your teeth to develop cavities. Can you think of a cereal that is good but is not sweet? What is a better snack to eat than candy?"

TV's portrayal of health behaviors

Most characters on TV are in perfect physical condition, but few are shown exercising. While many TV characters are shown eating, or drinking alcoholic beverages, few are overweight and even fewer are shown drunk or with hangovers. Point out to your child that unhealthy behaviors lead to unpleasant consequences in real life and that these consequences are not often shown on TV.

Television watching in itself can create poor health habits. Children who spend many hours in front of the television are not exercising, and many are snacking on the same sugary, salty, and empty-calorie foods extolled on the commercials. Consequently, children who watch many hours of TV per day are more likely to become obese than other children.

Children are more likely to adopt healthy habits if their parents demonstrate healthy life styles. This includes exercising and not snacking while watching TV. If you must snack while watching TV, eat fruit.

Pro-social, pro-learning programs

Some programs are meant to teach children about their world. These educational programs impart lessons about the world of nature, science, other cultures, or emotions. Other educational programs can teach young children about letters, colors, numbers, and other reading readiness skills. Some programs present valuable lessons for children and adults alike. Parents who watch with their children demonstrate that learning is enjoyable at all ages.

What can parents do?

Parents can limit the amount of television that their children watch each day. Watching television is a privilege; it is not a right. Parents should not use television as an electronic babysitter.

Young preschoolers should be limited to one or two short age-appropriate programs per day. Older preschoolers and young elementary school-age children might be allowed to watch one or two hours of age-appropriate programming a day. School-age children should be permitted to watch television only after homework and chores are completed. The hours of viewing can be liberalized on weekends, but children should be encouraged to spend more time outdoors and/or with other children than watching TV. If your child is shy or socially awkward, taking refuge in the fantasy life of television is easier than making friends. Don't let television become a crutch for your child.

Watch the effects of TV programming on your child. Children with marked fears and nightmares should be forbidden to watch frightening or stimulating programs, especially before they go to bed. If your child is frightened by a program, offer reassurance—and avoid teasing. Teasing does nothing to "toughen up" a frightened child, and makes the child lose self-esteem.

When a special program is aired, you might permit an extra hour or two of TV time. Be sure to tell your child why you are granting the privilege. If older children are permitted to watch more TV or different programs than younger children, be sure that the younger ones understand that certain privileges come with age and that TV viewing is a privilege in your home.

Children may complain if their friends are allowed to watch programs that they are forbidden to see; they may also feel left out. Parents must handle this in their own way. If your child really wants to see a particular program and you do not object to it, it might not be worth making an issue of it. However, if you do object to a program, you should explain why you will not permit it. One approach to a child who wants to watch a variety of programs (to which you have no inherent objection) is to let the child choose one or two, with the understanding that he or she can choose differently the next week.

In addition to these active TV viewing strategies, you should watch some children's programs yourself, including cartoons, to assess their quality. You can also plan an activity that is fun *and* interesting to most family members and have a "no TV" family evening now and then.

By your own example, you can diminish the importance of television in your family's life. It's well worth the effort!

Choosing a baby sitter

By Stella Chess, M.D.

Parents and children should occasionally spend time apart from each other. Parents should be able to enjoy an evening out, or a few days away from home, free from the demands made on them by their child. And a young child needs to learn to accept the temporary absence of parents without fear of being rejected or deserted. But this is possible only when you are completely at ease, confident that your child is being looked after by a friendly, efficient, and trustworthy baby sitter.

A friendly, efficient baby sitter can make parents and children feel at ease.

When you place your child in the care of a baby sitter, you should be as certain as possible that the sitter is fully able to assume responsibility for the safety and needs of your child. Whether the baby sitter is an adult or a teen-ager, and is needed for a few hours or a few days at a time, it is important that you choose the sitter carefully.

If you do not already know your prospective baby sitter, you should be certain to get a recommendation from someone whose judgment you trust. Depending on your child's age and the length of time you expect to be away, you will expect the baby sitter to have special qualifications. There are many things you will want to know about any baby sitter you engage.
- Does the sitter like and understand children?
- Do children like and respect the sitter?
- Is the person an experienced sitter?
- How will the sitter react to an emergency?
- Is the sitter physically and mentally healthy?
- Is the baby sitter clean and neat?
- Are the sitter's morals and conduct acceptable?
- Does the sitter have a sense of humor?
- Will the sitter refrain from gossiping?

A competent sitter should have little or no difficulty making your child feel at ease. But no child, with the possible exception of a tiny infant, should be expected to accept the care of a complete stranger without some objection. It is, therefore, a good idea to invite the sitter to your home so that you, the sitter, and your child can get to know each other. While the sitter is in your home, perform some activity in your child's daily routine such as playing, feeding, or dressing the child so that you and the child can begin to establish a friendly, personal relationship with the sitter.

If such an opportunity is not possible, arrange to have the sitter arrive early the first time. If you show that you like and trust the sitter, your child will be quick to sense this. The child can usually be counted on to relax and enjoy the quiet, pleasant atmosphere created by friendly conversation. Hurried, last-minute warnings and instructions to the sitter are likely to leave the child less relaxed.

During the sitter's first visit to your home, point out all exits, and special hazards such as electric heaters, electric outlets, open stairs, or swinging doors. Demonstrate how thermostats and other temperature regulators are operated. Show the sitter where to find a flashlight in case of electric power failure, and give instructions for the use of any appliances that the sitter may need while in your home.

Show the sitter where extra supplies of food, clothing, bed linen, and diapers are kept; where first-aid supplies can be found; and where you keep your permanent list of names and telephone numbers of people to call in an emergency. This list should include the name and telephone number of your family doctor (as well as the name of an alternate doctor to call if your family doctor is not available), the names and telephone numbers of several close neighbors, and the telephone numbers of the police and fire departments. Be sure to give the sitter the name and telephone number where you can be reached while you are away.

A baby sitter will do a much better job of caring for your child if you explain any special habits and problems your child has. Tell the sitter if your child is a restless sleeper, cries while asleep, sleeps with a favorite toy or blanket, or has to be awakened at a certain time to go to the toilet.

It is helpful for your sitter to know which books, stories, and records are your child's favorites. Sometimes a familiar song or story will comfort a child who misses the parents.

When a sitter is to supervise bedtime for children of varying ages, you should leave a list of their bedtimes. You should also tell the sitter what your child may have to eat or drink before bedtime. If the child is an infant, be sure to make enough formula to last the time you are away, and show the sitter how to heat and feed it to the baby.

To make the sitter feel more at ease, point out what foods she or he can eat and what other privileges she or he can take while in your home.

When a sitter is to take over your household for several days, you should leave a detailed list of your child's activities, duties, and privileges. The sitter should know whether you permit your child to have friends in after school, how many may visit at a time, and where they may play. If your child is required to wear special clothing when outdoors, the sitter should be informed. Also, tell the sitter if certain television programs are not permitted and what rules you expect your child to follow.

If you choose a baby sitter with care, and if parents and baby sitters respect the obligations and responsibilities each has to the other and to the child, then everyone concerned can be sure of a pleasant, satisfying relationship.

What your baby sitter should know

- Telephone number where you can be reached
- Family doctor's name and telephone number, and a substitute doctor's name and telephone number
- Telephone number and name of nearest neighbor
- How to operate any appliance that may have to be used
- How to set the thermostat
- Where extra food, clothing, and bedding are kept
- Where flashlights are kept if there is a power failure
- Telephone numbers for the police and fire departments
- Whether your child sleeps with a night light on
- Where first-aid supplies are kept
- Any special problems or habits your child may have
- Television programs your child is allowed to watch
- Privileges the sitter may take

Day care

By Patricia Fosarelli, M.D.

Substitute care is the care a child receives from a person other than a parent—a relative, babysitter, nanny, au pair, neighbor, day-care center teacher or director, or operator of a family day-care home.

A day-care center is a facility that can care for a number of children, from as few as a dozen to more than a hundred. Day-care centers are either for-profit or non-profit, but all are subject to state regulations regarding fire, safety, sanitation, and so on.

A day-care home is an actual private house in which up to 6 children can receive care. Some states also have large day-care homes, which can accommodate 7 to 12 children. In general, day-care homes are not licensed, and a number of states do not regulate them in any way.

In this country, 60 per cent to 75 per cent of the mothers of infants and preschoolers are in the work force. Due to the present divorce rate, the rising number of never-married mothers, and the number of women who need to work for financial reasons, the number of working mothers is not expected to decrease in the near future.

Postulated effects of day-care

The parent-child bond

Although many psychologists worried that children's relationships with day-care providers would weaken their relationships with parents, this apparently has not occurred. When children's bonds with parents are close and loving, there is *no* evidence that they will bond more closely to substitute care providers. Children with loving parents prefer them over all others. However, children who come from families in which the parent-child bond is weak or destructive might indeed prefer a more interested or kindly person.

Many parents think that if their children do not eagerly run to greet them at the end of the day, they prefer the provider to the parent or the day-care facility to home. This is not necessarily so. At certain ages, children like to display a bit of bravado and act as if they are fine without their parents. In the preschool years, it *is* an act, so don't be fooled!

Aggressiveness and assertiveness

In a number of studies, children who attended day-care programs were likely to be noisier, verbal, and more assertive than children cared for exclusively at home. This is not an unexpected finding. The rough-and-tumble of a group day-care setting encourages children to state their needs, air their grievances, and defend their rights.

However, assertiveness is not aggressiveness. Assertiveness means standing up for one's rights without interfering with another's rights; aggressiveness means getting what one wants irrespective of another person's rights, desires, or feelings. Having an assertive child is positive; having an aggressive child is not. If a previously placid child becomes aggressive after enrollment in a large day-care center, a parent should suspect that the environment is too stimulating for the child (the child needs to be with a smaller group) or that the teacher is not adequately supervising the group.

Change in sleep/eating/fears

Although children might normally experience sleep or eating disruptions in the first week or two of any major change in their routines (such as attending day-care for the first time or changing from one center to another), these should gradually improve after the first few days. A stable, high-quality care arrangement should not exert any lasting or even prolonged effects on a child's sleep or eating. Children who have secure, loving bonds with their parents and who attend a warm, supportive day-care facility are *not* likely to be highly fearful.

Learning advantages

Some day-care center directors promote their facilities as giving children a head start in life through their education programs. Studies have shown that quality day-care centers and preschools benefit children from disadvantaged homes more than children from affluent homes. This seems to be because children from affluent homes are already receiving the benefits of early education from parents, whereas children in disadvantaged homes frequently do not hear positive messages about education and do not have materials at home that facilitate learning. However, disadvantaged children who are exposed to quality day care or preschool may not benefit in the long term if they later attend mediocre elementary schools.

Pro-social behaviors

Children who are exposed to day care are more likely to be open to new situations and to meeting new people than children raised solely at home. However, day-care or preschool attendance does not necessarily predict children's ability to make friends, relate to adults, and handle new situations in elementary school and beyond.

Choosing a day-care center or day-care home

Many parents are confused about whether they should send their child to a day-care center or to a day-care home. What are the advantages (and disadvantages) of each?

A day-care center is a larger facility; its physical plant is dedicated to providing care for young children. Centers are licensed and must pass minimum fire, safety, and health code regulations. The personnel in centers frequently have degrees (or at least some training) in early childhood education or development. A well-prepared staff in conjunction with a well-maintained physical plant usually increases the likelihood that the care children receive is of higher quality. However, there is a price. Day-care centers are more expensive, because their professional staff requires appropriate wages and the overhead is high. Day-care centers are stricter about their hours of operation, because their care givers want a standard work day. Day-care centers are also more likely to exclude ill children and charge extra when parents are delayed in picking up their children. Finally, not all day-care centers are of the highest quality, and those of the highest quality are sometimes few and far between.

Day-care homes are smaller care facilities. Since day-care homes are not regulated in many states, there is no assurance that all the homes meet minimal fire, safety, and health codes. Since they are also private homes, the physical plant is not necessarily especially equipped for child care. Although many day-care home providers have some training in early childhood education or development, others have none.

Care in a day-care home is, on the average, less expensive than in a center. Overhead is low, and there is usually only one provider. Homes are less likely to exclude ill children and less likely to penalize parents for being late. They are also likely to be conveniently located near the children's own homes, necessitating less travel time and fewer early-morning awakenings for sleepy children. Most providers of family day-care homes are very dedicated people who truly wish to give the best care.

Which type of care is better? There is no easy answer. A child will thrive with a loving provider regardless of whether that person is in a center or home. Parents are usually deeply interested in providing love and care for their children—and most child-care providers feel the same way.

Parental finances, willingness to travel, and the types of care facilities available in the community are prime considerations in choosing the type of care. But the child's needs are paramount. If the child is quiet, dislikes large groups, enjoys having one person with whom to relate, and is most comfortable in a home environment, a good day-care home would be suitable. If the child is more gregarious, loves new situations, and likes meeting and being around lots of people, a good day-care center would be appropriate.

What to look for in a care facility

Frequently, parents rush into making a decision because they did not think that selecting care arrangements would be difficult. Take time to interview several providers before making a choice. Unless you are sure that you want a particular type of arrangement, investigate both centers and homes.

Visit prospective centers and homes when children are present, if possible. This might be more difficult to accomplish in a home, where the provider's attention will be divided between you and the children. However, it should be easy to arrange at a day-care center in which there are several providers and a director.

Observe the attitudes of the center personnel: Do they seem pleased to be working with children? Do they demonstrate kindness, humor, and affection? How do providers handle minor and major misbehaviors; are they gentle, but firm, disciplinarians?

Observe the attitudes of the children: Do they seem to like each other and their teachers? Do they seem to be happy? In what activities are they engaged? How frequently do they need to be reprimanded, and how do they (both the guilty party and the group) respond to reprimands? What kind of discipline is used? (Be sure to boycott any care provider who reserves the right to inflict corporal punishment.)

As you walk through the day-care center (or the area of the day-care home in which

the children spend their time), look carefully. Does it seem clean and appropriately lighted? Do you see any evidence of bugs or rodents (for example, a mouse trap)? If the children's play materials are not on display, ask to see them. Do they appear clean, in good repair, and appropriate for the ages of the children who attend?

Check also for the presence of a working fire extinguisher and working smoke detector; although the extinguisher might not be obvious in a day-care home, a smoke detector should be in plain view. Look for other safety and health provisions: clearly marked exits (at centers), gates on stairway entrances (if applicable), caps on electrical outlets, sinks that children can reach, appropriate storage areas for food, separate area (away from the children's main play area) for food preparation, harmful or dangerous products out of children's reach (preferably locked away), clean counter tops and eating surfaces, a separate area for diaper changes (if applicable) that is not the same as or next to the food preparation area, and a container, to which children have no access, for disposing of dirty diapers and soiled tissues. Remember to also walk through the yard or outdoor play area to assess its safety (fenced-in, fence and gates in good repair, uncluttered area, grassy or other "friendly" surface—*not* concrete, asphalt, gravel) and the safety of outdoor play equipment (in good repair, age-appropriate).

Ask to see the center's license (and its renewal date); it should be prominently displayed. If you live in a state that requires or encourages family day-care home registration, ask the owner if it is registered.

As you interview the center director or the home care provider, keep the following questions in mind:

1. What training have the provider(s) received to qualify them to operate a care facility? Does the provider take part in continuing education? How so?

2. How long has the center/home been in operation? Over time, how many children have been cared for?

3. How many children are enrolled now? What are the age ranges?

4. (For centers) How many teachers are there?

The answers to questions 3 and 4 will help you determine the teacher-to-child ratio. Different states have different permissible ratios, but education experts believe that optimal ratios are one teacher or provider to two or three children for infants, one to three or four for toddlers, and one to four or five for older preschoolers. The ratio in a day-care home should be no more than one to six.

5. (For centers) Will my child have the same provider each day?

A child needs one predominant substitute-care provider in order to feel secure.

6. How does the center or home respect your child's likes and dislikes?

There should be enough leeway to respect *basic*, cherished likes and dislikes.

7. Is parental involvement encouraged in the center or home activities?

In quality care arrangements, parental input is welcomed.

8. Are you permitted to drop in at the center or home anytime you wish, if your child is present?

You *have the right* to visit whenever your child is present in a center or home.

9. Does the provider have a policy about determining to whom a child can be released if the usual parent cannot be there?

To prevent a child being released to a hostile relative or noncustodial parent, the provider should have the names of the only people to whom a child can be released. If a person's name is not on that list, the child is not released. Beware of the provider who lightly dismisses such a request.

10. Is smoking prohibited at all times on the premises?

11. Are regular fire drills conducted with the children?

These should occur *even* in the smallest of day-care homes.

12. At which times are children and provider(s) encouraged to wash their hands?

To minimize the spread of infections, children should wash their hands before meals, after toileting, and after "dirty" play, especially outdoor play or play with animals. Staff should wash their hands before meals, before meal preparation (if applicable), after toileting, after changing diapers, after handling animals, and after outdoor activities.

13. To minimize the spread of infectious agents, does each child have an individual cot or mat for naptime?

14. Are naptimes usually at the same time each day? For how long? How does the provider manage a child who refuses to sleep?

This is important because naps (timing and duration) can affect the way a child sleeps at night; the same is true if there is fighting with a child over naptime.

15. Are menus posted in advance? Can children bring food from home? How does the provider handle individual food allergies and intolerances?

Advance menu posting, so that the parent knows not to serve the same meal for dinner, is helpful. Although providers cannot be expected to individualize each meal for each child, food allergies or intolerances must be respected and substitute foods provided. Whether or not children are able to bring foods from home depends on the ability of the center to store food.

16. How does the provider manage children who will not eat?

If the provider handles a refusal to eat differently from parents, the child might become confused and develop problems with meals at home. If refusal to eat is met with punishment or humiliation, the child might begin to act out at mealtimes, not only in day care but also at home.

17. What are the provider's policies on children who suddenly become ill or injured while at the center or home?

The parent should be called immediately. If the parent cannot be reached, there

should be a designated substitute who will
be called to pick up the child. An ill child
should be isolated from the other children,
but still closely supervised by the provider.
All centers and homes should request a preauthorization from parents for emergency
medical care for their children, so that
needed care is not delayed while the parent
is being located or en route.

18. What is the provider's policy on admit-
ting mildly ill children or children with
communicable conditions (such as ringworm) who are not ill?

If the provider will not accept mildly ill
children (for example, a cold without fever),
then you will need to have a contingency
plan for such occasions. To avoid spreading
communicable diseases, centers and homes
should not admit children with treatable
communicable conditions until they are receiving appropriate therapy.

19. Does the provider insist on proof that
each child is current on immunizations
for his or her age?

To prevent certain childhood diseases,
immunization is enormously important. Proof
of immunization is mandatory in licensed
centers; make sure a prospective day-care
home provider follows the rule, also.

20. Are the staff members in good enough
physical and emotional health to adequately care for active preschoolers?
Does the center director insist on periodic examinations by a physician and
skin testing for tuberculosis for all staff
members? Is the day-care home provider
in good health, and does the provider
have periodic examinations and skin
testing for tuberculosis? Do other family
members come in contact with the children? If so, they should observe the
same precautions.

Obviously, you want a provider with the
physical and emotional stamina to care for
your child. Periodic checkups help ensure
this. Tuberculosis testing is important because the disease is present in many communities. It is spread from adults to children—
not the other way around.

21. Does the provider keep a permanent
record of each child's (a) allergies, (b)
medical problems, (c) medications, (d)
physician's name and telephone number,
(e) parents' telephone numbers at work,
(f) relative's or designated substitute's
telephone numbers (to be called in an
emergency), (g) immunization record,
and (h) preauthorization for emergency
medical care?

22. Under what circumstances will the provider administer medicine to your child?

Medications should *only* be administered
with a doctor's or your permission. If you
permit a provider to administer a medication, be sure to explain the appropriate dose
for your child. Stay away from providers
who reserve the right to administer medications at their own discretion, without any
clear-cut guidelines.

23. Does the staff know how to read a thermometer and how to administer basic
first aid and CPR (cardiopulmonary resuscitation)?

In an emergency, failure to know these
might cost your child's life!

24. Does the provider seem interested in the
home lives of the children? Does the
provider seem eager to share information about a child's performance with the
parents?

25. Finally, do you like this person?

In addition, always ask for names of references or other parents who have used or are
using the center, so that you can contact
them. Although providers might have to ask
parents' permission to release telephone
numbers, be suspicious of any provider who
flatly refuses to give you any names.

Evaluating your child-care arrangement

Once you have chosen a care arrangement,
how do you know whether it's working out?
First of all, trust your instincts. If it seems
that you and the care provider disagree
frequently, especially about child-care decisions, it might be prudent to change provid-

ers. If you decide that you can't live with some of the provider's policies (or the lack of them), it might also be time to look for care elsewhere. Your child will be able to tell if you really don't like or trust the provider, and this knowledge will interfere with the child-provider relationship.

Many children experience brief sleep or eating disturbances as they begin a new care arrangement. If these do not improve in your child, meet with the provider. If the provider is too lax (or too rigid) about naptime, your child's sleep at night could be altered. If the provider is too lax (or too rigid) about mealtimes, your child might begin to act out at meals, not only during day care but also at home. This is especially true if you and the provider are at opposite ends of the spectrum in your philosophies about mealtimes and discipline in general.

If your child develops new sleeping or eating disturbances, think about *any* possible changes in home life before blaming the provider. If there are no changes at home, arrange a meeting with the provider. This is especially important if your child develops new complaints about the provider or the site. Always talk to your child about his or her day at the provider's center or home and what the child likes best and least about being there. Take all comments seriously, and respect your child's opinions. If your child reports abuse, investigate immediately.

If your child incurs numerous minor injuries at the center or home, the site might not be safe or the provider might not be adequately supervising the children. Talk to the provider about your concerns, but do not be accusatory, especially if your child incurs a lot of minor injuries at home, as well. Major injuries at a center or home, however, demand your immediate investigation.

Children get three to six colds per year. If you and your child's doctor believe that the child is getting more than a fair share of colds and other illnesses, meet with the provider and talk to other parents to see if their children are having the same problem. If they are, the center or home might lack proper hygienic measures.

Most child-care providers are deeply interested in loving and caring for children. Most parents feel the same way. Together, providers and parents can provide an optimal environment for children's physical, mental, and emotional growth.

Divorce

By Stella Chess, M.D.

Divorce is an upsetting experience for everyone involved. It is especially difficult for children to accept the threat to the security that comes from living with united and loving parents. But divorce need not permanently damage children's emotional development if parents learn to handle the problems that may arise from this major change in the children's lives.

Telling your child about divorce

When divorce becomes inevitable, children should be told about it. By the time parents have reached the point at which living together is no longer possible, even young children will be aware of the tension. If children are not aware of what is going to happen, they may be upset, believing the truth is too terrible to know.

It is not unusual for children to think that they are responsible for the split between their parents. They may remember times when they were the cause of disagreements between them. Or they may think of times they wished one of the parents would leave and never come back. Suddenly they see this wish coming true, and they feel guilty and ashamed.

How to explain the reasons for a divorce depends on the children's age and their ability to understand. Above all, they should be helped to understand that the divorce is not their fault. A 3-year-old will probably be satisfied with "Daddy is not going to live with us any more." An older child may want to know why and can be told, "Your father (or mother) and I are not happy together and so we are going to try living in different houses to see if we will be happier that way. If we are, we will get a divorce. We will tell you about it as soon as we are sure." When parents take their children into their confidence and let them know what is happening each step of the way, the children feel less bewildered and shut out. At the same time, children should be made to understand that parents, even if divorced, do not stop loving and being responsible for their children.

When you break the news of a divorce to your child, do it as calmly as you can. No matter how bitter or angry you may be, try not to speak of the other parent in an unfavorable way. There is no harm in explaining why you and the other parent could not get along, but don't burden your child with all the details. Never force the child to take sides. It is unfair, especially when the child needs to know that he or she is still loved by both parents, even though they no longer love each other.

If a parent deserts the family, do not hold out false hopes that the parent will return. Waiting for a thing that may not happen is harder on the child than being told the truth.

Sharing feelings

No one who has been through the emotional shock of a divorce can act as though nothing has happened. Do not weep on your child's shoulder, but if you are unhappy at times, there is no reason why you should not share your feelings. If you can convince yourself and the child that you will be happier as time passes, both of you will adjust to the situation more easily.

Now and then all children feel anger toward their parents, even if there has been no divorce. But divorce may bring out an unusual amount of resentment. Children should express their anger. No matter how understanding of the divorce they seem to be, they may secretly feel that if their parents had tried harder, they could have kept the family intact. Sometimes children will not voice their resentment because they think the parents may "divorce" them as well. Instead, children may act out their resentment. They may refuse to eat, bite their fingernails, or begin to lie.

Let your child know that you understand how he or she feels, and assure the child that no matter how angry you may become with each other, it is not the same kind of anger that led to the divorce. Children need to be able to act out their "bad" feelings and to know that it is safe for them to be angry.

Visiting the other parent

Unless it is impossible, your child needs to be able to visit the other parent. There are no set rules regarding the amount of time to be spent with each parent, but it is generally believed that an equal division of time may confuse the child. The child will feel more secure if there is one home where the greater part of time is spent—a place to belong. The child should be able to say, "This is where I live," and "This is where I visit."

In most cases, it is best to have the court set up visiting arrangements. Visits should be regular, and parents should try to keep to the schedule. For the child under 4, daytime visits are usually more satisfactory. An older child may want to spend the night with the other parent. This may be good, if the experience is a happy one and does not increase strain between the parents.

As a child grows older, the legal arrangements concerning visits—and possibly custody—may well be reviewed and revised to fit the child's changing circumstances, interests, and needs.

A parent shouldn't compete for a child's love by giving expensive presents and making every visit a holiday. This is unfair to the "stay-with" parent. It is obviously easier for a parent to make a child feel that the child is more fun to be with when the parent is not bothered by the responsibilities of living with the child daily.

If after visits your child makes unfavorable comparisons between you and the other parent, perhaps you are taking the weight of your responsibilities too heavily. Perhaps you should spend more time enjoying and less time trying to improve your child. Both parents must keep in mind that down-to-earth caring, understanding, and discipline when needed are more valuable gifts than anything that can be bought.

When a parent remarries

A parent's remarriage is another change in the child's life. If you plan to remarry, let the child know what to expect.

Some children adapt easily to suddenly having a new parent, relatives, and perhaps brothers and sisters. Other children feel that the change means being left out or taking second place in a parent's affections. It is important for children to know that the change will not affect the way their parents feel about them.

When visiting a parent who has remarried, the child needs to spend time when just the two of them can talk, read, and enjoy things together. The child also needs time to get to know the stepparent. It is not unusual for a child to resent the stepparent at first. But if the stepparent is patient and loving, the resentment will disappear.

When a new baby arrives in any family, there is bound to be some jealousy and bad feeling. Half brothers and half sisters are no more immune to rivalry than full brothers and sisters. Allow your child to express any bad feelings about the baby. The child may say, "You spend all your time with the baby and every time we go anywhere you take the baby with us. I liked it better before. I'm going to stay with my daddy." Don't scold or lecture the child. The storm will blow over. Help your child find new interests and friends to alleviate the child's dependency on you.

Each parent of a divorce must help the child adjust to changing circumstances, but neither parent should dictate to the other how the child is to be treated. If there are problems, and if both parents are willing, they may get together to discuss them. Both parents must try to make their child feel loved and comfortable no matter which parent the child happens to be with.

Julie Giesy, R.N., M.S.N.
Consulting Editor

The drug problem

By Thomas E. Cone, Jr., M.D.

The use of chemical substances to alter mood, perception, and behavior has become part of growing up in Western society. In recent years, drug and alcohol abuse by young people has markedly increased. Some surveys indicate that over 80 per cent of schoolchildren in the United States have used one or more substances (drugs) for nonmedical purposes. Today, young people have access to a wide variety of potentially dangerous and sometimes addictive drugs.

Why young people misuse drugs

There is no single reason why young people turn to drugs. Some try them out of curiosity or for "kicks." Others consider drugs the "in" thing to do. Many children feel isolated from their families and from a society they consider to be infested with hypocrisy, materialism, and distorted values. The misuse of drugs or alcohol is thus a way to rebel against parents and other authority figures. Some teen-agers even experiment with drugs because they perceive adolescence to be a time for living dangerously.

Other children may have emotional or psychological problems for which they receive little parental understanding or help. Still others may be congenitally predisposed to have a high initial tolerance to alcohol or other drugs and therefore find them relaxing or stimulating, according to their needs. To these youngsters, drugs provide an escape from a fast-moving world where they feel insecure and confused, unable to cope with the problems and pressures of everyday living.

Studies among young teen-agers show that a constantly increasing number drink alcohol, not only for social reasons, but also to relieve boredom and anxiety. The "shift to alcohol" among adolescents may represent a trend toward reconciliation with society's "drug of choice."

There is no good reason to misuse drugs. But in a world where pills and other drugs are available for the relief of many ills and alcohol is socially acceptable, experimentation with drugs is understandable, though not justifiable.

Habit-forming and addictive drugs

Marijuana, PCP, and LSD are *habit-forming*. This means that if used at regular intervals, they can cause psychological dependence. Users develop a mental or emotional need for the drug, even though their bodies do not develop a physical craving for the drug.

Heroin, cocaine, amphetamines, barbiturates, nicotine, and alcohol are *addictive* drugs. They create both a psychological *and* a physical dependence. Addicts actually become physically ill if they cannot get the drug to which they are addicted. Furthermore, the body becomes so used to the drug that doses must be increased to achieve the desired effect.

Sudden withdrawal from addictive drugs is painful and dangerous. On the average, about 18 hours after taking a last dose of heroin an addict may have severe leg and stomach cramps, chills, nausea, and diarrhea. The body may shake uncontrollably and perspire a great deal. Sudden withdrawal from barbiturates or amphetamines is extremely dangerous. It can cause convulsions, mental disturbance, and even death. Withdrawal from cocaine can produce prolonged periods of depression or even psychosis. Withdrawal from nicotine is often accompanied by an increase in nervousness, irritability, and fatigue. Withdrawal from any drug should be gradual and done under a doctor's supervision.

Withdrawal from alcohol may cause tremors, convulsions, hallucinations, and delirium. The symptoms develop after a period of relative or absolute abstinence from alcohol.

Experimentation does not necessarily lead to drug dependence. Alcohol is one example of this. Most people who try alcohol do not become dependent on it. It would be untrue to say that one or even a few tries of a habit-forming drug will "hook" a person, with the exception of heroin, cocaine, and maybe amphetamines. Yet all experimentation must be regarded as risky. The drugs to which children are most commonly exposed can lead to psychological dependence or addiction. It is important that children understand the dangers involved.

Commonly misused habit-forming drugs

Marijuana, also known as "pot," "grass," and "dope," is most often smoked in a homemade cigarette called a "joint" or a "reefer." Heavy doses can alter perception, impair judgment, and slow down reflexes and motor coordination.

PCP (phencyclidine), known as "angel dust" and "hog," is an animal tranquilizer. It can be inhaled, injected, or swallowed. A small amount can produce a state similar to drunkenness, ranging from euphoria to depression and hallucinations. Larger doses can cause convulsions, psychosis, rage, coma, cardiac irregularities, and death.

LSD (lysergic acid diethylamide), also known as "acid," is a psychedelic drug. If unadulterated, it is colorless, tasteless, and odorless, and so powerful that a very tiny amount (0.2 mg) can cause strange mental images and distort hearing, sight, smell, and touch. Greater doses may induce an anxiety or rage so strong as to lead to suicide or homicide. LSD may remain in the body for weeks, and persistent adverse reactions may recur long after the initial dose is taken, the so-called flashback phenomenon.

Both PCP and LSD are rarely available anymore, since they are relatively difficult to produce and not made in quantity.

Commonly misused addictive drugs

Heroin, also known as "H," "junk," or "smack," is a narcotic. It is related to morphine, but is more addictive. Usually, it is mixed with lactose (milk sugar) or quinine. Heroin addicts are always in danger of death from an overdose, because they can never be sure how much heroin there is in the mixture "bag" they buy. Most heroin addicts inject the drug into their veins, a method known as "mainlining." Adolescents may use the subcutaneous or "skin popping" route. Unsterilized needles can lead to hepatitis or acquired immune deficiency syndrome (AIDS). Heroin addicts usually suffer from chronic liver infections and malnutrition. They are also at high risk for AIDS.

Cocaine, also known as "snow" and "coke," is usually sniffed. It can also be injected, rubbed on the gums, or free-based (chemically concentrated and smoked). It produces a feeling of well-being, depression of appetite, a deceptive feeling of unbounded energy, rapid heartbeat, and increased blood pressure. Chronic use causes emaciation, insomnia, tremors, and convulsions.

Cocaine is very addictive, according to most drug abuse experts. One form, called "crack," is especially addictive. The drug is boiled down into crystalline balls, about the size of peas, which can be smoked. It is a far more potent form of cocaine than the powder used for sniffing. Because there is a marked psychological dependence on cocaine, its use tends to become compulsive.

Amphetamines, also known as "uppers" and "speed," are stimulants. They are sometimes prescribed by doctors for obesity, narcolepsy, fatigue, attention deficit disorder, and hyperactivity. Large doses can induce extreme talkativeness, irritability, hallucinations, and other dangerous or unpredictable actions, sometimes indistinguishable from acute paranoid schizophrenia.

Barbiturates, also known as "downers" and "barbs," are depressants and sedatives. Doctors prescribe them to induce sleep and to relieve nervous tension. Barbiturates are extremely dangerous when misused. Large doses distort vision, slow down reactions, lessen the ability to think and to concentrate, and cause staggering and slurred speech. The effect of a large dose is similar to intoxication. An overdose, or a mixture of barbiturates and alcohol, may cause death.

Alcohol is a depressant, although the initial effect may be that of a high, since drinking often breaks down inhibitions that regulate acceptable behavior. Studies done in the United States and Canada report a precipitous increase in the use of alcohol by young teen-agers. Alcohol has been "rediscovered" by some adolescents as an alternative to marijuana. Further, the social acceptance of alcohol among adults has lessened the anxiety of parents toward drinking by their children. Many adults tend to be far more permissive in their attitude toward alcohol than toward marijuana. Using marijuana is often considered drug abuse, while using alcohol is ignored. Yet alcohol continues to be the most dangerous and most abused drug in the United States and Canada.

Signs to look for

The sooner parents and teachers act when they suspect a youngster of experimenting with drugs, the better the chances are of preventing addiction. It is not easy to tell when children are misusing drugs. Those who do so become adept at hiding the fact. But there are a number of telltale signs, none of which are absolutely conclusive, that should alert parents and teachers to the possibility that a youngster may be taking drugs and in need of help:
- Change in a child's behavior, such as increasing aggressiveness or sluggishness,

unusual flare-ups of temper, or uncharacteristic passivity.
- Change in school attendance (frequently absent or late).
- Change in work habits (sloppy homework, apathy).
- Shying away from family activities and a general withdrawal from former pastimes.
- Poor physical appearance.
- Associating with known drug misusers.
- Stealing or borrowing money, needing more money than before.

Where to get more information and help

As soon as parents suspect that a child is misusing drugs, they should get in touch with the family doctor. The doctor, if unable to deal with the problem, will refer them to someone who is qualified in the treatment of drug misuse. The family doctor may refer the child to an established Adolescents' Unit, a residential treatment center staffed by physicians who are specially trained in the management of drug misuse, including alcohol.

You can obtain the hot lines to drug information and treatment centers by dialing Directory Assistance for the telephone number of the local Poison Control or Poison Information centers. For problems related to cocaine and other drugs, you can call the toll-free cocaine hotline, 1-800-COCAINE. To find a drug-treatment center in your area, you can call the National Family Resource Center, 1-800-241-7946. And the National Institute on Drug Abuse, 1-800-662-HELP, will refer you to local programs.

For help with alcohol abuse, Alcoholics Anonymous (AA) provides dedicated assistance and guidance 24 hours a day. Many AA chapters have teen-age members. Local chapters of Alcoholics Anonymous are listed in telephone directories.

If you suspect that your child is misusing drugs, keep calm and act intelligently. Remember, the problem is yours as much as it is the child's.

Explaining death to a child

By Stella Chess, M.D.

Even when there is no direct contact with death, it is not unusual for children to ask, "What does it mean when you're dead?" or, "Will I die, too?" The children may want to know why and how a pet or a flower dies. They may have seen a funeral procession or heard news about the death of a well-known person.

Many parents who are willing and able to discuss almost any subject with their children become evasive and ill at ease when questioned about death. Perhaps it is because most of us would rather not think about death. But death does occur. And when a loved one dies, it is especially important that parents be prepared to talk about it. Children usually have mixed emotions about death. They may have feelings of sorrow, fear, resentment, and even guilt. They may become confused and bewildered. How parents explain death, and how they answer children's questions about death, are important. Parents should be aware that children's concepts of death change as they get older.

All children do not react to death in the same way. However, research into how children view death has shown that the following concepts are common at specific ages.

Between 3 and 5, children tend to think of death as a kind of journey from which a person will soon return. Or, they may think that death is a kind of going to sleep, and then waking up. When told of a death, a child in this age group may express sorrow and then seem to forget about it soon afterward. Parents who are unaware of this common reaction may worry that their child is self-centered and heartless.

Between the ages of 5 and 9, most children accept the idea that death is irreversible, but they believe that death happens only to certain people and that it cannot happen to them. Around the ages of 9 or 10, children begin to understand that death happens to all living things, and that they, too, will die eventually.

Some ways to answer questions

No matter how difficult it may be for you, a direct, honest answer about death is the best one. Evasive answers may make a child's feelings of grief, fear, and resentment stronger and longer lasting. Children are not nearly as afraid of what they can understand as they are of things that are cloaked in mystery. Even death can be less terrifying if it is discussed openly and calmly.

In explaining death, you usually have to deal with such facts as illness, accident, or old age. The amount of detail you include in your explanation should relate to the child's capacity for understanding. For instance, if a 3-year-old wants to know why a grandparent has died, it is usually enough to say, "She was very old and very tired." A 6-year-old might be told that the grandmother was very old and tired, and that eventually everyone grows old and tired and can no longer go on living.

Some parents evade an honest answer in the mistaken belief that they are guarding their child against the pain that may be caused by the truth. But a child cannot go through life constantly protected from pain and grief. Sometimes, evasive answers may even be dangerous. When a beloved grandfather dies, a 6-year-old might be told that he has "gone to sleep." But the child sees that the "sleep" is one from which the grandfather never wakes. What will be the child's reaction? It may happen, and it has happened, that the child becomes afraid to go to bed, fearing that he or she, too, will never wake up.

Even a religious explanation, which seems desirable to many adults, is not always helpful. Few children find comfort in such explanations as "God took him" or "He has gone to heaven to be with the angels." Such explanations may build feelings of resentment, fear, and even hatred against the God who can strike without warning.

Naturally, children are more deeply affected by some deaths than they are by others. When a playmate dies, a child needs more reassurance. The child suddenly realizes that a person need not be old to die, and may, therefore, feel threatened. It is important that parents answer the child's questions about such deaths, so that the child understands that because someone the same age has died of an illness or an accident, it does not mean that the child, too, will share a similar fate.

When a playmate's father or mother dies, children are likely to think that they might also lose a parent. Such fear can be lessened by stressing the fact that very few young parents die. Parents might also add that should anything happen to them, they have made arrangements for the children to be cared for.

The death of a parent is especially difficult for a child to face. Not only does the child suffer grief but, understandably, he or she also feels the loss of security. The child may even feel deserted. Sometimes the surviving parent is in no condition to comfort the child, and this may reinforce the sense of rejection.

Sometimes, in the hope that the child will feel needed and, therefore, more secure, the child may be mistakenly told, "Now you are the man of the family," or "Now you must take your mother's place." No child, no matter how willing, can take the place of the lost parent. Such a responsibility should not be thrust on the child.

This is a time when an adult relative or close friend of the family can be a source of strength by reassuring the child about the future.

Guilt feelings

Children often feel that in some way or other they may be responsible for the death of a member of the family or a playmate. If a sick grandparent has lived with the family for a while, it is quite likely that the child was constantly "shushed" during the illness. Understandably, the child has not always been completely quiet. This in itself may make a child feel guilty when the grandparent dies. If the child is overly sensitive, such feelings can be most disturbing. Should a brother or sister die, some of the natural feelings of hostility among brothers and sisters may haunt the child. It is as though something the child did or thought contributed to the death. Parents can help their child overcome such feelings of guilt if they are aware that they may occur.

Mourning

There are differences of opinion and practice about children's participation in family gatherings of mourning relatives and in funeral ceremonies. A common practice in many families is to send the children to stay with friends so that they will be spared the upsetting effects of grief. In some instances, this may be wise, but often this makes the child feel alone and shut out. It may add to the child's feelings of fear. To be with the family, yet to be protected from the more extreme demonstrations of grief, is often more reassuring for the child than being spared the experience.

If, then, you find yourself facing the necessity of helping your child understand a death in the family or the death of a close friend, be honest. Help the child realize that life holds some sorrow as well as much joy for everyone. And recognize that the child needs special love, affection, and understanding to get through the experience in a positive way. The value of the feeling of belonging, in sorrow as well as in joy, cannot be overemphasized.

Parents may be called upon to face the very difficult task of explaining death to their own dying child. This situation usually arises when their child has a serious, chronic disease, such as cancer, which is no longer responding to treatment. Here the parents not only must bear their own grief over their impending loss, but comfort their child as well.

The subject of death will seldom come as a complete surprise to dying children, and it may even be raised by the child. This is because dying children usually have some awareness that they will die, although each child's understanding of death varies with age, as explained earlier. This awareness may develop because they may not feel as well as before, hospitalizations may be more frequent or prolonged, they may listen to conversations between their parents and doctors, and they may detect attitude changes on the part of their parents. Here again, no matter how difficult it may be for you, direct, honest responses about death are the best ones. From the onset of an illness from which death may result, parents are encouraged to foster a loving, secure home environment in which questions, fears, and anxieties can be voiced by their child and discussed openly. This kind of environment sets the stage for honest, much needed communication when the child's death later becomes more imminent. A child who is met instead by silence concerning the subject of death will experience unnecessary loneliness or isolation from loved ones, unwarranted anxieties or guilt, or the worry that he or she is being punished.

Sometimes parents will need to bring up the topic of death themselves, since their children may not want to upset or hurt them by voicing their concerns. Parents' comments should be related to the children's capacity for understanding. For children who are five or more years old, parents can begin by asking whether they have thought at all about dying. Younger children may be told that the treatments are not working anymore, and that after dying there will be no more suffering. It should be noted that children of all ages tend to have rather concrete worries that include whether they will be alone or in pain when they die. It is important that children be reassured that their physical needs will be met in every possible way with the help of doctors and nurses, whether they are hospitalized or at home. Most important, children will find great comfort in their parents' presence and expressions of love and caring.

If the process of a child's death can be experienced as a family with affection, acceptance, and open communication, many parents have found, in these difficult days, precious moments that they cherish as memories forever.

David R. Freyer, D.O.
Consulting Editor/Contributor

The gifted child

By E. Paul Torrance, Ph.D.

For many years, the term "gifted child" usually meant a child with a high intelligence quotient (IQ). But a few leaders in the field of education for gifted children thought otherwise. They insisted that the term should apply to any child who performs much better than others in any field of endeavor highly prized by society.

This definition is now widely accepted by educators, and six types of giftedness are generally recognized:
- General intellectual ability
- Specific academic aptitude, as in science, mathematics, or languages
- Creative or productive thinking
- Leadership ability
- Visual and performing arts ability, as in music, drama, painting, or sculpture
- Psychomotor ability, such as mechanical or manipulative skills

Educators are finding new ways to identify gifted children in these areas, and developing specialized programs for them. Many states require that school systems provide programs for all gifted children. Some provide only for the academically gifted—children identified on the basis of intelligence tests and grades. In some states, provisions are also made for the creatively gifted, using tests of creative thinking ability, the production of creative products, or solutions to problems as a guide for identification.

A few school systems have developed excellent programs for gifted children in the visual and performing arts. Identification for inclusion is usually through auditions or other performances, portfolios of products, and the like. Sometimes tests are used that

may identify outstanding talents which might otherwise go unnoticed.

School programs for gifted children vary greatly. In sparsely populated areas, the program may consist of an itinerant teacher in a bus filled with resource materials. In large cities, there may be separate schools for children gifted in different ways. In most special programs, however, gifted children spend part of their time in regular classes and the balance in separate classes with specially trained teachers. In some programs, gifted children remain in the regular classroom and the teacher adjusts some part of the program for them.

Intelligence tests are often used to identify the academically gifted. There is, however, no standard score. Some programs require an IQ of 120, while others require 130 or 140. Some academically gifted children are also creatively gifted—but not all. And not all creatively gifted children are academically gifted.

Characteristics of gifted children

People once thought of most gifted children as small, sickly, and wearing eyeglasses. Obviously, this is not true. Just as some academically gifted children are also highly creative, others are gifted in social leadership. Some are also outstanding in athletics, dance, or the like. The following characteristics of the intellectually or academically gifted child are generally accepted:
- Early and accurate use of a larger vocabulary than that of the average child
- Early use of sentences

- Early interest in calendars and in telling time
- Keen observation and unusual retention of facts
- Insatiable curiosity
- Early attraction to picture books
- A long attention span
- Early discovery of an interest in cause and effect relationships
- Early interest and skill in reading

Creatively gifted children may also have some of these characteristics. These children are also noted for their high energy level, questioning, experimenting, manipulating, and insistence on discovering the truth.

While gifted children have a great deal of energy, and may even be hyperkinetic, they are also able to sit still longer than the average child. Their absorption in what they are doing may be intense. The creative child insists upon examining things closely and seems to have an irresistible tendency to manipulate and explore objects.

Parents' role

Although gifted children tend to be superior in social development, they are by no means as advanced socially as they are mentally. There may be a marked gap between the child's mental ability and his or her social, emotional, and physical development. The child may know the meaning of such words as *loyalty* and *cooperation*, but not be loyal or cooperative. Patient understanding and guidance are needed to help the child translate language into deeds.

Like all children, the gifted child needs security, affection, encouragement, recognition, and praise from sympathetic parents. Parental insight is needed to nourish a child's gifts and to help the child develop harmoniously. Some children never fully develop their gifts because strong emotions or a feeling of insecurity at home block expression of growth.

Parents of a gifted child should encourage their child's gifts, not exploit them. A good way to encourage the child is by reading aloud before the child learns to read independently. Some gifted children learn to read before they start school and should be encouraged to read when ready. Even so, parents should continue to read aloud. As the child's interests expand, parents can help the child satisfy these interests.

If your child shows an interest in the arts, encourage participation. Only through performance can a child gifted with creativity and imagination be recognized.

At age 8 or 9, an intellectually gifted child usually reads many books and makes use of encyclopedias and dictionaries. The child may read about special subjects or pursue hobbies. Provide related books and magazines. Encourage the use of school and public libraries. Discuss favorite books and the discoveries made in them, both about one's self and about other people.

The gifted child constantly asks questions. If you do not know the answer, say so, and help find the answer. Occasionally, instead of answering a question, encourage the child to find the answer independently.

Parents need to give special attention to helping the gifted child learn problem-solving skills. Many gifted children actually lag behind less gifted classmates in these skills because they remember solutions and are not challenged to solve problems for which there are no learned solutions.

Parents can provide opportunities for creative problem solving and constructive responses to change and stress. They should prepare their children for and develop creative ways of coping with new experiences. Above all, the family should offer purpose, commitment, and courage. Without these, giftedness is likely to wither or turn in wasteful directions.

Mark S. Puczynski, M.D.
Consulting Editor

Growth

By Deborah Rotenstein, M.D.

For every child, a primary task of childhood is to grow and develop ultimately into a mature individual. Physical growth begins with conception. It is influenced by a variety of factors, many of which we are only beginning to understand. The interaction between genetics and environment results in a range of possibilities for children's height, and the rate at which children attain their genetic potential varies.

Growth rates

The most rapid growth and development take place during the 40 weeks prior to birth. The fetus, which begins from a single cell, develops into a group of cells, which become subspecialized. When a sufficient number of cells have developed, organ systems emerge.

Birth usually occurs when the fetus is 40 weeks old, but some infants are born earlier or later. So, even at birth, some infants are more mature physically than others.

After the first 2 years, children begin to assume their individual growth patterns, and after age 2 or 3, they assume the growth rate that they will follow until just before puberty. For the first 6 months of life, children grow at a rate of 7.2 to 8.8 inches (18 to 22 centimeters) per year. By 1 year, they grow at a rate of 4.4 inches (11 centimeters) per year. At 2 to 3 years they grow 2.8 to 3.2 inches (7 to 8 centimeters) per year, and between 4 and 9 they grow 2 to 2.4 inches (5 to 6 centimeters) per year. Growth rates of less than 2 inches or 5 centimeters per year after age 2 signal the need for medical assessment. Because absolute heights at any given age may vary, it is the pattern of growth that needs to be assessed.

The growth in height and weight for boys and girls at different ages is shown on the accompanying growth charts. Typical growth in height and weight is shown by the heavy center line, and faster and slower rates by the lines above and below it. The variation in the curves of the lines shows that there are periods of rapid and slow growth. After the fast growth of the first few years, the changes become more gradual and then fairly steady. Thin layers of cartilage called growth plates, found in all long bones, are active throughout childhood in making the bones grow. There is a spurt of rapid growth just before growth stops and the growth plates fuse.

The most valuable tool for assessing a child's growth is a well-kept growth chart. A child's height and weight should be measured and recorded on the growth chart at each visit to the physician. The most widely used growth charts are made up for boys and girls of all ages and are divided into ranges of height and weight by per cent. The age in years is marked along the bottom of the chart, and height (inches and centimeters) and weight (pounds and kilograms) are marked along the sides.

Growth differences

Growth patterns of boys and girls differ. In the first 2 years, boys are slightly taller than girls. After that, until puberty, the heights are relatively similar. Girls' skeletal ages—the degree to which their bones have matured—are generally more advanced at any given age than are those of boys. Children who are overweight often have a faster rate of growth and reach puberty earlier than nonobese children.

A child's rate of growth is not even; it may vary from year to year and even from season to season, and is often fastest in the spring and summer. For this reason, growth evaluations should always include observation for six months to a year.

Short stature

About 3 million children in the United States are shorter than 97 per cent of their peers. Most of these children are normal in every way except that they are small. Not all short children have abnormal growth. However, children who are not growing at an appropriate rate should be evaluated by their pediatricians.

Some children may be short because they come from a short family, and the genetic potential for height is small. Other children have a delay in puberty or a delayed growth spurt, a condition called constitutional growth delay. These children are shorter than their peers, but ultimately will reach normal adult height.

World-wide, malnutrition or undernutrition is the most common cause of short stature. Severe stress or a deprived environment can also cause shortness. Many systemic illnesses, such as diseases of the heart, lungs, pancreas (diabetes mellitus), kidneys, and digestive tract, can cause poor growth, as can endocrine disorders, such as a lack of thyroid hormone or lack of growth hormone. Growth hormone, which is one of the hormones involved in the control of growth, can be completely or partially deficient. Too much cortisol, a stress hormone, can also cause shortness.

Children may be small for other reasons. Intrauterine growth retardation— slow growth before birth—is one factor. It may be caused by infection, or the mother's use of alcohol, tobacco, or drugs during pregnancy. Chromosomal abnormalities can cause shortness and other genetic problems, such as Down's syndrome or Turner's syndrome. Skeletal abnormalities or bone disease can affect the size and shape of bones.

Occasionally a child is short for reasons that are totally unclear, and no specific causes can be found. It is not unusual for children who are under the age of 2 or 3 to cross percentiles in either direction on their growth curves. However, after age 2 or 3, a fall away from the growth curve signals that there may be a problem.

Therapy for shortness is directed at correcting the underlying medical condition. Most children who are deficient in growth hormone can be treated with growth hormone only by a pediatric endocrinologist. Children who are short because of delayed puberty, especially boys, can also benefit from medical intervention. Psychological support and/or counseling can often be very helpful to the treatment process.

Tall stature

Just as there are many children who are small, there are about as many who are taller than 95 per cent of their peers.

Most tall children have tall parents. Tall boys rarely complain about their size. However, tall girls may feel ill at ease. Children who are greater than the 95th percentile or who are growing—and continue to grow— at an abnormally rapid rate should be checked by a physician.

Abnormal height is most often caused by an endocrine disease or a genetic condition. There are several endocrine causes of abnormal height and rapid growth. One is growth hormone excess, which may be caused by a small tumor in the pituitary gland. A more common cause of unusually fast growth is early puberty. Genetic conditions that cause abnormal height are rare, and they often include abnormal body proportions.

Emotional factors of growth

Many short children adapt well to their size and may never have psychological problems, but others do not. Our society places a great value on height. Short children often face emotional stress from teasing and may have difficulty coping. In fact, parents of short children frequently have difficulty accepting a child's height and treating the child according to age level.

Teen-age years are often more difficult for the very short or very tall child. Often problems of short stature are made more difficult by the lack of sexual development. For short teen-agers, one problem is being treated as if they are younger than their actual age, and some of them react by behaving immaturely. Tall teen-agers may feel conspicuous and become very self-conscious.

Of course, a child who has a medical problem should be treated. But children also need to feel loved whether they are short or tall. For parents and other adults, one of the most important steps in making life easier, for a short or tall child, is to accept the child's size.

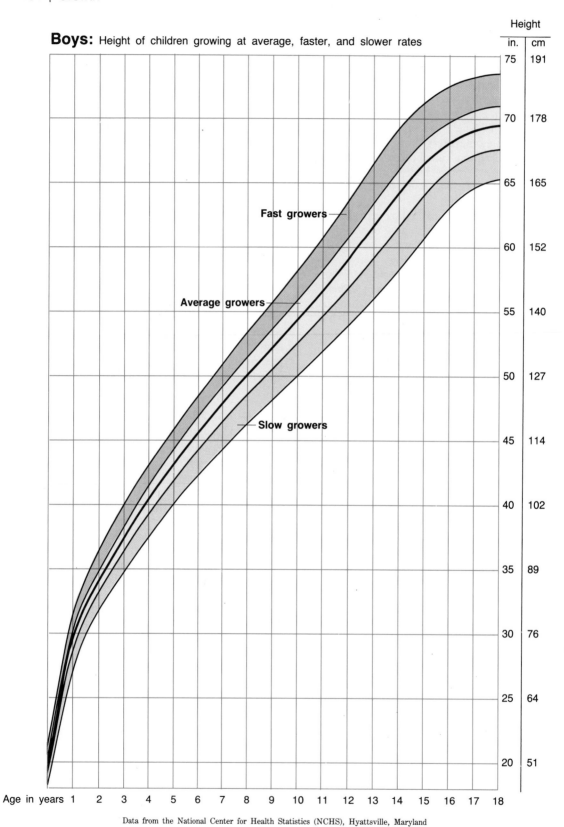

Boys: Height of children growing at average, faster, and slower rates

Height
in. | cm

Fast growers

Average growers

Slow growers

Age in years 1 2 3 4 5 6 7 8 9 10 11 12 13 14 15 16 17 18

Data from the National Center for Health Statistics (NCHS), Hyattsville, Maryland

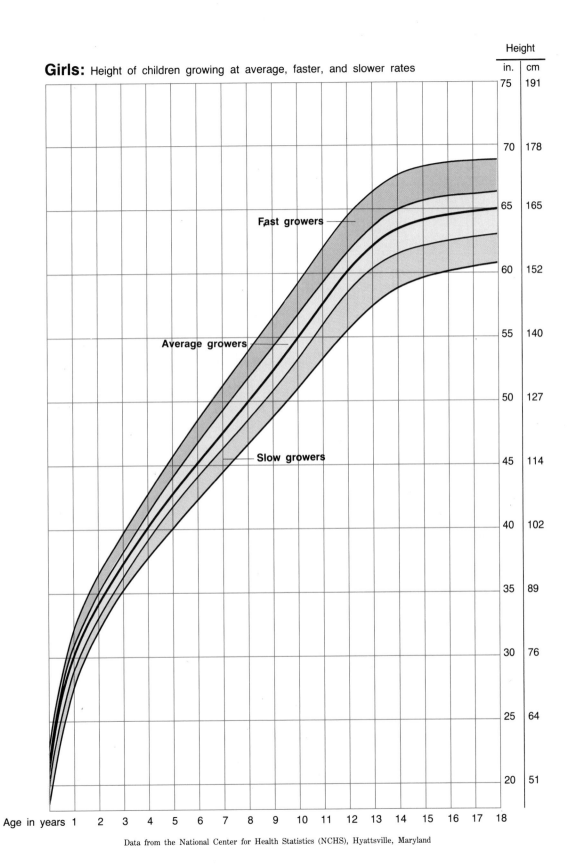

Girls: Height of children growing at average, faster, and slower rates

Height

| in. | cm |

Fast growers

Average growers

Slow growers

Age in years 1 2 3 4 5 6 7 8 9 10 11 12 13 14 15 16 17 18

Data from the National Center for Health Statistics (NCHS), Hyattsville, Maryland

Boys: Weight of children growing at average, faster, and slower rates

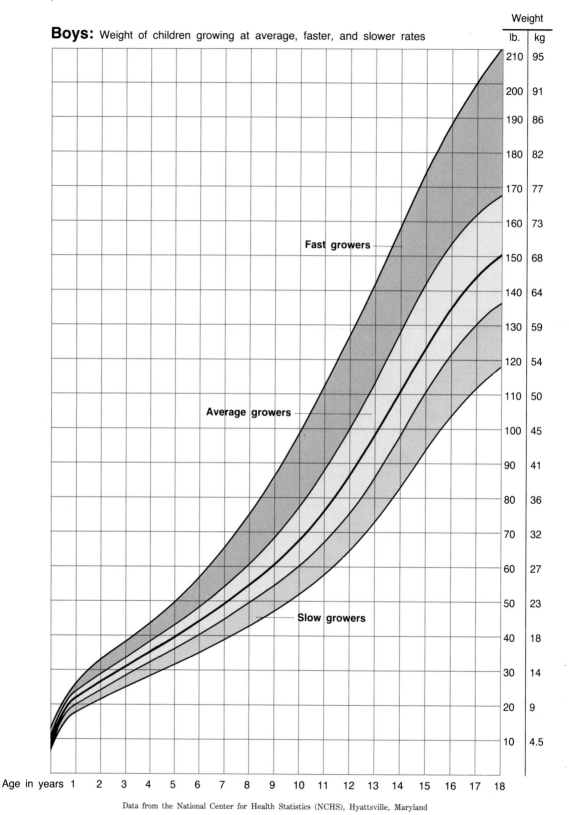

Age in years

Data from the National Center for Health Statistics (NCHS), Hyattsville, Maryland

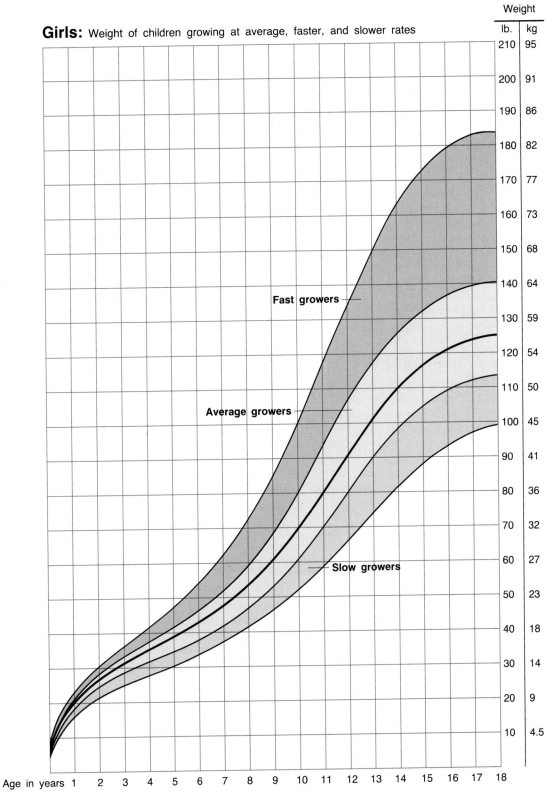

Girls: Weight of children growing at average, faster, and slower rates

Weight

lb.	kg
210	95
200	91
190	86
180	82
170	77
160	73
150	68
140	64
130	59
120	54
110	50
100	45
90	41
80	36
70	32
60	27
50	23
40	18
30	14
20	9
10	4.5

Fast growers

Average growers

Slow growers

Age in years 1 2 3 4 5 6 7 8 9 10 11 12 13 14 15 16 17 18

Data from the National Center for Health Statistics (NCHS), Hyattsville, Maryland

Latchkey children

by Stephen H. Sheldon, D.O., F.A.A.P.

"Latchkey children" is a term for youngsters less than 13 years old who care for themselves for significant periods of time before and/or after school and during vacations. In some families, these children may also be called upon to care for younger brothers and sisters when parents are not at home. "Latchkey" refers to the house key some of these children wear around their necks.

Self-care has increased dramatically over the past decade. It is estimated that about 13 per cent of all children between 5 and 13 are regularly left to care for themselves during a significant portion of the day. This translates into approximately 2 million to 4 million children in self-care.

Why are so many children left in self-care?

The "latchkey" phenomenon has grown in recent years for many reasons. As the number of single-parent households increases, the number of children in self-care can be expected to increase.

Single parents are parents without partners to help them share the responsibility of supporting the family and caring for their children. Often these parents are isolated and have few resources. Financial responsibilities require single parents to work at jobs that are less personally satisfying, and they often find it necessary to work at jobs in which there is little control over hours.

School hours often overlap with times parents are required to be at work. Hours when school ends usually do not coincide with job-quitting times. This mismatch of the parent's and child's responsibilities has created a need for alternate plans for school-age children before and/or after school. Single-parent families with younger children who are not yet old enough to attend school must find appropriate day care or baby-sitting for the entire day.

In two-parent families, more options exist, but parents often do not have the option of sharing responsibilities for child care before and after school. Two incomes are required to support the family, and often both jobs require parents to be at work and away from home before school starts, at the children's lunch hours, or after school. Therefore, these families also face the dilemma of mismatched beginning and ending times for school and work.

Options for working parents

In many situations, parents cannot be home to care for their children at certain times of day. Other options exist, however, and the variety of options often depends upon the community in which the family lives. Day care for children under 5 years old is available in most communities. Appropriate day care can range from formal private enterprises or businesses, which utilize well-trained professional staff and which are inspected and certified by health departments and agencies, to individuals who care for children in their own homes. Often, private homes also require certification and inspection. Friends, neighbors, and relatives may care for children in their homes or in the family's home. Similar day-care situations may also be available for older children. (For additional information, see DAY CARE in For Special Consideration.)

For school-age children, formal before-school and after-school programs may provide transportation to and from school, home, and special after-school activities. After-school programs are available through many school systems. Neighbors or relatives may also be able to care for children whose parents are at work.

Some schools and communities provide sports activities, breakfast, lunch, and snack programs. Others provide enrichment programs and other activities that complement children's schoolwork. Community agencies, the YMCA, and park districts may also provide these services.

Children in self-care

Despite all efforts, some families may not have the resources to provide before- and after-school alternatives for their children. Even if the family has enough financial resources, services may not be available in the community. Children must then care for themselves until parents get home. For some children, self-care times are a small part of each day, but other children face long periods of caring for themselves. Some children in self-care may have to learn to perform such tasks as preparing lunch or dinner.

Parents rarely find these self-care situations comfortable, but they have no other choice. Concerns and fears of parents and children vary from victimization, accidents, and injuries to the psychological stress family members experience during these times.

A decision to leave a child in self-care should be based on the developmental and emotional maturity of the youngster, rather than on the child's chronological age. Some 9-year-old children are better able to care for themselves than some 12- or 13-year-olds are. Parents should consider their child's maturity first and should make the decision together with the child.

Some hazards in self-care may be minimized by forethought, structured guidance that anticipates problems, and emergency-procedure practice sessions that introduce the child to self-care experience and that develop contingency plans.

Following are some problems and hazards that might occur during self-care and some ways to minimize these risks.

Victimization

A special fear for parents and children is the danger of physical and sexual molestation when children are caring for themselves. Whether or not self-care is involved, children may be particularly vulnerable during the walk home from school.

Children should be taught never to talk with strangers and never to accept rides from people they do not know, regardless of the story given. Children should avoid people who know them but whom they do not know. Children—and parents, as well—should understand that the worst thing that can happen if a child runs away from a stranger, refuses to talk to a stranger, or hollers for help may be slight embarrassment. The alternative is much worse.

Some communities have developed "Safe House" programs. A bright, easily recognizable sign is placed in a window of the home of each participating family, indicating that children can ring the bell and get help. These families welcome children who are being bothered by a stranger, are frightened, cannot reach their parents, and feel they need an adult's help.

Children in self-care should learn to lock the doors once inside the home, and they should be instructed not to open the door for anyone unless they and their parents have previously arranged it. Children should know how to call the police or a neighbor when they are frightened by a persistent stranger—and they should learn always to call parents if there is any question about visitors to the home.

Children in self-care should also learn how to respond to strangers who call on the telephone. Children should not tell anyone that they are home alone. An appropriate response might be, "My mom (or dad) can't come to the phone right now, but I'll have her (him) call back as soon as she's (he's) free." As soon as they are able, children should learn to write down the name and phone number of the caller. If necessary, a parent can be telephoned and given the message so the call can be returned.

Accidents and injuries

Accidental injuries occur with staggering frequency among children and young adults and are a major concern of parents whose children are left in self-care. Parents of "latchkey" children are anxious about accidents because it is difficult for them to reach their children quickly. In addition, working parents are more frightened by accidental injuries because they learn of the injuries through phone calls from a neighbor, school nurse, or relative.

Data appear to indicate, however, that children caring for themselves are not often accidentally injured, and parents of "latchkey" children report remarkably few accidents. Parents' attitudes are important in determining if and when they will work out and use accident-prevention strategies. Physical distance from their children and the fear of accidents tend to encourage parents to teach children how to prevent injuries when they are home alone. Children in self-care tend to take charge of themselves and take responsibility for the outcomes of their behavior, rather than place the responsibility on an older sibling or any other single person. They are frequently taught what to do and rewarded for successful behavior with praise, increased responsibility, increased allowance, and other kinds of recognition. For this reason, classical discovery learning and simple behavior-modification techniques may be very helpful in decreasing the frequency of accidents and injury. Some accident-prevention techniques parents can employ are:

Anticipating outcomes of behavior

Teach children to anticipate what might result from various behaviors. Playing outside should be limited to the yard. Children should not play in the street or alley, and should understand what the dangers are. (Falls and pedestrian injuries are common dangers in these areas.) Inside the home, electric appliances and the stove should be off limits to younger children.

Learning basic first aid

Children in self-care should be taught basic first aid for minor injuries. They can learn to control bleeding from minor cuts by simply applying pressure over the wound, and to place ice over simple bumps and bruises. When injuries do occur, children should also know how to get help. They should be familiar with using the telephone to call for help. They should memorize important phone numbers (parents, relatives, neighbors, police and fire departments) or have them listed in a prominent place, and should call if they are injured.

Understanding basic emergency procedures

Children should be taught basic emergency procedures, such as escaping from the home if a fire breaks out. Parents should identify at least two escape routes and should have practice fire drills regularly, so that children will be familiar with the procedure if it is needed. Children should also learn and practice the "drop and roll" procedure to extinguish flames in case their clothing catches fire. They should know that they are never to run under those circumstances.

Anticipating problems that might occur when children are caring for themselves, preventing them from happening, and practicing emergency procedures are the best ways to decrease the risks and fears of children and parents.

Psychological problems

Some experts believe there are certain psychological risks for children left in self-care. These include developing excessive fear of being left alone, feeling rejected, and becoming alienated from the family. Other experts argue the positive effects of the self-care experience. These include increased sense of responsibility, increased self-esteem, and increased self-worth. Much of the psychosocial and developmental impact of leaving children on their own is related to the level of maturity and development. Some children thrive on the self-care experience, while others are paralyzed by it. It is important for parents to gauge their children's readiness for self-care and gradually introduce them to it by arranging for a graded increase in responsibility, slowly extending the time of self-care, and providing appropriate guidance for anticipated problems and practice sessions for emergencies. Using appropriate feedback and rewards for successful performance increases the children's confidence in handling situations when they arise and their ability to support increasing levels of responsibility.

The self-care experience is not for every family. Some children and parents are ready for it. Others are not. Alternatives should be made available, both at home and through school or community groups, and children should not be hurried into a situation for which they are not prepared. Gradual introduction, careful preparation, and appropriate rewards can minimize risks and maximize benefits for all members of a family.

Learning disabilities in children

By Mark S. Puczynski, M.D.

Over the past decade, child health providers have become more aware of mild impairments in development, which are often identified as learning disabilities. These impairments are often first noted when children enter school and have trouble meeting the academic and social challenges of their new environment. The school setting presents the child with increased demands and expectations, and the child must learn new social as well as developmental skills. For the child with a learning disability, faced with mastering academic tasks and becoming familiar with new buildings and strange adults, school can become a center of struggle.

Each child is born with a unique developmental profile and can exhibit strengths and weaknesses in different aspects of development, such as fine and gross motor activity, attention span, memory function, language, perception, and productivity. Weaknesses in any of these areas may affect the ability of a child to function well in a regular classroom environment.

Disabilities related to these developmental areas are often expressed in a variety of symptoms, and at times it is difficult to distinguish between normal variations in a child's learning style and a true learning disability. Although the number of children affected by learning disabilities has not been determined, it does appear that boys are more frequently affected than girls.

Through the past years, many labels have been suggested to describe children with learning disabilities, including such terms as minimal brain damage, minimal cerebral dysfunction, hyperactivity, hyperkinesis, and developmental dyslexia. The use of these terms is often misleading and is not beneficial in the treatment of children with learning disabilities.

To date, a specific cause for learning difficulties in children has not been identified. We do know, however, that certain risk factors may predispose a child to learning difficulties. Some children may have a genetic abnormality. Others may have experienced serious medical problems that damaged the central nervous system and affected development. Exposure to toxins and infections while still in the uterus may have adversely affected the development of the central nervous system before birth, and the resulting developmental disabilities may not be noted until later in life. However, with the vast majority of children who have school-related difficulties, the cause of the learning disability is not easily identified.

Developmental skills

In order to function well in school, a child must acquire a variety of developmental skills, including auditory and visual memory, expressive and receptive language, motor skills, attention, higher order reasoning, and motivation. The presence or absence of these skills in the developmental profile of a child can affect the child's performance in such academic areas as reading, spelling, science, mathematics, and social development. The child who has not acquired these developmental skills may have difficulty with academic subjects and may experience early failure in school.

The desire to be accepted by other children in the classroom is an important goal for any school-age child. When children enter school, they leave the security of the home for an environment where they face peer pressure every day. For most children, this change produces positive results. By interacting with other children in this new environment, they learn more about themselves, as well as about patterns of socially accepted behavior. But for the learning-disabled child, the change can be painful. The main goal of any child in the classroom is not to be embarrassed by one's performance. "Looking bad" can cause the child with a learning disability to lose confidence in his or her abilities—and, consequently, to lose self-esteem.

Children who constantly experience failure in the classroom express their frustration and unhappiness in different ways. Some children become socially withdrawn and depressed. Others may "act out" in class in undesirable ways. This can lead to problems with other children and with teachers. Children may also experience such symptoms as headaches, stomachaches, limb pains, nail-biting, wetting, and soiling.

In later school years, the learning challenges increase. Junior high school students are expected to begin to think on more abstract levels and to reason in certain ways. Some children whose academic performance has been average in earlier years may blossom and excel when they can exercise their superior ability for abstract thinking. On the other hand, some children who have done well during earlier school years may begin to experience problems caused by an inability to work at a more abstract level. It is important for parents to recognize that early academic success does not predict success in later years.

What parents can do

A parent's own observations of the child's development in the years before school begins are often important in identifying a child who may be at risk for school failure. Children who are delayed in reaching developmental milestones, especially in language

skills, are more likely to fail in school. Parents who feel that language skills, attention, and basic self-help skills that involve organization, such as dressing, are developing slowly should contact their pediatrician. Early identification and intervention can help a child develop his or her full capabilities.

In most cases, however, the problems of children with learning difficulties do not become obvious until the children are in school. A teacher's concerns about a child's difficulties in paying attention or learning a specific skill, such as recognizing letters, may be a parent's first clue that a learning disability exists. If a child is unable to master skills that are readily learned by classmates, a complete evaluation of the child should be performed. This evaluation should include a battery of tests to identify a child's academic achievements and identify the developmental skills needed to function efficiently in a classroom setting. The child should also have a physical examination, including vision and hearing screening, in order to rule out any medical causes of learning impairment. A thorough social evaluation should also be included, since environmental factors may also adversely affect the child's performance.

When the evaluation is completed, parents and teachers can be provided with a description of the child's developmental strengths and weaknesses, and recommendations can be made for an appropriate classroom environment and for changes in the home that would benefit the child, as well.

Medications are sometimes prescribed as part of the treatment of children with an attention deficit disorder. It is important for parents and teachers to understand that medications will not cure a learning disability, even though they sometimes do help children who have serious problems with inattention and impulsive behavior. Counseling for a child and family is also sometimes recommended in order to help a child deal with problems as they are encountered. With these kinds of support, and with continued observation and help, children with learning disabilities can be expected to develop academically and socially to their full capabilities.

The mentally retarded child

By Laura Dittmann, Ph.D.

About 30 of every 1,000 children born in the United States are diagnosed during infancy or later as mentally retarded. The most severely retarded are often discovered in infancy. Some are identified in their early formative years. Others are found after they enter school.

The term *mental retardation* covers a range of children with subnormal mental ability—from nearly normal to totally dependent. Children are considered mentally retarded if they perform far below average, both intellectually and behaviorally. They do not think, reason, remember, and learn as well as other children the same age.

A number of other terms have been used to describe this condition, such as mental deficiency, learning impairment, subnormal intelligence, and incompetence. They all mean the same thing. But mental retardation and mental illness are *not* the same. Mental retardation means that a person has subnormal mental ability. Mental illness means that a severe emotional disturbance prevents a person with normal mental ability from using the higher centers of the brain in a normal way. (See BEHAVIORAL DISORDERS IN CHILDREN in For Special Consideration.)

A mentally retarded child who is neglected, treated badly, or forced into unmanageable situations, may develop emotional problems and become mentally ill.

Mentally retarded children are not just "slow learners." They can never catch up to the average child. In fact, they fall further behind as they grow older. But, except in cases of extreme retardation, parents and teachers can help mentally retarded children develop strategies so that they need not be totally dependent on others to survive. The way the family and others treat a mentally retarded child has a lot to do with whether or not the child can remain emotionally healthy and well adjusted.

What causes mental retardation?

Many causes of mental retardation have been discovered. A child may be mentally retarded as the result of heredity, birth defects, illness, or accident.

For example, if a child inherits certain defective genes from one or both parents, the brain may not develop completely. Brain damage may also be caused by an infection of the central nervous system before birth, during infancy, or in early childhood. If a pregnant woman contracts German measles or if she experiences severe malnutrition, her baby's development may be seriously damaged. Extensive injury to the baby's brain during an extremely difficult birth may also cause mental retardation.

Even a child who has a healthy start in life may, in the formative years, have an illness that produces a high, long-lasting fever or a brain injury that interferes with mental development.

Some experts in the field of mental retardation believe that neglect, malnutrition, surroundings that are dull and monotonous, and lack of love and attention may also retard a child's normal ability to learn. In some instances, when these abnormal life conditions are improved, the child's mental development also improves.

Types of mental retardation

Mental retardation is classified as severe, moderate, or mild.

Severe retardation can often be detected in infancy, possibly at birth. The severely retarded infant may have difficulty learning to suck and to swallow. The child may be slow to hold up the head, roll over, and sit up. Some degree of independence in eating, toilet habits, dressing, and self-care may be achieved. But usually, the severely retarded remain dependent throughout life. Sometimes, blindness, impaired hearing, heart disease, epilepsy, or malformation of limbs are also present.

Moderate retardation causes a child to develop more slowly than normal. A few moderately retarded children may seem normal, except that they are much slower to learn to speak, or their speech may be unintelligible. Generally, they can learn to take care of their personal needs, and those who are well adjusted may be able to live semi-independently. They can be trained to do simple work.

Mild retardation may not be recognized until a child begins to have difficulty at school. The child may not be able to pay attention as well as other children. Simple directions may be impossible to follow. The child may be unable to use scissors, crayons, pencils, and other materials the way normal children do. These children often require special classroom placement, where some can achieve fourth- to sixth-grade reading levels.

What parents can do

Whenever parents are puzzled by their child's development, they should seek professional help. The family doctor or pediatrician can refer parents to a special clinic for a detailed diagnosis and evaluation of the child's condition. As a rule, a good diagnosis will include a thorough study of physical, psychological, and social factors involved in the child's behavior. When a thorough study has been made, parents feel less compelled to go from one doctor to another in the hope of finding an easy cure for the condition.

Retarded children, like normal children, should get good medical care and attention.

They need nourishing food, plenty of sleep, scheduled immunizations, correction of any physical defects that can be corrected, and careful nursing during illness. A periodic reassessment of the child's condition is important.

Few parents adjust easily to the idea that their child is mentally retarded, but some react more extremely than others. Many parents find that talking to others in the same situation can be a great comfort. The National Association for Retarded Citizens has parents' organizations in most cities. Parents and others who are interested in retarded children meet to exchange ideas, discuss problems, set up camps or schools, and promote understanding of mental retardation. The local health and welfare council or the department of health will supply information about such groups in the community. (See AGENCIES AND ORGANIZATIONS INTERESTED IN THE WELFARE OF CHILDREN.)

Living with the retarded child

The retarded child, like all children, needs to begin life with parental love in family surroundings. Today there is greater understanding of retardation and more help available in the community. Most experts recommend keeping the child at home rather than in an institution. If parents can help the child do more and more alone, they will begin to see the child as a learning individual rather than a family burden.

The mentally retarded child's day should be kept simple and orderly. Let the child know what is expected from day to day. Patient teaching is required to help the retarded child learn what the average child of that age learns quickly. You may have to repeat the same instructions, activities, and simple lessons many times before a simple idea is grasped. Do not push the child beyond ability. If overloaded, the child may become confused and any efforts to learn will be blocked.

To determine ability, watch the child's behavior and concentrate on whether the child is ready to do certain things. When the child is physically and mentally able to do one task, think of a related or slightly more complex task that you can teach next. Does the baby reach for the bottle when it is offered? Then try to teach the baby to hold the bottle. Can the child take off shoes and socks? Then maybe it's time to learn to put them on. If a hand can move to the mouth, chances are the child can learn to eat unaided. Begin with small bits of food and don't discourage the use of fingers. The child can be taught to manage a cup if there is only a small amount of liquid in it and the cup is easy to hold. In time, increase the amount of liquid and change the type of container. Tell the child what you want in clear and specific terms. But remember to ask the child to do only one thing at a time.

After a while, most parents come to accept the fact that their retarded child will never have normal mental ability. They begin to find satisfaction with their child's progress, even if it seems slow and the accomplishments are small. They no longer make comparisons with other children in the family. They judge progress by what the retarded child can do today compared to last month or last year. In some cases, however, there may be no progress at all.

Parents need patience to discipline the retarded child. The child needs to learn rules, but what is expected should be based on the child's ability and development. Sometimes, parents demand better behavior from the mentally retarded child than from the other children in the family. They do not want the retarded child to "act" retarded. They expect far more in the way of control and cooperation than the child can possibly offer. As with any other aspect of learning, the demand for more than the child is capable of giving will hinder rather than help.

The retarded child's effect on the family

All retarded children are not alike. Some are easy to care for. Others cannot be trusted out of sight for a minute. Some need special care and equipment from the time they are born. Others seem normal at birth, and do not show retardation until later. One child may be attractive and physically healthy. Another may have physical as well as mental handicaps.

While it is not always the case, the severity of the retardation may determine its effect on the rest of the family. If the retardation is severe, it may be necessary to leave the child in the care of a sitter occasionally so that the rest of the family can get out. The other children may become resentful if their activities are curtailed by the retarded sibling.

It is a good idea to train a special caretaker, and to keep the same one if possible. Students enrolled in special education courses at nearby colleges are often eager to experience caring for a retarded child.

Usually the brothers and sisters reflect the attitudes and behavior of their parents toward the retarded child. The mentally retarded child can become the scapegoat for any problems, even those the family would have if the child were not present.

On the other hand, the retarded child can become a valued member of the family, around whose needs the others can rally and become united more strongly than ever.

Schools and institutions

Many people have been long concerned about the educational needs of mentally retarded children. In 1975, the United States took a major step forward in this area when a new public law was passed. The law protects the rights of these children and their parents or guardians. What's more, through federal aid to the states, the law assures that all handicapped children—regardless of how they are categorized—have a free public education that is designed to meet their individual needs.

This law makes it possible for more mentally retarded children to attend nursery and regular schools in their own neighborhoods. Nevertheless, there are some retarded children and some families for whom a special school or institution is a better choice.

In deciding what is best for all concerned, parents of a mentally retarded child may find it worthwhile to talk with a family counselor, a pediatrician, a public health nurse, or school personnel.

Mark S. Puczynski, M.D.
Consulting Editor

Moving

By Gladys Gardner Jenkins, M.A.

Moving can be an exciting adventure or an uncomfortable disruption in your child's life. But since children usually follow the lead of their parents, the degree of excitement or uneasiness that your child feels will depend largely on your attitude toward the move and how you explain it.

Most children, especially those who have close friends or who have formed strong ties to people, places, and the routines of the old neighborhood, will feel sad at leaving. But beyond such normal regrets, how you act can give your child either a dread of the unknown or an eagerness to tackle a new and interesting life experience.

A move can be a valuable educational benefit. It can help your child learn to meet new situations and adapt to new ways of doing things. The challenge of adjusting to a new situation is probably better preparation for life than the false sense of security that often results from a lack of change.

Preparing your child for the move

If your child is old enough to understand, you should explain why the family is making the move. Perhaps it is necessary because a parent has a new job, or is being transferred. Maybe someone in the family is ill and must have change of climate. Or maybe you are just moving to a different neighborhood. Whatever the reason for a move, children will probably accept the fact that they are leaving much that is familiar and dear to them if they understand why the move is necessary.

If it is possible, parents should go to the new community, visit the neighborhood in which the family will live, and talk to some of the people who live there. They should also investigate housing and school facilities. They can then give their children a clear picture of what it might be like to live in the new place. If a trip such as this is not possible, it is still a good idea to find out as much as possible about the family's future home. If the family is planning a move to another part of the country, or to another country, it will be helpful to get together to study maps and read stories and articles about the area where they will live.

Also, the family should discuss any aspects of the move that may present problems for them, such as difference in climate, difference in attitudes and customs of the people who live in the new neighborhood, or a lack of the kind of facilities to which family members are accustomed in their present neighborhood. Whenever possible, parents should explain unfamiliar local customs to their children so that the children will become interested in the many different ways people do things, and will respect rather than scorn such differences.

If you are moving to an area where you anticipate real hardships because of climate, inadequate housing, or inadequate schools, you should give your child some idea of what the hardships are likely to be. At the same time you should make the child understand that as a family in which each member helps, there is no reason why your family will not be able to cope with any difficulty that may be encountered.

Problems you may meet

Even with the best preparation, your child may have some deep emotional reaction to moving. Often, anxiety over the welfare of a pet that cannot be taken along may precipitate an emotional crisis. You can relieve your child's anxiety by letting the child help find a good home for the pet.

Your child's attachment to friends may be so genuine and intense that the child will be distressed by leaving them. You can help lessen this distress by suggesting that an exchange of letters and postcards will keep the friendship going, and that later on perhaps there can be visits.

Leaving friends may be especially hard on a child to whom a close friend or membership in a club, special group, or an athletic team has meant the security that goes with the sense of really belonging. The child in the last year of elementary school may be quite upset by the move. The child has probably been looking forward to this last year in the old school. A child this age may feel strange in the new school and may have difficulty becoming part of already formed groups. Membership in some of the smaller community, church, or synagogue groups which usually welcome newcomers may help the child feel more at ease.

Usually, social groups in an elementary school are not so exclusive or as tightly knit as they are in a high school. In general, a child who is good at games or who is friendly and outgoing will be accepted into a group almost casually. Also, it is easier for parents of younger children to get to know each other through informal neighborhood meetings or through the PTA. It is a rare community where neighbors will not welcome you. Most people have had some experience with moving and establishing their families in a new community, and they expect to welcome newcomers. The friendly atmosphere makes it easier for your child to meet other boys and girls and to develop new friendships and interests.

If your child is shy or timid or shows much uneasiness in the new situation, the child will need your support when entering the new school. Take the child to school before he or she is to begin classes and introduce the child to the principal, the teacher, and if possible some future classmates. If the child has difficulty with schoolwork, or has physical problems such as poor coordination, vision, or hearing, the school should know about them. The school should also know about any special abilities. Most teachers want to be helpful, but they can do their best only when they are aware of your child's special needs.

Sometimes a child appears to have adjusted to the move without any difficulty. But after the initial excitement has worn off, there is an emotional slump. It may be that school is not as challenging or as stimulating as it was in the old community. It also may be that the new school is quite a bit more challenging than the previous one, so that the child is having trouble keeping up with the new classmates. Or it could be that there is trouble finding compatible new friends. Help the child make the best of circumstances. Talk to the teachers. They might be able to help the child find more interests, or they might be able to help the child find more congenial friends. If the school is inadequate, provide books and materials the child can use at home. Encourage personal hobbies, and increase family trips to places of interest.

It is not unusual for a well-adjusted child to feel lonely, restless, and moody after a move. But if your child was already unhappy, the move may increase the anxiety. You may have to turn to someone trained to help you understand the basic causes of your youngster's unhappiness.

Most youngsters, however, settle into the new community within a period of months. Their adjustment is helped considerably if the experience of the move has given the secure feeling that, "Wherever we live we are a family. We can make a home and meet all kinds of circumstances." This is a fine way to establish the emotional security that will support a child throughout life.

Julie Giesy, R.N., M.S.N.
Consulting Editor

The physically handicapped child

By Edward F. Lis, M.D.

Most physically handicapped children with normal intelligence have a good chance for a useful and satisfying life, within limits. But their parents must love and accept them, and help them develop self-confidence by concentrating on what they *can* do rather than on what they *cannot* do.

Many parents of handicapped children are overwhelmed by the responsibility of caring for them. When problems become acute, they may even begin to resent the children. Some parents feel guilty. Some, ashamed of their handicapped children's looks, make them feel unloved. Feelings of guilt and resentment may cause parents to treat their children in ways that are harmful to growth and development.

Some parents try to shield their handicapped children from situations they think might cause hurt feelings. The result is that the parents do things for their children that the children could do for themselves. Such treatment can make children dependent and self-conscious.

Some parents go to the other extreme. They ignore disabilities and push the children beyond their limits. If these children fail often, they may be afraid to try anything, since they may not readily succeed.

Children who feel unloved because of their parents' attitudes toward them may become emotionally as well as physically handicapped.

Causes of some common physical defects

Parents of a handicapped child should have as much reliable information as possible about their child's condition so that they know how to deal with the child's capabilities and limitations.

Physical defects may result from many causes and may involve any part of the body. A child may be born with defects that stem from abnormal genes passed on to the child from either or both parents at the time of conception. Such hereditary defects may include cleft lip and cleft palate, congenital heart disorders, improper closure of the spinal canal, and various bone and joint disorders.

A child may be born with a physical defect if the mother had an infection such as German measles during pregnancy, if she misused drugs, or if she had toxemia (blood poisoning) during pregnancy.

Some physical defects result from premature birth or complications during delivery. Such abnormal births do not always result in defects, but they can cause cerebral palsy, epilepsy, hearing and seeing difficulties, and mental retardation.

Many children who are born with one or more physical defects may develop further disabilities. For example, a child with a cleft lip and a cleft palate may also have teeth and ear problems. A child with a hearing defect may also have visual problems. Similarly, a child with defective vision may also be hearing impaired.

Infection, an accident, or poor nutrition may produce physical disability. For example, meningitis or encephalitis may cause brain damage. A streptococcal infection may cause rheumatic fever and rheumatic heart. An accident may cause paralysis or loss of

Many physically handicapped children are able to attend school.

limb. A burn may cause disfigurement, and insufficient vitamin D may cause rickets.

Treatment

Severe birth defects and acquired disabilities require the services of specialists experienced in treating the particular defects. The family doctor or pediatrician can best determine the appropriate specialist for treatment and for continuing medical care.

Clubfoot and other bone and joint defects are treated by an orthopedist. Facial defects, such as cleft lip and cleft palate, are treated by a plastic surgeon. Brain and spinal cord defects are treated by a neurosurgeon. Physical medicine is used to treat people with neurological and muscular disorders. It includes physical therapy, occupational therapy, special braces, and other means of improving disorders without the use of drugs or surgery.

Caring for the handicapped child at home

The physically handicapped child has needs that go beyond special medical attention to the defects. A handicapped child, like a normal child, needs good nutrition and immunization against disease. The child needs periodic visits to the family doctor or the pediatrician. A handicapped baby needs the same amount of cuddling and attention as a normal baby. A handicapped toddler needs to explore, and the preschool child who is handicapped should be stimulated with new experiences.

A handicapped child, like a normal child, must be given responsibilities and tasks appropriate to age and ability. This gives the child the feeling of being trusted and needed. A handicapped child also needs discipline—neither more nor less than that needed by all children—to learn the limits of socially acceptable behavior. Handicapped children feel more secure knowing that they are expected to be as well behaved as normal children.

Parents should refrain from rushing to help their handicapped children do things they can do for themselves. But there is no harm in making things easier for them. For instance, parents can alter clothes so that children can dress and undress themselves with as little difficulty as possible. They can arrange furniture so that the children can get around the house more easily.

Depending on the nature of the handicap, a child may need additional attention in the home. Parents may have to learn special skills and techniques to carry out treatment prescribed by the doctor. At times, they may have to make changes in the home to accommodate a wheelchair or other necessary equipment. Parents should not hesitate to inform their doctor when problems arise in treating the child at home. The doctor may be able to suggest ways to ease or correct the problems.

Educating the handicapped child

Medical treatment and special education during early childhood help many physically handicapped children lessen or even overcome a handicap. For example, special education can give the child with cerebral palsy a chance to improve coordination and speech defects. It also provides the opportunity for a physically handicapped child to relate to people outside the family, and to learn to handle reactions to the handicap.

Some physically handicapped children can attend regular classes in a private or a public school. Some public schools have classrooms adapted to the special needs of handicapped children, and trained teachers to instruct them. Some communities provide bus service for handicapped children who need wheelchairs, braces, or other equipment to get around.

When a child is too severely handicapped to attend school, the public school may send a teacher to the home, or it may provide electronic or other teaching equipment. Residential schools may provide medical and educational services in cases where parents are unable to cope with handicapped children

at home, or where local facilities are either inadequate or nonexistent. Such schools are similar to boarding schools in that the children may return home for holidays and other school vacation periods.

Parents who want information about special educational services should contact their school district or the division of special education in their state.

Help for parents

The cost of providing treatment and special education for the handicapped child may become a financial burden. Each state has an official department that serves the handicapped and that has federal and state funds to help parents in financial need or those who require help in planning a program of education for their child.

Many agencies and groups that deal with handicapped children have parent-education programs to help parents face problems and understand their own attitudes. Lectures help parents understand the nature of their child's disability and its cause. Perhaps most important, parents learn they are not alone when they share experiences with other parents of handicapped children.

Parent-education programs are led by qualified people in the fields of medicine and special education. Discussions, lectures, visual aids, and trips to schools and institutions for the handicapped give parents information on health care, discipline, and physical and psychological adjustments necessary in caring for a handicapped child. Where such groups do not exist, some agencies have mobile units to provide parents of handicapped children with counseling.

A child like all others

In time, parents become aware that their handicapped children are in most ways like all other children. They learn that other children have similar handicaps and that their children need the medical and educational services that are available to such children. Finally, the parents of handicapped children discover that their children are individuals in their own right.

Mark S. Puczynski, M.D.
Consulting Editor

Sex and your child

By James Walters, Ph.D., and Lynda Walters, Ph.D.

Increasingly, parents want their children to develop the attitude that sex is a normal, natural part of life, and that sexual feelings are healthy and desirable. Sexual behavior, however, requires responsibility, not only because it can result in pregnancy, social disease, and AIDS, but because it can result in guilt feelings that are damaging to sexual functioning in adulthood.

Infants spend considerable time touching and exploring their bodies. We smile at the sight of a baby chewing on a toe, but our response may be less accepting if the infant rubs his or her genitals. It is important for parents to understand that rubbing the genital area—masturbation—is natural and does not reflect precocious sexuality.

Having pride in one's body contributes to a healthy self-concept. If children are taught that nudity is shameful, they may conclude that the body is something to be ashamed of. This feeling may be carried into adulthood.

Discussing sex with your child

Sex should be talked about. Many people believe that if they avoid discussing sex, their children will not become sexually active. But not discussing sex only means that parents will not know about their children's sexual values and behavior. A wall of silence between parents and children is particularly unfortunate in the light of research indicating the misconceptions children and youth have about sex.

For one thing, many young people believe that they are more sexual than their par-

ents. Because they think their parents do not understand their feelings, young people often find it difficult to discuss their sexuality. Part of the problem is that many adults have learned to keep their sexual feelings hidden, and they convey this idea to their children.

Another problem is that we tend to live with a number of myths. For example, many people believe that sex education for children may lead to less responsible sexual behavior. There is no evidence to support this belief. For another, some fathers believe that an open show of affection toward a son is unmanly and may cause the boy to grow up preferring sexual responses from people of his own sex. Again, there is no evidence to support this belief. But these myths persist, and actually prevent us from creating the kind of environment that will contribute toward the healthy sexual development of our children.

People have different values about sex. Children will understand your values only if you clearly indicate *what* they are and *why* you hold them. Of course, for very young children you'll need to keep your explanations simple. Older children, however, will profit from an explanation.

Parents who do discuss sex with their children are often too serious. They label and describe body parts and functions without communicating the most important message of all: sex is a means by which grown people share their love.

Other parents teach about the birds and flowers in order to avoid talking about human sexual intercourse. Yet, describing sexual intercourse isn't all that difficult. You can do it.

Your child may ask, "Where is your vagina?" or "Where is your penis?" Simply say, "My vagina (or penis) is right here," and place your hand there.

Remember, the exact words you use aren't as important as the feelings you convey. If you reflect embarrassment, your child will think that sex is something to be embarrassed about. If you reflect shock, your child will think that there is something shocking about sex.

Specific details about menstruation can be left to preadolescence, at which time both boys and girls need to be informed.

Helping a child accept his or her sexuality, and so grow into a sexually responsible adult, is an important responsibility of parents. Letting someone else do it will not ensure a satisfactory result.

Sexual influences of the media

Children learn a great deal about sexual behavior from television, motion pictures, magazines, comic books, and newspapers. But it is difficult for them to sort out the facts. Some of what they learn is likely to be in error. Even if the information is not wrong, the values communicated may violate those of parents.

Parents can guide movie and television viewing by setting rules. Make a point of knowing what movies or television programs your child wants to see. When you believe that something is objectionable, you might say, "This is an adult film (or program). It isn't meant for children."

You may discover that your child has a magazine with highly explicit sexual material to which you object. To explain how you feel, you could say, "This magazine really bothers me. I feel that love is an important part of sex. This magazine leaves out the most important part of all."

Guidance should lead to increasing self-direction. If you attach too much importance to what you forbid, you may inadvertently stimulate your child's curiosity. And, in so doing, you may lead the child to satisfy this curiosity behind your back.

Sexual problems in our society

In the course of growing up, children learn that some forms of sexual expression are more acceptable than others. But, without some guidelines from their parents, children may respond with naiveté, fear, or disgust.

Realistically, children must be taught some caution in their interactions with strangers. However, not all child molesters are strangers. Frequently, children are acquainted with the people who make sexual advances toward them. Teach your child to say, "Leave me alone or I will tell my parents!" In many cases, fear of exposure will deter the offender.

If the offender is a stranger, fear of exposure may not be so great. Tell your child to scream and run to an adult. In every case, children should report such incidents to their parents. They should never be made to feel guilty if overtures are made to them.

A thought to remember

The most important thing to remember in educating children sexually is that parents do not have to convey to them many of the negative messages the parents themselves may have learned as children.

There are better ways. Hiding sex, or pretending it doesn't exist in children, doesn't contribute to the development of responsible sexual behavior. Recognizing that sex is important, and preparing your children for it, does.

Julie Giesy, R.N., M.S.N.
Consulting Editor

Traveling with children

By Michele Prior, R.N., M.S.N.

A family vacation is a special time, but it may take some creativity to make traveling to your destination fun for your child. Fortunately, there are some activities you can plan to help keep your child contented on a long trip.

It may be beneficial to start at a time when your child will be likely to sleep for all or part of the trip. If that is not possible, plan time-passing activities. Of course, paper and crayons or markers for drawing are favorites with most children. Take along a tray with legs to make it easier for your child to use his or her artistic talents. A tray will also come in handy for putting puzzles together and for building with blocks. Modeling with clay can also help to keep your child busy.

Pack a small cassette recorder along with some of your child's favorite music and story tapes. Children also love blank tapes for recording songs they sing or stories they make up along the way.

Playing games can help the trip go faster, too. Many popular children's games come in travel-sized editions, and card games are easy to take along. Children also enjoy having a list or pictures of things to look for along the ride and seeing how many they can find.

Other things to include on your packing list are snack foods such as dry cereal, raisins, and juice; moist wipes; a change of clothes; and your child's favorite stuffed animal or blanket. Always have a first-aid kit available. Childhood accidents occur when traveling because of changes in the child's routine and environment.

Take along small, wrapped surprises for your child to open and play with on the trip to reward him or her for behaving well. When traveling by car, plan to stop often to let your child run off pent-up energy. Knowing that there will be frequent breaks will help your child remain safely seated. One of the most difficult parts of traveling with children is having to confine them to their car seats or seat belts, but remember that "buckling up" is the only safe way to travel, both close to and far from your home.

With plane travel, there are additional factors to consider. Whenever possible, plan to take a nonstop flight and request seats in the first row or aisle, where there is more room. Although airlines provide earlier boarding when flying with children, this may not be the best option with active infants or toddlers, because they will be confined longer. If you have a seat assignment, it may be better to board later and let the child run off energy.

During take-off and landing, encourage your child to drink liquids or to suck on candy or chew gum (if age appropriate) to equalize pressure and prevent ear discomfort. If your child has cold symptoms and is prone to ear infections, be sure to have the child's ears checked before flying.

Children are usually thrilled about traveling and going on a vacation, but keep in mind that changes in their routines, coupled with added excitement, may alter their sleeping patterns and also cause changes in behavior. Enjoy your trip—these are temporary disruptions. Life will go back to normal after you are home for a couple of days.

The working mother

By Eda LeShan, B.S., M.A.

Some mothers feel worried and guilty if they hold jobs that take them away from their families. Others, who find personal fulfillment in homemaking and motherhood, are made to feel like second-class citizens. Neither of these negative attitudes is valid. The truth is that women can find personal fulfillment whether they are full-time homemakers or have a job outside the home.

Some preschool children thrive on group experience in a first-rate nursery school.

The young mother who considers working away from home is most likely to be influenced by four major factors:
▪ She is concerned about the psychological effect on her children, especially if they are quite young.
▪ She is experiencing a new consciousness of her needs and rights as a woman because of the growing influence of the Women's Liberation Movement.
▪ She is aware that she is living in a climate that discourages large families, and may have to think seriously of other avenues of personal fulfillment.
▪ Finally, today's young mother can expect to have better health and live longer than did her mother. Even if she finds complete fulfillment as a mother and homemaker, she may want to prepare herself for the years when her children are grown and no longer require as much of her time and energy.

Whatever social forces influence the young mother, going to work will create many special and practical problems.

Concerns of all working mothers

The question that often occurs to working mothers is whether they are short-changing their children. In general, the working mother is concerned about the *quality* of the time she spends with her children because she knows how limited the *quantity* of time is. Mothers who stay at home are less likely to worry about this. And, sometimes, a mother's mere physical presence at home may become a substitute for emotional involvement in her children's lives.

Often the working mother is so conscious of the pitfalls of psychological neglect of her children she may go overboard in the other direction. For example, mothers who feel guilty about working tend to read most often to their children, to "play house" when their feet are killing them, or to play endless games with a sick child.

Children do not need constant attention to know they are loved. No child will grow up suffering from nervous and mental damage because mother sometimes says, "Darling, I can't play with you now, I'm too tired." Mothers who stay home say the same thing after cleaning a stove or waxing a floor. What children need most of all is the abiding sense that they count most when the chips are down.

Of course, there are times when a mother should recognize that her own needs must be set aside—that her greatest responsibility is to her child. A mother's job may be very important to her, but when her child is in real trouble, priorities become very clear.

Another serious concern for all working mothers is the fact that there are so few satisfactory resources for the care of young children, as well as planned and properly supervised after-school play programs for older children. Fine nurseries and day-care centers are in short supply. There are a great many that are inadequate at best and may be damaging at worst. At present, many working mothers are involved in trying to get their communities to provide better child-care facilities for children of all ages. (For additional information, see DAY CARE in For Special Consideration.)

Some preschool children thrive on early group experience in a first-rate nursery school. Some are not ready for such an experience until they are 4 or 5 years old. Most young children catch many colds and childhood illnesses during the first year at school. Then they begin to build up better immunity. Some 2-year-olds thrive on an eight-hour day in a group setting, but some become overtired and cranky after an hour and a half.

Children differ greatly in how early they can be separated from their mothers or from a mother substitute in the home. This means that the working mother needs time to evaluate her child's needs and possible reactions so that she can make the best possible arrangements for child care. She also needs a list of reliable baby sitters. She may need an experienced grandmother with free morning hours who can be called on when a child is sick, or an energetic teenager who is willing to play outdoors with a child after school.

There is no way of knowing in advance when children will need their mother's attention most. Sometimes young children are quite happy with a baby sitter or attending nursery school or a day-care center, and then begin having learning problems when they start school. Some mothers work until their children are teenagers, then quit because they feel this is the most crucial time—the time their children need them most.

The single working mother

Single mothers are mothers without partners to help share the burden of supporting and caring for their children. They may be widowed, separated, divorced, or unmarried.

The single working mother's concern for her children's welfare is usually very intense, because she is isolated and completely responsible for her children's welfare. When she or her children are ill, or when she is exhausted at the end of a day, she has no one to whom she can turn for help at all times.

The single working mother needs to think of ways to provide loving father substitutes for her children—a favorite uncle to baby-sit on a Saturday afternoon; a retired grandpa who can take a child to an after-school dental appointment or to the barber shop; a neighbor father who is willing to include her children in the backyard games he plays with his own children.

Because she has to work, the single mother tends to take less satisfying jobs than the mother who has a choice. This, combined with the burden of full parental responsibility, often results in what one mother called "a life that is never for me." The single working mother needs to devote thought to how she can nourish her own life. She cannot be a good mother to her children unless she cares about herself.

The married working mother

Many married women also have little or no choice about taking an outside job. A husband may be working part-time while studying for a profession. He may be unemployed for a long period, or have a long illness. When there is no choice about the wife's working, both parents need to explore ways to help each other with child care and household chores.

However, couples should do some genuine soul-searching about the phrase *have to work*. Sometimes a woman who *wants* to work for her own fulfillment feels guilty. She may feel that she is selfish and unfair to her family, yet at the same time she will convince herself and her husband that she *has* to work because the family income is inadequate even when it is not. If this is the case, she damages herself and her children by denying an important truth about her nature. She may also unnecessarily damage her husband's self-esteem.

The mother who has a real choice about whether to work needs to take a hard look at the situation before she decides to take a job. Will the additional income really make a difference? Or will the cost of baby sitters, nurseries, additional taxes, extra clothes, lunches out, and transportation actually make taking a job a luxury? Is the cost too high in terms of the family's emotional needs at this particular time?

Husbands of working mothers

Husbands should not feel that their masculinity is threatened by changing a diaper, washing dishes, or cooking a meal. In a true marital partnership both parents can find ways to share in all areas of child care and household chores.

The mature woman will consider her husband's needs. Some men feel threatened by a wife who has a rich, rewarding life of her own. Husbands and wives need to keep lines of communication open between them at all times so that they can work out any conflicting feelings they may have, arrive at acceptable compromises, and show continuing respect for each other's needs.

Time and changing roles

Women need a sense of perspective about time and changing roles. The period when children are truly dependent is short. It is wise to think in the broadest terms about how to plan one's life.

Women must accept the fact that no matter what their decision about working, there will be frustrations, fatigue, boredom, and uncertainty. A crowded subway at the rush hour, impatient demanding bosses, and TV dinners three nights in a row may be no less harrowing than colicky babies, sleepless nights, and lack of adult stimulation.

Indeed, having a job outside the home may sometimes seem mad, especially on the day your child cries because you can't get to the school play or you come home tired and realize you forgot to defrost the meat you were going to have for dinner.

Having two careers is not for everyone. Many talented and energetic women enjoy their professions so much that to cut them off from this, even briefly, would play havoc with their lives. These women must follow their own needs and understand that if they stifle their needs they may become emotional cripples. And such people cannot be good influences on their children. They cannot feel truly loving toward others unless, first of all, they care about their own lives.

If we care deeply about teaching our children those ethical values that will lead to good human relationships, the first lesson must be that only when we respect our own talents and possibilities are we capable of offering equal respect to others. To want to fulfill oneself is not selfish—on the contrary, the fulfilled person feels a deep joy in being alive and communicates it to everyone. If we want our children to search for their own best potentialities, the best way to help them is to be this kind of person ourselves

Michele Prior, R.N., M.S.N.
Consulting Editor

Agencies and organizations interested in the welfare of children

Hundreds of agencies and organizations in the United States and in Canada provide information and counseling to anyone seeking help with special problems relating to family and child health, welfare, and education. Some of these agencies and organizations are privately sponsored. Others are sponsored by city, state, or federal governments in the United States, or by provincial or territorial governments in Canada.

Telephone directories usually list local agencies and organizations and, where they exist, the local chapters of state, national, provincial, and territorial agencies and organizations. Whenever possible, get in touch with a local chapter or agency first.

The following list contains names of some of the major agencies and organizations in the United States and in Canada. The list also contains a brief description of what each does. To make it easier for you to find the one you think may be able to help you, the agencies and organizations are grouped under general headings.

United States

Diseases and
  physical handicaps

Health

Learning and
  social development

Mental health

Welfare and safety

Canada

Diseases and
  physical handicaps

Health and welfare

Learning and
  social development

Mental health

If this list does not include an agency or an organization that seems equipped to meet your special need, your doctor, the nearest hospital, the local health department, or your spiritual adviser may be able to suggest others.

United States

Diseases and physical handicaps

Allergy/asthma

Asthma & Allergy Foundation of America
1717 Massachusetts Avenue, Suite 505
Washington, DC 20036
(202) 265-0265

Has support groups throughout the U.S.; sponsors the Asthma Care Training (ACT) asthma self-management program for children, and disseminates publications regarding asthma and allergic diseases. Publications are available on request.

National Foundation for Asthma
P.O. Box 33069
Tucson, AZ 85751
(602) 323-6046

Provides medical care for asthmatics referred by their physician, including those who cannot afford private care. Write for further information.

Arthritis

American Juvenile Arthritis Organization
1314 Spring Street, N.W.
Atlanta, GA 30309
(404) 872-7100

Seeks the cause, prevention, and cure of juvenile arthritis and related diseases. It helps patients and doctors through research, patient and community services, public health information, and education.

Birth defects

March of Dimes Birth Defects Foundation
1275 Mamaroneck Avenue
White Plains, NY 10605
(914) 428-7100

Provides information on research, medical services, and centers. Pamphlets on birth defects prevention and prenatal care are available.

Blindness

American Council of the Blind
Adelphi House, M-5
1229 Chestnut Street
Philadelphia, PA 19107
(800) 424-8666

Offers a forum for the support and education for the sighted parents of the blind or visually impaired, for blind or visually impaired parents, and others. It publishes a quarterly newsletter.

American Foundation for the Blind
15 West 16th Street
New York, NY 10011
(212) 620-2000

Publishes a directory of about 800 nonprofit agencies serving the visually handicapped in the U.S.

Cancer

American Cancer Society, Inc.
19 West 56th Street
New York, NY 10019
(212) 586-8700

Provides education, research, and service to individuals and families. Filmstrip kits, pamphlets, and manuals are available upon request.

Leukemia Society of America
733 Third Avenue
New York, NY 10017
(212) 573-8484

Seeks to control leukemia through research, education, and service. Local chapters offer counseling, guidance, and aid to patients and families affected by leukemia. Information available upon request.

National Leukemia Association
585 Stewart Avenue
Garden City, NY 11530
(516) 222-1944

Dedicated to promoting leukemia research and public awareness. The association provides financial aid to leukemia patients and families based upon need.

Cerebral palsy

United Cerebral Palsy Associations, Inc.
66 East 34th Street
New York, NY 10016
(212) 481-6347

Oversees local affiliates that offer medical, educational, recreational, counseling, therapy, and other services to patients and their families. Pamphlets and films are available.

Cystic fibrosis

Cystic Fibrosis Foundation
6931 Arlington Road, #2
Bethesda, MD 20814
(800) FIGHT-CF

Oversees local chapters that provide community services and referrals. A nationwide network of CF medical centers provides diagnosis and treatment. Literature and audio-visual materials are available from the foundation and local chapters.

Deafness

Alexander Graham Bell Association for the Deaf
3417 Volta Place, N.W.
Washington, DC 20007
(202) 337-5220

Encourages the teaching of speech, lip-reading, and the use of residual hearing to deaf children. Furnishes free information kits on speech, hearing, and education of the deaf to individual parents and teachers.

The John Tracey Clinic
806 West Adams Boulevard
Los Angeles, CA 90007
(213) 748-5481

An educational center for preschool deaf and hard-of-hearing children and their parents. Offers both hearing and psychological examinations for preschool children with suspected hearing loss. Offers a special summer program for families the world over; correspondence course in English and Spanish to help parents teach children to understand and communicate with language; and a course for parents of a child with both hearing and vision loss. All services are free.

Diabetes

American Diabetes Association
P.O. Box 25751, 1660 Duke Street
Alexandria, VA 22313
(703) 549-1500

Conducts education programs and funds research in diabetes. Local affiliates sponsor meetings for people with diabetes and camps for diabetic children. Booklets, a free quarterly newsletter, cookbooks, and other materials are available.

Disabled

National Easter Seal Society
2023 West Ogden Avenue
Chicago, IL 60612
(312) 243-8400

Provides rehabilitation to children and adults with disabilities from any cause. Programs include medical rehabilitation, recreation, housing, transportation, equipment loans, and other services for the treatment and management of disabling conditions. Booklets and pamphlets are available upon request.

Epilepsy

Epilepsy Foundation of America
4351 Garden City Drive

Landover, MD 20785
(301) 459-3700

Conducts programs in research, public and professional education, and patient services. There are local chapters in many states. Free literature is available upon request.

Genetic diseases

National Genetics Foundation
P.O. Box 1374
New York, NY 10101
(212) 586-5800

Encourages prevention and treatment of genetic diseases through service to physicians and to families who have, or suspect, an inherited disorder. There is a small charge for this service.

Heart

American Heart Association
7320 Greenville Avenue
Dallas, TX 75231
(214) 373-6300

Offers educational programs and materials about cardiovascular diseases and their prevention through local chapters.

Kidney

National Kidney Foundation
Two Park Avenue
New York, NY 10016
(800) 622-9010

Provides information; local affiliates provide referral services, information, and community programs. Call the toll-free number listed for referrals and other information.

Multiple sclerosis

National Multiple Sclerosis Society
205 East 42nd Street
New York, NY 10017
(212) 986-3240

Is concerned with research into the cause, prevention, and cure of multiple sclerosis. Local chapters provide client services that may include special clinics, aids to daily living, and counseling and referral services. Public and professional educational materials are available from the society and its chapters.

Muscular dystrophy

Muscular Dystrophy Association
810 Seventh Avenue
New York, NY 10019
(212) 586-0808

Sponsors international research seeking effective treatments and cures for muscular dystrophy and related neuromuscular disorders; maintains nationwide network of clinics for diagnosis, medical care, and counseling. Through affiliates, provides wheelchairs, lifts, braces, and other orthopedic aids; offers educational and recreational programs adapted to patients' needs; provides professional and public health education. Literature is available on request.

Respiratory

American Lung Association
1740 Broadway
New York, NY 10019
(212) 315-8700

Helps eradicate tuberculosis, control other respiratory diseases, discourage cigarette smoking, and eliminate air pollution through research and education. Local affiliates help parents and teachers develop child health programs. Booklets, films, and filmstrips are available from local affiliates upon request.

Health

American Academy of Pediatrics
P.O. Box 927, 141 Northwest Point Road
Elk Grove Village, IL 60009
(708) 228-5005

Provides information and assistance on child-health problems to parents and teachers.

American Dental Association
211 East Chicago Avenue
Chicago, IL 60611
(800) 621-8099

The national professional organization for dentists. Provides literature on dental health upon request.

American Medical Association
535 North Dearborn Street
Chicago, IL 60610
(312) 645-5000

The national professional physician membership organization. Answers general inquiries directed to its library.

American Podiatric Medical Association
9312 Old Georgetown Road
Bethesda, MD 20814
(301) 571-9200

A national association of podiatrists. Provides literature, films, filmstrips, and slides about the growth and care of feet to parents, teachers, and children upon request.

Learning and social development

American Camping Association, Inc.
5000 State Road, 67N
Martinsville, IN 46151
(317) 342-8456

Promotes the improvement and development of organized camping for children and adults. Furnishes information about accredited camps for children. A publications catalog is available on request.

Association for Children and Adults with Learning Disabilities
4156 Library Road
Pittsburgh, PA 15234
(412) 341-1515

Offers guidance concerning a wide range of learning disabilities, including dyslexia, hyperactivity, attention deficit disorder, and poor motor coordination. A free information kit is available.

Boys Club of America
771 First Avenue
New York, NY 10010
(212) 351-5900

An association of 275 North American Jewish community centers and Young Men's and Young Women's Hebrew Associations (YM-YWHA). Local centers conduct nursery schools and educational programs for preschoolers, summer day camps, physical education programs, and social work programs for school-age children.

National Federation for Catholic Youth Ministry
3900-A Harewood Rd. NE
Washington, DC 20017
(202) 636-3825

Founded in 1982 to replace and expand services of previous groups. The Federation provides national leadership, support, and direction for adults and youth in youth ministry. Its goals are met through a variety of programs and services.

The National Conference of Christians and Jews, Inc.
71 Fifth Avenue
New York, NY 10019
(212) 206-0006

A national organization that educates people about racial, religious, and nationality prejudices. Conducts a five-part program to better human relations in the United States. This organization provides a variety of guided workshops and institutes on community relations and the administration of justice, youth programs, courses in how to rear children without prejudice, human relations seminars and institutes for teachers. It also conducts interreligious programs for better interfaith understanding.

Play Schools Association, Inc.
19 W. 44th Street
New York, NY 10036
(212) 921-2940

Holds workshops and discussion groups for parents, teachers, and volunteers concerned with recreational facilities for children. Conducts after-school learning centers for "latchkey" children. Pamphlets and films are available.

United States Department of Health and Human Services
Office of Human Development Services
Administration for Children, Youth, and Families
Hubert Humphrey Building
3rd and Independence SW
Washington, DC 20201
(202) 472-7257

Deals with welfare of children from birth through adolescence, particularly children from low-income or troubled families; children and youth in need of foster care, adoption, or other child welfare services; handicapped children; runaway youth; and children from Native American and migrant families. Provides technical help to local groups with programs to meet the problems of domestic violence. The Head Start Bureau helps children from low-income families with educational, health, nutrition, and social services. The Children's Bureau helps state and local agencies develop programs for families in crisis; adoption of children with special needs; foster care; prevention of child abuse and neglect. The Family and Youth Services Bureau helps runaways and their families; it funds shelter programs which include family counseling and family reunification. The national magazine *Children Today* is published for parents, professionals, and others interested in children and youth.

Mental health

American Association of Psychiatric Services for Children
1133 15th Street, NW, Suite 1000
Washington, DC 20005
(202) 420-9713

A membership organization of psychiatric clinics for children. Local approved clinics (both inpatient and outpatient) vary as to age range and services. The association guides parents and teachers in selecting an appropriate clinic.

National Catholic Educational Association
1077 30th Street, NW, Suite 100
Washington, DC 20007
(202) 337-6232

Coordinates Catholic treatment facilities and programs for the handicapped, including treatment for autism, deafness, hearing

impairments, learning disabilities, mental retardation, and visual handicaps. Publishes a directory of facilities nationwide.

National Down's Syndrome Congress
180 Dempster Street
Park Ridge, IL 60068
(800) 232-NDSC

Oversees 500 local groups that provide aid to parents of children with Down's syndrome; coordinates the activities of local parent organizations. Booklets and an extensive bibliography are available.

National Mental Health Association
1021 Prince Street
Alexandria, VA 22314-2971
(703) 684-7722

Works for the care and treatment of people with mental illnesses. Local affiliates provide referrals and information about community services, special education, and treatment programs for children with mental illnesses. Information is available upon request.

U.S. Bureau of Community Health Care Delivery and Assistance
Health Services Administration
5600 Fishers Lane
Rockville, MD 20857
(202) 625-8400

Operates outpatient medical facilities providing evaluation, treatment, and follow-up services to children suspected or diagnosed as mentally retarded.

Welfare and safety

American Public Welfare Association
1125 Fifteenth Street NW, Suite 300
Washington, DC 20005
(202) 293-7550

A national organization of public human service employees, agencies, and others interested in public human services. Provides information about public human services.

American Red Cross

A national nonprofit organization reliant on volunteers to carry out its congressionally chartered responsibility of providing disaster preparedness and relief as well as assistance to members of the armed forces, their families, and veterans. More than 2,900 chapters carry out programs in blood donor services; health, including a donor organ and tissue transplant service; safety; and various community assistance programs. More than ten million volunteers, including blood donors and schoolchildren, help the Red Cross.

Contact local chapters for various publications on services or to volunteer.

Big Brothers / Big Sisters of America
230 N. 13th Street
Philadelphia, PA 19107
(215) 567-7000

A national organization that matches school-age children in need of mature friendship and guidance with adult volunteers on a one-to-one basis. Volunteers are screened and supervised by social work professionals.

Child Welfare League of America, Inc.
440 First Street NW
Washington, DC 20001
(202) 638-2952

A national, privately supported federation of private and public agencies serving children and their families. Develops and upgrades standards for child welfare services. Sponsors annual regional training conferences, collects and disseminates information, publishes professional material, works with other national and international organizations to improve conditions affecting the welfare of children.

OURS, Inc.
3307 Highway 100 N.
Suite 203
Minneapolis, MN 55422
(612) 535-4829

Offers problem-solving assistance and information about adoption—including transcultural and transracial adoption—and parenting resource information for all kinds of situations.

Canada

Diseases and physical handicaps

Arthritis

The Arthritis Society of Canada
250 Bloor Street East, Suite 401
Toronto, Ontario M4W 3P2
(416) 967-1414

Provides funding for research, patient care, and public education. Helps establish patient support groups. In some provinces, the society develops services such as pool therapy and home-visit programs for patients of all ages.

Blindness

The Canadian Council of the Blind
510-220 Dundas Street
London, Ontario N6A 1H3
(519) 433-3946

Seeks to aid the blind and visually impaired through social association, recreation, and advocacy throughout Canada.

The Canadian National Institute for the Blind
1931 Bayview Avenue
Toronto, Ontario M4G 4C8
(416) 480-7580

Seeks to improve the condition of the blind and partially sighted of Canada, to prevent blindness, and to promote sight enhancement. Conducts a program of rehabilitation and prevention of blindness for children and adults. Aids parents of blind and partially sighted children with counseling and services designed to supplement the child's education. Provides guidance and counseling for those entering the labor force or planning a university education.

Cancer

The Canadian Cancer Society
130 Bloor Street West, Suite 1001
Toronto, Ontario M5S 2V7
(416) 961-7223

Seeks to control cancer through an educational program of considerable scope. Offers material and emotional support to people living with cancer and to their families. Finances cancer research projects. Films, filmstrips, posters, and pamphlets are available.

Cystic fibrosis

Canadian Cystic Fibrosis Foundation
2 College Street
Toronto, Ontario M4P 1P2
(416) 960-6268

Conducts research into the basic causes and treatment of cystic fibrosis, and aids those afflicted with cystic fibrosis. Films and literature are available from the foundation.

Deafness

The Canadian Hearing Society
271 Spadina Road
Toronto, Ontario M5R 2V3
(416) 964-9595

An organization serving deaf and hard-of-hearing children and adults. Provides information to parents on options for communication and education, such as sign language or oral interpreting, technical devices, audiological services, and vocational rehabilitation and employment services.

Disabled

Canadian Rehabilitation Council for the Disabled
1 Yonge Street, Suite 2110
Toronto, Ontario M5E 1E5
(416) 862-0430

An association of nonprofit organizations, including Easter Seals and Ability Funds, at the national, provincial, and regional levels directed toward ensuring comprehensive rehabilitation services for physically disabled children and adults.

Heart

Canadian Heart Foundation
1 Nicholas Street, Suite 1200
Ottawa, Ontario K1N 7B7
(613) 237-4361

A federation of provincial heart foundations throughout Canada. Information on heart and blood vessel disease is available to parents, teachers, schools, and other interested parties through the provincial foundations. Requests from the U.S. for materials not available from the American Heart Association should be made to the national office of the Canadian Heart Foundation.

Muscular dystrophy

The Muscular Dystrophy Association of Canada
150 Eglinton East
Toronto, Ontario M5H 2T7
(416) 488-0030

Supports research programs. Provides direct services to MDAC clients and their families through a network of regional offices and local chapters. Literature is available.

Respiratory

Canadian Lung Association
75 Albert Street
Ottawa, Ontario K1P 5E7
(613) 237-1208

A national voluntary health organization concerned with the prevention and control of lung disease. Carries out programs in medical research, rehabilitation, and public education. For information, contact the provincial lung association.

Health and welfare

Canadian Dental Association
1815 Alta Vista Drive
Ottawa, Ontario K1G 3Y6
(613) 523-1770

The national organization of members of the dental profession in Canada. CDA seeks to advance the practice of dentistry and to improve public dental health. Services include dental health pamphlets and booklets.

The Canadian Red Cross Society
460 Jarvis Street
Toronto, Ontario M4Y 1H6
(416) 923-6692

A national voluntary organization dedicated to the improvement of health, the prevention of disease, and the mitigation of suffering throughout the world. Its activities are aimed at assisting victims of war and natural disasters; at providing water safety devices, blood, emergency services, and first aid; and at meeting the health and welfare needs of the community. Publications on all Red Cross programs are available at national, provincial, and branch levels.

Department of National Health and Welfare Public Affairs
Brooke Claxton Building
Ottawa, Ontario K1A 0K9
(613) 957-2991

Provides advisory and consultative services. Prepares educational material—booklets, manuals, posters, pamphlets—for parents and professionals. Prominent among these is *The Canadian Mother and Child*, a handbook for mothers. Provincial departments distribute all materials.

Learning and social development

Canadian Council of Christians and Jews
49 Front Street East
Toronto, Ontario M5E 1B3
(416) 364-3101

A national organization seeking to educate people about religious, racial, linguistic, and cultural prejudices. Among its many human relations programs, it sponsors a project to promote better understanding between urban and native youths.

The Canadian Education Association
252 Bloor Street West, Suite 8-200
Toronto, Ontario M5S 1V5
(416) 924-7721

A national association whose membership is drawn from senior educational administrators, trustees, etc., and is supported by tax funds. Its information service prepares and distributes reports on current education activities and projects; publishes *Newsletter*, *Le Bulletin*, and *Education Canada*, annually publishes *CEA Handbook* listing names and addresses of senior education officials in school boards and departments of education; and publishes *Directory of Education Studies in Canada* and *Canadian Education Index*.

Canadian Home and School and Parent-
 Teacher Federation
323 Chapel Street
Ottawa, Ontario K1N 7Z2
(613) 234-7292

The federation of provincial and local associations. Publications on parent education are available from the federation.

Young Women's Christian Association of / du Canada
80 Gerrard Street East
Toronto, Ontario M5B 1G6
(416) 593-9886

A national voluntary organization serving 46 YWCA's and YM-YWCA's across Canada. Dedicated to the development and improved status of women and their families. Services include child care, residences and shelters, fitness activities, wellness programs, and adult education.

Mental health

Canadian Mental Health Association
2160 Yonge Street
Toronto, Ontario M4S 2Z3
(416) 789-7959

Concerned with improving services for people with mental disorders. Conducts programs promoting prevention. Provides support through speakers, literature, and films for parents of children with emotional and learning disorders and for professional groups working with them.

G. Allen Roeher Institute
York University
4700 Keele Street
Downsview, Ontario M3J 1P3
(416) 661-9611

A federation of groups working on behalf of the mentally retarded in Canada. Local associations operate summer camps and other recreational programs, and provide strategies for community living and self-determination.

Books for parents

A great many people have had a great deal to say about child development and related subjects dealing with child guidance, family living and the changing family, education, sex education, special needs, and health. The books and video cassettes listed here are but a small sampling of the wealth of interesting literature to help you in raising your child. The article AGENCIES AND ORGANIZATIONS INTERESTED IN THE WELFARE OF CHILDREN lists some of the specialized sources that offer pamphlets and other literature.

Before You Were Three: How You Began to Walk, Talk, Explore and Have Feelings by Robbie H. Harris and Elizabeth Levy. Delacorte, 1981. Paperback.

Between Parent and Child by Haim G. Ginott. Avon, 1969. Paperback.

Childbirth and Marriage: The Transition to Parenthood by Tracy Hotchner. Avon, 1988. Paperback.

Child of Mine: Feeding with Love and Good Sense by Ellyn Satter. Bull Publishing, 1986. Paperback.

Childhood Stress: Don't Let Your Child Be a Victim by Barbara Kucsen. Dell, 1986. Paperback.

Children in the Crossfire: The Tragedy of Parental Kidnapping by Sally Abrahms. Atheneum, 1984. Paperback.

A Child's Journey: Forces That Shape the Lives of Our Young by Julius Segal and Herbert Yahraes. McGraw, 1979. Paperback.

The Conspiracy Against Childhood by Eda J. LeShan. Atheneum, 1967. Paperback.

Crisis in the Classroom: The Remaking in American Education by Charles E. Silberman. Random House, 1970.

Dare to Discipline by James Dobson. Tyndale, 1977. Paperback.

Dialogues with Mothers by Bruno Bettelheim. Free Press, 1962. Also Avon, paperback.

Dr. Spock's Baby and Child Care: Fortieth Anniversary Edition by Benjamin M. Spock, M.D. and Michael B. Rothenberg, M.D. Dutton, 1985. Paperback.

Dr. Spock Talks with Mothers: Growth and Guidance by Benjamin M. Spock, M.D. Greenwood, 1982.

Doing Drugs by Bruce Jackson and Michael Jackson. St. Martin's, 1983. Paperback.

Don't Push Your Preschooler by Louise B. Ames and Joan A. Chase. Rev. ed., Harper, 1981.

The Erosion of Childhood by Valerie P. Suransky. Univ. of Chicago Press, 1982. Also in paperback.

Feeding Your Child: From Infancy to Six Years Old by Louise Lambert-Legacé. Rev. ed., Beaufort Books, 1983. Paperback.

The First Three Years of Life by Burton L. White. Rev. ed., Prentice-Hall, 1987. Also in paperback.

The Games Children Play by A. H. Chapman. Berkley Publishing, 1978. Paperback.

Good Schools for Young Children by Sarah H. Leeper and others. 5th ed., Macmillan, 1984.

The Handbook for Latchkey Children and Their Parents by Lynette Long and Thomas Long. Berkley, 1984. Paperback.

Helping Children Overcome Learning Difficulties by Jerome Rosner. Rev. ed., Walker, 1979. Also in paperback from same publisher.

Helping Children with Problems: What Parents and Teachers Can Do by June M. Schasre. Walker, 1978.

Helping Parents Help Their Children by Eugene L. Arnold, M.D., ed. Brunner-Mazel, 1978.

Hide or Seek by James Dobson. Expanded and updated, Revell, 1974. Paperback.

How Children Fail by John Holt. Rev. ed., Delacorte, 1982. Also in paperback from Dell.

How Children Learn by John Holt. Rev. ed., Dell, 1988. Paperback.

How It Feels to Be Adopted by Jill Krementz. Knopf, 1988. Also in paperback.

How to Parent by Fitzhugh Dodson. New American Library, 1973. Paperback.

The Hurried Child: Growing Up Too Fast Too Soon by David Elkind. Addison-Wesley, 1981. Also in paperback from same publisher.

Infants and Mothers: Differences in Development by T. Berry Brazelton, M.D. Delacorte, 1983. Also Dell, paperback.

The Intimate Environment: Exploring Marriage and the Family by Arlene S. Skolnick. 4th ed., Scott, Foresman, 1987.

Jane Brody's Good Food Book by Jane Brody. Bantam, 1987. Paperback.

Mind and Media: The Effects of Television, Video Games, and Computers by Patricia M. Greenfield. Harvard, 1984. Also in paperback from same publisher.

Mister Rogers' Playbook: Insights and Activities for Parents and Children by Fred Rogers and Barry Head. Berkley, 1986. Paperback.

Mister Rogers Talks with Parents by Fred Rogers and Barry Head. Berkley, 1985. Paperback.

Mothers, Fathers, and Children: Explorations in the Formation of Character in the First Seven Years by Sylvia Brody and Sydney Axelrod. International Universities Press, 1978.

Our Special Child: A Guide to Successful Parenting of Handicapped Children by Bette M. Ross. Walker, 1981.

Parent's Guide to Child Nutrition by Boston Children's Hospital Staff. Addison-Wesley, 1986.

A Parent's Guide to Children's Reading by Nancy Larrick. 5th ed., Westminster, 1983.

The Read-Aloud Handbook by Jim Trelease. Rev. ed., Penguin, 1985. Paperback.

Real Men Enjoy Their Kids! How to Spend Quality Time with the Children in Your Life by Steven Shechtman and Wenda G. Singer. Abingdon, 1983. Paperback.

79 Ways to Calm a Crying Baby by Diana S. Greene. Pocket Books, 1988. Paperback.

Sexual Abuse: Let's Talk about It by Margaret O. Hyde. Rev. ed., Westminster, 1987.

Signals: What Your Child Is Really Telling You by Paul Ackerman and Murray Kappelman. New American Library, 1980. Paperback.

Something's Wrong with My Child: A Parent's Handbook about Children with Learning Disabilities by Milton Brutten and others. Harcourt, 1979. Paperback.

Teaching the Child under Six by James L. Hymes, Jr. 3rd ed., Merrill, 1981. Paperback.

These Are Your Children by Gladys G. Jenkins and Helen S. Shacter. 4th ed., Scott, Foresman, 1975.

Toddlers and Parents by T. Berry Brazelton, M.D. Dell, 1976. Paperback.

Twin Care by Marci Cunningham. Backwoods Books, 1987. Paperback.

Understanding Your Parents by Harold Rashkis, M.D., and Levon Tashjian, M.D. Stickley, 1978.

What Every Baby Knows by T. Berry Brazelton, M.D. Addison-Wesley, 1987.

What Every Child Would Like His Parents to Know to Help Him with the Emotional Problems of Everyday Life by Lee Salk. Simon & Schuster, 1984. Paperback.

Whole Child-Whole Parent by Polly B. Berends. Rev. ed., Harper, 1987. Paperback.

Why Isn't Johnny Crying? Coping with Depression in Children by Donald H. McKnew, Jr., and others. Norton, 1983.

Working and Caring by T. Berry Brazelton, M.D. Addison-Wesley, 1987. Also in paperback.

Your Child's Self-Esteem: The Key to His Life by Dorothy Briggs. Doubleday, 1975. Paperback.

Video Cassettes

Baby Basics. Vida Health, 1987.

Diapers and Delirium: Care and Comfort for Parents of Newborns. Lifecycle Productions, 1987.

Infant Health Care and *Infant Development* by Johnson & Johnson and T. Berry Brazelton, M.D. Whittle and A. Eric Jones Productions, 1987.

Medical Guide

It is always best to have a medical doctor on whom you can call if your child becomes ill. A continuing relationship with your child's doctor, a relationship that starts with the in-hospital examination of your baby at birth, has many advantages. Through periodic examinations and immunizations, the doctor gets to know your child intimately and establishes a rapport with the child. The doctor's abilities to diagnose a condition and treat your child whenever necessary gains your confidence.

This guide is not meant to replace your family doctor, dentist, or other health care professional. There is, of course, no substitute for consulting a trained professional on matters involving the health or well-being of your child.

What this guide can do is help you recognize and treat those symptoms that call for immediate first aid—as in the case of shock. It can help you recognize symptoms that require diagnosis and treatment by the doctor—a rash and sore throat, high fever and lethargy. Above all, it can help make communications between you and the doctor clearer and more complete.

Caring for a sick child

By Morris Green, M.D.

All parents try to keep their children healthy. But in spite of all efforts, a child is bound to become ill occasionally. Suddenly, for no apparent reason, the child has a high fever, has an earache, or complains of a stomachache. The child may catch chicken pox or some other communicable disease.

When your child becomes ill, keep calm. Remember that most children quickly bounce back to normal after an ordinary illness. It is quite natural for a child to worry about not feeling well. The child may be listless and irritable. Be sympathetic, but not unduly so. If you look grim and anxious, your child will react to your obvious anxiety by becoming even more upset.

Before you call your doctor, be prepared to answer questions and give certain information about your child's condition. Take the child's temperature before calling the doctor, and tell the doctor whether you used the thermometer orally or rectally. The doctor will want to know if the child has a rash, a sore throat, swollen glands, or aching muscles. Report rapid breathing or any other symptoms that you think are serious. Any clues you can give the doctor about your child's condition will help with the diagnosis and prescription.

Explain that getting plenty of rest and doing what the doctor says will help your child get well soon. Be reassuring. If your child is seriously ill and must be confined to bed for a time, usually it is a good idea to explain enough about the illness to lessen any fears a child may have. Do not burden your child with all the details, but do not lie, either.

Making a sick child comfortable. Ideally, the sickroom should be a room that is easily reached from any other part of the house and from which you can hear your child call you. Keep the room uncluttered, softly lighted, and well ventilated. Ideally, room temperature should be kept between 68° and 72° F. (20° and 22° C). At this temperature, the child will not need heavy blankets to stay warm.

Give your child sponge baths and wash only one part of the body at a time. Keep the rest of the child's body wrapped in a large towel to prevent chills. Be sure to dry the skin thoroughly.

Giving medicine to the child. Your child may balk at taking medicine, especially if you indicate by words or facial expressions that it tastes bad. The best way to give medicine is to be matter-of-fact. If the child continues to fuss, mix the medicine with some fruit juice. If the medicine is a pill, crush the pill and mix it with a spoonful of jelly, honey, or syrup in order to make it easier for the child to swallow.

Always follow your doctor's instructions. If you have any questions, be sure you understand the doctor's answers. Write down the times you are to give your child medicine and any instructions about diet and special treatment. Keep all medicine out of your child's reach. Never give the child medicine that is left over from a previous similar illness without consulting your doctor.

Some day-care centers and child-care providers will accept children who have colds or other mild illnesses. These facilities and care providers usually have an area set aside for these children so that other well children will not be exposed to the illness. Some hospitals provide daytime care for sick children of working parents. For a fee, parents can drop their children off at the hospital in the morning. The children are cared for during the day by professional caregivers. Then the parents can pick up the children after work.

When the child goes to the hospital. Sometimes it is not possible to care for a sick child at home. The child may need an operation, or the illness may be so serious that the child requires hospitalization. Most children become concerned if they must go to the hospital. Usually, it is anticipation and uncertainty that worries children—not the actual experience. Even when they do not seem concerned, they may have many anxieties about being in the hospital.

It is wise for parents to prepare children for hospitalization by telling them what to expect from the time they enter the hospital to the time they are ready to go home. If you are not familiar with hospital procedure, take the time to find out. Many hospitals provide this information in brochures. A prehospitalization visit may also be possible. The child will accept the situation better if convinced that you know about the place and that he or she will be well treated while there. Do not promise the child that the hospital stay will be an enjoyable experience. On the other hand, do not stress the possibility that it may be unpleasant. Be as matter-of-fact as possible.

You need not go into great detail, but you can describe those parts of hospital procedure that are usually most reassuring to a child. For instance, you can mention the name bracelet that the child will wear while in the hospital. If possible, you should stay with your young child during the hospitalization. If this is not possible, you can tell the child that nurses will be there to help when help is needed.

Children who are going to have surgery can be told that they will fall asleep before the operation and wake up after the operation.

School-age children who are accustomed to spending time away from the family and who adjust easily to new situations may look forward to the hospital stay as a new adventure. It may not, however, be so simple for preschoolers. In spite of knowing what to expect, they may become frightened if the parents are not there with them. If parents leave, preschoolers may feel that their parents are deserting them at a time when they need the parents most. Very young children may not be sure that their parents will return. If it is impossible for you to stay, a hospital staff member should be present during your leave-taking. Your child will feel less abandoned if someone is at hand to provide comfort and cuddling after you leave. Never slip away without telling your child that you are leaving, but you will come back again.

Help your child select one or two favorite toys to take to the hospital. Take the child little surprises when you visit. Visit and call your child as often as you can so that the child feels loved and missed.

While your child is recovering, whether after returning from the hospital or from an illness at home, you can make the recovery less tedious. See that the child has enough suitable toys, games, and books to keep busy. If school has been missed, ask the teacher for work that the child can do at home. Then set aside time for study periods when you have the time to help the child study.

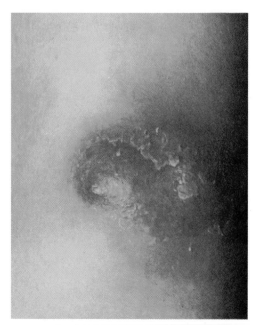

Abscesses of the skin are usually red, warm, swollen, and painful. Hot compresses often can be used to bring the abscesses to a head so that they open and drain.

Abscess is a collection of pus in any infected part of the body. Abscesses occur most commonly in the skin. They also may form around the appendix as a complication of appendicitis, or around a tooth. Perhaps the most common types of abscesses are pimples and boils.

Abcesses occur when bacteria infect body tissue. Blood flow to the area increases to fight the infection, and pus forms. Blood vessels expand to make room for the increased fluid, and the infected area swells.

Many abscesses open and drain naturally or with the application of hot compresses. Some have to be opened by a doctor. Some subside and do not have to be opened. Do not squeeze abscesses, because bacteria can get into the bloodstream and cause infections elsewhere.

Keeping all parts of the body clean helps to prevent infections that can cause abscesses. Antibiotics may clear up an infection, but should be used only as a doctor directs.   T.M.H.

See also **Acne; Boil**

Accidents. Every child gets bruises, bumps, and scrapes. And minor injuries, although momentarily upsetting, may be educational in the long run. They teach the child valuable safety concepts. Of course, serious accidents are another matter.

Do all you reasonably can to protect your child from accidents. But be careful not to overprotect and give your child the idea that the whole world is a dangerous place. Fit the precautions you take to the child's age and surroundings. Certain precautions are especially necessary if you have an infant or a curious toddler. Others are important if you live close to a busy traffic area, or if you have a lot of power machinery.

Protecting your baby. The younger children are, the more they need to be protected. A baby, of course, requires almost total protection. The high chair and stroller should have straps to keep the infant from tumbling out. Do not leave a baby alone in an infant seat on a table, couch, bed, or car seat. The plastic seat may slide off and fall to the floor. The crib should have sturdy sides. As soon as the baby starts to crawl, put safety gates at the top and bottom of stairways. A playpen may also be used selectively when you are busy in the kitchen. However, do not pen a child in too much. Do not use baby walkers, which can be unsafe. Instead, be sure your child has adequate "crawl and explore" time under your supervision.

Make sure all toys are safe. Do not give the baby beads or rattles that can be swallowed. Avoid stuffed animals with tiny button eyes that can be pulled off and swallowed. Toy manufacturers' age suggestions are usually accurate.

Thin plastic, such as that used by dry cleaners, can quickly suffocate a baby. Never cover a crib mattress with it or leave it where your baby can get to it.

Surprisingly, more children drown at home than in public pools. These are usually young children left alone in bathtubs, in wading pools, or near swimming pools—sometimes for only a few minutes. Never leave your child alone in the bathtub, even to answer the phone or the door.

Pails of water, and even the toilet bowl, may be dangerous, depending upon the child's age. Some deaths from falling into pails of water and toilet bowls have been reported.

Curiosity and caution. As soon as children can creep, they peek into every corner and try to stick their fingers and toys into electrical wall outlets. Eliminate this hazard by covering the sockets with caps that are available at most hardware stores. Remove extension cords when not in use.

To guard against electric shock, repair frayed cords and damaged appliances promptly. Have large appliances and power tools equipped with ground wires that divert current harmlessly into the earth. Then, if a short circuit develops, there is no danger to a child who touches the faulty appliance. Do not allow electric appliances near water, especially at bath time. Your child may touch the appliance with wet hands or pull it into the tub and be electrocuted.

Street and automobile safety. Automobile accidents are the greatest threat to children. From the time your child is able to understand, gradually teach traffic safety—to look both ways for cars before crossing a street, to cross only with the green light or the "walk" sign, to obey school patrols and crossing guards, and to walk on the left side of the road when there is no sidewalk. Point out the hazards of playing in the street and running into the road without first looking in both directions.

You should have a proper child safety restraint for your automobile to protect your child in case of an accident or a sudden stop. Up to about the age of 1, a child should ride in an infant seat. For a child age 1 to 4, use a child safety seat. Do not buy any restraint that does not meet federal safety standards. Children more than 4 or 5 years of age and weighing more than 40 pounds can use the car's safety belt.

Do not allow your child to stand on the seat, climb over seats, lean out of windows, or play in the rear of an open station wagon or truck. Special safety catches on doors are not necessary if the child is strapped in. Do not remove the inside door handles. In an emergency, a child might be trapped.

Bicycle safety. A bicycle provides pleasure, exercise, and transportation. But it can be a hazard for your child if it is not the right size, and if the child does not know how to use it safely. Be sure the bicycle is sturdy, has good brakes and tires, and is equipped with all the safety devices required by law.

Check the bicycle to be sure it is suitable for the child's height. Adjust the seat so that it is parallel to the ground. Then, have your child sit on the bicycle with one thigh, leg, and heel extended down in a straight line. The foot should rest comfortably on the pedal at its lowest point. The handlebars should be about as wide as your child's shoulders. The handlebar grips should be at right angles to the handlebar stem and a little higher than the seat.

Never buy a bicycle that is too big in the hope that the child will grow up to it. A bicycle that is too big or too small is hard to handle and may be the cause of an accident.

Your child should learn to ride the bicycle in the backyard or in a playground—not on the sidewalk, where pedestrians may be hit, or in the street, where there are cars.

While learning to handle a bicycle, children should also learn the importance of courtesy and safety. They should be able to recognize traffic signs and signals. They should know and obey all traffic regulations and safety rules pertaining to bicycles in your city. Local programs of bicycle safety will be successful only if parents support them, and if they insist that their children obey all rules.

Caution your child against showing off on a bicycle by jumping curbs or riding "no hands." Your child should not ride a bicycle at night, but if for any reason it is necessary, the bicycle should be equipped with front and rear lights and the child should wear light-colored clothing and a helmet.

Teach your child to keep the bicycle in top condition. Check periodically to be sure the brakes are in good working order and that the handlebars are securely fastened. A well-cared-for bicycle is safer than a neglected one and will last longer.

Burns are a hazard. Small children are fascinated by fire and sense little danger, and so they will walk right up to flames. Never leave your child in a room with an open gas fire or a burning fireplace. Make

Protect your child

Birth to 4 months
(Wriggles, rolls over)

Dangerous objects
Do not allow very small or sharp objects near your baby. Do not use objects not intended for play, such as a can of baby powder, to distract the child. Do not place a string or necklace around the baby's neck.

Fire
Do not smoke around the baby. Do not buy baby clothing or blankets that are flammable. Install smoke alarms in your house.

Motor vehicles
Never park a buggy where it might roll into traffic. Your baby's safest spot in a car is strapped in an infant safety restraint seat on the rear seat. Do not leave the baby alone in the car.

Play areas
The best play areas are a padded playpen or a blanket on the floor.

Stairs, doors, windows
Do not put your baby near an open door or window that is so low that the baby could roll out. Do not park the buggy near an open stairway.

Toys
Give your baby only large, soft toys and sturdy rattles. Do not give the baby toys with sharp points or edges.

Water
Before your baby's bath, check the water temperature with your elbow. While bathing the baby, hold the infant securely. Never leave the baby alone in a bathtub.

Special hazards
Keep crib sides up. Do not leave the baby alone in an infant seat on a couch or bed. Do not leave the baby alone on a changing table, bed, sofa, counter top, or chair. Do not put pillows on your baby's bed. Do not use filmy plastic sheets or coverings on the crib mattress. Do not carry, drink, or eat anything hot while you are holding your baby.

4 to 7 months
(Begins to sit and crawl)

Dangerous objects
Keep buttons, pins, beads, and pieces of hard food out of your baby's reach. Check the floors and the playpen for small objects before letting the baby play there.

Fire
Never leave your baby alone in the house. Do not smoke around the baby.

Motor vehicles
Keep your baby strapped in an infant safety restraint seat attached to the rear seat. Never leave the baby alone in a car.

Play areas
Your baby will love to play in the yard or on the porch, and possibly in a playpen. Keep these areas clean and free of things that might cause harm.

Poisons
Do not leave poisons, medicines, or other materials such as bleach, detergents, or baby powder within reach. Remove all harmful substances from the cabinet under the sink and other storage spaces.

Stairs, doors, windows
Put gates at stairways and porch steps. Never leave your baby alone near an open stairway, door, or window that is not securely screened.

Toys
Give your baby only soft rubber and soft plastic toys. Beware of toys small enough to swallow. Do not put strings of beads across the crib.

Water
Follow the same bath routine. Never leave your baby alone near water. A baby can drown quickly in only a few inches of it.

Special hazards
Do not put pillows on your baby's bed or filmy plastic sheets or coverings on the mattress. Do not leave your baby unattended on a bed or other high place.

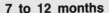

7 to 12 months

(Crawls, sits, stands, walks)

Dangerous objects

Put knives, scissors, pins, coins, and breakable objects high out of your baby's reach. Beware of dangling tablecloths and appliance cords. Do not give the baby such foods as peanuts, popcorn, or raisins that are easily breathed into the windpipe. Do not use baby clothing that has bells, pompons, or loose buttons that can be swallowed. Beware of sharp-edged furniture.

Fire

Empty ashtrays before your baby does. Never leave the baby in a room with an open, burning fireplace. Use a fireplace screen. Never let the baby crawl or walk around hot stoves or heaters. Do not leave hot liquids on table or counter tops where the baby may reach them. Do not carry hot liquids or foods near your child.

Motor vehicles

Keep your child strapped in an infant restraint seat. At home, never leave your child alone outside near driveways or traffic.

Play areas

The playpen is still the safest place for a child, especially when you are cooking.

Poisons

Lock up everything poisonous. Do not keep household chemicals under the sink. Do not keep lye drain cleaners in the house. Do not leave medicines where your baby can get them, not even in your purse. Keep syrup of ipecac in the home.

Stairs, doors, windows

Keep all gates closed. Keep screens locked or nailed in place.

Water

Watch your baby in the bath, wading pool, or even around a pail of water. In a boat, every child should wear a life jacket. Even if taught to swim, babies are not safe around water.

Special hazards

Put safety caps on wall sockets. Prevent your baby from chewing on cords. Do not leave plastic bags lying around.

1 to 2 years

(Crawls, walks, runs, climbs)

Dangerous objects

Keep sharp tools and glass objects out of your child's reach. Do not let a toddler eat popcorn, peanuts, or candy with nuts.

Fire

Keep matches and lighters out of reach. Never let your child near a trash burner or leaf fire. Teach your child that fire is hot and will burn.

Motor vehicles

Use a child safety seat. Teach your child not to run into the street or play in the driveway or near the street. Teach your child the importance of "buckling up."

Play areas

Fence the section of the yard where your child plays so that the child cannot wander into traffic. Supervise the child outdoors.

Poisons

Your child will eat anything and will climb great heights to get it. Lock up medicines (including aspirin), insecticides, and household chemicals (including kerosene and furniture polish). Never get your child to take pills by saying they are candy.

Stairs, doors, windows

You may need taller gates now. Watch your child carefully. Lock gates and doors to any dangerous areas. Use window guards on the upstairs windows. Do not use wax on stairs.

Toys

Everything your child picks up will go into the mouth. Avoid toys with removable parts (check the wheels on toy cars). Do not repaint toys with lead paint.

Water

Safety precautions are the same as for a younger child. Also, fence in ponds, pools, and cisterns.

Special hazards

Keep all hot appliances—toasters, irons—out of reach. Put a guard around heaters and radiators. Do not leave a chair where a child might use it to climb to a dangerously high place.

Protect your child

2 to 3 years
(Always investigating)

Dangerous objects
Turn in handles of pots on stove. Lock up power-operated tools. Do not allow your child near operating machinery, including power lawn mowers.

Fire
Do not let your child play with matches. Never let your child poke a fire. Beware of fluffy skirts around fire.

Motor vehicles
Your child should be kept in a safety seat. Teach your child how to cross the street, but not to cross it alone. Teach the meaning of traffic lights and walk signs. Do not let the child play near streets.

Play areas
Keep the play area in the yard free of dangerous debris. Check play equipment for slivers and loose bolts and nails. Supervise the child outdoors.

Poisons
Keep all poisonous substances locked up. Never leave empty containers where your child can find them. If your child swallows a poison, call the nearest poison control center. Keep the telephone number for the center handy for fast reference. Keep syrup of ipecac on hand, but do not use unless directed to do so by a physician.

Stairs, doors, windows
Your child can now open doors and possibly windows. Lock those that may lead to a dangerous situation. Keep stairs clear.

Toys
Balls, blocks, and stuffed animals (without bead eyes or other ornaments that can come loose and be swallowed) are good toys for this age.

Water
Supervise the bath closely. Do not leave your child alone in the bathroom. Begin to teach the child how to float. Never leave a child alone near a body of water.

Special hazards
Teach your child to play gently with pets and to avoid stray animals.

3 to 4 years
(Always in motion)

Dangerous objects
Same as for 2-year-old.

Fire
Same as for 2-year-old.

Motor vehicles
Teach your child never to chase a ball into the street. Make sure the child is kept in a safety seat.

Play areas
Teach your child that a closed gate means to stay in the yard. Check the child's activities frequently. Your child is now good at climbing fences and opening locked gates.

Poisons
Same as for 2-year-old.

Stairs, doors, windows
Never let your child lean out open windows. Caution about running up and down stairs. Tack down carpeting. Avoid using throw rugs that might be slipped on.

Toys
Your child can use simple playground equipment. Check all toys for sharp edges.

Water
Start teaching your child to swim. Do not let your child use an inner tube or inflated toys alone.

Special hazards
Never leave trunks or large picnic coolers where your child may crawl into them and suffocate. Warn about the dangers of abandoned refrigerators. Do not keep such refrigerators around; if you do, remove all their doors. Advise your child to be careful around strange animals.

4 to 6 years
(Getting independent)

Dangerous objects
Caution your child about picking up sharp or rusty objects. Tell him or her to avoid broken glass.

Fire
Store flammables out of reach. Begin to teach safety rules about fire. Children should not go near brush fire. Children should not turn on the stove.

Motor vehicles
Teach your child to obey traffic signals, crossing guards, and police officers. See to it that your child uses the car safety belt.

Play areas
Take your child to park playgrounds. Teach safe use of swings and slides. Supervise your child carefully.

Poisons
Same as for 2-year-old.

Stairs, doors, windows
Teach your child never to lock the door to any room, including the bathroom. Teach the child not to pound glass. Protect the glass in storm doors with an adequate glass guard, or replace the glass with plexiglass.

Toys
Keep your child's toys in good repair, or discard them. The child can throw and catch a ball. Warn your child not to dart into the street after the ball.

Water
Never let your child swim alone. Watch your child closely.

Special hazards
Let your child participate in home fire drills and practice escaping out the bedroom window. For second floors, get a portable ladder that attaches to a window and teach the child how to use it.

6 and older
(Goes to school)

Dangerous objects
Continue to lock up hazardous objects. Do not let your child use dangerous tools or power mowers. Stress that safety rules also apply away from home.

Fire
Teach your child first aid for burns, what to do if clothes catch fire, and how to call the fire department.

Motor vehicles
Be sure your child looks both ways before crossing a street. Teach the rules of bicycle safety.

Play areas
Warn your child about playing in construction areas, around large holes, in caves, and in abandoned or empty houses. Do not let your child play in the car.

Poisons
After 6 years, the child usually loses appetite for distasteful substances that can poison, but take no chances—tell your child what substances around the house are poisonous.

Stairs, doors, windows
Tell your child to sleep with the bedroom door closed to keep out smoke in case of fire.

Toys
Games, puzzles, creative toys, sports equipment. Teach your child to handle balls and bats safely.

Water
Sign your child up for formal swimming lessons. Stress that children should "always swim with a buddy."

Special hazards
Be sure your child knows what to do if lost, never to go with strangers, and how to handle emergencies.

your child keep a safe distance from burning trash, bonfires, and barbecues. Protect your child from hot substances—turn the handles of pots and pans toward the back or center of the stove, and put the cords of electric appliances out of reach.

Hot radiators and registers are especially hazardous to infants and toddlers. A brief contact can cause a serious burn.

Tap water scalds can also occur. Water heaters should be set below 120° F. (48° C.), and parents should test the bathwater before placing the child in it.

Fire safety. What can you do about your child's fondness for fires? First, do not provide the chance to experiment. Keep matches and cigarette lighters out of reach. Teach your child about fire and its dangers.

Never leave a young child alone in the house. A child can start a fire, or a fire can spring up and trap the child. A child panics easily in fire and may hide under a bed or in a closet. When your child is old enough, demonstrate how to escape from a fire, especially from the child's room. If the child sleeps on the second floor, buy a rope ladder that fastens to a window so the child can climb down in case of fire. Encourage your child to sleep with the bedroom door closed, because a door provides a barrier against fire and smoke. Teach your child never to open a door if a fire is suspected. Tell the child to first feel the doorknob and panels. If they are warm, the door should not be opened, because there are flames and superheated air on the other side. One whiff of hot air could fell a child in an instant. Equip your home with smoke detectors, and have your child inspect the detectors with you to ensure that they are in good working order.

Protection from poisons. Put locks on medicine cabinets, and keep other potentially dangerous materials safely out of reach. Until children are about 6 years old, they will eat anything, including bleach, medicines, insecticides, and cosmetics. Crawling children easily invade low spaces, such as under-sink cabinets, so never keep household chemicals there. Older children often search for pills that they think are candy. Flavored aspirin for children is a great menace. A child can swallow a lethal dose of 30 to 40

tablets in minutes. Do not leave drugs in a nightstand, briefcase, or purse, and never encourage your child to take medicine by calling it candy.

If your child swallows poison, call the nearest poison control center or your physician. Keep the telephone number of the poison control center in a handy place for reference. Have syrup of ipecac on hand, but do not use this unless directed to do so by a physician.

A child of 6 is less likely to drink bad-tasting substances, but develops new fascinations just as dangerous, such as guns, machinery, and fire. The 6-year-old is intensely serious about discovering how things work.

Guns are deadly. It is not enough just to hide a gun. Many children have found not only the guns, but also the ammunition. Often children insert the bullets, fire the guns, and kill playmates or themselves. Lock up empty guns and ammunition in separate places, so that your child cannot discover both at once. Never allow a loaded gun in the house.

Power machinery is treacherous. A young child should not be allowed around farm machinery, power tools, and power mowers unless carefully supervised. Do not allow your child near a power mower while it is being operated. The mower may throw off stones, wire, or even broken blades at tremendously high speeds. You can lessen the hazard by picking up loose objects before mowing.

Do not let an older child operate a power mower, power tools, or other hazardous machines without close supervision. Remember that a child may sneak into a workshop, and equip stationary tools with key-operated switches or plugs. Lock portable tools in a cabinet.

Swimming safety. One of the most important lifesaving skills children will learn, either from parents or in a class, is swimming. Children should follow strict swimming rules—they should never swim in quarries or other unsupervised places and never swim without a responsible person who can swim. Older children who swim should know how to administer CPR and other elementary first aid.

Avoiding animal bites. In many instances, the child, and not the animal, is the cause of a bite. To protect your child from animal bites, teach these safety precautions:

- Never touch a sick or injured animal.
- Never try manually to stop a fight between animals. Call an adult or use a stream of water from a hose.
- Never take food away from an animal.
- Never pet strange animals. M.G.

Acne is a condition in which the sebaceous (oil) glands become overactive and inflamed, causing a breakout of pimples on the skin. In severe acne, infections and abscesses form in the oil glands. Now, with present-day acne treatment, these problems can be avoided.

Acne develops mainly on the face, but it may also appear on the chest and back. It can occur at any age, but it develops most often during adolescence, when hormones produced by the adrenal and sex glands increase the activity of the oil glands. Why some children develop acne and other children do not is unknown.

Severe acne and consequent scarring can be avoided if the child carefully cares for the skin and follows a doctor's advice. With proper care, the acne should become less severe or disappear after a few years.

- The affected skin should be cleansed thoroughly at least two or three times a day with warm water and mild soap.
- The child should not squeeze or pinch pimples.
- Hair should be kept clean and dandruff free.
- The child should not take any medicine unless the doctor advises it.

A balanced diet is important, as are a happy environment, proper exercise, and adequate rest.

Encourage your child to follow the doctor's instructions. The doctor may advise oral or topical antibiotics, benzoyl peroxide, and/or vitamin A acid applications daily. In severe acne, oral retinoids may be prescribed or the doctor may refer the child to a dermatologist. Special surgery for acne may be helpful for removal of blackheads, pustules, and cysts.

Many young people worry excessively about skin disorders and become discouraged while trying to clear them up. You can reassure them by pointing out that acne is a common problem that can now be treated effectively. A.M.M.

See also **Abscess; Endocrine glands; Hair care; Nutrition; Vitamins**

Adenoids are clusters of lymphatic tissue located high up in the back part of the throat, directly behind the nasal cavity. Healthy adenoids may help prevent or overcome infection.

If the adenoids swell (usually because of an infection), they may block the passage from the nose and force mouth breathing. Or they may block the opening to the Eustachian tube (the passage leading to each middle ear). This may cause ear infections or impair hearing.

Location of the adenoids

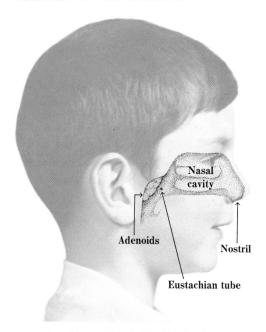

The adenoids are located in the back of the throat, behind the nasal cavity. They help fight infection.

The adenoids may have to be removed surgically if they obstruct nasal breathing, obstruct the Eustachian tube, cause recurring nasal or ear infections, or impair hearing. c.f.f.

See also **Anesthetics; Earaches; Swollen glands; Tonsillitis**

AIDS

AIDS stands for acquired immune deficiency syndrome. AIDS is a disease that causes people to suffer from opportunistic infections, which are serious infections caused by germs to which healthy people are resistant.

The human immunodeficiency virus (HIV) is the cause of AIDS. A person who has the human immunodeficiency virus is said to be HIV positive. People with AIDS related complex, or ARC, are HIV positive and have some symptoms, but do not have full-blown AIDS. AIDS in some cases is not preceded by ARC. The number of people who will develop ARC or AIDS because they are HIV positive is not known.

AIDS is one of the least transmittable communicable diseases of childhood. HIV is spread through transfusion of contaminated blood, use of contaminated hypodermic needles, or intimate sexual contact with a person who has the disease. It can also be transmitted from mother to baby while the baby is in the womb. In recent years, the blood supply has, for the most part, been made safe from HIV transmission.

In school, children with AIDS need no routine quarantine or isolation, although they may be exposed to germs that can cause opportunistic infections. Exclusion of a child with AIDS from day care is dependent upon how well the child can control secretions and the circumstances of the day-care facility. s.w.

Albinism is the absence of a pigment or coloring (melanin), in the skin, eyes, and hair. This inherited disorder results when a child lacks the enzyme needed to produce normal skin pigment. Albinism may be total or partial. In total albinism, the child's skin and hair are milk-white or platinum colored. The child's eyes are extremely sensitive to light, and the pupil and iris have a pinkish color. The eyes are weak and may also waver from side to side in a searching motion.

A child with partial albinism may have white skin patches that are usually present at birth. The child might have a triangular- or diamond-shaped white patch on the forehead and a streak of white hair immediately above the forehead. In ocular albinism, the pigmentary defect is confined to the eyes.

There is no specific treatment for albinism. An albino child may wear tinted eyeglasses if the eyes are sensitive. The child should wear proper clothing to protect the skin and sunglasses to protect the eyes from excessive exposure to sunlight. m.g.

Allergy is an abnormal reaction to substances that are neither harmful nor infectious to most people. Children of parents who are allergic inherit the tendency to become allergic, but do not necessarily inherit the same allergy that the parents suffer.

Substances that cause allergic reactions are called allergens. They include foods, drugs, pollens, airborne mold spores, animal dander (particles from hair, feathers, or skin), household dust, bacteria, viruses, parasites, and other substances. Light, heat, and cold may also cause allergic reactions. Emotional factors aggravate allergies. A doctor will take these factors into consideration when treating a child who suffers from such allergic diseases as hives, eczema, or asthma.

Allergens may enter the body by being inhaled, eaten, drunk, touched, or injected. When they enter the body, the allergic person develops antibodies. The interaction of the allergens and the antibodies releases histamines and other chemical substances that circulate throughout the body and cause allergic symptoms.

Allergic symptoms may occur in any part of the body. When they occur in the respiratory tract, the child may appear to have a cold. The child sneezes and has a runny or stopped-up nose, or wheezes, coughs, and has trouble breathing. When allergic symptoms appear in the skin, the child may have a rash or wheals (flat, hard ridges on the skin that usually itch). When symptoms occur in the central nervous system, the child may be irritable and have headaches or seizures. When they occur in the gastrointestinal tract, the child may have cramps, nausea, vomiting, or diarrhea. These reactions are often completely reversible so that no permanent damage results. Doctors often prescribe antihistamines and other drugs to relieve symptoms.

An allergy may develop at any time during a person's life. It usually develops gradually. At first, the body does not react to the substances. But, as exposure continues, an allergy results. Doctors do not know why one child develops an allergy to a substance that is harmless to another child.

Common allergies. Four common allergic diseases that children develop are asthma, eczema, hay fever, and hives.

Asthma affects the bronchial tubes. Common symptoms are coughing, wheezing, and labored breathing. These often worsen with exertion. The coughing commonly occurs at night. In children older than 9 months, the wheezing usually occurs when they exhale. In infants, the labored breathing is rapid and the child seems short of breath. Children 3 years old or older also feel tightness in the chest, or breathlessness. Common causes of asthma are airborne allergens and respiratory infections.

Eczema is a rash that occurs in patches on the skin and itches intensely. The patches may be red and oozing or crusty. Or they may be thickened, dry, and scaly. Foods, drugs, inhalants, and allergens that touch the skin are common causes.

Symptoms of hay fever include sneezing, stuffiness or blockage of the nose, runny nose, watering of the eyes, and itching of the eyes, nose, ears, and the roof of the mouth. Pollens, airborne molds, and house dust are usually responsible for hay fever.

Hives are raised, whitish wheals with reddened edges. The wheals usually itch. Food, drugs, and insect bites are common causes of acute (sudden and severe) hives.

Some children's allergies improve as the child grows older. Other children develop complications and become worse. About one half of all allergic adults developed allergies before they were 11 years old. If you think your child has an allergy, consult the doctor. Treatment depends on the severity of the symptoms.

Determining allergies. A doctor begins the search for the cause of an allergy by compiling a detailed history of the illness, especially the events preceding the first attack. The doctor tries to relate the symptoms to foods, substances inside and outside the home, the time of day, the season, and other factors. Usually a doctor can determine the possible allergen through this history. The doctor will then prescribe removing the suspected allergen from the child's diet or environment in order to determine if the substance is causing the reaction. For example, a child who coughs when going to bed and for a short time in the morning may stop coughing when a feather pillow or down comforter is replaced with one filled with synthetic fibers.

Unfortunately, treatment is sometimes complex. Often allergic symptoms are caused by a combination of several allergens. Also, house dust, animal dander, and airborne molds may be persistent factors. The attack may also be triggered by infections, emotional upsets, weather changes, or simply an overload of allergens.

Skin tests help identify possible allergens. These tests are simple and can usually be done in one or two sessions:

■ Using the prick test, the doctor makes small, light pricks, usually on the child's arms. With each prick, the doctor places a small amount of a suspected allergen. If the child is allergic to a substance on a test area, that area becomes red, swollen, and itchy.

■ In another method of testing, the doctor injects a small amount of the possible allergen under the child's skin and waits about 10 to 20 minutes for a reaction.

■ With an infant covered with eczema, or with a highly emotional older child, the doctor may use the indirect, or enzyme assay, method. A blood sample is taken from the child and, after preparation, it is tested in an allergist's laboratory. When monoclonal antibodies are used, results can usually be

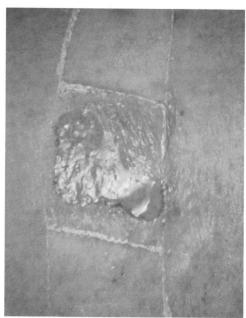

Doctors sometimes use patch tests to determine if a child is allergic to a substance upon contact. Possible allergens are placed on unbroken skin, covered, and left touching the skin. These pictures show two different reactions. The one on the left is moderately severe, the one on the right is very severe.

determined and interpreted for the patient or parents in less than two days.

■ In the patch test, the doctor places the possible allergens on unbroken skin and covers them, usually for 48 hours, to determine what substances may produce an allergic reaction upon contact.

Skin tests may be useful, although their uses are limited. There is no correlation between the size of the reaction and the child's sensitivity. And not every positive skin test is significant, because irritants such as tobacco, cow hair, mustard, cottonseed oil, and spinach can cause false positive tests. Also, with few exceptions, food allergies are not reliably detected. The food may cause an allergic reaction only after it has been altered by digestion. Consequently, foods are often tested through a controlled diet as well. Avoiding the suspected food allergen should bring relief from allergic symptoms. Including it again in the diet should produce the symptoms. Eggs, fish, nuts, beans (which include peanuts), pork, and milk are common food allergens.

Treatment. Doctors may treat allergic disorders such as hay fever and asthma with a series of shots over a period of years. Repeated injections of gradually increasing doses of the responsible inhaled allergens help build up resistance to these allergens.

Doctors usually treat an allergy by eliminating the allergen from the child's surroundings. For instance, it may be necessary to remove a dog or cat, feather pillows, or wall-to-wall carpeting from the child's home, because otherwise immunization is generally ineffective.

When a particular food is the allergen, the doctor may suggest eliminating it from the child's diet. For example, if milk is the allergen, all foods that contain milk—such as ice cream, cheese, and butter—must be eliminated. Immunization against food allergens is not practical, because there is no proof yet that it is effective.

In rare instances a child is so allergic to the venom of bees, wasps, yellow jackets, hornets, spiders, or ants that a serious or fatal reaction may result from a sting or bite. Such an allergic child should have a special medical kit for emergency treatment if bitten or stung. The doctor may advise shots to desensitize the child to insect venom.

If your child suffers from a respiratory allergy, your doctor may also suggest some of the following procedures to help reduce airborne allergens in your home and make the child's bedroom as dust-free as possible:
- Use an air conditioner that filters out pollen and decreases humidity.
- Eliminate wall-to-wall carpeting, stuffed toys, upholstered furniture, and feather pillows from the child's room.
- Enclose the child's mattress and box spring in a zippered, allergen-proof cover to prevent dust from escaping into the air.
- Do not keep pets that have either fur or feathers.
- Do not use Venetian blinds, curtains, bookcases, or upholstered furniture, or keep plush animals and other dust-collecting objects in the child's room.
- Avoid smoking in the house or automobile, because smoke irritates the mucous membranes in the respiratory tract.

Children who are extremely sensitive to certain foods or drugs should wear a warning bracelet or necklace bearing this information. A bracelet may be purchased from the Medic Alert Foundation through your pharmacy.

Preventing allergic reactions. If you have a strong family history of allergy, consult your doctor to attempt to prevent allergies in your child. The doctor may recommend breast-feeding or starting your infant on prepared milk formula or cow's milk substitutes. The doctor may also recommend that you introduce new foods slowly, and that you not give the baby food of high allergy potential, such as uncooked cow's milk, eggs, and wheat, until the infant is 10 to 12 months old. J.S.H.

See also **Asthma; Eczema; Hay fever; Hives**

Anemia is a condition that results from a reduction in the number of red blood cells, or a reduction in the amount of hemoglobin in the red blood cells. Hemoglobin is made up of iron and protein and gives the red color to red blood cells. The hemoglobin in the red blood cells picks up oxygen from the air that a child breathes into the lungs and carries the oxygen to all body tissue. When either the number of red blood cells or the amount of hemoglobin in these blood cells is reduced by anemia, the child's body does not receive enough oxygen and does not function properly.

In some mild cases of anemia, the child may not have symptoms. That is why your pediatrician will routinely screen the child with a blood count at age-appropriate times. A child with anemia may be pale and may not feel as energetic and playful as usual. If anemia is severe and comes on suddenly, the child may be without energy, short of breath, and critically ill. If you think your child may be anemic, consult your pediatrician.

The most common cause of anemia is insufficient iron in the child's diet. Between the ages of 6 months and a year, a baby who receives only milk may become anemic, because milk lacks iron. Meats, iron-fortified cereals, egg yolk, and vegetables are necessary and should be added to the child's diet. If iron deficiency anemia occurs, iron may be prescribed.

Sometimes a child's diet contains plenty of iron, but the child's body does not absorb enough of it. During certain long-lasting diarrheas, iron is not absorbed by the intestines. The diarrhea must be controlled before the anemia can be corrected by iron tablets or tonic. In rare instances, injections of iron may be necessary.

Loss of blood from an injury, from an ulcer, from hemophilia, or from other bleeding diseases may also cause anemia. This anemia is cured by stopping the bleeding and, if necessary, by giving the child transfusions.

Some anemias, called hemolytic anemias, are caused by the destruction of red blood cells. Hemolytic anemias may be inherited or acquired. Sickle cell anemia is an inherited hemolytic anemia. Some acquired hemolytic anemias are caused by sensitivity to certain drugs or plants. F.O.

See also **Bleeding; Blood count; Hemophilia; Leukemia; Nutrition**

Anesthetics are commonly used to eliminate the feeling of pain. Doctors usually give
them to a child who is having an operation.

There are two kinds of anesthetics—local
anesthetics and general anesthetics. Local
anesthetics eliminate pain in a small area of
the body, but they do not cause unconsciousness. The anesthetic is usually given by
injection. Doctors use local anesthetics for
such operations as stitching a cut or pulling
a tooth. This is the safest form of anesthetic,
but it can seldom be used for large operations.

General anesthetics eliminate pain over
the entire body. They cause partial or complete unconsciousness. General anesthetics
affect the brain directly and block reception
of pain. The most common way to administer a general anesthetic is to have the child
breathe it in the form of a gas. Intravenous
drugs such as sodium pentothal, often used
with older children and adults, are seldom
used for infants and young children.

Before receiving a general anesthetic, a
child is not given anything to eat or drink
for several hours. This allows the stomach to
empty so that while unconscious the child
won't vomit and possibly breathe food into
the lungs.

Preanesthesia medications are often (but
not always) given thirty minutes to two
hours before an operation to cause drowsiness, relieve apprehension, and decrease
airway secretions. These are given by injection.

Parents can ease a child's apprehension
before an operation by explaining the purpose of the surgery, the sequence of events
before, during, and after the operation, and
any discomfort involved.

Major operations, and in small children
many minor operations, are carried out under general anesthesia. Administering anesthesia is no more risky in children than in
adults. Even premature, newborn infants
can be safely anesthetized. Prior to an operation, the person who will give the anesthetic usually explains how it will be done.

Many lesser operations in children are
performed under general anesthesia as an
outpatient. After completely awakening
from anesthesia, the child can go home to
finish recovering from the operation. This is
quite safe and allows the child to be in the
more secure, familiar surroundings of the
home. T.M.H.

Anorexia nervosa is an emotional illness.
It is an extreme form of very poor appetite
or self-starvation. *Anorexia* means "without
appetite," but anorexics may be very hungry
much of the time. Anorexia occurs mainly in
adolescent girls and young women. The
cause is emotional or sociocultural.

The condition may begin when the child
goes on an extreme diet because of fear of
being fat. This may lead to a refusal to eat,
self-induced vomiting, or laxative abuse after
eating. The amount of weight loss may not
be noticed by parents until it is extreme.
The patient herself will have an altered body
image—that is, she will see herself as fat—
and will have little concern for her wasting.
The condition may be accompanied by a
failure to menstruate.

There is a relentless pursuit of thinness.
In spite of the loss of weight, the child may
not only continue normal activities, but also
may exercise quite vigorously. The child
maintains an active interest in food and food
preparation. Some patients show signs of
depression.

Although anorexia nervosa may be mild, it
is generally a severe and chronic problem. It
may even result in death. Children are usually hospitalized under the care of a physician and a psychiatrist.

See also **Appetite; Diets; Overweight;
Underweight**

Antibiotics. *See* **Drugs**

Antidote. *See* **Poisoning and poisons**

Antihistamine. *See* **Allergy**

Appendicitis is an inflammation of the
appendix, a narrow tube in the lower right
part of the abdomen. One end of the tube is
closed. The open end of the tube is attached
to the large intestine. If the appendix be-

Location of the appendix

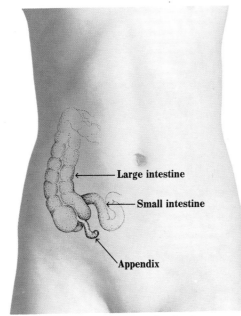

The appendix is a small sac in the lower right abdomen. One end of the appendix is attached to the large intestine.

- Large intestine
- Small intestine
- Appendix

comes infected, it becomes inflamed. It swells and fills with pus. If there is a delay in diagnosis and surgery is not done, the appendix may burst and cause peritonitis, an inflammation in the abdominal cavity.

Appendicitis occurs most commonly in school-age children and young adults, but it can occur in younger children, too.

Acute (sudden and severe) appendicitis usually begins with vague, general abdominal pain which may localize within hours to the right lower abdomen. The abdomen may become tender. The child may vomit, have fever, and feel constipated. Laxatives may increase the dangers of appendicitis. Never give laxatives or cathartics (such as Epsom salts or castor oil) for abdominal pain unless advised to do so by a doctor.

Children complain of abdominal pain often, but the pain is usually caused by something other than appendicitis. It is important that you contact the doctor if your child is ill with abdominal pain. Delay in diagnosing appendicitis leads to a longer illness. Doctors estimate that about one-third of the small children with appendicitis have ruptured

appendixes before they reach a hospital.

A child who has an unruptured appendix removed usually stays in the hospital for 3 to 5 days. Normally, the child can return to school 7 to 10 days after the operation. A child who has a ruptured appendix removed stays in the hospital about 10 days. Normally the child can return to school a week or two after coming home.

See also **Laxatives; Stomachache**

Appetite. Whether a child has a good or poor appetite depends mainly on the child's age and health and the emotional climate of the home. Of course, appetite may be temporarily affected by an illness, such as a cold or chicken pox, or by an emotional upset. Babies experience hunger pains when they need food. When they eat, the hunger pains stop, so babies' first reactions to food are pleasant. Gradually, they recognize their mothers as givers of food. If their mothers are loving and tender when they feed their babies, the babies begin to associate food with love. But if the mothers fail to feed their babies when they are hungry, appear uninterested in their babies, or force the babies to eat when they are not hungry, the babies may have mixed feelings.

How can you promote good appetite?
- Give food only to satisfy your child's appetite. Do not force the child to eat, and do not use food (especially sweets) as reward and punishment.
- Respect your baby's appetite as the best indicator of how much food the infant needs. For several months after the first birthday, children generally need less and eat less food. Parents often think their children are not eating enough because they are no longer growing at a tremendous rate. However, parents are usually surprised to discover that their children are gaining weight.
- Respect your baby's continuing development in feeding practices. Parents should let babies feed themselves when they want to, even though the youngsters may be messy for a time.
- As your child gets older, do not let the child drink milk at the expense of other foods. Once cow's milk is started, limit consumption to 3 glasses per day.

- Give your child finger foods. Small children like foods that they can handle easily—foods that they can eat with their fingers and foods that are cut into bite-sized pieces.
- Present new foods in small quantities. And be patient. It may take several times before a child gets used to the new food.
- Remember, mealtimes should be happy occasions, free of struggle. M.G.

See also **Nutrition; Vitamins**

Arthritis is an inflammation of body joints. A joint may swell and become painful, and the skin covering the joint may be red and feel warm. The joint becomes stiff and its movement limited. Arthritis can result from injury or infection. Usually, its exact cause is unknown. If you suspect that your child has arthritis, consult your doctor.

Rheumatoid arthritis is a common form of arthritis in children, especially children between the ages of 2 and 6. Doctors do not yet know what causes rheumatoid arthritis. Usually, only one or two joints, such as the knee or ankle, are affected. However, the disease may affect many joints. The joints can become dislocated, deformed, or fused. A high fever is also a common characteristic of the condition. Rheumatoid arthritis usually lasts for several years. Your doctor may prescribe drugs to reduce inflammation and relieve pain, and may also suggest exercises that concentrate on using the joints afflicted by arthritis.

Infectious arthritis, which also affects children, usually follows an infection somewhere in the body, often in the upper respiratory tract. Bacteria cause pus to form in joint cavities. Usually, only one or two of the larger joints, such as the hip, shoulder, or knee, are affected. The child may also have fever and chills. Doctors treat this condition with antibiotic drugs and by draining the pus from the affected joint.

Rheumatic fever is a serious childhood disease that may cause temporary arthritis. This form of arthritis is not connected with rheumatoid arthritis. Usually, the larger joints, such as the ankles, knees, hips, wrists, elbows, and shoulders, are affected. The arthritis tends to move from one joint to another, with any one joint being affected from a few days to several weeks. This type of arthritis is generally treated with drugs to relieve pain and reduce inflammation.

Other forms of temporary arthritis may also affect children. For example, a child may injure a joint—most commonly a knee joint—and develop arthritis in that joint. Occasionally, a young child develops a brief episode of arthritis of the hip from an unknown cause. M.G.

See also **Osteomyelitis; Rheumatic fever**

Artificial respiration. *See* **CPR**

Asphyxiation. *See* **Suffocation**

Aspirin poisoning. *See* **Poisonings and poisons**

Asthma is an allergic disease that affects the bronchial tubes. It causes coughing, wheezing, and labored breathing. Breathing is obstructed by the swelling of the mucous membranes of the bronchial passages, by muscle spasms in the walls of the bronchial tubes, and by the excessive secretion of a thick, sticky mucus. The onset of asthma may be abrupt or gradual. An attack may be mild, or it may require hospitalization.

Childhood asthma is usually caused by respiratory infections or by inhalants (substances that float in the air, such as house dust, molds, pollen, and animal dander, *i.e.*, particles from animal skin, hair, and feathers). House dust mites eat dander, molds, and natural fibers and, after a few days, die, leaving excrement, carcasses, and baby mites, all of which may trigger asthma. Less often, emotional problems or foods may bring on or aggravate an asthmatic attack. Air pollutants, low barometric pressure, humidity, changes in temperature, and other factors may also provoke asthma.

Any child with asthma should be under a doctor's care. Asthma rarely improves without treatment from a doctor. If asthma is neglected, it often recurs for many years, and it may permanently change the child's lungs and chest wall.

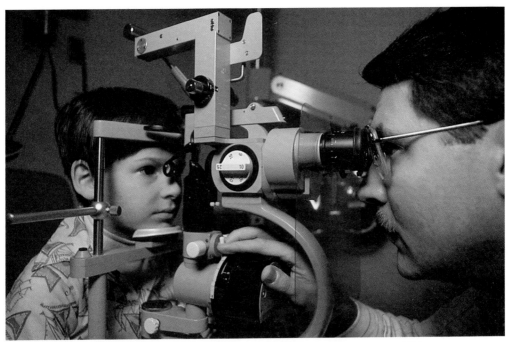

An eye examination is necessary to determine accurately whether or not a child has astigmatism. Astigmatism can be corrected by glasses or contact lenses.

In treating asthma, the doctor tries to determine the substance or substances causing the attack. The doctor will want to know if the child has had previous or associated allergies, and know about other family members with asthma or other allergic diseases, since these tend to run in families. The doctor will also want to know the frequency of the asthma attacks, foods the child eats, pets the child is exposed to, and other details of the child's life—for example, does exercise or cold air cause the child to wheeze? The doctor may perform prick tests or intradermal tests to determine what airborne substances the child is sensitive to.

Drugs may be prescribed to widen the bronchial tubes by relieving bronchial spasms and shrinking the mucous membranes. Breathing and physical fitness exercises may be prescribed. The doctor will probably suggest eliminating pets, house dust, feathers, cigarette smoke, and other substances from the child's surroundings. Immunization to build up a child's resistance to airborne substances is also helpful. J.S.H.

Astigmatism is a defect of the eye that makes images appear distorted or blurred. It occurs when the lens or the cornea of an eye is improperly curved. Because of this defect, not all the rays of light from an object fall evenly on the retina. Some rays focus in front of the retina, some on it, and some behind it. Both near-sighted and far-sighted eyes can be astigmatic. The condition is a common one and seldom is a serious handicap. It can be corrected by glasses or contact lenses. Eight out of 10 children have some degree of astigmatism.

Astigmatism is difficult, if not impossible, to diagnose without a careful eye examination. But there are some signs that may indicate the condition. Occasionally, in more severe forms, a child may hold the head at an angle to make up for a blurred image. In milder forms, the constant effort of the eye to overcome the irregularly blurred images may result in headache, fatigue, irritability, or eyestrain. R.O.S.

See also **Eye health; Far-sightedness; Headache; Near-sightedness**

Ataxia is a lack of muscle coordination. A child with ataxia moves unsteadily and staggers when standing or walking. The child may turn awkwardly and may frequently bump into objects such as tables and chairs. All children have an ataxic gait when learning to walk, but children who are developing normally should have a smooth gait by the time they are 3 years old. If you suspect your child has ataxia, see your doctor.

Ataxia usually indicates that the part of the nervous system that controls balance and coordination is not functioning properly.

Here are some causes of ataxia.
- Infection of the nervous system
- A tumor in the nervous system
- A hereditary disease that affects the nervous system
- Accidental poisoning
- Lead poisoning
- Hysteria
- Overdoses of sedatives, or of medicines that prevent convulsions or vomiting. A.G.S.

See also **Cerebral palsy; Hysteria**

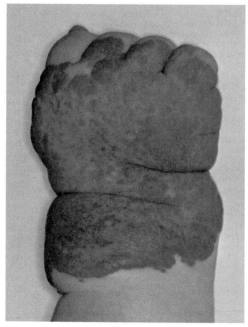

Some birthmarks (hemangioma) disappear by themselves. The baby shown above was born with a birthmark on his hand and wrist.

Athlete's foot. *See* **Ringworm**

Bandage. *See* **Bleeding; Cuts and scratches; First aid**

Bed-wetting. *See* **Wetting**

Birthmark. Many children have birthmarks, but most birthmarks are small and do not impair a child's health in any way. Many disappear if they are left alone. Others last throughout a person's life.

Strawberry, or vascular, birthmarks are the most common. They are caused by slightly enlarged or prominent blood vessels in the skin. Black or brown birthmarks, often called moles, occur because of increased amounts of pigment in the skin. If a new mole (nevus) appears, or if an old one suddenly seems to be growing, bleeding, ulcerating or changing color, or is painful, consult your doctor. The doctor will want to examine it to be sure it is not harmful to the child's health.

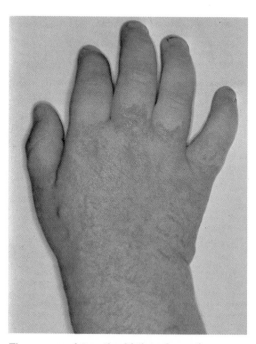

Three years later, the birthmark on the baby's hand and wrist had almost disappeared even though it was not treated in any way.

Salmon-patch birthmarks are light red or pink blotches commonly found on the back of the neck, on the forehead, and on the eyelids. They usually disappear by themselves during childhood.

Strawberry birthmarks are bright red, spongy in texture, and elevated from the skin surface. Most of these birthmarks disappear by the time the child reaches 3 to 5 years of age. But if one starts to grow rapidly, consult your doctor. The doctor may treat strawberry birthmarks by compression therapy. Occasionally, a doctor may remove the birthmarks surgically.

Port-wine birthmarks are flat and purplish-red. They are commonly found on the face or neck. A few may become lighter in time, but they rarely disappear. You may wish to use a special cosmetic to cover them.

Mongolian spots are blue marks on the buttocks or lower back. They usually disappear during childhood.

Some mothers of children with birthmarks wonder whether experiences or thoughts they may have had during pregnancy could have caused the marks. No evidence supports such a notion.   A.M.M.

See also **Moles**

Bites and stings are common hazards of childhood. Some bites and stings require little treatment—nothing more than washing with soap and water. Others are serious injuries that call for treatment by a doctor.

Mammal bites. The mouths of animals contain a variety of germs that may cause infection or a serious disease. Rabies, one of the most serious diseases, destroys nerve cells in part of the brain and almost always results in death. The rabies virus lives in the saliva of many kinds of animals. The disease is most commonly transmitted by dogs, but it may also be spread by other mammals, including cats, bats, foxes, and skunks. To prevent rabies, have pet dogs and cats vaccinated. Also report all strays to the police or health authorities.

The circumstances surrounding the animal bite help determine the treatment. The child may be bitten by a family pet that has been vaccinated against rabies. For minor wounds that are no more than a scratch, wash with soap and plenty of warm water, and rinse

thoroughly. Then cover the wound with a bandage. If the scratch becomes inflamed, call your doctor. If the bite is a puncture wound, wash the wound with soap and water, and call your doctor.

If your child is bitten by a stray mammal, wash the wound with soap and water and call your doctor. If your child has a cut, scratch, or other wound that comes in contact with the saliva of a stray mammal, follow the same procedure. If the animal can be captured, it is usually kept under observation by a veterinarian to find out if it has rabies. If your doctor suspects that the animal has rabies, the doctor will start rabies inoculations for the child immediately. If the animal cannot be captured, the doctor may give the injections as a precaution.

Ratbite fever is also transmitted through a bite. If your child is bitten by a rat, wash the wound with soap and water, then call your doctor or take the child to a hospital emergency room. The doctor may administer antibiotic and tetanus shots.

A human bite that breaks the skin can also cause a severe infection. Wash it with soap and water and see a doctor.

Snakebites. If your child is bitten by a snake, it is important to know whether the snake is poisonous. A nonpoisonous snakebite is no more harmful than any other animal bite. Wash the bite with soap and water, then call your doctor.

Recognizing poisonous snakes. There are two types of poisonous snakes in the continental United States—coral snakes; and pit vipers, which include rattlesnakes, copperheads, and cottonmouths (water moccasins). Rattlesnakes are the only poisonous snakes found in Canada.

Poisonous snakes can often be identified by the following characteristics.
- Both pit vipers and coral snakes have two fangs along with their normal teeth.
- A pit viper has a pit on each side of its head, between its eye and its nostril.
- Most rattlesnakes have noise-making rattles on the end of their tails.
- Coral snakes have black snouts and fairly wide red and blackish-blue bands, separated by narrower yellow bands.

If you cannot find the snake that bit the child, you may be able to tell if the snake was poisonous by asking whether the child is in pain, or by observing the bite area for swelling and discoloration.

The bite of a harmless snake may produce mild pain, but the pain rarely lasts and it does not spread. A child bitten by a poisonous snake almost always feels deep, burning pain. If the bite is that of a pit viper, the pain usually spreads. If the bite is that of a coral snake, the pain does not spread.

A nonpoisonous snakebite rarely produces swelling. If swelling does occur, it does not spread. The bite of a pit viper produces swelling within three to five minutes. The swelling usually spreads rapidly toward the trunk of the child's body. The bite of a coral snake does not cause swelling.

A perfect bite pattern of two fang marks generally indicates the snake is poisonous. However, the bite pattern is not always a reliable sign because it may be obscured by marks inflicted by the snake's other teeth.

Poisonous snakebites. If your child is bitten by a poisonous snake, the child needs immediate medical attention. Call a doctor or take the child to a hospital. If possible, kill the snake and keep it for identification.

Activity causes the poison to spread more rapidly, so keep the child as still as possible until medical help arrives, or until you can get to a hospital. Keep the bitten part of the body in a lower position than the heart.

If the child develops mild symptoms of poisoning and if the bite is on an arm or leg, tie a bandage above the wound, between it and the heart. Make sure that you can wedge a finger under the bandage. Do not put the bandage around any joint. Release the bandage for 90 seconds every 10 minutes to prevent damage from lack of blood circulation.

If the child develops severe symptoms—pain, swelling, numbness, difficulty breathing—and you cannot get the child to a doctor or a hospital within 30 minutes, continue first aid. Sterilize a knife or razor blade and make an "I" shaped cut through—and slightly below—each fang mark along the *length* of the arm or leg. Make the cut no longer than ½ inch (12 millimeters). Cut through the skin, but not deep enough to sever muscles and nerves. Do not make cuts on head, neck, or torso.

Apply suction to the cut or cuts with a suction or bulb syringe found in many first-aid kits. Or, if you have no cuts or open sores in your mouth, suck and spit out the poison. Rinse your mouth. Continue suction for 30 to 60 minutes, or until the swelling stops spreading. Take the child to a hospital.

Insect, spider, and tick bites. Most insect and spider bites are more annoying than serious. Put calamine lotion, an ice cube, a drop of household vinegar, or a thick paste of baking soda and water on the bitten area.

Two dangerous spiders are the brown recluse spider and the female black widow spider. The brown recluse spider is found in at least 17 states—Alabama, Arkansas, Colorado, Georgia, Illinois, Indiana, Kansas, Kentucky, Louisiana, Mississippi, Missouri, North Carolina, South Carolina, Ohio, Oklahoma, Tennessee, and Texas. Because it hides in dark places—wadded-up newspapers, bedding, clothes, or shoes—it can be easily transported by travelers to new areas. The black widow spider is found in nearly every state and in Canada.

Bites from either of these spiders produce a burning sensation, followed by severe cramps in the abdomen, chest, and legs. If you suspect that your child has been bitten by a brown recluse spider or a black widow spider, call your doctor.

Ticks are parasites that suck blood through a hooked beak that they fix tightly in their victim's skin. Children who have been in tick-infested areas should be examined carefully for ticks, especially along the hairline.

A few drops of turpentine or alcohol will make a tick loosen its hold. Holding a hot match or lighted cigarette near the tick may also be effective. Working gently and slowly, remove the tick with tweezers or a piece of paper. If you tear the tick loose, its mouth or other body parts may stay in the skin and cause festering sores. Also avoid crushing the tick. Ticks often carry germs, which they transfer to their victims. Scrub the area from which the tick is removed with soap and water for five minutes. If the bite becomes inflamed and swollen, or if the child runs a fever, becomes weak, or develops a rash, call your doctor. M.G.

See also **Allergy; Lyme disease**

Common poisonous spiders and snakes

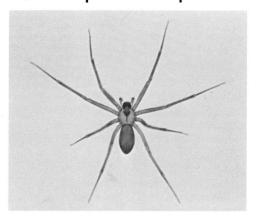

Both the brown recluse spider (left) and the black widow spider (right) have
distinguishing marks. The brown recluse spider has a dark violin shape on its back.
The black widow spider has a red or yellow hourglass shape on its abdomen.

The best way to identify a coral snake is to
remember the distinctive color pattern—
red bands touch yellow bands.

The body of the western diamondback
rattlesnake has a pattern of brown diamonds,
edged with a light-colored border.

The copperhead has broad, brown, X-shaped
bands on its light-colored body.
The top of its head is copper colored.

The eastern cottonmouth usually has broad
dark bands on its body. This pattern may
become obscure as the snake grows older.

Bleeding, if excessive, must be controlled promptly because it can be fatal. Stop excessive bleeding before you take precautions against infection. An infection can be treated later with antibiotics, but profuse bleeding is an immediate threat.

You can control severe bleeding by firmly pressing a folded towel, handkerchief, or other cloth pad directly over the bleeding wound. Hold the pad of cloth in place with your hand until you can fasten it in place with a bandage. Do not remove the cloth. If blood seeps through, cover the first cloth with another pad of cloth.

If bleeding is severe, and the blood is red and spurting, do not wait to find a bandage or pad. Use your hand to apply pressure. And try to remain calm—both to reassure your child, who will probably be frightened, and to ensure that the steps you take are the proper ones.

Bleeding of the foot, leg, hand, or arm will stop sooner if you elevate the limb. Have the child lie down, and place a pillow or a folded blanket or coat under the limb. Then, apply direct pressure to the wound and bandage it.

If pressure does not control bleeding, and the bleeding is in a limb, a tourniquet may be necessary. Use a tourniquet only as a last resort.

Make a tourniquet from a wide strip of cloth. Wrap the cloth tightly around the limb two or three times, between the wound and heart. Knot it, but leave the ends long enough to tie a stick in place on top of the knot. Then twist the stick until the bleeding stops. Do not remove the tourniquet. Get the victim to a doctor immediately.

Activity encourages bleeding. Keep the child quiet. If the bleeding seems to be severe or persistent, or to come from a large blood vessel, take the child immediately to a hospital emergency room.

Bleeding may come from injured arteries, veins, or small vessels called capillaries. Blood from arteries is bright red. It comes in spurts if the artery is large. Blood from veins is darker and flows more evenly and slowly. Blood from capillaries is usually a minor oozing. M.G.

See also **Blood clotting; Cuts and scratches; Hemophilia; Nosebleed; Shock**

Blister is a collection of fluid under the skin that causes the top layer of skin to puff out. Blisters can be caused by many things. Here are the most common causes:
- Burns, including sunburn
- Poorly fitted shoes
- Chafing or pinching of the skin
- Skin diseases, such as chicken pox, impetigo, poison ivy, insect bites, and genetic disorders.

Infants sometimes get blisters on their lips from sucking. A severe pinch or bruise may injure a blood vessel and cause a blood blister (blister filled with blood).

Most blisters require no special treatment. The body usually absorbs the fluid. It is best not to open a blister, because the covering protects underlying tissues from infection. If the blister opens accidentally, wash the area several times daily with mild soap and water, and cover with a bandage to keep it clean. If a blister becomes inflamed, or if it does not heal, consult your doctor. A.M.M.

See also **Burns; Chicken pox; Fever blisters; Frostbite; Impetigo; Poison ivy, oak, and sumac; Sunburn**

Blood clotting helps to stop bleeding. Bleeding starts when a blood vessel is broken, usually because of injury. The body's first response to such injury is made by blood elements called platelets. These disklike elements stick to the damaged area of the vessel wall and form a soft plug or patch. This plug is then reinforced by the clotting factors of the blood's plasma. These factors and the platelets form a thick covering over the loose plug and prevent further bleeding. If this thick covering is on the skin surface, it appears as a scab. Eventually, the plug is dissolved as the injured tissue heals.

Bleeding from small blood vessels usually stops within 5 to 10 minutes. You can help clotting by applying cold compresses to the injured area. The cold shrinks the blood vessels that supply the injured area, reducing the flow of blood. The pressure of the compress helps the plug to form. But if you continually wash the damaged area, the platelets and clotting factors are bathed away and no clot can form.

How to stop bleeding

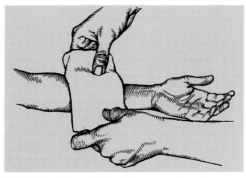

1. Fold a piece of cloth into a pad and place it on the bleeding wound.

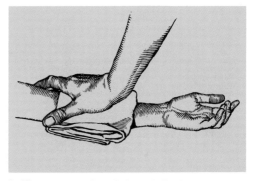

2. Then, press the cloth pad firmly against the bleeding wound.

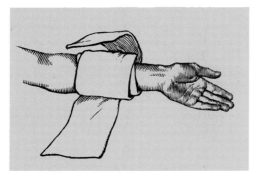

3. Wrap a strip of cloth around the pad and the injured part of the body.

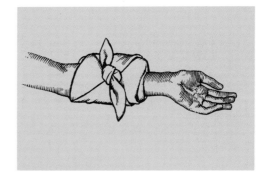

4. Tie the cloth strip to hold the pad in place over the wound.

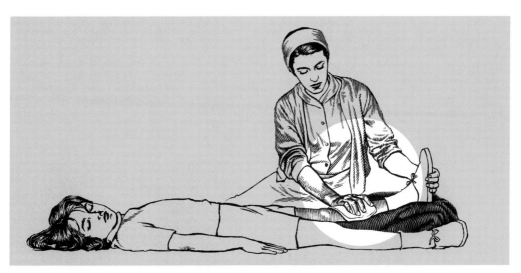

You can stop bleeding from a limb more quickly if you have the child lie down. Next, elevate the limb by placing a pillow, a folded coat, a folded blanket, or some other object under the injured limb. Then place a folded cloth pad over the wound and apply direct pressure.

If your child injures a large blood vessel, the blood clotting process cannot form a plug. Severe bleeding results. To stop the bleeding, apply direct pressure to the wound. Fold a towel or handkerchief into a pad, and hold it on the wound. If you cannot find a cloth quickly, apply pressure with your hand. If the bleeding persists, take the child immediately to a hospital.

Sometimes blood clotting occurs in blood vessels that have not been injured physically. This clotting is called thrombosis. Thrombosis blocks blood vessels and reduces the flow of blood. The reduction of blood flow to a vital organ can result in permanent injury to the organ.

Unusual bleeding—for example, bleeding without injury, excessive bleeding from a slight injury, or bleeding that will not clot—occurs for a variety of reasons. A child may have excessively fragile or diseased blood vessels, not enough platelets or defective platelets, or plasma that may lack clotting factors. The lack of clotting factors is known as hemophilia. F.O.

See also **Bleeding; Blood count; Hemophilia; Nosebleed**

Blood count is an actual count of the cells in a precisely measured drop of blood. The blood sample can be taken from one of the child's fingers or an earlobe, or from a blood vessel. The count is done by examining the drop of blood under a microscope or by a machine. Blood contains many different cells that perform specific jobs in the body. The most important cells are the red cells, the white cells, and the platelets. Healthy blood contains these cells in certain proportions.

Red cells get their bright coloring from hemoglobin, which contains iron. Hemoglobin absorbs oxygen from the lungs and carries it to the body tissues. White cells attack germs to prevent infection. Platelets, which look like tiny disks, assist in blood clotting.

A blood count can give a doctor vital information. For instance, a low count of red blood cells may show that a child has anemia. An increase in white blood cells may indicate an infection. A normal blood count is one sign of good health. F.O.

See also **Anemia; Blood clotting; Blood type**

Blood poisoning is an infection of the bloodstream caused by microbes such as bacteria, fungi, and protozoa. Although microbes may enter the bloodstream directly at the time of an injury, they usually get into the blood by way of an infection that already exists in the body—for example, appendicitis, pneumonia, a boil or a pimple, a sore throat or tonsillitis, or an infected tooth.

A child with blood poisoning may have chills and fever, and may complain of an aching body and feeling of weakness. The child's skin may show a rash, and the lymph glands in the armpits or groin may become tender. This is an emergency. Call your doctor immediately, or take the child to the nearest hospital, where antibiotics can be administered to fight the infection.

Blood poisoning occurs more frequently in babies than in older children because babies seem less able to keep infections from spreading. In rare instances, a child's body cannot produce the antibodies needed to protect against infection, and the child has bloodstream infections repeatedly. H.D.R., JR.

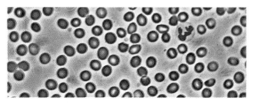

This blood sample is magnified and stained for examination. It is taken from a child who has a normal blood count. The red blood cells are doughnut shaped. The large cell in the upper right corner is a white blood cell. A normal blood count is one sign of good health.

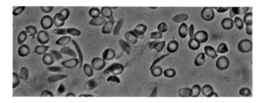

This magnified, stained blood sample is from a child with sickle cell anemia—a hereditary, permanent anemia. In this type of anemia, from 50 to 90 per cent of the red blood cells are shaped like sickles.

Blood type. Everyone's blood contains inherited chemical substances known as "blood factors." Combinations of these factors determine a person's blood type. You should know your children's blood type.

One type of blood is just as healthy as another. But if a blood transfusion is necessary, it is important to know that the blood of patient and donor will mix without serious reaction. If they do not mix, certain combinations of factors may cause red blood cells to clump together. This clumping blocks small blood vessels and can cause serious illness or even death. Blood typing makes safe transfusion possible by ensuring that the blood of donor and patient will blend.

There are four major human blood groups —A, B, AB, and O—and many subdivisions. Blood is further classified as Rh-positive and Rh-negative. F.O.

See also **Rh factor**

Blue baby. *See* **Cyanosis**

Boil is a painful abscess under the skin that develops when a sweat gland, an oil gland, a small wound, or a hair follicle (the sac containing the hair root) becomes infected and fills with pus. If one boil develops, others often follow. Several boils formed close together constitute a carbuncle. The bacteria that cause boils are almost always present on the skin, but they cause infection only occasionally. Squeezing pimples or failing to keep the skin clean may cause boils.

When a boil is developing, the area first is red and tender. Considerable swelling and pain may develop. Gradually, pus forms and the center of the boil becomes yellowish.

Moist heat helps keep the infection from spreading and draws the pus to a head so it will drain. Soak a towel in warm water and apply it to the boil for 20 to 30 minutes every 4 or 5 hours. Be careful that the towel is not so hot that it burns the skin. The boil may subside, or it may come to a head, erupt, and drain. If your child has boils frequently, consult a physician. T.M.H.

Bowlegs. Almost every new baby appears to be bowlegged. The knees are held out, and the feet are slightly turned in. Although the bones themselves are usually well formed and straight, the legs tend to remain

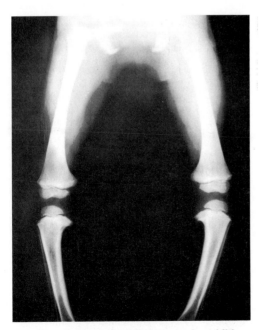

This X ray shows the leg bones of a child who was born with bowlegs.

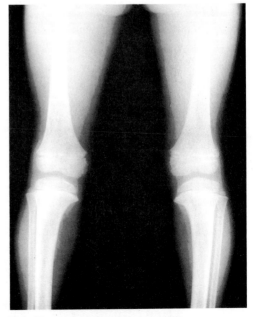

This X ray shows the same child after 4½ years of medical treatment.

in the position they were in before birth. This condition is called physiologic bowing and tends to gradually disappear as the child grows and begins to walk.

It takes a bit of time for the foot, ankle, knee, and leg muscles and ligaments to strengthen. As these muscles and ligaments become stronger with walking, the legs gradually look straighter and the knees come closer together. Physiologic bowing usually disappears when the child is between 1 and 2 years old.

If you are concerned that your child may be too bowlegged or if the child's legs have not straightened themselves by 2 years of age, have your doctor check the position of your child's legs to make sure they are developing properly.

In some children, bowlegs may result from rickets, caused by a vitamin D deficiency, or from a disturbance in the growth centers of the bone. In a few children, bowlegs may require medical treatment of braces or even surgery for correction. J.J.G.

Braces, dental. If your child has malocclusion (poor bite), the dentist will probably suggest that you take the child to an orthodontist (a dentist who specializes in correcting irregularities of the teeth and jaws). Malocclusions are corrected with braces, which gradually realign the teeth.

The orthodontist will X-ray the child's teeth and make study models of the mouth to be sure of the irregularity that needs correction. The orthodontist will make regular and thorough examinations, adjusting the braces as the teeth move into their proper positions, and will give instructions for keeping the teeth and braces clean. For instance, a child with braces will be told not to chew gum or eat sticky candy.

Many parents worry that their child will suffer severe pain during orthodontic treatment. A child may occasionally experience some discomfort, but at no time should there be severe pain. Some parents worry that continued use of braces may cause tooth decay. If the child practices good dental hygiene, this should not happen. M.G.

See also **Malocclusion**

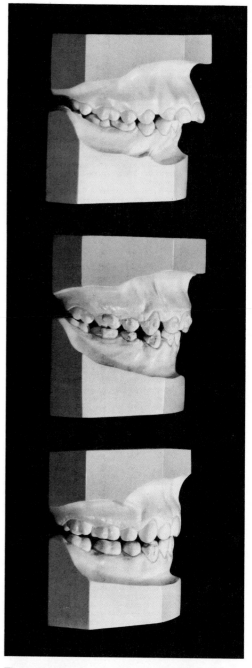

These three sets of plaster casts were made from the same boy at various times during treatment for malocclusion. The first set shows the position of the boy's teeth before braces were applied. The second casts, made about a year later, show the progress of straightening. The third casts show the position of the teeth after treatment was completed.

Dentists use braces to correct irregularities of a child's teeth.

Breath-holding spells are not uncommon in children about 1 year old. The spells usually begin with vigorous crying. Children then suddenly gasp and hold their breath until they turn blue or pale. They may begin to twitch, or may even pass out briefly. Reflex mechanisms of breathing will then take over, and they will come to in a few moments.

Few things frighten parents more than seeing their children hold their breath. There is one good rule to follow when this happens: Do nothing at all. Usually the spells are not dangerous. If a child passes out, elevate the feet, turn the head, and open the mouth so that excess saliva will flow out and not choke the child. As the child recovers, try not to show concern. If your child is a frequent breath-holder or has convulsions, consult the doctor. The doctor may be able to help you discover the reason for the breath-holding and tell you how to prevent it. M.G.

See also **Convulsions; Fainting**

Broken bones, also called fractures, are fairly common during childhood, particularly among boys. There are several types of fractures:
- In a closed fracture, the broken bone does not cut through the skin.
- In an open fracture, a sharp end of the bone sticks through the skin. Open fractures are considered medical emergencies and are serious because of the danger of bone infection.
- A greenstick fracture is a type of closed fracture in which there is a partial break in a bone. It occurs most frequently in younger children. Children's bones are soft and, like a stick of green wood, may bend and splinter on one side only.
- In an epiphyseal fracture, the growing ends of the long arm and leg bones break off or separate. This type of fracture can occur only in children, and involves the wrist and ankle most frequently.

Some fractures are not immediately apparent. But if the area around an injury swells, becomes very painful, and is tender to touch, call your doctor. All obvious fractures require immediate attention. All open fractures demand emergency treatment in a hospital as soon as possible. Here are some emergency first-aid measures:
- Do not move the injured part, and do not let the child move it. Moving the sharp, broken ends of a long bone may injure nerves, blood vessels, and muscles, or cut through the skin. It is especially important not to move the child if you suspect a back, neck, or head injury.
- Encourage the child to lie still and quiet.
- Cover open skin wounds with clean or sterile dressings, if possible.
- To treat for shock, cover the child with a blanket or extra clothing.
- Call the police or fire department for emergency help in getting the child to a hospital. If no trained emergency help is available, put a splint on the injured part to prevent further injury when the child is moved. Do not try to straighten the injured part. Gently bind it to a board or firm object, such as a tree branch or a piece of cardboard. If possible, pad the splint by wrapping cloth around it to avoid pressure on nerves.

Emergency splinting

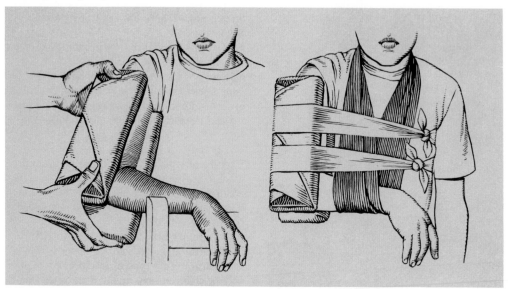

If you must apply a splint to the upper arm, and the arm is bent, use splints that reach from the armpit to below the elbow. Use a sling to support the lower arm. Then tie the splints snugly around the child's body with strips of cloth.

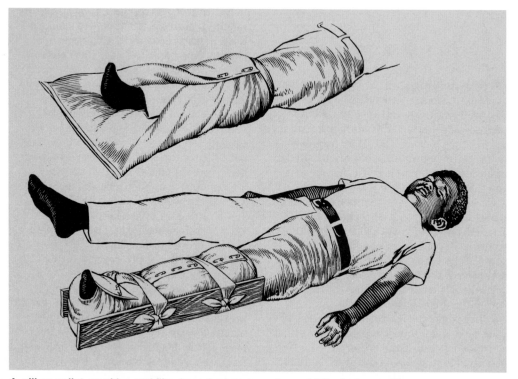

A pillow splint provides stability for a broken bone in a child's foot or ankle. Gently wrap the pillow around the foot and leg. Next, secure the pillow with safety pins. Then tie the splints snugly around the child's leg with strips of cloth.

- If there is a broken bone in the upper arm and the arm is in a bent position, use a splint that extends from the armpit to below the elbow.
- If there is a broken bone in the upper arm and the arm is straight, use a splint that extends from the armpit to the child's fingertips.
- If there is a broken bone in the lower arm, use a splint that extends from the armpit to the fingertips.
- For a broken wrist, use a splint that extends from the fingertips to the elbow.
- For a broken bone in the thigh, use a splint that extends from the foot to the child's armpit.
- If a bone in the lower leg is broken, use a splint that extends from the foot to the hip.
- If a bone in the ankle or foot is broken, use a splint that extends from the foot to the knee.

If it is essential that a child be moved after a back injury, use a wide board to lift the child so the child's back will not bend. Also, if it is essential that you move a child with a suspected neck injury, support the head firmly so the child's neck does not move. J.J.G.

See also **Dislocation of joint; shock**

Bronchitis is an inflammation of the lining of the bronchial tubes. It may be caused by allergy, bacteria, a fungus, viruses, or chemical substances. In most cases, bronchitis is caused by a cold or a lingering virus infection. Most cases are mild and do not last long. If the child's bronchitis lasts for more than a few days, consult your doctor.

The most bothersome symptom of bronchitis is coughing. The cough may be worse during the night. In severe cases, the cough may start the child vomiting. Do not give medicine to reduce the cough unless your doctor prescribes it. Coughing usually rids the bronchial tubes of irritating material. In severe cases, a chest X ray and other studies may sometimes be necessary.

Wheezing sometimes occurs in infants and young children with bronchitis. M.G.

See also **Allergy; Colds; Coughing; Humidifying**

Bruises (contusions) are injuries that usually do not break the surface of the skin but are severe enough to cause small blood vessels to break under the skin. The blood oozes into surrounding tissues. Swelling and pain occur. The skin may turn red at first, then turn black and blue as the blood seeps into the tissues. As the blood is gradually absorbed into the blood system, the skin of the bruised area becomes yellow and then returns to its normal color. The darker a child's skin is, the less noticeable are the color changes.

An ordinary bruise does not need any treatment. But you may reassure and comfort your child by putting cold cloths on the injured area. Severe bruises should be treated by a doctor.

Bruises are usually caused by falls, blows, or bumping against sharp or hard objects. If a child bruises easily, or if bruises appear without any obvious reason, the child's blood may not be clotting normally. Inform your doctor. M.G.

See also **Blood clotting; Hemophilia**

Burns range from minor annoyances to serious injuries that can cause permanent crippling or even death. Burns are classified according to degree of severity. A first-degree burn is one that reddens the skin but does not produce blisters. A second-degree burn reddens the skin and blisters it. A third-degree burn destroys skin and tissue, and may penetrate deeply into the body.

Small first- and second-degree burns usually are not serious and require only minor treatment. But consult your doctor about all second-degree burns, because an infection may start when a blister breaks. To relieve pain and decrease injury, put the burned area under cool running water for a few minutes, pat dry, and cover with sterile gauze or a clean bandage. If pain continues, apply petroleum jelly and a light gauze covering. This may relieve the pain. Do not use any greasy substance.

First- and second-degree burns that cover a large area are more serious. Wrap the child in a clean sheet to avoid infection and take the child to an emergency room. If this is not immediately possible, immerse the

burned area in cool water (70° F.; 21° C). If
you cannot immerse the burn in water, apply wet compresses. Cool water or a cool
compress lessens pain and helps diminish
tissue destruction. Do not apply oily mix-
tures, tea poultices, or other home remedies.
Consult your doctor at once.

Never use water on a third-degree burn.
Cover the burned area with a thick, sterile,
dry gauze bandage to keep out air. If the
burn covers a large area, wrap the child in a
clean sheet. Consult your doctor and get the
child to the hospital at once.

A child who is burned seriously may go
into shock. To counteract this, keep the
child lying down and covered with a light
blanket. If possible, raise the legs by resting
them on a folded blanket, a pillow, or other
object. If the child is conscious and can swallow, give the child a drink of water.

If your child is burned by chemicals, immediately wash the affected area with running water. Use a hose, put the child under
a shower, or pour the water from a bucket
or other container. Remove the clothing
from the burned area while continuing to
wash with water. Then continue first aid as
for other burns.   T.M.H.

See also **Accidents; First aid; Shock;
Sunburn**

Cancer is a disease in which there is a
rapid, uncontrolled growth of abnormal cells
in the blood or other body tissue. The abnormal cells destroy normal ones and take their
place. Although cancer in children is not
common, it kills more children between the
ages of 1 and 14 than any other disease.
Scientists do not yet know exactly what
causes cancer.

If cancer attacks the blood, abnormal
white blood cells are produced. This condition is called leukemia. It is the most common type of cancer in children. First signs
of leukemia may include anemia, easy bruising, bone pain, tiredness, loss of appetite,
enlargement of lymph glands, and prolonged
and unexplained low-grade fever. Leukemia
is no longer uniformly fatal.

If cancer attacks the body tissue, it appears as a tumor (a lump or swelling). Not

First aid for burns

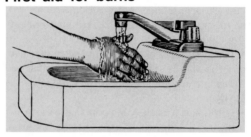

For minor burns, run cold water on
the burn for several minutes. If pain
continues, apply petroleum jelly and a
light gauze dressing over the burn.

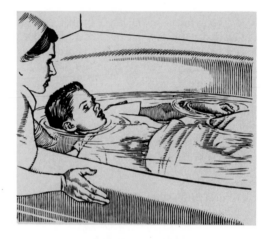

If the burn is a major one and you
cannot get the child to a hospital
immediately, immerse the child or the
burned part of his body in cool water.

For chemical burns, immediately flood
the burn with flowing water. Remove the
child's clothing while rinsing the burn.

all tumors are cancerous. Those that are not are called benign tumors.

Cancerous tumors may occur anywhere in the body—the bones, the eyes, the lymph glands, the muscles, the skin, the testes. Any lump or swelling which can be seen or felt and which is growing rapidly may be a sign of cancer. Other symptoms include weight loss, unexplained anemia, unexplained fever, and failure to thrive.

Tumors of the brain may cause a child to walk unsteadily. They may also cause severe headaches, repeated vomiting, convulsions, cross-eye, double vision, and unconsciousness. Tumors of the spinal cord often cause trouble with walking, stiffness of the back, or difficulties with urinating.

Doctors use blood counts, X rays, computerized tomography (CT), magnetic resonance imaging (MRI), radionuclide imaging, and bone marrow examinations to diagnose cancer. Physicians may prefer to remove tumors—both benign and cancerous—surgically. If the tumor is cancerous, the surgeon often removes surrounding tissue to be certain of removing all cancer cells. Otherwise, the cancer may begin to grow again. Doctors also use radiation therapy and chemotherapy to help fight cancerous tumors. The curing of a tumor depends on the type it is, where it is located, and its stage of development. M.G.

See also **Leukemia**

Canker sores are tender ulcers on the inside of the mouth. One or several canker sores may develop at a time. Canker sores heal by themselves slowly over a period of 8 to 12 days. Doctors do not know what causes them.

Canker sores may first appear as tender, small blisters on the inside of the cheeks, on the tongue, or on the gums. The child may complain of a sore throat or refuse to eat or drink. After one or two days, the blister breaks and a shallow, tender ulcer appears. During the first few days, the child may have a fever (101° to 103° F.; 38° to 39.5° C). If the child is uncomfortable, or a fever greater than 103° F. (39.5° C) persists, give acetaminophen in age-appropriate doses. The glands below the chin may become tender.

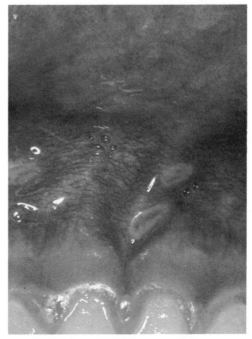

The gums are a common place for canker sores to develop.

The child may be able to drink nonirritating beverages such as apple juice (avoid citrus juices) through a straw. After eating, the child should use a mouthwash of plain water or salt water (one level teaspoonful of table salt in a glass of water). A.M.M.

Car sickness. *See* **Motion sickness**

Carbon monoxide poisoning.
See **Poisonings and poisons**

Carbuncle. *See* **Abscess; Boil**

Cerebral palsy is a general term referring to a variety of motor disabilities that result from brain damage. The damage may occur before, during, or shortly after birth.

Control of muscles and motion is governed by the cerebrum (the largest and most complex part of the brain) and the cerebellum (a portion of the brain that is responsible for coordination). The cerebrum and the cerebellum send signals through the spinal cord and peripheral nerves to the muscles. When there is damage in these areas of the brain, the child's muscles receive badly organized signals from the brain. Paralysis, weakness, incoordination, lack of balance, trembling, and involuntary and unorganized movements may occur.

Brain damage sufficient to cause motor disabilities usually is so extensive that other defects in brain function occur. There may be seizures, problems with speech, and visual impairment. If damage is severe, there may be intellectual impairment.

The lack of muscle control that accompanies cerebral palsy often interferes with language skills. Because of this, it may be difficult to assess the overall intelligence of a child with cerebral palsy. It is also difficult to determine whether a child's performance on an intelligence test is affected by cerebral palsy or by mental retardation.

The cerebrum and the cerebellum may be injured in a variety of ways. Lack of oxygen reaching the infant's brain, hemorrhage into the brain, or infection of the mother by German measles or other virus diseases early in her pregnancy are suspected causes. Usually, cerebral palsy is not recognized at birth because the cerebrum and the cerebellum of a newborn have almost no control over crying, sucking, or moving. During the first year, as the cerebrum and cerebellum develop in the child without cerebral palsy, .sitting, directed hand movements, standing, and walking appear. As these fail to develop normally in a child with cerebral palsy, a doctor can estimate the degree of injury. By that time, clues about the cause are difficult to find. Detailed information about pregnancy, delivery, and the early newborn period may provide enough information for a doctor to speculate as to the cause. But a definite diagnosis is often impossible.

Although children with cerebral palsy continue to develop and grow, the acquisition of developmental skills comes later than for normal children. In some instances these skills never develop.

Cerebral palsy cannot be cured, but medical treatment, physical therapy, speech therapy, special education, training, and counseling may help increase the skills of afflicted children. The type of help children with cerebral palsy should receive depends on the type and degree of disability they have. Medical treatment may include drugs or surgery. Physical therapy may include braces and exercises. The learning ability of children with cerebral palsy varies. One may only be able to accomplish self-feeding and dressing. Another may graduate from college and enter a profession.   A.G.S., M.S.P.

Chafing and chapping are two kinds of skin irritations. Chafed skin is red and often moist. Chafing results when clothing rubs against the body—at the belt line, for example—or when two skin surfaces rub together—as in the armpit or groin. Sand, perspiration, or other irritating substances may make the chafing worse.

To clear up chafing, try to eliminate the cause. If tight clothing is the cause, dress your child in loose-fitting clothes. If a child is fat, the child may have to lose weight before the chafing disappears.

Careful cleansing of the skin and application of a soothing cream or lotion are helpful in treating chafing. If the chafed area is moist, apply cornstarch or zinc oxide paste or powder two or three times daily to promote drying. When the child's skin is drier, discontinue the cornstarch and use talcum powder. If the chafed area is dry, apply cold cream three or four times a day. If itching occurs, cut the child's fingernails short so that the child will not get hurt by scratching the area. Apply cool tap water compresses for 20 to 30 minutes, four times a day. Or give the child tub baths for the same amount of time. If home treatment does not clear up the chafing, consult your doctor.

Chapping is a reddening, scaling, or cracking of the skin caused by a loss of oil in the skin. Exposure to cold, wet, windy weather may cause a child's cheeks, lips, and hands to chap. Staying indoors when the weather is bad prevents chapping. But exposure cannot always be avoided. Mittens and mufflers will help, as will an effort on the child's part not to lick the lips. If your child's skin chaps easily, apply cold cream to the

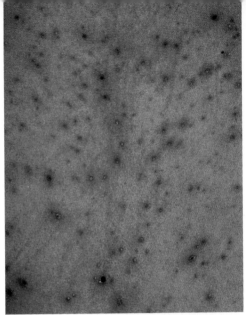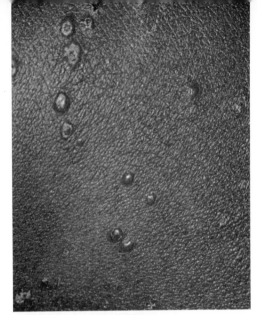

In the rash that accompanies chicken pox, new pimples form while old ones change to blisters. As the blisters dry up, scabs form and then fall off. Skin color (white, left; black, right) can affect the appearance of a chicken pox rash.

chapped areas several times daily, especially after washing, to lock in the moisture. This not only soothes chapped areas, but also helps prevent chapping.

Harsh soap, failure to rinse thoroughly, and careless drying can also cause chapping. Have your child use a mild soap or a cleansing lotion or cream. Encourage the child to rinse and dry thoroughly after washing.

Chapped skin rarely requires medical care. But if chapping is persistent and severe, consult your doctor.   A.M.M.

Charley horse is a sudden, involuntary, and often painful contraction of a muscle or a group of muscles, especially in the leg or arm. Children often suffer such leg cramps at night, after going to bed. A charley horse may also be caused by overuse of muscles or by a strain.

The stiffness and soreness caused by a charley horse can be relieved by bending or straightening the knee or elbow so as to stretch the muscle. Rubbing liniment on the affected part may also help to relieve some of the soreness.

Do not confuse a charley horse with a muscle bruise. A muscle bruise is caused by a blow or strain that crushes and tears the muscle fibers and causes internal bleeding.

The bruise may turn black and blue, and a hard lump may form. The torn muscles may bleed internally for several days. Ice packs on the bruised area will help to relieve the pain and reduce the bleeding. Warm baths will also help a child gradually regain full use of the muscle.

See also **Bruises; Cramps; Growing pains; Rheumatic fever**

Chicken pox (varicella) is an extremely contagious disease. It is caused by the varicella-zoster virus.

A rash usually appears first on the chest and the back, and then spreads rapidly over the rest of the body. The rash changes to pimples within a few hours and then into blisters. The blisters break in one to three days and dry into scabs. The rash occurs in successive crops—new pimples form while old ones change to blisters. This condition lasts for three to four days. The blisters dry up by the fifth to the seventh day. Most of the scabs fall off by the 10th day, but some may remain up to the 20th day.

Most children do not become very sick with chicken pox, although some may have a mild fever. Some children may also vomit, and have backache and headache. Treating fever with aspirin is not recommended because this may result in the development of Reye's syndrome.

Chicken pox occurs most often in children between 2 and 8 years of age, but it can occur even in the newborn child. Call your doctor if you suspect your child has chicken pox.

While your child has chicken pox rash, try to keep the child from scratching. Scratching can open and infect the blisters, causing scars. Wash the child's hands at least three times a day and keep the fingernails short. Baking soda or cornstarch baths once or twice a day may help relieve the itching. Use one or two cups of soda or starch for each bath. If the itching is severe, your doctor may be able to prescribe medication. Call the doctor if any of the blisters become infected.

Chicken pox appears from 14 to 21 days after exposure. Usually, a child can go back to school about a week after the disease begins. Chicken pox is contagious from about one day before the symptoms appear until the blisters have formed into scabs. A child is immune to it after one attack.

Children who are immunodeficient because of serious illnesses such as leukemia, or children receiving cortisone or X-ray treatment, must be protected from chicken pox as it can produce serious complications. Recently two antiviral drugs, acyclovir and vidaraline, have been shown to be effective against varicella-zoster virus; these drugs can be used to treat certain serious cases of chicken pox. Temporary protection can be induced by the use of varicella-zoster immune globulin. Preliminary results with a new live-virus chicken pox vaccine indicate that it is effective in both healthy and immunodeficient children. H.D.R., Jr.

See also **Communicable diseases; Reye's syndrome; Virus**

Choking. A child may choke from accidentally breathing food or other objects into the windpipe. If the child is coughing violently but can still breathe, go to the nearest hospital immediately. If possible, have someone telephone your doctor to meet you there. If the child is choking and cannot breathe, waste no time. Use one of the following procedures, depending upon the age of the child and the situation:

Baby less than 1 year old

- Hold the baby on your forearm, head down, at a 60-degree angle.

- With the heel of your hand, slap the baby's back, high between the shoulder blades, *four* times to force the object out of the windpipe.

- If the airway is still obstructed, place the baby faceup on a firm surface.

- Using two fingers, give *four* rapid thrusts over the breastbone.

- If the baby still does not breathe, open the baby's mouth and move the jaw forward. This will lift the tongue.

- Look in the baby's mouth for a foreign body. If you find one, remove it. (Do not, however, blindly sweep the mouth and throat with your fingers.)

- If you find no obstruction, apply CPR (see **CPR** for detailed instructions).

- Continue CPR until the baby starts to breathe or until emergency medical care arrives.

Child more than 1 year old

- Lay the child faceup on a firm surface. Face the child and kneel, straddling the child's hips.

- Place one of your hands over the other, with the heel of the bottom hand on the child's abdomen (slightly above the navel and below the ribcage).

- Press your hands into the child's abdomen with a quick upward thrust. Repeat this action *four* times. (This action—the Heimlich maneuver—forces air out of the child's lungs and blows the object from the windpipe. If the child is older and is standing, this same maneuver can be performed as shown in the illustration.)

- If the obstruction remains, open the child's mouth and move the jaw forward. This will lift the tongue.

- Look in the child's mouth for a foreign

First aid for choking

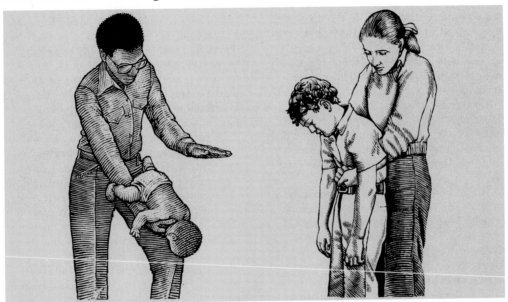

If a baby or very young child is choking (left), hold on your forearm, as shown, and slap the back repeatedly. If an older child is choking (right), wrap your arms about the waist, lock your hands together, and thrust upward.

body. If you find one, remove it. (Do not, however, blindly sweep the mouth and throat with your fingers.)

■ If you find no obstruction, apply CPR (see **CPR** for detailed instructions).

■ Continue CPR until the child starts to breathe or until emergency medical care arrives.

Babies and toddlers can choke on small objects they place in their mouths. Encourage your child to give you any such objects found, then thank the child and substitute a safer object. Make sure that stuffed toys and dolls do not have eyes made of buttons, beads, or glass.

Children can also choke on food particles. Train your child to chew food thoroughly and not to talk while eating. Do not give a child under 4 years of age small, hard foods, such as peanuts, hard candy, popcorn, raisins, coin-sliced carrots, or carrot sticks. Grapes and hot dogs with smooth skins may also cause choking. M.G.

See also **Accidents; CPR; Coughing; Gagging; Swallowed objects**

Chorea (formerly called St. Vitus's dance), is a disease of the nervous system which causes uncontrollable twitching of muscles in the face, arms, legs, or of the entire body. An attack of chorea usually lasts about six weeks, and it gradually subsides without damaging the child's nervous system. The disease most commonly affects children from 7 to about 15 years of age. Doctors do not know what causes chorea.

The twitching may be mild and infrequent, or it may be severe and almost continual. Children with chorea may have difficulty in writing or in feeding themselves. They may walk awkwardly and be clumsy when carrying things. In severe cases, the muscular jerking may cause children to fall out of bed. Children with chorea may become nervous, irritable, and emotionally upset.

Call your doctor if you suspect your child has chorea. The doctor may prescribe sedatives and bed rest. A.G.S.

See also **Ataxia; Rheumatic fever; Tic**

Chromosomes. *See* **Heredity**

Cleft lip is a cleft (split) in the upper lip. It is congenital (present at birth). The cleft may be just a small notch on the lip or it may extend to one or both sides of the nose. A cleft lip may occur by itself or it may appear along with cleft palate or other body defects such as deformed, additional, or missing teeth.

Doctors cannot always determine the cause of a cleft lip. Sometimes it is inherited, but often something has happened during the course of the mother's pregnancy to affect the normal development of the child's lip.

If the child has no other abnormalities, a cleft lip can be treated by plastic surgery, usually when the baby is a few weeks old. Treatment is more difficult if the cleft occurs on both sides of the nose, but the defect can be corrected. Sometimes more than one operation is needed to correct the abnormalities. If the child also has a cleft palate or other defects, care of all the problems must be planned together. T.M.H.

See also **Cleft palate; Heredity**

Cleft palate is an opening in the roof of the mouth that keeps the nose and mouth from being adequately separated. The opening may be very small, or so large that the mouth and nose are practically one cavity. Often the cleft extends through the upper lip as well as the palate. Sometimes cleft palate is hereditary, but often something has interfered with normal development of the mouth before the baby was born.

An infant with cleft palate may have difficulty in nursing and may need special feeding. Also, a child with cleft palate tends to have middle-ear infections, and so should be watched carefully for this complication.

Your physician may recommend surgery to correct the cleft palate, but may delay surgery until the child is 2 years old. (See photographs on page 205.) Or the doctor may suggest the use of a dental appliance instead. The aim is to give the child a good appearance, to enable the child to eat and speak normally, and to promote normal physical, emotional, and social growth. T.M.R.

See also **Cleft lip**

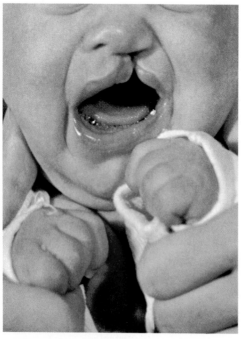

A cleft lip is a split in the child's upper lip. It is present at birth.

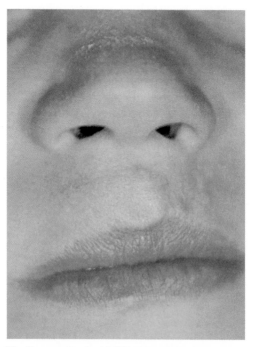

Plastic surgery is highly successful in the correction of a cleft lip.

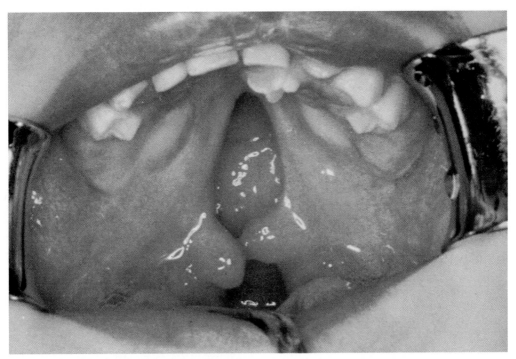

A cleft palate is a split in the palate (roof of the mouth). It is present at birth.

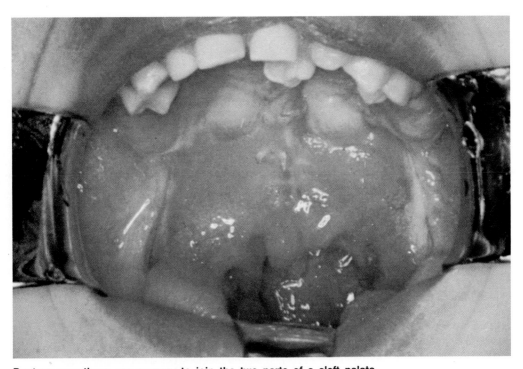

Doctors sometimes use surgery to join the two parts of a cleft palate.

Clubfoot is the most common foot deformity a baby may be born with. Usually, a clubfoot is twisted inward and downward, making the entire leg resemble a club. Clubfoot tends to run in families, and occurs about once in every 1,000 births. It is more common in boys than in girls.

Clubfoot may occur in one or both feet, and it varies in severity from a very mild deformity requiring little treatment to a severe case requiring extensive care, including surgery. An orthopedist (bone specialist) usually directs the care of a child with a clubfoot. Treatment may include stretching exercises, the use of plaster casts or foot splints, and, later, special shoes. Severe foot deformity usually requires surgical treatment. The best results are obtained when care is started early, sometimes in the first week of life. When treatment is delayed, it takes longer to correct the deformity, and the results may not be as successful. J.J.G.

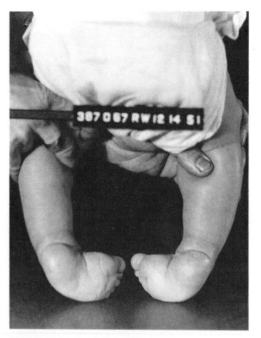

This infant was born with clubfeet. Corrective treatment was begun before the child was a year old.

Coagulation of blood. *See* **Blood clotting**

Colds. Sneezing, a stopped-up or runny nose, sore throat, and a cough usually are signs of the "common cold," a malady with which parents are all too familiar. Children under 2 years old usually get about 7 colds per year. The number of colds decreases as the child grows older. Colds may be caused by many different viruses. These viruses are spread through the air in droplets from sneezes and coughs.

For mild colds with no fever or only a slight fever, you do not have to call your doctor. However, you should call your doctor if your child has a fever of 102° F. (39° C) or higher, if there is a fever accompanied by sore throat, if the cold seems severe, or if the cold lasts more than a few days.

Because colds may be complicated by ear infections, sinusitis, or other illnesses, your doctor may prescribe antibiotics to treat such complications. But the antibiotics have no effect on the cold virus. In fact, there is no way to cure a cold. All you can do is make the child as comfortable as possible, follow the doctor's instructions, and remember the following points:

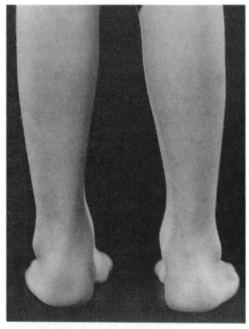

By the time the child was 6 years old, the clubfoot condition was corrected to an almost normal position.

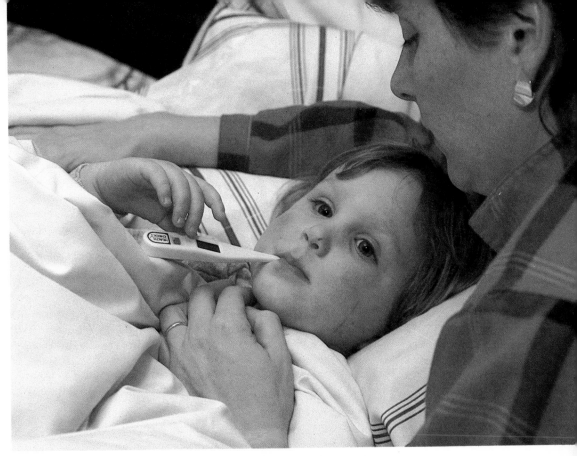

If your child has a fever of 102° F. (39° C) or higher, or a fever and a sore throat, call your doctor. Try to make the child as comfortable as possible.

■ A child with a cold who does not feel very sick and has only a slight fever does not have to stay in bed. A child who feels ill may wish to be in bed.

■ Relieve a child's fever with an aspirin substitute in doses appropriate for the child's age or with other fever medicine recommended by your doctor.

■ Generally, coughing should not be suppressed. It helps rid the bronchial tubes and windpipe of mucus and other irritating material. However, if your child coughs frequently enough to grow tired, irritates the throat, or cannot sleep, your doctor may want to prescribe a cough medicine.

■ Increasing the humidity in the child's room may soothe an inflamed nose and throat. A cold mist vaporizer should be used.

■ Gently wipe the child's runny nose to prevent the skin from becoming chafed. Use nose drops or nasal sprays only when your doctor advises them. If a baby's nose is stuffed up, your doctor may recommend using salt water nose drops and a rubber syringe to suck the mucus out of the baby's nose. Salt water for nose drops can be made by adding ¼ teaspoon of salt to ½ cup of warm water.

■ Let the child decide if and how much to eat or drink. Do not force food or liquids on the child.

Infants usually suffer only mild colds—a runny nose and a slight cough. However, a baby may be very uncomfortable because eating is difficult when the baby cannot breathe through the nose. A baby also is more likely to develop middle-ear infections, pneumonia, and other complications. So anyone with a cold, including members of the immediate family, should stay away from a baby. If you have a cold and you must care for a baby, do not breathe directly into the baby's face. Also, wash your hands before you handle anything—teething ring, foods, the bowl of a spoon, toys, nipples—that goes into the baby's mouth.   M.G., S.G.

See also **Allergy; Bronchitis; Communicable diseases; Coughing; Croup; Drugs; Earaches;**

Fever; Hay fever; Humidifying; Laryngitis; Measles; Nose drops; Pneumonia; Sinusitis; Sneezing; Sore throat; Strep throat; Virus; Whooping cough

Cold sore. *See* Fever blisters

Colic

Colic is a common, uncomfortable condition that some babies experience from the first 2 to 4 weeks of life to the third month. (Sometimes colic lasts until babies are 6 months old.) These babies cry hard and seem to be in great discomfort, as if they have a severe stomachache. Their legs may stiffen, or they may pull them up against the abdomen. Often the abdomen is hard and tense, and they may pass gas. Colic occurs more often in the evening, and, with a few babies, almost every night. If you think your baby has colic, consult your doctor.

No one is certain what causes most colic. It occurs both in breast-fed babies and in bottle-fed babies. Some doctors believe that colic is due to immaturity of the baby's intestinal tract, because colic almost always disappears by the time a baby is 3 months old. Colic may be, but usually is not, caused by allergy.

High-strung babies are more prone to develop the condition than placid ones. Anxiety or tension in the family may increase the frequency of colic. Whatever the causes, colic does not interfere with the baby's health or development. Here are some of the things you can do to prevent or lessen your baby's colic:

- If your baby is formula-fed, have your doctor review the formula. The doctor may want to change it.
- Check rubber nipples to make sure the holes are the proper size.
- Do not feed the baby too rapidly, for too long, or too frequently.
- Burp the baby frequently during feedings to release swallowed air.
- During an attack of colic, humming, quiet rocking, walking, or holding the baby firmly against your chest, either wrapped snugly in a blanket or supported by a pouch, may soothe the baby.
- Sometimes a colicky baby is more comfort-

able lying on the stomach on a warm hot-water bottle.
- A pacifier often relieves colic.

If the mother is breast-feeding, elimination of such foods as cabbage or onions from her diet may be tried.

If your baby has colic, have some part-time help, if at all possible, so that you can take an afternoon nap. An afternoon away from home once a week may also help. M.G.

Colitis

Colitis is an inflammation of the colon (the large bowel). Colitis may be either acute (of short duration) or chronic (lasting for a long time). Consult your doctor if you suspect that your child has colitis.

Acute colitis is a sudden irritation or infection of the colon, accompanied by diarrhea. Some cases are caused by bacteria, parasites, and viruses. A child with acute colitis should eat bland foods, drink plenty of liquids, and rest.

Children with chronic colitis have symptoms either continuously or recurrently over several weeks or months. There are two common forms of chronic colitis—ulcerative and mucous, or spastic.

Ulcerative colitis can endanger a child's life. While doctors do not know what causes it, they do know how to manage it. The inflamed lining of the colon bleeds easily and becomes ulcerated. The most common symptom is diarrhea that may contain mucus and blood. The child may also have a poor appetite, recurrent abdominal pain, arthritis, fever, and anemia.

A child with ulcerative colitis may have to be hospitalized. Doctors prescribe drugs to fight the inflammation and infection. Surgery may be necessary in extreme cases.

Mucous, or spastic, colitis tends to occur in emotionally sensitive children. It may be caused by anxiety or other emotional factors. Symptoms are recurrent abdominal pain and either diarrhea or small, hard stools.

Regional enteritis (Crohn's disease) is a long-lasting disease similar to colitis. Regional enteritis is usually an inflammation of the small bowel, but the inflammation sometimes extends to the colon. The symptoms include fever; recurrent abdominal pain, particularly after eating; diarrhea; constipation; a feeling of rapid fullness of the stomach at meals; weight loss; and retardation of growth. Ulceration of the small bowel may cause fistulas (abnormal channels within the body).

Doctors do not know what causes regional enteritis. Drugs may relieve the symptoms, but sometimes the inflamed section of the bowel must be removed surgically. M.G.

Color blindness is an inability to tell certain colors apart. Some children cannot identify green or red or both. Other children cannot distinguish between blue and yellow. Only a very few children see all colors as gray. Some color-blind children fail to recognize pastel shades.

In most cases, color blindness is inherited. Women are less likely to be color blind than men are. About 8 out of every 100 men are color blind, while about 1 of every 200 women is color blind. No cure has yet been found for color blindness.

Color-blind people often do not realize that their eyesight is defective because they learn to use the color names that everyone else uses. They do not realize that they are not seeing the colors as others see them.

If you notice that your 5- or 6-year-old child has difficulty identifying colors; wears mismatched socks; or cannot take the correct crayon from a box when asked to select one by color, you should have your child's vision checked. R.O.S., S.G.

See also **Heredity**

Coma is a state of unconsciousness caused by injury, poison, drugs, or disease. A coma may occur suddenly, or it may be preceded by confusion, disorientation, or stupor. A coma is always an emergency situation that demands immediate first aid and immediate medical attention.

Here are the steps to take if your child goes into a coma:
■ Be sure that nothing obstructs the child's breathing.
■ Lay the child on one side with the mouth open and slightly downward so that saliva and any vomit may roll out of the mouth.

■ If the child's tongue falls toward the back of the mouth, pull it forward. You may have to use a handkerchief or a towel to get a grip on the tongue.
■ If the child has a convulsion, place a folded handkerchief between the teeth so that the tongue will not get bitten.
■ Call your doctor. If you cannot reach a doctor, take the child to the nearest hospital emergency room.

Severe head injury is a common cause of coma. A child may lose consciousness immediately after the injury or may go into a coma hours later. Rarely, a child may go into a coma days, or even weeks, later. Always consult your doctor when your child receives a severe head injury. The doctor will decide if the child should be hospitalized immediately or can be cared for safely at home.

If your child is in a coma and you suspect that a poisonous substance has been swallowed, take the child to a hospital immediately. Also, take along the container the substance was in to help the doctor identify the poison and perhaps determine how much the child has taken.

Coma in children may also be caused by a brain hemorrhage, a stroke, a brain tumor, or drugs. Diseases such as diabetes, meningitis, encephalitis, Reye's syndrome, and hepatitis may also cause coma.

A child who is in a coma requires hospital care. Coma is treated according to its cause. For example, if the coma is caused by diabetes, the doctor will give the child insulin and fluids. M.G.

See also **Convulsions; Diabetes mellitus; Fainting; Head injuries; Meningitis; Poisonings and poisons**

Communicable diseases. Most communicable diseases of childhood begin in much the same way. A child may wake up in the morning with a miserable case of sniffles, or may come dragging home from school, aching and irritable. At this stage, there is a big question about what the symptoms mean. It could be just a cold. But there is no question about what you should do:
■ Put the child to bed and keep everybody else out of the room.

Communicable diseases

Disease	Incubation period	Common symptoms
Chicken pox (Varicella)	14 to 21 days.	Mild fever, headache, blisterlike rash that appears suddenly. Blisters become encrusted in 1 to 3 days.
Diphtheria	2 to 6 days; can range from 1 to 9 days.	Severe sore throat, fever, yellowish-gray patches on tonsils, throat, or palate. Breathing may become tight and difficult.
German measles (Rubella)	About 14 to 21 days.	Sore throat and headache. Rash on face and head, spreading to neck and trunk. Slight fever during rash. Rash lasts 2 or 3 days. Glands at back of head and neck and behind ears become enlarged.
Influenza	1 to 3 days.	Fever, chills, muscular aches and pains.
Measles (Rubeola)	Fever, 10 days after exposure. Rash, 14 days after exposure.	Resembles cold. Fever, runny nose, watery eyes, cough. White spots on inside of cheeks. Rash begins near the ears and on the side of the neck and spreads downward.
Mumps (Infectious parotitis)	About 14 to 21 days (average, 18 days).	Fever, swelling, and pain in one or more salivary glands. Difficulty in chewing and swallowing.
Poliomyelitis (Infantile paralysis)	7 to 14 days; can range from 3 to 35 days.	Fever, sore throat, dull pain on bending neck, headache, muscle spasms, stiff back. Symptoms may begin suddenly or gradually.
Scarlet fever	2 to 5 days.	Begins very suddenly with headache, chills, fever, sore throat, vomiting. Neck glands enlarged and tender. Tongue coated and pitted looking at first, then becomes red and rough. Rash appears about 3 days after first symptom.
Whooping cough (Pertussis)	5 to 21 days (average, 10 days).	Increased nose and throat secretions. Spells of coughing, which are worse at night. Slight fever. Whooping develops in 2 weeks. Coughing spasm may end in vomiting.

Isolation period of infected child	Isolation period of exposed child	Preventive measures
Isolate for 6 days after rash appears and until *all* blisters are crusted over.	None.	None. One attack usually gives immunity. A vaccine is available for individuals who are at risk for serious disease.
Isolate until doctor has taken 3 consecutive bacteria-free cultures, one every 24 hours.	Quarantine 7 days and until 2 consecutive bacteria-free cultures have been taken, with a 24-hour time span between them.	Shots of diphtheria toxoid (usually begun as part of 3-in-1, DPT shots in infancy). One attack usually gives immunity.
Isolate from first symptoms to 5 days after rash.	None.	Vaccination. One attack usually gives immunity.
Isolate from first symptoms until 7 days after.	None.	Influenza vaccine protects for only a few months.
Isolate from first symptoms to 5 days after rash.	Quarantine 7 to 14 days under some conditions, but quarantine of no value during epidemic.	Vaccination of all susceptible children. Gamma globulin in special cases for temporary immunity. One attack usually gives immunity.
Isolate until swelling subsides, 7 to 10 days.	None.	Mumps vaccine. One attack involving one or both sides usually gives immunity.
Isolate for 7 days from onset, or for duration of fever.	None usually, except to avoid exertion.	Oral polio vaccine should be given beginning in infancy.
Isolate about 7 days, or longer if doctor advises.	None. But should have throat culture.	None.
Isolate for 4 weeks from onset, or 3 weeks after coughing begins.	Quarantine for 14 days after exposure.	Shots (usually begun as part of 3-in-1, DPT shots). Early immunization important. One attack usually provides immunity.

- Take the child's temperature.
- Look for a rash on the child's arms, face, neck, and chest.
- Follow the child's condition.
- Keep the child home from school.
- Call the doctor if your child appears seriously ill, has a high fever (102° F.; 39° C), or develops a rash.

Do not think you are being overcautious by following this procedure. The child may indeed have only a cold. But, if the illness does turn out to be contagious, the earlier and more complete the isolation, the better for other members of the family, especially for babies and elderly relatives. The sooner you get medical advice, the better the chance to determine the nature of the illness and treat it.

The table on pages 210 and 211 provides information about the incubation period, common symptoms, isolation period, and preventive measures for nine communicable diseases. The listing is alphabetical, with medical names of the disease in parentheses. Each disease is discussed more completely in a separate article in the Medical Guide.

"Incubation period" means the length of time between exposure to a disease and the appearance of the first signs or symptoms. This is the time usually required by the viruses or bacteria, once they are in the body of a susceptible person, to grow and reproduce in sufficient quantity to cause illness.

"Common symptoms" are the signs that alert parents to call a doctor to make a diagnosis and prescribe any treatment.

Isolation of the child who has the disease is recommended for each communicable disease. Quarantine of the child who has been exposed to the disease is recommended for some of the diseases.   H.D.R., JR.

See also **Fever; Immunization; Rash; Shots; Virus**

Conjunctivitis is an inflammation of the membrane covering the outer, front layer of the eyeball and the lining of the eyelid. It may be caused by bacteria, viruses, fungi allergies, or chemical irritants such as smoke or soap. Conjunctivitis usually occurs by itself, but it may appear in connection with

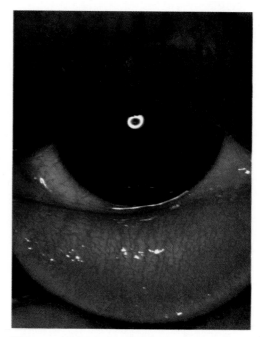

When a child has conjunctivitis, the lining of the eyelid and the membrane covering the eyeball become inflamed.

colds, measles, chicken pox, ear infections, and other diseases. Some forms of conjunctivitis are contagious.

If your child complains of "something in my eye," look for conjunctivitis. This feeling is often a first symptom, followed by a discharge of water or pus, or swelling accompanied by itching, burning, and discomfort from light. Symptoms are usually more intense in the evening after the eyes have been used and will vary with the amount of inflammation. In the morning, a child's eyelids frequently will be stuck together from the discharge that has dried during the night. Wash the eyes open, but apply no other home treatment. If the inflammation does not clear soon, see your doctor.

Conjunctivitis in newborn babies may be an indication of a serious problem. Babies often have a chemical conjunctivitis from the eye drops administered shortly after birth. This condition should last only 2 or 3 days. If your newborn has conjunctivitis that persists past the fourth day of life or begins in the first few weeks of life, consult your doctor immediately.   R.O.S.

See also **Allergy; Eye health**

Constipation is a bowel disorder in which bowel movements are hard, dry, and difficult to pass. You cannot tell if your child is constipated just by watching the child during a bowel movement, because some completely healthy children grunt, strain, and get red in the face just before and after they have a bowel movement.

Some parents worry unnecessarily about constipation and become overly concerned about the "regularity" of their child's bowel movements. Babies, like adults, vary a great deal in the frequency of bowel movements. Most young babies have one to three movements a day, but some have four or five regularly every day. Occasionally, a breast-fed baby has one bowel movement every two or three days, but breast-fed babies usually have four to eight movements each day.

Most babies have an occasional, mild episode of constipation with some discomfort for a day or so. This is common in illnesses with fever. Usually, no special treatment is necessary except to offer the baby an extra amount of water.

If your baby's stools are especially dry, try a few changes in diet. Cereal may be mildly constipating. If the baby eats other solids, give more fruit (except bananas). Occasionally, one-half ounce (15 milliliters) of prune juice mixed with an ounce (30 milliliters) of water will help. Add pureed prunes to your baby's diet. Begin with two teaspoons a day. Never give your baby laxatives, suppositories, or enemas without consulting the doctor.

Occasionally, an extremely hard stool may cause a small tear in the anus. This may, in turn, cause some pain in the passage of stools and some bright red blood on the outside of the stools. Consult your doctor if this occurs.

Quite frequently, older children will be constipated for short periods of time. Occasionally, this condition represents some resistance to toilet training, but most often it starts around the age of 2, when children are learning to exercise their own will and to say "no." They even say "no" to their own body needs, ignoring them while they continue to play. Or they say "no" because they are upset over the arrival of a new baby in the house. Never battle over this withholding of stools, because children who feel they must defend their right to exercise their own control can become very stubborn. Do not focus undue attention on bowel habits.

To avoid constipation, your child should have a balanced diet, regular exercise, and plenty of liquids. Consult your doctor if your child is persistently constipated, especially if the child resists going to the toilet and soils underpants repeatedly during the day. M.G.

See also **Appetite; Enema; Laxatives; Nutrition; Suppositories**

Contagious diseases. *See* **Communicable diseases; Immunization**

Contusions. *See* **Bruises**

Convulsions (seizures) are involuntary contractions of muscles. During a convulsion, a child's muscles may jerk or twitch, and the child may lose consciousness. Eyes may roll, stay open, or almost close, and the child may have brief spells of staring into space. Teeth may be clenched. The child may become rigid, with the neck arched, arms and legs stiff, and toes pointing. Sometimes during a convulsion, the child may urinate involuntarily or have a bowel movement. Although convulsions are frightening to watch, they usually are not dangerous.

If your child has a convulsion, try to remain calm and reassuring. Unless the child is in a dangerous place, let the child stay in the position in which he or she falls—on back, side, or stomach. Turn the child's head to one side to prevent choking if the child vomits. The convulsion usually stops within a few minutes. After the convulsion, the child generally sleeps deeply for a while.

If your child has a convulsion for the first time, it is important to call the doctor as soon as possible. Although fevers are the most common cause of convulsions, infectious diseases could also be the cause.

Convulsions are brought on by brain disturbances. The most common cause of convulsions for children between 1 and 3 is high

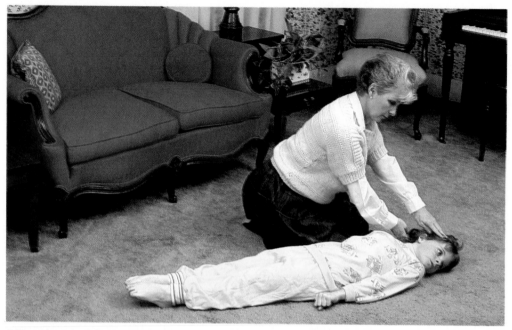

Although convulsions usually are not dangerous, there is always a chance of self-injury during a convulsion. Turn the head to one side to keep the child from choking, Remove nearby objects. Do not move the child unless the location is hazardous. Call a doctor as soon as possible.

fever. If high fever tends to bring on convulsions in your child, the doctor may prescribe daily doses of an anticonvulsant medicine for a couple of years. You should also take precautions whenever your child has a high fever (102° F.; 39° C) by giving the child appropriate doses of acetaminophen or other drugs your doctor may prescribe for fever, as well as a sponge bath in lukewarm water.

Convulsions may also occur in connection with diseases causing unusually low blood sugar or unusually low levels of calcium in the blood. In diseases such as tetanus (lockjaw) or infections of the brain, such as meningitis, convulsions are often frequent and severe. Convulsions may occur after birth injuries or after brain injuries resulting from accidents. Epilepsy is the name given to convulsions that occur repeatedly without any fever or disease. M.G.

See also **Epilepsy; Fever; Head injuries**

Cot death. *See* **Crib death**

Coughing usually indicates that something is irritating the breathing passages and that the body should be rid of it. Some of the most common causes of coughing are the following:
- Respiratory infections such as bronchitis, the common cold, croup, pneumonia, sinusitis, and whooping cough
- Allergies such as asthma and hay fever
- Accidentally breathing small objects such as coins, tiny toys, safety pins, beads, or small food particles into the windpipe or lungs
- Accidentally breathing chemical substances into the windpipe or lungs

Chronic coughing may be caused by cystic fibrosis or reactive airway disease (asthma). Occasionally, a child develops a cough habit.

The way you treat a cough depends largely on its cause. Consult the doctor to determine the cause. The doctor may advise chest X rays, blood tests, a sweat chloride test for cystic fibrosis, and allergy tests.

Usually, a child's coughing should not be suppressed. It is the normal way to get rid of irritating material in the respiratory system. But if coughing tires your child or interferes with sleep, the doctor may prescribe a cough medicine for the child or tell you to give the child cough drops. Never give cough medicine to a child unless your doctor prescribes it.

Here are some other steps your doctor may take to relieve your child's coughing:
∎ In case of a bacterial respiratory infection, the doctor may prescribe antibiotics and advise you to increase the humidity in the child's room. Moistened air makes breathing easier for the child.
∎ In case of nasal allergies, the doctor may prescribe antihistamine drugs to prevent or lessen allergic reactions.
∎ If a foreign object has been breathed into the windpipe or lungs, the object may have to be removed surgically.

See also **Asthma; Bronchitis; Colds; Croup; Cystic fibrosis; Hay fever; Humidifying; Measles; Pneumonia; Sinusitis; Swallowed objects; Tuberculosis; Whooping cough**

CPR (cardiopulmonary resuscitation) is an

emergency procedure that combines artificial respiration with manual heart (cardiac) massage. Instructions for both parts of the procedure are provided in this article.

CPR is used to open the passage from the lungs to the mouth, to move air in and out of the lungs by making the chest alternately expand and contract, and to force blood from the heart to other parts of the body by compressing the heart periodically. Using this procedure can prevent irreversible brain damage or death if the breathing and heartbeat have stopped.

If possible, CPR should be performed by someone who has been trained in the technique. Training is often available through community agencies. If you have not had CPR training yourself, the following explanation will help you become familiar with the procedure.

CPR is also more easily performed by two people. If possible, have one person administer artificial respiration and the other person perform cardiac massage.

When a child's breathing stops for any reason, quickly begin artificial respiration and check the child's pulse. If no pulse can be felt, apply CPR immediately (both artificial respiration and heart massage) while someone else calls the Emergency Medical Services (usually 911; check your local emergency number).

If the child's breathing has stopped because of drowning, lay the child stomach down on a flat surface, turn the child's head to one side, and press down on the back before you start CPR. This clears water from the child's throat and trachea (windpipe) so air can pass freely.

Turn the child faceup, turn the head to one side, and clear the mouth of any foreign object. Then put your hand under the child's neck and tilt the head back.

Artificial respiration. Begin CPR with mouth-to-mouth resuscitation. This provides positive air pressure to inflate a child's lungs immediately. It also enables the person administering CPR to judge the volume, pressure, and timing needed to inflate the lungs. When administering mouth-to-mouth resuscitation to a child, take relatively shallow breaths to match the child's own small breaths. Continue until the child's normal breathing resumes or until professional help arrives.

When handling an infant, be careful that you do not exaggerate the backward position of the head tilt. An infant's neck is so pliable that forceful backward tilting might block the child's breathing passages instead of opening them.

Do not pinch the nose of an infant who is not breathing. Cover both the mouth and the nose with your mouth and breathe slowly (1 to 1.3 seconds between breaths) to make the chest rise. For a small child, pinch the nose, cover the mouth with your mouth, and breathe as for an infant.

Check for pulse periodically. In an infant, the pulse is determined by feeling on the inside of the upper arm midway between the elbow and the shoulder. For children older than 1 year, locate the carotid pulse by sliding your fingertips down the side of the Adam's apple (voice box) into the groove next to it. If you cannot find a pulse, you will need to alternate artificial respiration with chest compressions.

How to give mouth-to-mouth artificial respiration

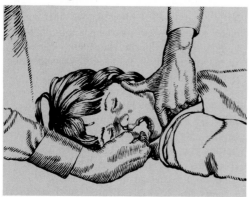

1. The victim should be lying on a firm surface with the head turned to one side. Use your fingers to remove any foreign object from the child's mouth.

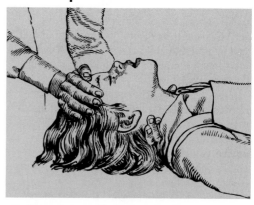

2. Place one hand under the victim's neck and the other hand on the forehead. Then tilt the head back. If the head is not tilted back, the tongue may block the throat.

3. If the victim is a small child or infant, take a shallow breath. Cover both the nose and mouth of the victim with your mouth. Blow into the mouth and nose every three seconds.

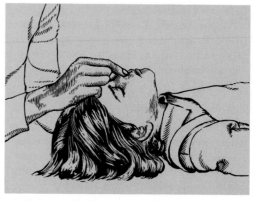

4. If the victim is a large child or adult, pinch the nostrils shut with the thumb and index finger of the hand pressing on the forehead. This will prevent any leakage of air.

5. Take a deep breath and cover the victim's mouth with your mouth. Blow into the victim's mouth. A large child or adult needs about one breath every five seconds.

6. Watch the victim's chest. When it rises, turn your head and listen for a return rush of air. When the victim has finished breathing out, repeat step 3, or steps 4 and 5.

Cardiac massage. In infants and small children, only one hand is used for chest compressions. For an infant, you may slip the other hand under the back to provide firm support. Use only the tips of the index and middle fingers to compress an infant's chest at the sternum (breastbone), pressing down one finger's width below the line between the nipples. Be sure not to depress the tip of the sternum. Depress the chest at least 100 times a minute.

For small children, use only the heel of one hand on the sternum where the bottom of the two halves of the ribcage meet in the middle of the chest. Depress the sternum 80 to 100 times a minute.

For both infants and small children, pause after every fifth chest compression and give the child a breath.

Cradle cap is a scalp condition that may occur during the first few months of a baby's life. Whitish scales form on the baby's scalp and then flake off. If the condition is not treated, the scales form a heavier crust that is yellowish and greasy. When cradle cap reaches this stage, the scalp may look a little red and irritated, and a rash may develop on the baby's face and chest, and in the armpits.

The best way to prevent cradle cap is to shampoo the baby's scalp thoroughly (including the soft spots) at the beginning of each bath. Use soap and water and a washcloth.

If your baby has already developed cradle cap, repeat the following steps once or twice a day:
- Comb the scalp with a fine-toothed comb.
- Gently scrub the scalp with a mild soap.
- Dry the scalp thoroughly.
- Apply several drops of baby oil to the scalp and rub it in thoroughly.

If the condition does not improve in a few days, consult the baby's doctor.   A.M.M.

Cramp is the sudden painful contraction of a muscle or group of muscles. A cramp is caused by some unusual event irritating muscle tissue. Although cramps may occur in any part of the body, leg and stomach cramps are the most common.

Leg cramps usually occur at night, after the child goes to bed. The child may be awakened by painful cramps in the calf and thigh muscles. You can usually relieve the pain by massaging the cramped muscles.

Muscle cramping may be caused by sudden overstretching or overactivity of muscles. The most common cause of muscular leg cramps in a child, however, is flat feet. The abnormal arch of the foot strains the leg muscles, and they develop cramps during rest periods. Consult your doctor if your child has leg cramps frequently.

Abdominal and intestinal cramps may occur in girls during the menstrual period. Applying heat and using acetaminophen may help relieve pain. Abdominal and intestinal cramps may also be caused by appendicitis, an ulcer, food poisoning, or emotional upset. If the cramps last longer than 24 hours or are accompanied by severe vomiting, call the doctor.   J.J.G.

See also **Charley horse; Colic; Colitis; Flat feet; Food poisoning; Growing pains; Menstruation**

Crib death (Sudden Infant Death Syndrome or SIDS) is the sudden and unexpected death of an infant, usually while asleep. Ongoing research has not yet established the cause or causes of death. It is estimated that more than 8,000 babies die in the United States each year because of crib death.

Some stricken infants are reported to have had a mild respiratory infection a week or two earlier. But most infants are apparently in excellent health just before death. Some even had a satisfactory physical examination on the day they died.

Crib death is the most frequent cause of death in infants between 2 weeks and 9 months of age, with most deaths occurring between 2 and 3 months of age. Most deaths occur between midnight and 9 A.M. Boys are affected more often than girls, and infants of low birth weight are more likely to be affected than those of average or high birth weight. While crib deaths may occur at any time during the year, they are more frequent in colder months.

Parents who have had a baby die from crib death often feel responsible for the death. Their guilt feelings, while natural, are not supported by facts. There is no way in which crib deaths can be predicted or prevented. These infants do not suffocate in their bedclothing. And they do not die because of poor care. Crib deaths can occur to infants of the most capable parents.

Parents who have had one child die from crib death usually worry about the possibility of a second baby dying in the same manner. There is an increased risk, which is considered to be five times greater than the risk of the general population. Parents who have experienced a SIDS death in their family may have concerns about their subsequent children. These parents should discuss their concerns with their doctor, who may arrange for an evaluation of the new baby.

Contact the National Sudden Infant Death Syndrome Foundation, 8240 Professional Place, 2 Metro Plaza, Suite 205, Landover, Maryland 20785 for information on crib deaths. M.G.

Cross-eye (strabismus). Many babies' eyes "drift" during the first few months of life. One eye or the other will turn in occasionally, making the child look cross-eyed. Let your doctor decide if the condition of your child's eyes requires attention. If the baby's eyes are not straight most of the time by one month or all the time by 3 months, the doctor will probably suggest that the infant be referred for a special eye examination.

If treatment for cross-eye is started early, chances of correcting the cause of the disorder are excellent. The doctor may recommend eyeglasses. The doctor may recommend that the child wear an eye patch over the good eye to make the crossed eye work harder to develop good vision. If these corrective measures fail to straighten the child's eyes, a surgical operation may be necessary.

If crossed eyes are not corrected, the child may lose the sight of the crossed eye. R.O.S.

See also **Eye health**

Croup is a respiratory illness characterized by a hoarse, barking cough and tightness in the child's breathing. A child with croup makes a harsh, wheezing noise when taking a breath (stridor). This may be the result of an inflammation of the larynx (voice box) or the bronchi (air passages) leading to the lungs.

Spasmodic croup, in which the child does not have a fever, is the most common and mildest form of croup. It comes upon the child suddenly at night and may be repeated for several nights. Humidify the child's room with a cool-mist humidifier or vaporizer. If neither is available, create a steamroom in your bathroom by running a hot bath or shower. Stay with your child to make sure the child does not get into the hot water. Twenty minutes in a steamy bathroom should greatly ease the child's symptoms. Giving the child plenty of water and fruit juice will also help. When you put your child back to bed, elevate the child's head and shoulders to make breathing easier.

Laryngobronchitis is a form of croup that is caused by a viral infection. This type of croup is accompanied by fever and other coldlike symptoms. The hoarse, barking cough and tight breathing can occur both day and night. Steam or mist will not adequately treat this kind of croup.

If your child has difficulty breathing, appears very ill, or does not improve with cool mist, take the child to the doctor as soon as possible. If you cannot reach the doctor, take the child to a hospital emergency room. M.G.

Cuts and scratches. The best way to treat small cuts and scratches is with soap and water. First, wash your own hands. Then, wash the cuts with plenty of soap and water, using cotton or a clean cloth. After this, rinse away the soap and cover the cut with a small sterile gauze square or a bandage to keep it clean. You do not have to apply any antiseptic to a wound that is thoroughly washed. If areas around the cuts or scratches become inflamed, consult your doctor. Inflammation is caused by infection.

If a cut is large and deep, take the child to a hospital emergency room. Stitches may

Treatment for cuts

 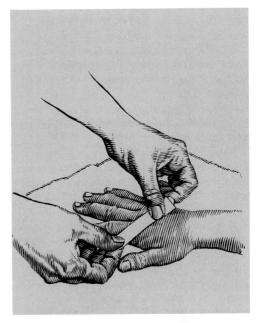

Wash a small cut with plenty of soap and warm water. Then rinse
the cut thoroughly and cover it with an adhesive bandage strip.

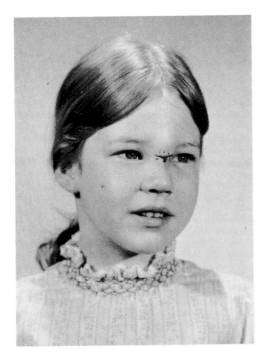 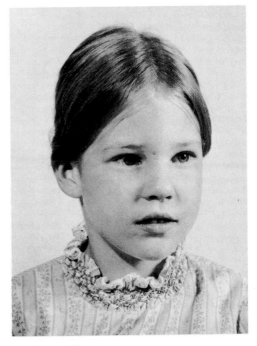

Some cuts require stitches to bring the edges of the cut together.
This helps the wound heal and usually prevents unsightly scars.

be necessary to close the wound. But in many cases a doctor can use strips of adhesive tape to bring the edges of the wound together.

A deep cut may bleed profusely. You can usually control bleeding by applying a sterilized dressing or clean cloth over the cut and pressing down until the bleeding stops. If the bleeding continues, do not remove the first dressing. Place another dressing on top of it and continue pressing.

Cuts in the scalp and face may bleed profusely for a few minutes. In most cases, the wound is not as serious as it appears. Wash away the blood, and then decide whether a doctor should examine the cut.

A cut on the inside of the finger, palm, or wrist may injure a nerve or a tendon. Have the child flex all the fingers on the hand to make a fist. If nerves or tendons have been cut, the child will not be able to make a fist. If you think your child has a cut nerve or tendon, take the child to the hospital emergency room immediately.

Always consult your doctor about puncture wounds; wounds that do not bleed readily; or wounds that may have been contaminated with soil from pastures, barnyards, lawns, gardens, or other areas fertilized with animal manure. These wounds may contain bacteria that cause tetanus (lockjaw), a disease that causes muscle spasms and convulsions. The doctor may want to give the child a shot of tetanus toxoid to safeguard against tetanus infection.   M.G.

See also **Bites and stings; Bleeding; First aid; Medicine cabinets; Tetanus**

Cyanosis is a bluish coloring of the skin and lips that results from a lack of oxygen in the blood. A "blue baby" has cyanosis because a congenital (present at birth) heart defect interferes with the circulation of blood through the heart. Cyanosis in a blue baby is not always apparent when the baby is resting, but it may become noticeable when the baby cries or is very active. In addition to cyanosis, the baby may also have a heart murmur and respiratory problems.

Congenital heart defects. Cyanosis due to congenital heart defects is usually caused by

A normal heart and an abnormal heart

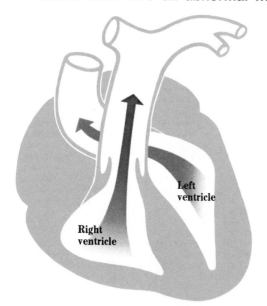

Normally, the right ventricle pumps blood to the lungs, where oxygen is added. The blood then flows back into the heart, and the left ventricle pumps it to the body.

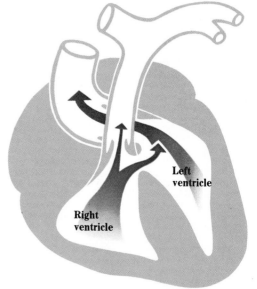

In this heart, much of the blood flows through a hole in the wall between the ventricles and by-passes the lungs. The left ventricle then pumps it to the body.

the passage of unoxygenated, bluish blood from the veins through an abnormal opening in the wall between the right and left ventricles of the heart. This defect is called a Ventricular Septal Defect (VSD). In a normal heart, the unoxygenated blood from the veins is pumped from the right ventricle through the pulmonary artery to the lungs, where oxygen is added. Then, the bright red, oxygenated blood is pumped into the left ventricle and into the aorta and other arteries. In a child with cyanosis caused by a congenital heart defect, part or all of the blood by-passes the lungs. Because of an abnormal opening between the ventricles, the unoxygenated blood is pumped from the right ventricle directly into the left ventricle, and then into the aorta.

In addition to an abnormal opening between the left and right sides of the heart, there may be an obstruction or narrowing of the pulmonary artery. This obstruction or narrowing also prevents the blood from being properly oxygenated.

Another congenital heart defect that causes cyanosis is transposition (change in the position) of the aorta and the pulmonary artery. Cyanosis may also indicate that the baby's heart has only one ventricle.

If your baby has a congenital heart defect, your doctor will probably refer you to a pediatric cardiologist (a children's doctor who specializes in the treatment of the heart and its diseases). The cardiologist will take a chest X ray and an electrocardiogram (EKG), which records the size and shape of the electrical impulses of the heart. This doctor may examine the heart by echocardiography and cardiac catheterization. A long tube is inserted in the heart through a vein in the arm, and the path of the tube is viewed on an X-ray screen. The cardiologist may also introduce a dye into the baby's circulation to help temporarily outline the defect.

Some heart defects can be corrected by surgery, but the timing of the operation depends on the baby. As long as the baby is gaining weight and does not have severe breathing difficulty, the operation will probably be delayed until the baby is 2 years old. Corrective operations include by-passing the narrow passage that impedes the flow of blood to the lungs and closing off the abnormal opening between the right and left sides of the heart. Many congenital defects can be completely corrected so that the child has no disability.

Other causes. Cyanosis can also be caused by a collapsed lung, pneumonia, suffocation, shock, or other conditions. Treatment consists of relieving the condition that is producing the lack of oxygenated blood, and, if necessary, giving the child oxygen.   M.G.

Cystic fibrosis is an inherited disease in which glands produce abnormally thick mucus that clogs up body organs and hinders their normal operation. Breathing and digestion are most often affected. Doctors do not know exactly what causes it or how to cure it completely. Early diagnosis and treatment have made it possible for many affected children to lead fairly normal lives until they are adolescents or young adults.

The most common and serious symptoms of cystic fibrosis are a persistent, hacking cough and repeated attacks of bronchitis or pneumonia. These are caused by blocked air passages. Some newborn babies who have cystic fibrosis may have difficulty with bowel movements because of an obstruction in the intestines. These infants may have frequent bowel movements that are bulky, loose, pale, and unusually foul-smelling. They may fail to gain weight even though they have a good appetite. A child with cystic fibrosis loses an excessive amount of salt through sweat.

If the disease has settled in the respiratory tract, your doctor may prescribe regular aerosol treatment through a face mask to help thin out the secretions in the child's breathing passages so that mucus can be brought up to the throat, and the child can spit it out. The child may also receive antibiotics or drugs that relax the chest bronchial airways.

The doctor may also prescribe physical therapy to promote draining of the secretions from the bronchial tubes.

The doctor generally prescribes a diet high in protein and calories. In the presence of abdominal cramps or frequent, oily stools, a diet moderately low in fat content may be recommended. Because pancreatic juices necessary for digestion become blocked in the pancreas, pancreatic enzyme preparations may have to be given by mouth. M.G.

Cysts are abnormal, fluid-filled sacs within the body. A cyst has no opening. Usually the lining of the cyst produces the material that fills the cyst.

Cysts are of all sizes and may occur almost anywhere in the body. They may be congenital (something the child is born with), or they may result when a gland opening becomes plugged. Sometimes, doctors cannot determine their cause. Only rarely are cysts malignant.

Some cysts are simple and harmless. They eventually disappear by themselves. Often, however, cysts have to be removed. Some, such as a thyroglossal cyst (in the neck), tend to become infected. Other cysts have to be removed because they interfere with proper functioning of a body organ. For example, cysts on the lungs may interfere with breathing.

Cysts that are close to the surface of the skin can be removed by simple surgery in the doctor's office. Cysts that are deep in the abdomen or chest require a major operation and hospitalization. T.M.H.

Deafness is the partial or complete inability to hear certain sounds. More specifically, it is the inability to discriminate speech.

In a child with normal hearing, sound waves pass through the ear canal. They strike the eardrum, a thin membrane that separates the ear canal from a tiny chamber. The eardrum and three small bones in the chamber are called the middle ear. When the eardrum moves, the movement is transmitted along a chain of the bones—the hammer, the anvil, and the stirrup—to the inner ear. There, the cochlea (an organ shaped like a snail's shell) changes the vibrations into nerve impulses, which are sent along the auditory nerve to the brain. Deafness may result if anything interferes with the healthy operation of any of these parts.

There are three main types of hearing loss. If sound waves are not conducted ade-

quately to the child's inner ear, the hearing loss is called conductive. If sound waves reach the child's inner ear, but they are not properly changed into nerve impulses, the hearing loss is called nerve deafness or perceptive deafness. If the child's hearing loss is the result of both conductive and perceptive impairments, the hearing loss is called mixed deafness.

Causes of deafness. Deafness can develop before birth. It can be inherited. It also can develop in an unborn child if the mother has German measles or other diseases during her pregnancy, or if she takes certain drugs.

Or, deafness can be caused after birth by a number of illnesses or injuries, especially head injuries such as skull fractures or concussions. German measles, measles, meningitis, mumps, scarlet fever, and whooping cough are some of the diseases that may cause perceptive deafness. Infected adenoids, tonsillitis, and the common cold can cause temporary deafness if the infection spreads to the middle ear. An obstruction in the ear canal—an accumulation of wax, a boil, a small object like a marble—may cause deafness. Deafness can also result if the eardrum is ruptured by a sharp instrument, a violent noise, or sneezing.

Detecting hearing losses. These signs can warn parents that their child may be deaf:
■ From birth to 6 months—The child is not startled by noises and is not responsive to pleasant or cross voices. The infant does not turn toward the source of familiar sounds.
■ From 6 months to 18 months—The child does not understand words. The baby babbles a few sounds, but does not turn the head in response to sounds.
■ From 18 months onward—The child does not speak words but makes wishes known by gesturing. The child does not identify objects when they are named. The child depends on sight more than on hearing.

If you have any doubt about your child's ability to hear, consult your doctor. The doctor may recommend that you take the child to an otologist (a doctor specializing in ear conditions) for examination.

Various tests can be made to determine the severity of hearing loss. These tests include the use of the voice, a watch, tuning forks, and an audiometer (an electronic de-

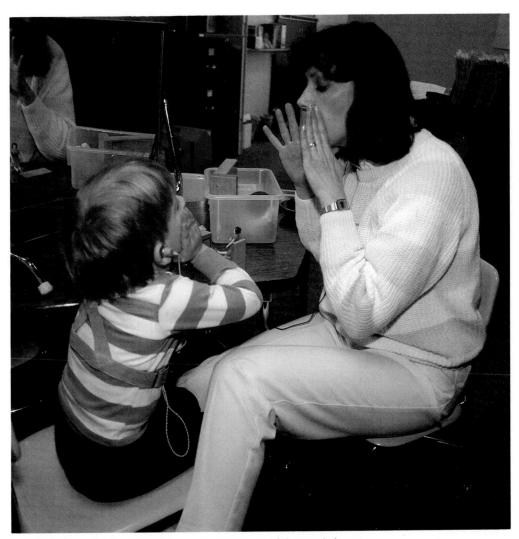

A child who is hard of hearing usually needs special speech lessons.

vice that measures the range of a child's hearing, from the lowest sound to the highest). An audiometric examination helps a doctor determine whether a child is deaf, how much hearing the child has, the character of the hearing loss, and whether a hearing aid will be helpful. Audiometric graphs or records also provide a means of measuring hearing loss for a particular child over a long period of time. A record of hearing loss can be kept and compared with new records, enabling the doctor to tell whether the child's hearing is unchanged, improving, or becoming worse.

Deafness and speech. Detecting a hearing loss is important at any age, but it is especially important in babies because speech normally develops from hearing. A child who is born totally deaf cannot learn to talk without special training. Early intervention is important. Families of children as young as 6 months can participate in a language-stimulation, auditory training program with their child, and amplification—the use of a hearing aid—should begin before the child is 2. The child usually enters a school when about 4 or 5 years old. Some schools also have parent education programs to help parents

A hearing aid does not restore hearing to a hearing impaired child, but it does amplify the sound so that the child can hear the sounds and discriminate between different sounds.

guide their child even before the child enters school. Excellent parent education programs are also available by mail. (See AGENCIES AND ORGANIZATIONS INTERESTED IN THE WELFARE OF CHILDREN.) With special schooling and guidance, a totally deaf child can grow into a mature, self-supporting person.

Children with only partial loss of hearing usually need special speech lessons, too. They cannot discriminate all the sounds in words and, consequently, cannot reproduce the sounds adequately.

Hearing aids. A hearing aid consists essentially of a microphone, an amplifier (also called a transmitter), and a receiver. The microphone picks up sound, and the amplifier makes it louder and transmits it to the receiver by means of a wire. The receiver is small and usually made to fit in the child's ear. Some amplifiers are made to be worn on a jacket lapel or some other place where they can receive sound freely. Others are small and are worn as part of an ear-level hearing aid.

There are two types of hearing aids—the air conduction aid and the bone conduction aid. An air conduction aid amplifies sound, transmitting it directly to the ear. Bone conduction aids transmit sound waves to the bony part of the head, usually in the mastoid region behind the ear. The air conduction aid is by far the more popular and usually the more effective, but the bone conduction aid may be better for some children.

A hearing aid will not restore or bring hearing to normal, but it will amplify sound so that it can be heard and so that the child can be taught to discriminate sounds. Many of the sounds will seem new or strange at first. Voices may sound different because they lack some of the qualities and timbre of normal speech. This is especially true if the child had normal hearing at one time and then lost it, either through disease or injury.

A child with partial deafness can frequently hear some tones better than others. The hearing aid can be adjusted to amplify tones the child has difficulty hearing. Hearing aids also help a child hear sounds in the immediate surroundings, such as approaching cars.

An ear specialist will tell you whether a hearing aid will help your child. The doctor can also tell you whether the child will benefit most by using a hearing aid at all times or only when it will help most—during school, for example.   C.F.F.

Dehydration is a condition that results when the water content of the body drops excessively. It is sometimes accompanied by a loss of certain body minerals, such as sodium and potassium.

Dehydration is caused by one of two things. The first is an increase in the loss of water from a child's body, as may occur with persistent vomiting, persistent diarrhea, excessive sweating, high fever, severe burns, or increased urination. The second cause of dehydration is a decrease in the intake of water, as may occur when a child does not or cannot drink sufficient fluids for the body's normal functions. Sometimes, both factors may cause dehydration. For example, a child who is vomiting is losing water from the body. At the same time, the child may not be able to drink any liquids.

The severity of dehydration depends upon the amount of water and the amount of minerals lost. Generally, the child's skin is dry, and the tongue and the lining of the mouth are parched. Skin may become less elastic. Babies and young children lose weight. Occasionally, the child may run a fever of 102° F. (39° C) or higher. In more severe cases of dehydration, the child may be listless and the eyes may be sunken. The soft spots (fontanels) in an infant's head may become depressed.

If your child shows signs of dehydration, call your doctor. If you cannot reach the doctor, take the child to a hospital. If the diarrhea, vomiting, or other cause of the dehydration has stopped, give the child water or cracked ice. If the child can keep this down, then give frequent small amounts of weak tea, a mixture of half water and half apple juice, or a carbonated soft drink. A teaspoonful at a time may be all a small child can take.

The doctor will judge the severity of the dehydration on the basis of what has caused it and on any signs of dehydration the child has. The doctor may also examine samples of the child's blood and urine to determine if there has been a mineral loss. If the dehydration is not severe, the doctor may advise oral rehydration. If it is severe, and especially if there is persistent loss of fluids, the doctor will probably advise hospitalization and giving fluids intravenously. M.G.

See also **Diarrhea; Fever; Soft spots; Urinary disturbances; Vomiting**

Diabetes mellitus is a disease in which the body fails to utilize sugar properly. In children with insulin-dependent Type I diabetes, the failure generally occurs because of destruction of the cells that produce insulin, the hormone that enables the body to store and burn sugar in its normal manner. Diabetes is more common in adults, but it can occur at any age.

A child with untreated diabetes usually eats a great deal more than is normal, drinks large quantities of water, and urinates frequently or in large amounts. A doctor can diagnose the child's condition by analyzing the child's urine and blood. A child who has diabetes will show an excess of sugar in both blood and urine. If the diagnosis is not made promptly and treatment begun, the child loses weight rapidly, breathes deeply and rapidly, is nauseated, vomits, gradually becomes weaker, and may become drowsy or go into a diabetic coma.

All diabetics should be under a doctor's care. Although diabetes cannot be cured, it can be controlled through the use of insulin injections and diet. Care must be taken to regulate the amount of insulin given, because too much may lower the blood sugar to a point where the child may feel unusually hungry or nauseated. The child may perspire and grow pale, or faint and lose consciousness—sometimes with a convulsion. This condition is called insulin shock. If a child appears to be developing insulin shock, offer orange juice or some other food that contains sugar and promptly call your doctor.

Although the diabetes will be lifelong, it should not interfere with the child's psychological and social development. Encourage the child to participate in the usual childhood activities and to take care of his or her own dietary and insulin needs. Diabetic children can grow to adult life able to carry on normal activities. M.G.

See also **Convulsions; Diets; Drugs; Endocrine glands; Heredity**

Diaper rash is so frequent in its mild form that almost every baby has it sometime. The skin in the diaper area looks red and chafed, and sometimes there are a few pimples and rough red patches on it. The rash may spread and the baby may be uncomfortable. Sores of severe diaper rash on the circumcised penis may result in painful urination.

Severe diaper rash usually results from friction and associated contact irritants (harsh soaps, detergents, acid stools, or topical medications). Sweat retention with excessive heat and moisture are other significant factors.

To treat diaper rash, change wet or soiled diapers frequently. Avoid using waterproof pants over the diapers, especially on very young babies or on those with sensitive skin. Rinse the diapers thoroughly after washing them. The "rinse" cycle of an automatic washing machine usually rinses the diapers adequately. Disposable diapers may be less irritating and should be tried.

When your baby's skin is chafed, let the baby lie without diapers for several hours after each diaper change. The air will help dry and heal the skin. Apply a protective preparation, such as zinc oxide paste or a baby lotion, after the skin has been cleaned with plain water. Your doctor may want to recommend a preparation.

For severe diaper rash, leave the diapers off for two to four days and use a fan to circulate the air. If cloth diapers are being used, rinse the diapers in a vinegar solution—use ½ cup of household vinegar in the tub of rinse water. Rinse the diapers in this solution after they have been completely washed and rinsed. After rinsing them in the vinegar solution, wring the diapers out, or let them go through the "spin" cycle of an automatic machine, and dry them in the usual way.

Occasionally, diaper rash occurs because enzyme- and bleach-containing detergents are used in washing the diapers. You can lessen the chances of this if you use a mild soap and rinse the diapers thoroughly.

If the diaper rash looks like a chemical burn, develops blisters, or becomes infected, consult the baby's doctor. Candidiasis (a fungal infection) and impetigo (a blister-forming skin disease) are fairly common complications of severe diaper rash.   A.M.M.

See also **Impetigo**

Diarrhea is an intestinal disorder marked by frequent loose, watery bowel movements. Diarrhea can be serious, especially when it is accompanied by mucus or blood in the stools, listlessness, failure to eat, dehydration, vomiting, or fever. If your child's diarrhea persists or appears to be serious, call your doctor.

Diarrhea in babies is often caused by problems in feeding. Sometimes the baby's formula is not sterilized adequately or is made in incorrect proportions. Check with your doctor about your formula preparation and the amounts you are feeding the baby. Sometimes one or two loose stools may occur when the baby starts eating new solid foods. To help your baby adjust more easily to new solid foods, cut down on the amount of the foods and start any new foods slowly. Occasionally, diarrhea may be caused by a food allergy.

Mild diarrhea may accompany a general infection. Your doctor may precribe medicine for the general infection. The doctor may also suggest that you give your child extra fluids (water, diluted formula, or other liquids) to help replace the fluid lost with the diarrhea. The doctor will probably tell you to feed the child a bland diet of such foods as applesauce, cereal, and gelatin.

Sometimes a specific bowel infection causes diarrhea. Be careful to prevent spreading the infection to other members of your family. Wash your hands after handling the baby or diapers. Place the diapers in a covered container and wash them separately from other clothing. Boil the diapers or iron them to kill germs.

In older children, diarrhea is usually milder, but it occurs for similar reasons— bowel infection or as part of a general illness. Diarrhea may also be a symptom of tension or anxiety that occurs at times of stress or excitement, such as a school examination or a special party. If these situations frequently cause diarrhea, consider ways to relieve your child of stress or help avoid too much excitement.   M.G.

See also **Allergy; Dehydration; Food poisoning; Influenza; Sterilizing**

Diets. A balanced diet contains all the food elements that a child needs to grow and stay healthy. A child requires proteins to build body tissues, fats and carbohydrates for energy, and minerals and vitamins for growth, maintaining body tissues, and regulating body functions.

Your doctor may prescribe a special diet for your child if the child has an illness, a metabolic disorder, a food allergy, or a weight problem. Be certain you know why the diet is being prescribed and how you can best carry it out.

Here are some questions you may want to ask when the doctor advises a diet:

- Is the quantity of food eaten important? If so, how can you keep a record of what the child eats?
- How urgent is it to follow the diet closely? In some metabolic diseases, where the child's body cannot digest certain component materials in foods, it is vitally important to follow the dietary prescription to the letter.

Encourage your child to stay on the diet. If there are choices among foods, use those the child prefers, especially if the child must remain on the diet for a long time. Let the child who can understand assume some responsibility for eating needed foods and avoiding others. Most children are happy to have this trust placed in them. Older children often can help plan what they will eat. Helping make such decisions may give them the incentive to carry them out.

Make diet foods as appealing as you can. For instance, a white cream soup, served in a colorful bowl or cup with a bright garnish, usually perks up the appetite of a child on a bland diet.

A child on a diet has to learn to go without eating certain foods, but try not to put an extra strain on willpower. For example, a child who is allergic to eggs has to accept the fact that he or she cannot eat eggs for breakfast even though the rest of the family has eggs. But serve eggless desserts so that the child can eat the family dessert.   M.G.

See also **Allergy; Anorexia nervosa; Appetite; Nutrition; Overweight; Underweight; Vitamins**

Diphtheria is a severe, contagious disease that causes a membrane to form in the throat or nose. This membrane may hinder breathing and eventually cause choking or even death. Diphtheria is caused by bacteria. Once common, diphtheria is no longer widespread because almost all children are immunized against it.

Diphtheria usually begins from two to four days after exposure. A child with diphtheria may have a sore throat, fever, headache,

backache, drowsiness, and vomiting. Yellowish-gray patches may appear on the throat, the tonsils, or the roof of the mouth. Sometimes the membrane so completely obstructs the throat that the child cannot breathe. A doctor may have to perform a tracheotomy (incision into the windpipe) to get air into the lungs. Call your doctor immediately if you suspect that your child has diphtheria.

Inoculations of diphtheria toxoid are routinely given in a single shot along with tetanus (lockjaw) toxoid and pertussis (whooping cough) vaccine. These inoculations, called DPT shots, are usually begun when the infant is 2 months old. The last infant DPT shot is given when the baby is 16 to 18 months of age. As further protection, a DPT booster is given at 4 to 6 years of age, or when a child enters kindergarten or first grade.

For nonimmunized children over 6 years of age, two Td shots (combined tetanus and diphtheria toxoids) are given eight weeks apart. A third shot a year later completes the immunization.

For continued protection, all immunized children should have a Td booster shot at 14 to 16 years and at 5- to 10-year intervals during adult life.

A baby who has received a DPT shot may have a fever and a loss of appetite, and will be cranky. The area around the injection may be sore and red. This reaction occurs because of the whooping cough vaccine. To relieve fever, give acetaminophen in doses appropriate for the baby's age. Your baby should feel better the next day. If your baby runs an excessively high fever or exhibits other abnormal behavior, notify your doctor. The doctor may wish to modify the immunization schedule.   H.D.R., Jr.

See also **Communicable diseases; Fever; Immunization; Shots; Tetanus; Whooping cough**

Disinfecting. *See* **Sterilizing**

Dislocation of a joint. A joint is dislocated when the two bone ends that make up the joint become separated and no longer work together. Most dislocations are caused by injury. They occur most frequently in the shoulder, elbow, ankle, or finger joints. A

Dislocation of shoulder joint

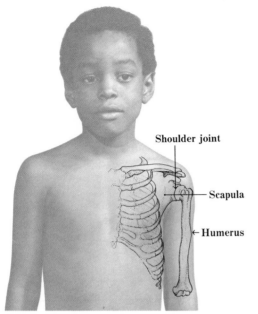
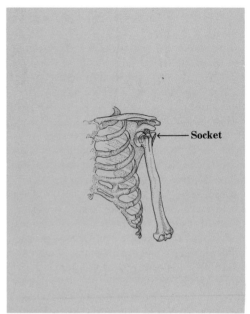

Shoulder joint

Scapula

←Humerus

Socket

The shoulder joint consists of two bones—the humerus and the scapula. When the humerus slips out of the socket of the scapula *(right)*, the shoulder is dislocated and the child experiences immediate pain.

dislocation causes immediate pain and rapid swelling of the injured part. There is usually a visible deformity, and the joint cannot be moved normally. In addition, one of the dislocated bones may be broken. A joint dislocation is serious and requires immediate medical treatment.

Call a doctor at once and do not move the child. If you cannot reach a doctor, protect the joint by putting splints on the injured part in the most comfortable position. Never pull on the bones or attempt to relocate the joint yourself. After applying the splint, take the child to a hospital immediately for X-ray examination and proper care. The child will probably be given an anesthetic, and the doctor will attempt to gently manipulate the bones of the joint back into their proper position. Most often this is successful. Rarely, an operation may be needed to correct the dislocation. The doctor will usually apply a splint, cast, or brace to protect the healing joint.

Sometimes a joint, usually the shoulder or kneecap, will dislocate periodically. Surgery is required to correct this condition. v.v.g.

Drowning. *See* CPR

Drugs are used to provide comfort and to prevent and cure disease. Drugs are obtained from plants, animals, and minerals, or they are produced synthetically.

■ Insulin, a hormone extracted from animal tissues, is also being synthesized using recombinant DNA technology. Doctors use insulin to control diabetes mellitus, a disease in which the body does not produce enough insulin.

■ Most antibiotics are produced from molds that live in the soil. Doctors use antibiotics to treat blood poisoning, boils, osteomyelitis, pneumonia, scarlet fever, and tuberculosis.

■ Sulfa drugs are synthetic drugs produced from chemicals. Doctors may use sulfa drugs against urinary tract infections.

■ Vaccines are made from the growth of bacteria or viruses. Vaccines have been developed to prevent diphtheria, poliomyelitis, measles, mumps, German measles, whooping cough, tetanus, hemophilus influenzae infections, and other diseases.

- Silver nitrate is a drug derived from a mineral. Doctors drop silver nitrate into the eyes of newborn babies to prevent infection.

The same drug often may be dispensed in different forms. For the child who cannot swallow capsules or tablets, a doctor may prescribe a syrup, drops, or chewable tablets. If a child is vomiting, the drug may be given as a suppository. A doctor injects a drug to get a rapid effect, or if the drug is ineffective when taken by mouth. Time-release capsules allow the action of the drug to be spread over a period of hours.

Many drugs can be bought without prescriptions, but there are dangers in giving them to children. Many illnesses have similar symptoms but are treated differently. Your doctor will diagnose the illness and prescribe the proper drug and dosage. An overdose of any drug may be harmful. Do not even give vitamins to your child without first checking with your doctor.

After your child recovers, discard any left-over drugs that were prescribed to treat the illness. Medicines often deteriorate with time. Also, they may be hazardous to a child exploring the medicine cabinet. M.G.

Drug abuse. Drugs are a serious problem in today's society. Children using drugs often have noticeable behavior changes, as well as changes in school performance and a decline in social interests. If you suspect your child is using drugs, you need to discuss this with both your child and your child's doctor.

The most common drugs and other illicit substances used by children and adolescents are cigarettes, alcohol, marijuana, cocaine, crack, and Phencyclidine (PCP).

You should also be sure that any babysitter you entrust your child to does not use any of these substances. (See also THE DRUG PROBLEM in For Special Consideration.)

Sharon Galli, M.D., Consulting Editor

Dyslexia. Significant confusion exists regarding the definition of this term. Many specialists define it as a severe level of reading impairment in a person of normal intelligence who does not have major neurological or physical abnormalities and is not environ-

mentally disadvantaged. People with dyslexia experience letter and word reversal. For example, they may not be able to distinguish *saw* and *was*, or the letters *d* and *b*. Some specialists believe that dyslexia results from a mild neurological disorder; however, this view is not uniformly shared by specialists in this area.

The evaluation of a child with a reading difficulty includes a battery of neuropsychological tests, a physical examination, and vision and hearing screening tests. Helping a child with dyslexia involves developing an individualized program that focuses on a child's developmental and emotional strengths and weaknesses. M.S.P.

Ear, objects in the. If your child says that something is in his or her ear, do not try to remove the object yourself. The attempt to remove a foreign object may injure the ear canal or eardrum, or the object may be pushed farther down the ear canal, making it harder to get out. Call your doctor. If you cannot reach the doctor, take your child to a hospital emergency room.

Children are prone to put such things as peas, beans, or corn kernels into their ears. These vegetables absorb moisture and swell, causing intense pain and blocking the ear. Paper also swells and causes pain and blockage. Beads, buttons, and stones that fit into a child's ears can cause painful irritation. Sometimes an insect lodges itself in a child's ear canal, causes discomfort because of its movement, and frightens the child with its buzzing. Matches or hairpins may break the skin and cause a painful infection.

Caution your child never to put anything into the ears. Try to keep small objects out of the child's reach. C.F.F.

See also **Earaches**

Earaches are usually caused by infections in the ear canal or middle and inner ear.

Infections of the ear canal. Excessive wetness (from swimming or bathing) or trauma (from fingers or foreign objects) can make the ear canal especially susceptible to infections. Symptoms include pain, itchiness, and some hearing loss.

Your child's doctor may treat your child with ear drops containing antibiotics and corticosteroids. Dry heat from a heating pad and acetaminophen may also help relieve pain.

Infections of the middle ear (Otitis Media). Otitis Media is one of the most common problems during childhood. Most ear infections occur between 6 months and 6 years of age. Children who develop ear infections early in life have an increased risk of recurrent or chronic infections. A middle ear infection can easily be diagnosed by the doctor. Oral antibiotics are usually prescribed for about 10 days. A follow-up ear examination is necessary to ensure that the infection has been cured.

Fever, vomiting, and diarrhea may accompany a middle ear infection. Acetaminophen for pain and fever and dry heat to the ear will ease some of the symptoms.   C.F.F.

Eczema is a rash that is usually caused by an allergy to a food, drug, or some irritating substance. Patches of skin become red and itch persistently. Often the itching is so intense that the child scratches until the skin breaks and bleeding occurs. Scratching opens the skin, a colorless fluid oozes from the rash, and the skin becomes thick, coarse, dry, and scaly. In an infant, the rash appears mainly on the cheeks, and in the folds of the neck, arms, and sides of the legs. In an older child, it appears mainly as chronic, thickened areas behind the knees, in front of the elbows, or in the creases of the neck. In severe cases, it may spread over the entire body. If you think that your child has eczema, consult your doctor.

The cause of eczema is often difficult to determine. Your doctor may suggest eliminating a certain food from the infant's diet to find out if that particular food is causing the allergic reaction. In more severe cases, the doctor may perform skin tests to determine which substances the child is allergic to. If the doctor is able to discover what is causing the baby's eczema, you can sometimes prevent the condition by removing the offending food from the baby's diet or by removing the irritating material from the baby's surroundings.

Eczema usually begins in infancy. It occurs more often in children with a family history of allergies. It usually clears completely by the time the child is 18 to 24 months old. Sometimes, however, it persists through puberty and into adult life. The skin of a child who has had severe eczema usually heals without any scars. However, some children may retain uneven pigmentation of the skin, which is exaggerated by sunburn. Many children with eczema develop hay fever or asthma as they get older. A child may also have both eczema and a respiratory allergy at the same time. If your child has eczema, certain precautions may reduce the discomfort produced by the rash:

- Do not let the child's skin come into contact with wool or clothing made of synthetic fibers. Cotton is preferable.
- Avoid clothing that causes excessive perspiration.
- Avoid irritating soaps, bubble bath, detergents, and excessive bathing.
- Keep the fingernails short to lessen damage from scratching.

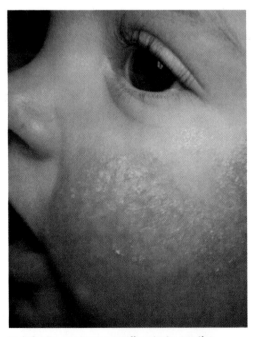

In infants, eczema usually starts on the cheeks and then spreads to the folds of the neck and other parts of the baby's body.

- Antihistamines and other drugs may reduce itching, but they should be used only when prescribed by a doctor.
- When the skin is red and oozing, wet compresses help relieve itching and inflammation. Your doctor may also prescribe lotions and ointments to lessen itching.
- Keep a baby with eczema clothed, because scratching becomes more violent when clothes are off.
- Keep the child occupied to help take the child's mind off the itching.

The skin changes caused by eczema make the child's skin more susceptible to infection. If a secondary infection occurs, the child may need to be treated with oral or topical antibiotics. J.S.H.

See also **Allergy; Itching**

Electric shock is usually much easier to prevent than to treat. It is very dangerous and can kill or seriously injure anyone.

If your child suffers electric shock, remember that while seconds count, do not be careless of your own safety. If you find the child unable to let go of an electric wire, keep calm. Do not touch either the wire or the child with your bare hands while electricity is still flowing. Pull the main switch if it is near, or jerk the plug from the socket. If you cannot turn the electricity off, you will have to move the wire off the child or the child off the wire. Use anything dry that does not conduct electricity—boards, branches, wooden poles, folds of cloth or newspaper, or rubber or heavy cloth gloves. And be sure that you are standing on a dry surface.

As soon as the child is free, start giving artificial respiration if breathing has stopped. (See CPR.) If possible have another person call the paramedics (usually 911).
If you are alone, restore breathing before calling for help. If an electric spark has caused a burn, treat it later.

A child suffers electric shock usually because an adult has forgotten how curious and investigative a child can be, or because the adult does not realize how little a child knows of danger or caution. To a child, an electric outlet is a fascinating hole in the wall, just right for poking with a stray

Freeing a child from a live wire

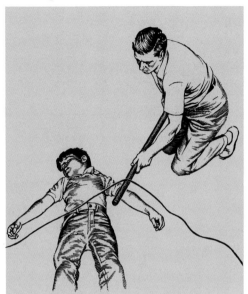

To get a live wire off your child, stand or kneel in a dry place and move the wire with a broomstick, or with any other object that does not conduct electricity.

bobby pin. To a child, an appliance cord is for pulling—a child doesn't know that it may be faulty. To a child, it is quite possible to find a favorite television character by poking into the rear of the television set.

Make your home safe, keep an eye on your child, and let the child understand that in dealing with dangers your "No" means "Positively no!" Even the crawler learns to stay away from outlets if you repeatedly pick the child up, say a firm "No," move the child to another spot, and offer a toy. For added safety, buy special plugs that cover the electric outlets. M.G.

See also **Accidents; Burns; CPR**

Electroencephalography (EEG) is a recording and study of brain waves. The most common reason for administering an EEG is to evaluate a child who has had a seizure. An instrument called the electroencephalograph records electrical impulses sent out by the cortex (the thin layer of nerve cells that covers most of the brain). The electrical impulses are picked up by wires

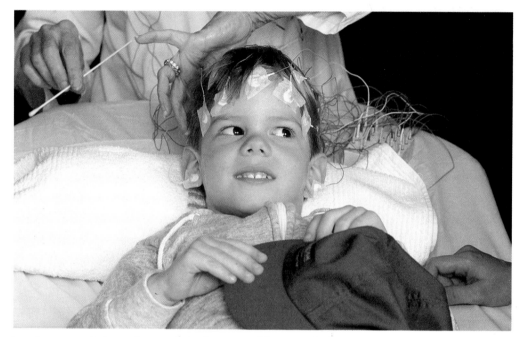

An electroencephalograph records brain waves. Wires attached to the child's head pick up electrical impulses from the brain.

attached to the scalp, either with glue or with needles, and recorded on a strip of paper. The record (the electroencephalogram, or EEG) looks like a series of wavy lines with varying patterns. The child's hair does not have to be shaved off, and the child feels no pain from the electroencephalograph.

Abnormal patterns may be recorded if the child has epilepsy, a seizure, a brain tumor, encephalitis, drug intoxication, or a dangerous disease of the brain. In some cases, especially in epilepsy, doctors can determine the cause of the abnormal electrical pattern from the electroencephalogram. If a child's EEG confirms the diagnosis of epilepsy, medications to control the seizures can be prescribed. In other cases the abnormal pattern indicates only that brain destruction or deterioration has occurred, and the electroencephalogram cannot be used to establish a definite cause of the destruction or deterioration.   A.G.S.

Emetics are medicines that cause vomiting. Inducing vomiting is a recommended treatment for certain types of poisoning. Do not induce vomiting until you have called the Poison Control Center, your doctor, or an emergency room. Never induce vomiting if the child is asleep, unconscious, semiconscious, or has convulsions; or if the child has swallowed a corrosive substance or a petroleum product.

Vomiting is more effective if the child first drinks some liquid. The best emetic is syrup (*not fluid extract*) of ipecac. If you do not have syrup of ipecac, put one teaspoon of mustard in half a glass of water, or three teaspoons of salt in a glass of warm water, and have the child drink the mixture.

Any time you induce vomiting, be sure to keep the child's head lower than the hips so that all the vomit flows out of the mouth and not back into the throat. Also, be sure to catch and save the vomit for the doctor to analyze.   M.G.

See also **Poisonings and poisons**

Encephalitis occurs when an inflammation of the brain alters normal functioning of various parts of the brain. There are many different signs and symptoms of encephalitis.

Location of endocrine glands

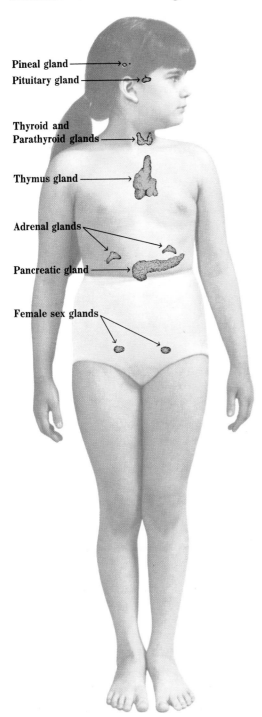

Pineal gland

Pituitary gland

Thyroid and
Parathyroid glands

Thymus gland

Adrenal glands

Pancreatic gland

Female sex glands

Endocrine glands produce hormones that regulate growth, sexual development, metabolism, and other body functions.

They include fever, headache, mental dullness, stiff neck, and convulsions. Hallucinations and coma may also occur. Call your child's doctor if you suspect that your child has encephalitis.

Encephalitis is caused by several kinds of viruses. These viruses can be transmitted by mosquitoes and other insects. Or, encephalitis may accompany mumps, measles, or certain other infections. Preventive measures include insect control and vaccinations, if available, against the specific viruses that cause encephalitis.

Care of a child with encephalitis is extremely difficult, especially when the child is in a period of sleep. Almost all children with encephalitis need to be hospitalized for an extended period of time. Recovery may be slow. Supportive and rehabilitative efforts and treatments are very important for the recovering patient.

Prognosis is varied and guarded. A few children do not survive encephalitis. Some who survive may have long-term motor, visual, or intellectual impairment. H.D.R., JR.

Endocrine glands produce vital chemical substances called hormones. Hormones regulate body growth and shape and various functions of the body. Endocrine glands are also called the ductless glands because their hormones enter the bloodstream directly instead of through ducts.

The "master" endocrine gland is the pituitary. This gland, approximately the size of the end of your thumb, produces many hormones. One hormone regulates a child's growth. Other hormones regulate other endocrine glands—thyroid, adrenal, and sex glands.

The thyroid gland produces thyroid hormone, which regulates metabolism (chemical process of utilizing foods). The adrenal glands produce hormones that regulate growth, sexual development, sugar metabolism, and the use of salt. Part of the pancreatic gland produces insulin, which regulates the use of sugar within the body. The sex glands produce hormones that affect growth and the development of masculine or feminine characteristics. M.G.

Enema is the introduction of fluid into the intestine through the rectum to flush the colon. The fluid remains in the intestine for a short time and, when eliminated, it washes out feces from the bowels. Enemas are usually given to empty the bowels before certain types of surgery.

Never use enemas unless a doctor has prescribed them. The doctor may do so in the rare case of an impaction (a severe piling up of feces in the bowels). But constipation is best treated by a prescribed diet and increased exercise. Regular use of enemas for constipation may have harmful effects.

- They may make a mild case of constipation more severe, because they tend to destroy the healthy muscle tone of the bowels.
- They may frighten a young child.
- They may make a child focus too much attention on the anus and bowels.
- They are uncomfortable physically. M.G.

See also **Constipation**

Enuresis. *See* **Wetting**

Epilepsy is a chronic (long-lasting) disorder of the nervous system. Some forms cause convulsions and loss of consciousness. The exact cause of epilepsy is unknown, but it may be the result of any condition or disease that affects the brain. Many epileptic patients have some brain damage due to infection or a tumor, or as the result of an injury.

Types of epilepsy. The two most common types of epilepsy are known as *grand mal* (pronounced "gran mahl") and *petit mal* (pronounced "petty mahl"). Some doctors prefer to use the term "convulsive seizures" for grand mal and the term "absence attacks" for petit mal.

A child who has a grand mal seizure loses consciousness and falls. The child's muscles may stiffen or become rigid. The child then begins to twitch and jerk, first rapidly, then more slowly but more violently. Saliva may flow more freely during convulsions and not be swallowed, and the child may lose bowel and bladder control. The convulsions usually last only a few minutes, but afterward the child may sleep for a time.

Seizures are dramatic and frightening, but children rarely suffer serious injury during them. You cannot do much for a child suffering an epileptic seizure except place a coat, pillow, or folded blankets under the head, loosen clothing, and remove objects from the path of moving arms and legs. After the attack, you should turn the child on one side.

In a petit mal seizure, the child loses consciousness for a few seconds, but usually can maintain balance and does not fall. The child may appear dazed momentarily after the seizure, but soon resumes conversation or normal activity. Petit mal seizures occur frequently, perhaps dozens in a single day. These seizures may interfere more with a child's learning than will the infrequent grand mal seizures, because they repeatedly interrupt the child's concentration.

Not all convulsions are caused by epilepsy. An infant with a high fever may have convulsions. If the child is younger than 4, and if the convulsions occur only with a fever—and not very often at that—the convulsions will probably cease to be a problem by the time the child is about 6 years old. However, if the convulsions occur without fever and continue after the child is older, the doctor will probably suspect epilepsy.

Any child suffering from convulsions should have immediate medical attention. Parents should be completely frank in describing the child's convulsions, in reporting head injuries or illnesses involving high fevers, and in recalling any history of convulsions in the family. The doctor, who seldom is able to observe the seizure, will need this information and the results of diagnostic tests to make a proper diagnosis. The doctor probably will request that an electroencephalographic study be made. This is a painless recording of the brain's activity picked up by sensitive wires that are pasted to the child's scalp. (See ELECTROENCEPHALOGRAPHY, pages 231-232.) The electroencephalogram, or EEG, appears on paper as an ink tracing of parallel, wavy lines.

Drugs can eliminate or reduce seizures in about 85 per cent of all epileptics, but some time may be required before the doctor can determine the proper combinations and dosages of drugs. Success of the treatment for epilepsy will depend largely upon how carefully and continually the doctor's instructions are followed.

Day-to-day living. Epileptic children need the same affectionate guidance, patient understanding, and satisfactions from life that all children need. Epilepsy itself is usually not a serious handicap, but the attitudes of adults and the child's playmates may create difficulties. Parents of an epileptic child should tell friends and neighbors about their child's condition and give them accurate information about epilepsy.

However, epilepsy, if not properly controlled by medication, may impose some restrictions on a child's life. Swimming, bicycle riding, climbing, driving, and other activities may have to be limited. Most epileptic children can go to school. However, the parents of an epileptic child should inform the principal, teacher, and school nurse about the child's condition. An explanatory note from the child's doctor may also be helpful in case the child has a seizure at school and needs help.   A.G.S.

See also **Convulsions; Electroencephalography; Fever**

Eye, objects in the. Your child will tell you immediately if there is something in his or her eye, because it hurts. An infant will probably cry and rub the eyes.

Do not try to remove an object from your child's eye. Most foreign objects are washed out in a few moments by the extra tears the irritated eye produces. If the object does not wash out, call a doctor or take the child to a hospital. Many amateur attempts to remove objects from an eye result in loss of sight, usually from infection.

If a harmful fluid gets into your child's eye, wash the eye immediately with plenty of water. After you apply first aid, call your doctor. If you cannot reach the doctor, take the child to a hospital emergency room.

If an eye is injured by a sharp object such as a dart, an arrow, or a knife, do not try to open the eyelids. Cover the injured eye with a clean cloth and take the child to a doctor or to the emergency room of the nearest hospital.   R.O.S.

See also **Eyelids**

Eyeglasses. Eyeglasses cannot cure poor eyesight, but in many cases they can help a child see better. Even when a child has no obvious eye defect, parents should be alert to signs of eye trouble. This is especially true of 2-year-olds. By this age a child's eyes should be functioning effectively. But if the child overreaches or underreaches when trying to grasp objects, seems overly sensitive to bright light, or squints or rubs the eyes excessively, there may be some visual deficiency.

Children should have a complete eye examination by the time they reach 3 or 4 years of age. They should have frequent reexaminations as they grow and their eyes change. If a serious visual deficiency is neglected in a preschooler, by the time the child is ready for school even glasses may not be of much help.

Parents should remember that often young schoolchildren with blurry vision may not complain about it, because they think everyone sees as they do. A schoolchild who is mentally, emotionally, and physically healthy, but fails to keep up with classmates, may have a visual problem. The child may misbehave in class because of frustration over the inability to see clearly. Often, parents and teachers find that when such a child begins to wear glasses, learning and behavioral problems tend to lessen and disappear.

Children who wear glasses need not wear them all the time unless the doctor tells them that they should. Some children need to wear glasses only when reading or doing close work. If this is the case with your child, let the teacher know so that the child can be helped to use the glasses to the greatest advantage. Teach your child to take care of the glasses. Show the child how to put them on and take them off without stretching the earpieces, how to keep the glasses clean, and how to handle them without scratching the lenses.

Eye health. A good rule for the care of normal eyes is to leave them alone except for periodic medical examinations. When eyes seem abnormal in any respect, a complete eye examination is in order. Attempts at self-diagnosis and self-treatment of eye disorders can be disastrous.

Contrary to popular opinion, no known exercises will correct near-sightedness, far-sightedness, or defective color vision. Also, extra vitamins or special foods rarely help. The varied diet of food available to most people in the United States and Canada contains all the vitamins needed for eye health.

Infants. For the first several weeks of life, a baby sheds no tears when crying. Infants produce only enough tears to keep their eyes moist. Tears drain through two small openings in the inner corner of each eyelid into a tiny sac and then enter the nose, causing it to "run." Occasionally, this tear system becomes blocked and tears constantly run over the edges of the lid. Or the tear sac near the nose may swell. If this happens, call your doctor.

In the first few weeks of life a baby's eyes look crossed at times. Do not be alarmed at this lack of eye coordination. Let your doctor decide if the condition warrants attention. But if the baby's eyes are constantly out of line at 6 months of age, your doctor will probably refer your child for a special eye examination. If treatment is started early enough, it can often eliminate the need for surgery.

Older children. All children should have a complete eye examination before they enter the first grade. About 1 out of 5 of the children examined will need help with some visual problem. In most states, children receive visual screening tests when they enter school. However, rather than count on the tests at school to discover if your child has a visual problem, it is wiser to have your child's eyes examined beforehand. Then have your child's eyes examined every two years.

Also, be alert to the following danger signs which can indicate eye difficulty:
- The child frequently stumbles or bumps into furniture.
- The child squints, frowns, or blinks excessively while reading.
- The child holds reading material close to the eyes.
- The child has sore or unusually red eyes or eyelids.

Good lighting and correct posture ensure more efficient use of the eyes and often prevent eye discomfort. Do not restrict reading to save your child's eyesight. Restrictions can actually prevent the development of visual ability. Like muscular ability, visual ability improves with practice and use.

Distinct contrasts in lighting may contribute to eye fatigue, as when a child watches television in a darkened room or studies at a desk where a single lamp leaves the rest of the room in darkness. Some other light should be on in the room.

To read well, a child must be able to see well. But if tests show the eyes to be normal, if the child's I.Q. is normal, and if the child still is having difficulty in reading, the child should be checked for a learning disability. Because of some learning disabilities, some children who see words clearly find it almost impossible to understand their meanings. If this appears to be true of your child, consult your doctor.

Accidents. In the United States alone, children suffer about 95,000 serious eye accidents each year. About a thousand of these cases are so severe that the child loses the sight in one or both eyes. Most of these accidents could have been prevented.

Do not allow your child to handle sharp-pointed scissors, a bow and arrow, or sharp tools until mature enough to understand the dangers involved.

If your child suffers an eye injury, get professional help immediately. Do not put liquid into the eye (except to wash out irritants such as acid or gasoline). Gently cover the eye, and take the child to a doctor. R.O.S.

See also **Astigmatism; Color blindness; Conjunctivitis; Cross-eye; Dyslexia; Eyelids; Far-sightedness; Near-sightedness**

Eyelids protect the eyes and help keep them clean. Any disease of the eyelids should be checked by a doctor.

A sty, a common disease of the eyelid, is an infection in one of the glands in an eyelid. It is a small boil that forms at the lid edge. Usually it comes to a head, breaks, drains, and cures itself. Warm compresses held against the sty may hasten the process and relieve minor irritations.

One sty often leads to another because as a sty breaks and drains, it can infect other areas of the eyelid. To avoid this, your doctor may recommend antibiotic eye ointments or drops. If your child has one sty after another, consult your child's doctor.

Other diseases of the eyelids may produce redness, burning, itching, crusting, or swelling of the lids. There may also be tumors or notches in the eyelids, or the lid margin may be red. Any persistent change in this area should be seen by a doctor. R.O.S.

See also **Conjunctivitis; Eye health**

Eyestrain. *See* **Eye health; Far-sightedness; Near-sightedness**

Fainting is a brief period of unconsciousness. It usually occurs suddenly, when the blood pressure falls to a point at which the brain does not get enough blood to maintain consciousness.

Children may feel weak and numb just before fainting. They may become nauseated

A child who faints easily should be taught to place his or her head between the knees as soon as fainting symptoms start.

and light-headed, have blurred vision, and appear pale. They may salivate excessively and sweat, yawn, or sigh. Sometimes these symptoms end in a fainting spell, but other times they do not.

If your child faints, he or she will probably remain unconscious for only a few seconds. Place the child flat on the back. Do not put anything under the child's head. Loosen clothing and elevate the legs slightly. Blood will flow back into the brain, and the child will regain consciousness. Call a doctor if the child has fainted and does not regain consciousness promptly.

A sudden fright or threat often causes a fainting spell. For example, fainting may occur as a reaction to pain, or to an unpleasant sight. Fatigue; fasting; standing motionless for long periods; hot, crowded quarters; and many other conditions may also cause fainting. The fainting spell usually occurs when a child is standing. It rarely happens when the child is lying down.

Some children faint more easily than others. If your child faints easily, teach the child to lie down or sit and place the head between the knees as soon as the symptoms start. If in a very hot room, the child should walk to a cooler place if possible. Children who faint easily should be taught to avoid situations which they know may cause them to faint.

Usually, fainting is not a sign of any serious condition. However, if your child faints repeatedly, tell your doctor. The doctor will want to determine the cause.

Fainting is only one cause of unconsciousness. Diabetic coma, head injury, and poisoning are others. M.G.

See also **Breath-holding; Coma; Convulsions; Diabetes mellitus; Head injuries; Poisonings and poisons**

Fallopian tubes. *See* **Menstruation**

Far-sightedness (hyperopia). A child who is far-sighted sees distant objects fairly well, but near objects are blurred. The reason for this is that a far-sighted eye is shorter from front to back than a normal eye. Light rays from an object strike the retina of the eye before they can be brought into focus.

Most far-sighted children see well at the beginning of a task involving reading or other close work. But if the task is prolonged, they may complain of blurred vision, eye discomfort, and headaches. A far-sighted child may become inattentive and cranky after studying or watching television or movies for too long a time.

Some children are poor readers because they are far-sighted. It is work for a far-sighted child to see because the child must focus the lenses of the eye more than a person with normal vision in order to see clearly. Because it is difficult to read, the child may daydream instead.

If you suspect your child is far-sighted, consult your doctor. A complete eye examination for all children over the age of 3 is in order. R.O.S.

Fever. The normal oral temperature of the human body is about 98.6° F. (37° C). A child's temperature goes up and down a little during each day, depending on the time of the day and what the child is doing. Usually, a child's temperature is slightly lower in the morning and slightly higher in the afternoon. Exercise, a hot bath, drinking warm liquids, wearing too much clothing, or merely being out in the sun may raise a child's temperature by several tenths of a degree, or even an entire degree. If your child has a fever after any of these activities, wait about half an hour before taking the temperature.

A below-normal temperature (around 97° F.; 36° C) may occur at the end of an illness. As long as the child feels well, do not be concerned.

A fever is present if a child's temperature is 101° F. (38.3° C) or higher rectally, 100.2° F. (37° C) orally, or 99° F. (37.2° C) by armpit. Call your doctor promptly when a fever occurs in an infant under 3 or 4 months of age.

Reducing a fever. If your child has a fever and is uncomfortable, you may give acetaminophen (aspirin substitute, sold under brand names such as Liquiprin®, Panadol®, Tempra®, and Tylenol®) in age-appropriate doses. (Use the table accompanying this article as a guide.) Aspirin has been linked to Reye's syndrome and is not recommended for treatment of children who have a fever. Call your doctor if the acetaminophen does not control the fever; if the child has a rash, a sore throat, an earache, is in pain, or appears ill.

Proper dosage of acetaminophen (aspirin substitute)
Avoid overdosage. Check with your doctor before giving more than two doses.

Age of child	Amount	Frequency
6 months old	.08 cc acetaminophen drops (brand names: Liquiprin®, Panadol®, Tempra®, Tylenol®), or ½ teaspoon of acetaminophen syrup or elixir	Every 4 to 6 hours
1 year old	1.2 cc of acetaminophen drops, or ½ teaspoon of acetaminophen syrup or elixir	Every 4 to 6 hours
2 to 3 years old	1.6 cc of acetaminophen drops, or 1 teaspoon of acetaminophen syrup or elixir	Every 4 to 6 hours
4 to 5 years old	3 chewable 80 mg acetaminophen tablets, or 1½ teaspoons of the acetaminophen syrup or elixir	Every 4 to 6 hours

How to take a child's temperature

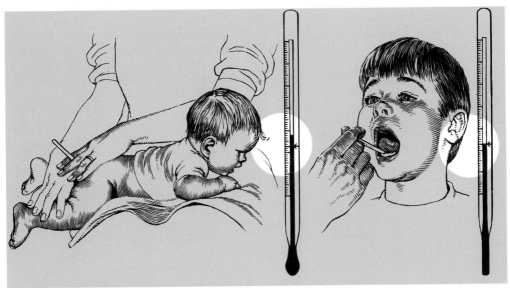

To use a rectal thermometer, lay the child facedown. Insert the bulb of the thermometer about an inch (2.5 centimeters) into the rectum and hold it in place gently. Normal rectal temperature is about 99.6° F. (37.5° C). Use an oral thermometer for older children. Place the bulb under the tongue. Then the mouth should be kept closed. Normal oral temperature is about 98.6° F. (37° C).

Some children have convulsions if a fever develops rapidly. If your child tends to have fever convulsions and is running a high fever, try to lower the temperature. Give the child acetaminophen in doses appropriate to age. Also, sponge the skin with cool or lukewarm water. If the child has a convulsion, call the doctor.

Taking a child's temperature. The three most common ways of taking a child's temperature are by rectum, by mouth, or by armpit. Rectal temperature registers about a degree higher than oral temperature. The temperature by armpit registers about a degree lower than oral temperature. When you report the temperature, tell your doctor how you took it.

Take the temperature of an infant or young child rectally, using a rectal thermometer. Check the mercury-filled bulb of the thermometer to be certain it is not cracked. Then lubricate the tip with petroleum jelly or cold cream. Lay the child stomach down across your knees. Gently insert the thermometer about an inch (2.5 centimeters) into the child's rectum. Let the thermometer find its own direction. Then, place your hand on the child's buttocks and hold the thermometer between your index finger and middle finger so that the child will not be injured when moving. Leave the thermometer in place for two or three minutes.

When the child is a year old, you may want to start taking the temperature in the armpit. Undress the child so that there are no clothes between the arm and chest. Use either an oral or a rectal thermometer. Place the bulb in the armpit and hold the arm against the side for three minutes.

Temperatures can be taken orally with school-age children. Place the thermometer under the child's tongue for three to five minutes. Be sure the child's mouth remains closed around the thermometer.

To read a thermometer, hold it at the end opposite the mercury bulb. Do not hold it by the bulb, because the heat of your fingers may raise the temperature. Rotate the thermometer until the mercury column appears. After you have read the temperature, wash the thermometer with alcohol or cool, soapy water. Hold the thermometer tightly by the end opposite the bulb. Shake it down by snapping your wrist. Keep shaking it until the mercury falls. M.G.

See also **Convulsions; Dehydration**

Fever blisters (herpes simplex) usually form on the lips or around the mouth, but they sometimes form inside the mouth. Fever blisters are also called cold sores. They are caused by a virus.

Fever blisters often occur along with certain illnesses that cause fever, such as the common cold or the flu. The blisters also tend to recur, particularly when the child is subjected to physical or emotional stress.

The blisters are infectious, so the infected child should have his own washcloth and towel and should avoid spreading the fluid in the blisters. The blisters usually dry in three or four days and develop a crust. The crust drops off in another three to five days. M.G.

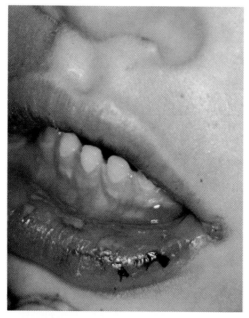

A fever blister starts as a patch of red, burning skin. Then yellowish blisters develop. When these blisters break, they ooze and form a crust.

Fingernails. *See* **Nail care**

First aid. (NOTE: First aid for particular emergencies is described in separate articles—BITES AND STINGS; BLEEDING; BROKEN BONES; BURNS; CPR; CHOKING; CONVULSIONS; CUTS AND SCRATCHES; DISLOCATION OF JOINT; ELECTRIC SHOCK; FROSTBITE; NOSEBLEED; POISON IVY, OAK, AND SUMAC; POISONINGS AND POISONS; SHOCK; SPRAIN AND STRAIN.)

Most home accidents result in minor injuries, and the needed first aid is obvious. In more serious cases—severe bleeding, stoppage of breathing, and poisoning—act quickly, because each second is important.

First-aid rules. Here are some general steps to follow in giving first aid:
- Keep calm.
- Have the child lie down.
- Check for injuries and do what is immediately needed to stop bleeding. If breathing has stopped, administer CPR.
- Call the doctor. If possible, have someone else call the doctor while you give first aid.
- Keep the child quiet and continue first-aid treatment until the doctor arrives.

First-aid kits. To do its job properly in the home, in the family car, or on a hike through the woods, a first-aid kit should contain sufficient materials for its probable use. It should be arranged so that you can quickly remove any item without scrambling the contents of the entire kit. Individual items should be wrapped separately, so that unused materials do not become soiled or contaminated.

Surgical supply manufacturers package first-aid kits according to Red Cross specifications. First-aid kits available in most drugstores and department stores are not standardized. Examine the contents and packaging of a kit before buying one.

To meet most emergencies, you should have the following items:
An assortment of adhesive bandage strips
Several gauze pads
A roll of adhesive tape
A roll of sterile gauze bandage
A tube of burn ointment
A package of folded, sterile gauze totaling one-half square yard (0.5 square meter) or more. M.G.

Fistulas are abnormal tunnels or openings in the body. Generally, they connect one organ with another organ, or an organ with an abnormal opening in the skin.

Fistulas occur in three ways:
- They may be congenital.
- They may result from infection when an abscess ruptures into two organs, or into an organ and the skin.
- Or, they may result from an injury that penetrates the body.

Symptoms of fistulas include pain and a discharge of pus or other matter.

Congenital fistulas. In rare cases, a child is born with a fistula leading from the navel to either the bowel or bladder. If the bowel is involved, contents from the intestines ooze from the navel. If the bladder is involved, urine oozes from the navel. Another fistula that may be present at birth connects the trachea (windpipe) and the esophagus (tube that carries food to the stomach). When the baby is first fed, milk gets into the trachea and causes breathing difficulty.

Infections. Anal fistulas are commonly caused by infections and abscesses near the rectum. This fistula (called fistula in ano) leads from the rectum to the anus. Pus, and occasionally excrement, oozes through the abnormal opening. Regional enteritis (an inflammation of the intestine) sometimes causes fistulas to develop between loops of the intestine, from the intestine to the abdominal wall, or from the intestine to the bladder.

Injuries. An injury, such as a gunshot wound or a fall onto a sharp object, can harm an artery and a vein and result in an arteriovenous fistula. Blood runs directly from the artery into the vein, putting an increased workload on the heart.

If your child has a draining sore on the skin, consult your doctor. Most fistulas are corrected by surgery. The complexity of the operation depends on the organs affected. Some, such as the fistula in ano, may close spontaneously and heal. Sometimes, fistulas are cured by a minor operation requiring only about a day in the hospital. Those that involve blood vessels or the trachea are more complicated and require major operations for correction. T.M.H.

See also **Colitis**

Normal foot and flat foot

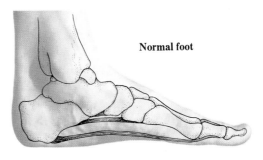

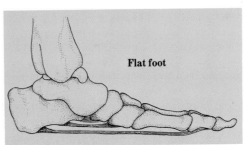

The bones in the arch of a normal foot are supported by muscles and ligaments. When these muscles and ligaments are weak, the arch flattens.

Flat feet. The arch of the foot consists of several bones, all fitting next to one another in a curve that is supported by muscles and ligaments that attach to the bones. When these muscles and ligaments are weak, the arch relaxes and flattens out, and the child appears to have flat feet. Soreness, pain, and fatigue in the legs may develop.

Most babies look as though they have flat feet. This is because their feet are naturally plump, and fat partially hides the foot arch. With use, and the ability to walk, the child's muscles and ligaments strengthen and hold the bones of the foot in a firmer arch. If your child still appears to have flat feet at about 2 years of age, or if your child has complaints of pain in the feet or legs or of tiring easily, consult your doctor. The doctor may suggest using corrective devices in the shoes.

When your child is about 2 years old, it is best to have the child wear shoes with flat, flexible soles. These soles allow the muscles and ligaments of the child's feet and ankles to move and become stronger.

At any age, it is best to have a child wear shoes with flat, flexible soles. Babies do not need hard-soled or high-top shoes when learning to walk. J.J.G.

Flu. *See* Influenza

Food poisoning can result from eating food that is contaminated by bacteria or by chemicals. Some mushrooms and other plants can also cause food poisoning.

Symptoms of food poisoning include nausea, vomiting, diarrhea, and stomach cramps. Younger children and infants may have convulsions. Call your doctor if you suspect food poisoning. Serious cases of food poisoning may require hospitalization. However, most types of food poisoning are rarely fatal. Botulism, a rare type of food poisoning that is caused by a toxin produced in bacteria, may paralyze the muscles used in breathing and cause death by suffocation.

Food poisoning usually occurs because food has been prepared, canned, or stored under unsanitary conditions. Potato salad, meat salads, custards, chicken, and similar foods easily become contaminated by bacteria. Keep these foods refrigerated until they are served. M.G.

See also Poisonings and poisons

Foot care. Probably the most common questions parents ask about their child's feet are, "When should the child start wearing shoes?" and "What type of shoes should be worn?" For the first year, a baby does not need shoes. A child does not even need bootees or socks on the feet unless the house or floor is unusually cold. Buy the first pair of shoes for your child when the baby begins active, unassisted walking.

The proper first shoes should have flat, flexible soles. There is no longer believed to be any specific advantage in letting your child go barefoot for prolonged periods once active, unassisted walking has begun.

Does the shoe fit the child properly? When the child stands, the longest toe should be from ¼ to ½ inch (6 to 13 millimeters) from the end of the shoe. To check the width of a shoe, lightly pinch the material over the child's toes. It should form a little fold if the shoe is wide enough. Later, when your child wears sturdier shoes, you can check the width by pressing in the sides of the shoe while the child is standing. If the shoe is wide enough, a slight bulge should form.

Proper fitting socks are important, too. Your child's socks, like the shoes, should have from ¼ to ½ inch (6 to 13 millimeters) extra room at the end. Cotton and wool are the best materials for socks, because they cushion the foot and absorb moisture. Change your child's socks every day. When children are old enough to put on their own socks, parents should check to see that they are put on correctly, with the heel of the sock covering the heel of the foot.

Until your child is about 5 or 6 years old, check the shoes every few weeks to be certain they are still long and wide enough.

The average toddler needs a new pair of shoes about every three or four months. Children usually outgrow their shoes before they wear them out, but never let a child wear a pair of shoes that are run-down at the heels or on the soles. Run-down shoes put extra pressure on parts of the child's feet and may cause aching feet, calluses, and other foot disorders.

Children may not always tell you that their shoes do not fit or that they hurt their feet. Look for certain signs. The shoes are probably too small if children appear to walk with discomfort or tend to take the shoes off on coming into the house. Another indication of short shoes is redness at the base of the big toenails. Red spots or blisters indicate that the shoes may be rubbing the feet.

Do not pass shoes down from an older child to a younger child. Feet have different shapes, and the older child's shoes will be impressed with the shape of the child's feet. Even though hand-me-down shoes may be the correct size, they can force the younger child's feet out of their own individual shape and into the shape of the shoes. J.J.G.

See also Bowlegs; Flat feet; Hip, congenital dislocation; Knock-knee; Nail care; Ringworm; Warts

Fracture. *See* Broken bones

Frostbite results when the body is exposed to extreme cold. It usually occurs in the ears, fingers, nose, and toes. The immediate effect of frostbite is that the frostbitten area becomes whitish and numb. This occurs because the blood and moisture in the tissues freeze and circulation is cut off. Further damage varies. The tissue of a frostbitten finger may be completely destroyed. Or the child may experience no more than a mildly painful burning sensation every time the finger is exposed to cold, even months after the original injury.

If you think your child has frostbite, follow these procedures:

- Consult a doctor as soon as possible.
- Do not massage the frostbitten area, because you may damage the tissues.
- Do not rub the frostbitten area with snow or ice, because you may remove the skin and injure the tissues.
- Take the child indoors and let the frostbitten area warm gradually.
- Do not apply hot pads, heating pads, or hot-water bottles.

If your child's hands or feet become frostbitten, warm them gradually by soaking them in lukewarm water.

- Do not put the child close to a hot stove or under a heat lamp.
- Soak frostbitten fingers or toes in lukewarm water (90° to 100° F.; 32° to 38° C). Apply warm (not hot), wet towels to frostbitten nose or ears.
- If blisters occur, cover them with a bandage to protect them from infection.

Frostbite can be prevented by following certain precautions.

- Dampness increases the chance of frostbite, so teach your child to come indoors to change wet or damp clothing, particularly mittens, shoes, and socks.
- Be certain that ears, hands, and feet are adequately protected in cold weather.
- The child should wear a protective face mask when ice-skating, skiing, or otherwise exposed to the cold for a long time.   M.G.

See also **Blister**

Fungus diseases. *See* **Ringworm; Thrush**

Furuncle. *See* **Boil**

Gagging is a reflex action at the back of the throat. Sometimes it produces vomiting. When babies gag, it is a sign that they are not able to cope with what is in the mouth and that they may need help.

Many young babies gag easily, and this may cause "spitting up." Occasionally, a baby may gag because a bit of dust or lint gets into the mouth, or because a nipple has been pushed too far into the mouth. Sometimes babies gag during feeding simply to show that they have had enough to eat. Children also gag if they are nauseated and about to vomit.

Babies often gag when first offered solid food, such as cereal. This is quite natural, because the solid food is strange in consistency and is difficult for them to swallow. To avoid the gagging, make the food more fluid and offer it in smaller amounts.

Gagging is an important protection against the entry of solids into the larynx and breathing passages, where they could cause choking and suffocation.   M.G.

Gamma globulin is one part of plasma, the liquid part of blood. Gamma globulin contains antibodies that help the body fight infection. When an infection begins, the body manufactures gamma globulin that includes antibodies to fight that infection. In some cases, after the infection has cleared up, enough of the gamma globulin remains in the body to prevent the child from getting that disease a second time. That is why it is rare for a child to have a disease like measles twice.

Antibody deficiencies may be treated effectively by replacement. The antibody present in the gamma globulin fraction of blood is isolated from a large population of human donors. The antibodies isolated represent the antibody response normally generated by this large group of people. Therefore, the antibodies received by a patient have the advantage of representing a broader spectrum than any one individual could produce. Screening of potentially ill donors in addition to the standard isolation technique for gamma globulin has resulted in a product essentially free of the risk of accidental infection. Gamma globulin may be given by injection either into the muscle or directly into the bloodstream. Although the latter route results in initially higher blood levels of antibody, it appears that attaining a gamma globulin two-thirds of normal will significantly reduce the risk of infection in antibody-deficient individuals. ɪ.ꜱ.ʜ.

See also **Allergy; Communicable diseases; Immunization; Shots; Virus**

Genes. *See* **Heredity**

German measles, also called rubella or three-day measles, is a contagious disease caused by a virus. It is preventable. A child is usually immunized against German measles at 15 months of age.

German measles occurs most frequently in children between the ages of 5 and 15. Outbreaks of German measles usually occur during late winter and the spring.

First symptoms of German measles are low fever, sore throat, headache, and a swelling and hardening of the glands in the

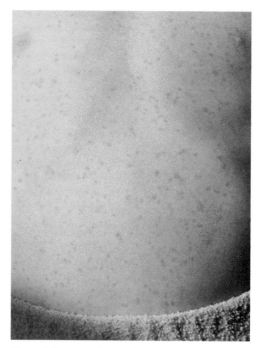

One of the symptoms that may accompany German measles is a rose-colored rash.

neck and behind the ears. These symptoms appear from 14 to 21 days after exposure. A rose-colored rash may appear next, although some cases are so mild that they produce no rash. The rash begins on the face, spreads over the rest of the body, and lasts two or three days. The spots are separate at first, but then run together, causing a flushed appearance. In young children, the rash may be the first symptom. On darker skins, the rash may not be apparent.

If you suspect that your child has German measles, call your doctor. Most cases of German measles are so mild that the child usually does not have to stay in bed. German measles is contagious from about seven days before the rash appears until about five days after. A child who has had German measles can usually go back to school one week after the rash appears. An attack of German measles usually gives a child permanent immunity to the disease.

German measles can harm an unborn child. If a woman gets the disease during the first three months of pregnancy, the child may be born with cataracts, deafness, mental retardation, and other defects. Before becoming pregnant, all women of childbearing age should have a blood test to see if they are immune to German measles. If a pregnant woman is exposed to German measles, she should see her doctor as soon as possible. H.D.R., JR.

See also **Communicable diseases; Immunization; Shots; Virus**

Glands. *See* **Endocrine glands; Swollen glands**

Glandular fever. *See* **Mononucleosis**

Goiter is an enlargement of the thyroid gland. This gland is located in the front of the neck between the top of the breastbone and the Adam's apple. The goiter is usually visible as a prominent bulge. In children, goiters most frequently develop just before the beginning of puberty, and they are more common in girls than in boys. If you suspect

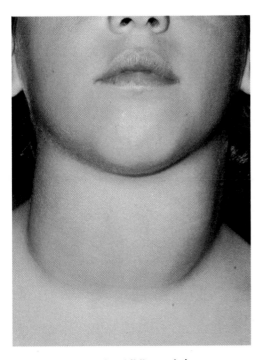

The swelling in this child's neck is caused by a goiter.

that your child has a goiter, consult your doctor.

One type of goiter is called a simple goiter. Several conditions can cause simple goiters:

■ The thyroid does not produce enough thyroid hormones. Goiters caused by this can usually be treated with medication.

■ Certain medications or foods may contain goiter-producing agents. Treatment requires discontinuing the use of those medications or foods.

■ The thyroid may be chronically inflamed. Doctors do not know what causes the inflammation. The goiter generally disappears without treatment, but thyroid medication is usually prescribed.

■ The diet may lack a sufficient amount of iodine. This condition is rare in the United States and Canada because of the widespread use of iodized salt.

Another type of goiter is called a toxic goiter. This type of goiter causes an excessive production of thyroid hormone (hyperthyroidism).

Toxic goiters may produce emotional instability, increased nervousness, an increase in appetite, and weight loss. Children may lose weight even though they eat large amounts of food. They may sweat excessively, their hands may tremble, and their eyes may protrude. The goiter may cause a feeling of pressure in the neck or even some difficulty in swallowing.

Thyroid-suppressant drugs are generally used to treat toxic goiter. The drugs must be taken regularly for a number of years. However, they may not effectively control and eliminate the goiter. In some cases, an operation is needed to remove part of the thyroid gland. M.G.

Growing pains. Doctors do not believe that growth causes pain in the feet or legs of children. If your child complains of pain in his feet and legs, try to find the cause.

Poor alignment of the bones, ligaments, and muscles of the feet and legs causes the body's weight to be carried unevenly by the feet and legs. This is the most common cause of foot and leg pains in young children. A doctor should examine a child who limps because of pain or a child who complains that one or both hips or knees hurt.

Occasionally, a child may have fleeting pain and swelling—sometimes with redness—in one or more joints. If your child has these symptoms, call your doctor. This condition may indicate arthritis, osteomyelitis, rheumatic fever, or other diseases.

Also, a child who exercises a great deal may become fatigued and complain of painful feet or legs, or may have cramps in them during the night. Sprains, bruises, and bumps are also possible causes of pain in the feet and legs. M.G.

Hair care.

The color of your child's hair, its texture, and its abundance are physical characteristics for which you and the child's ancestors are responsible. But its luster, vitality, and attractiveness depends mostly on the child's general health and on the kind of hair and scalp care the child receives.

Your child's hair needs a daily brushing of at least 100 strokes to give it gloss, to remove loose scales, and to stimulate the scalp. Boys with short hair require less brushing. Begin brushing the child's hair regularly as soon as there is enough hair to brush. Be sure to use a brush with soft bristles that will not scratch or irritate the tender scalp. Separate the hair into sections and brush up and away from the scalp, one section at a time. Move your wrist with each stroke so that the brush goes through a rolling motion.

If you use a comb, pick one with blunt teeth, because sharp edges may injure the scalp and hair. Take a small section of tangled hair and start combing it about two inches from the free end of the hair. When the comb passes freely to the end, place it a little higher in the section and comb through to the end again. Repeat the procedure until the comb passes freely from the scalp to the end of the hair.

Combs and brushes are as individual as toothbrushes. Each child should have his or her own. Wash combs and brushes frequently in warm soapy water to keep them clean and fresh.

If your child's hair is brushed and combed each day, a shampoo once a week or every

A good brushing is important for healthy, shiny hair. Use a soft brush and brush up from the scalp with a rolling motion. If hair is tangled, brush the ends first and work upward.

ten days is probably enough. Use only gentle shampoos. Until puberty, most children do not have much oil in their hair, and strong shampoos may irritate the scalp and make the hair unmanageable. And if some lather runs into a child's eyes, a strong shampoo will burn or sting much more than a specially prepared gentle one.

Brisk towel drying may break and split a child's hair, so blot the hair dry. A cream rinse may help your daughter if her hair snarls and tangles after shampooing. If she has long hair, avoid styles such as tight pony tails that pull excessively on the hair.

As adolescence approaches, your child may develop dandruff—small, whitish scales that form on the scalp and then flake off. Simple dandruff, with or without mild itching, is not regarded as a scalp disease. A shampoo once a week usually controls dandruff. If dandruff is excessive, uncontrollable, and accompanied by itching and inflammation of the scalp, consult a doctor.

Children should be encouraged to take care of their own hair as soon as they are willing to do so. Girls, especially, benefit from learning to care for and arrange their own hair. Children should also be complimented on their hair care. Compliments will further encourage children to do a good job. M.G.

Hard of hearing. *See* Deafness

Hay fever (seasonal allergic rhinitis) is an allergic reaction of the nose and eyes caused by pollen, molds, and other substances floating in the air. Common symptoms include sneezing; stuffiness; difficult nasal breathing; runny nose and eyes; and itching of the eyes, nose, ears, and the roof of the mouth. A fever is not one of the symptoms. Some children who have hay fever also develop asthma.

Hay fever occurs at certain times of the year and is usually caused by pollens from grass, trees, ragweed, and related weeds, or by airborne molds.

If typical hay fever symptoms last all year, your child may have perennial allergic rhinitis. Substances in the air other than pollen, such as dust and animal dander (particles from skin, hair, and feathers) are some of the substances that cause perennial allergic rhinitis. If your child seems to have a constant cold, the child may be allergic to something.

If you think your child has either seasonal or perennial allergic rhinitis, consult the doctor. The doctor may recommend sending the child to an allergist (a doctor specializing in the treatment of allergies). The allergist will probably perform tests to determine what substances (called allergens) are causing the reaction. Once the allergens are identified, you may be able to eliminate them from the child's surroundings, or at

The pollen from ragweed causes hay fever in many children. One ragweed plant can produce a billion pollen grains.

least reduce them. Sometimes the allergist can immunize the child against the allergens. The allergist may also prescribe drugs to relieve symptoms.

The allergist may suggest that you do several things:
- Eliminate stuffed toys, wall-to-wall carpeting, upholstered furniture, and feather pillows from the child's room—possibly from the entire home.
- Encase the child's mattress and box spring in an allergen-proof cover to reduce dust.
- Keep windows closed to minimize entry of pollen.
- Use an air conditioner with a good filter or an air-cleaning device to clean the air, and keep the humidity low.
- Avoid smoking in the home or car.
- Keep no pets that have either fur or feathers. J.S.H.

See also **Allergy; Asthma**

Head injuries are fairly common among children, but relatively few are serious. However, if your child loses consciousness—either at the time of a head injury or later—call a doctor immediately. Any blow that knocks the child unconscious could cause brain injury from bleeding inside the skull.

A child who has a severe bump on the head should be kept quiet for a while and watched closely for these danger signs:
- Severe headache.
- Persistent vomiting. If the child vomits more than once or twice after a head injury, call the doctor.
- Difficulty in speaking. If the child's speech is slurred or if the child is not able to talk as well as usual, call the doctor.
- Unequal pupils. If the pupils of the child's eyes are not the same size, call the doctor.
- Double vision. If your child complains of double vision, or if you notice that the child squints one eye to prevent seeing double images, call the doctor.
- Weakness of one side. If the child is unsteady in walking, or limps, call the doctor. If the child cannot use one arm or leg as well as the other, call the doctor.
- Excessive sleepiness. The child may go to sleep after a head injury. If you cannot awaken the child easily, call the doctor.

- Convulsions. If convulsions start, turn the child's head to one side so that vomit can run out. Call a doctor as soon as possible.

If the child shows none of these symptoms for 12 hours after a head injury, the child is probably all right. In some cases, intermittent headaches can persist up to a few weeks as a result of a head injury. In rare cases, persistent headache, drowsiness, and a change in the child's normal behavior may develop days or weeks after a head injury because of a slowly accumulating blood clot. If any of these symptoms do appear, call the doctor immediately.

See also **Coma; Convulsions; Fever**

Headaches can usually be relieved by pain medicine in doses appropriate for the child's age. If your child has a headache that does not respond to acetaminophen, call the doctor. Headaches have many causes:
- A child with a sudden infection and fever may develop a headache. The headache usually subsides as the infection clears up.
- Fatigue and overexposure to sun can cause headaches.
- Emotional tension can cause persistent or recurrent headaches in children.
- Eyestrain can also cause recurring headaches. If headaches occur frequently, have your child's vision checked.

A few children have quite severe headaches called migraines. A child with a migraine may see spots before the eyes, become nauseated, and even vomit. Unusual excitement, nervous strain, emotional upset, or excessive fatigue may cause migraines. The child may feel better lying down in a quiet, darkened room. A doctor can prescribe medicine for migraine headaches. M.G.

Hearing aid. *See* **Deafness**

Heart murmur is an unusual sound produced by an abnormal flow of blood through the chambers of the heart. A normal heart makes "lub-dub," "lub-dub" sounds every time it beats. The "lub" sound occurs when two valves inside the heart close. The "dub" sound is made when the valves in the aorta and the pulmonary artery close. A heart murmur is a rumbling or scratchy noise.

A very common group of heart murmurs is called functional or innocent murmurs. These murmurs are completely harmless and tend to disappear when the child reaches adolescence.

Other murmurs are caused by abnormal blood currents flowing through channels narrowed by disease, through defective channels present at birth, or through holes in walls within the heart.

Usually, heart murmurs are discovered during a doctor's examination. Most heart murmurs are harmless and do not interfere with the child's normal life. M.G.

Heat exhaustion is one of the body's reactions to overheating and inadequate fluid intake. It usually occurs during strenuous exercise when sweating makes the body lose too much water. Heat exhaustion is not the same as heatstroke. A child with heat exhaustion continues to sweat; a child with heatstroke usually does not.

The symptomatic onset of heat exhaustion is often gradual. A child may become pale and weak. Body temperature remains normal. The child may complain of headache, dizziness, weakness, and cramps, may become nauseated and vomit, and may seem disoriented. Skin feels moist and clammy, and the pulse may be weak and irregular. Move the child to a cooler place. Cover the child with ice-water-cooled towels and offer drinking water. Call the doctor.

To prevent heat exhaustion, dress your child in lightweight, loose-fitting clothing that is light in color. Keep strenuous play to a minimum during extreme heat, and see that the child drinks a lot of cool fluids before and during periods of activity. M.G.

See also **Heatstroke**

Heatstroke (sunstroke) results when the body's heat-regulating system stops functioning normally. Heatstroke is caused by excessive heat, not by the sun itself.

One way the body normally cools itself is by sweating. A child with heatstroke usually

If a child is suffering from heat exhaustion, first move the youngster to a cooler place and offer cool water. Call a doctor as soon as possible.

First aid for heatstroke

If you cannot put the child into a tub of cold water, put wet cloths directly against the child's skin. If possible, put ice packs against the back of the child's neck.

stops sweating. This is not, however, always the case. The child's skin may become flushed, hot, and dry; and the child may become agitated, confused, lethargic, or convulsive, or lose consciousness. When the child stops sweating, the body temperature rises. The temperature is usually over 105° F. (41° C); at this level, it is necessary to lower the child's temperature immediately.

Place the child in a bathtub of ice-cold water until the temperature goes down to 102° F. (39° C) or lower. If this is not practical, take off the child's clothing and put wet cloths and ice bags directly against the skin. Call a doctor and arrange for transportation to an emergency medical facility at once. Infants, especially, are at great risk of heat-related illnesses; *never* leave an infant in a closed automobile on a warm day. Heat-stroke can be fatal. M.G.

See also **Heat exhaustion**

Hemoglobin. *See* **Anemia; Blood count**

Hemophilia is a hereditary disease in which the blood does not clot properly and bleeding is difficult to stop. Hemophilia occurs almost entirely in males. Women rarely show signs of the disease, but they carry it and transmit it to their sons.

Hemophilia varies from severe forms in which bleeding occurs after almost any activity, to milder forms in which only major injuries or surgery produce excessive bleeding. The bleeding may occur internally as well as from a cut on the skin. Internal bleeding usually occurs in body tissues, in muscles, or in joints such as those at the knee, ankle, elbow, or hip.

No cure has yet been found for hemophilia, but bleeding can be controlled with normal blood plasma or with concentrates of clotting factors (medicines that help clot the blood). Prompt medical treatment can prevent large hemorrhages that might permanently damage joints, tissues, or organs. Surgery and dental extractions can be performed without danger of hemorrhage if the child with hemophilia is first treated with plasma or the concentrates of the clotting factors.

Hemophilia is sometimes apparent in new-born infants. They bleed excessively from the umbilical cord or following circumcision. More commonly, the disease becomes evident when the child begins to crawl or walk. Small bumps cause large bruises and swelling, which are signs of large areas of hemorrhage. If this happens, have the child examined immediately by your doctor. If you know there is a history of hemophilia in your family, report this to the doctor who will deliver the baby and to the baby's pediatrician. The baby's doctor will probably want to examine the child at about 3 months.

Once hemophilia is diagnosed, doctors usually recommend protecting the child from activities that might produce injury—for example, discouraging tree climbing or physical contact sports such as football. F.O.

See also **Blood clotting; Bruises; Heredity**

Hemorrhage. *See* **Bleeding; Hemophilia**

Hepatitis is a disease that involves inflammation of the liver. The two major types of hepatitis are viral and toxic.

There are two main forms of the viral type: hepatitis A, or infectious hepatitis, and hepatitis B, or serum hepatitis. Symptoms of both include headache and loss of appetite and energy. A child may also be nauseated, vomit, and have abdominal pain. Urine may look greenish-yellow and stools may be pale. Older children may have a temperature of 100° to 104° F. (38° to 40° C) for two to five days. As the fever subsides, jaundice (a yellowing of the skin and whites of the eyes) usually appears. Normally, jaundice lasts from 8 to 11 days.

Most cases of hepatitis A, or infectious hepatitis, are caused by contaminated food or water. Symptoms appear in about four weeks. Most cases of hepatitis A last about two to six weeks.

Symptoms may be lessened—or even prevented—if injections of gamma globulin are given within a week after exposure. A child should be isolated for at least one week after the onset of the disease.

Take every possible care to protect others in the family. Be certain that everyone washes his or her hands before meals and after bowel movements.

Provide separate eating utensils for the sick child and sterilize them after use. One attack of infectious hepatitis usually gives permanent immunity.

Hepatitis B, or serum hepatitis, is less common than hepatitis A, or infectious hepatitis. Once commonly transmitted through a transfusion of blood, hepatitis B is now mainly spread by use of improperly sterilized medical instruments.

Symptoms appear in from 60 to 180 days, with an average of about 90 days. Children with hepatitis B do not have to be isolated. Hepatitis B immunoglobulin is recommended for those patients exposed to hepatitis B. The hepatitis B vaccine may also be administered. Those at risk for hepatitis B exposure should be immunized.

Toxic hepatitis results from exposure to certain chemicals, including carbon tetrachloride and a variety of medications. Such chemicals can enter the body by being swallowed, inhaled, absorbed through the skin, or received in injections. Treatment depends upon the cause.

See also **Gamma globulin; Jaundice**

Heredity. The kind of person your child will be is determined to a great extent at the moment of conception, when the sperm from the father unites with the egg from the mother. If scientists could translate the chemical code inside the tiny fertilized egg, they could tell whether the child is to be a boy or girl, blue- or brown-eyed, blond or dark-haired. The storehouse of this information lies in the chromosomes. Under a microscope, chromosomes appear as dark strings in the nucleus of each body cell. With the exception of the sex cells (the sperm and the egg), 46 chromosomes are in each cell of the human body. Egg and sperm cells each have 23 chromosomes. In fusing, they give the fertilized egg the total of 46 chromosomes.

Whether the fertilized egg develops into a boy or a girl is determined by two special chromosomes—the sex chromosomes. Every egg bears a chromosome known as the X chromosome and every sperm bears either an X or a Y chromosome. When the sex

chromosomes meet in the fertilized egg, an XX baby will be a girl and an XY baby, a boy.

When an egg cell is fertilized by a sperm cell, it starts to grow. First, it divides into two cells; then into four cells; then into eight cells, and so on—until it produces all the cells in a baby's body. During each cell division, the 46 chromosomes in a cell duplicate themselves so that each new cell gets an identical group of 46 chromosomes. The 46 chromosomes are composed of two sets— one set of 23 chromosomes from the individual's father and one set of 23 from the mother. Each chromosome in one set of 23 can be matched to a particular chromosome in the other set. In a girl, the 23 pairs of chromosomes look alike. In a boy, one pair of chromosomes, unlike the other 22 pairs, does not look alike. In a girl, the two sex chromosomes (XX) look alike. In a boy, the chromosomes (XY) do not look alike.

Genes determine heredity traits.
Hundreds of tiny particles called genes are arranged in a line along the length of each

Identical twins look almost exactly alike because they develop from a single egg cell and, therefore, inherit the same genes.

chromosome. Genes control a child's inherited traits, such as the blood group, blood-clotting ability, sensitivity to certain tastes, and hair color.

DNA (deoxyribonucleic acid) is the key chemical compound of a gene. DNA is a molecule that consists of two threadlike strands that are connected by crosspieces. The two strands are wound around each other. The structure (called a double helix) looks like a rope ladder twisted into a spiral. A DNA molecule makes an exact duplicate during cell division.

Except in certain instances of sex-linked traits, there are two genes for every trait—one gene on a chromosome in the set of 23 from the individual's mother, and one gene on the matching chromosome in the set of 23 from the father. In many traits, the action of one gene overpowers the action of the other. The more powerful gene is called dominant, and the other gene is called recessive. The gene for brown eyes is dominant over that for blue eyes. If a child gets a gene for brown eyes from the father and a gene for blue eyes from the mother, the child will have brown eyes. Except in certain instances of sex-linked traits, it takes two recessive genes to make a recessive trait show up. Both chromosomes must carry the gene for blue eyes for a child to have blue eyes. The individual with one gene for blue eyes and one for brown may transmit either gene to the next generation, because only one chromosome from the pair (and therefore only one gene), goes into the sperm or egg cells.

Genes are not always either dominant or recessive. This situation is called incomplete dominance. Three genes—which may be designated A, B, and a—control the inheritance of blood-group types. (Even though there are three genes, the most any person can have is two.) A and B are dominant to a, but they are incompletely dominant to each other. If a child inherits a dominant A gene from each parent or a dominant A gene from one parent and a recessive a gene from the other, the child has blood type A. If the child inherits a dominant B gene from each parent or a dominant B gene from one parent and a recessive a gene from the other, the child has blood type B. However, if the child inherits an A gene from one parent and a B gene from the other, the child's blood type is neither A nor B. It is type AB because of incomplete dominance between genes A and B. If the child inherits a recessive a gene from each parent, the child's blood type is O.

Sex-linked traits. The genes on the X and Y chromosomes determine traits that are called "sex-linked" because these genes are carried on the sex chromosomes. Color blindness is one sex-linked trait.

Color vision is controlled by a gene located on the X chromosome. The Y chromosome has no gene for color vision. A boy (XY) has only one X chromosome, and, therefore, only one gene for color vision. A girl (XX) has two X chromosomes, and, therefore, two genes for color vision. If a boy inherits a gene for color blindness, he is color-blind. But, since the gene for normal vision is dominant and the gene for color blindness is recessive, a girl is color-blind only when she inherits two genes for color blindness—one from her mother and one from her father. If she inherits only one gene for color blindness, she has normal vision, but she is a carrier of color blindness. Since a father does not pass on his X chromosomes to his sons, the sons of a color-blind father never have the disorder unless their mother is a carrier. However, his daughters are carriers and transmit the defective X chromosome to about half their sons and half their daughters.

Another example of a sex-linked trait is hemophilia, a disease in which blood does not clot normally. Queen Victoria was just a carrier and did not have the disease. Because she was XX, the gene on her "good" X chromosome overcame the recessive hemophilia gene on the other X chromosome. Those of Queen Victoria's male descendants who received her defective X chromosome had the disease, and those who received the good X chromosome did not. Those of Queen Victoria's female descendants who received her defective X chromosome became carriers of the disease.

Not all hereditary diseases are caused by sex-linked genes. Some hereditary diseases, such as sickle cell anemia, always require two recessive genes.

Hereditary diseases. Scientists are studying hereditary diseases, trying to discover how body chemistry sometimes goes wrong. If the mistake can be corrected—by a drug or a change in diet—the person with an inborn defect of metabolism, for example, can lead a normal life.

Diabetes mellitus is a condition in which the body does not utilize carbohydrates normally. It can be controlled by giving insulin, a hormone that the diabetic does not produce in sufficient quantity.

Phenylketonuria (PKU) is a hereditary disease in which the newborn child cannot properly use part of the protein in milk. If this abnormality goes unchecked, it eventually causes mental retardation. A blood test or a test of a diaper wet by urine shows the doctor whether the disease is present. If it is, the doctor immediately prescribes a special diet to help the child develop normally.

Another important area of genetic research is the detection of carriers of hereditary diseases. The carrier of a recessive gene that causes a hereditary disease is apparently different from the normal person. In the case of the phenylketonuria gene, a blood test indicates that individuals with one gene for the disease can be identified, even though they are not sick in any way. Scientists are searching for tests to detect carriers of bad genes, because if one carrier marries another, the chances are one out of four that any child of theirs will have the disease in question. Marriage between cousins is more likely to produce a child with a hereditary disease. If one partner carries a recessive gene, a member of the same family is more likely than usual to carry it, too. Because the field of hereditary disease is changing so rapidly, parents should discuss any questions with their doctor.

Mutations and abnormalities. Occasionally, changes take place spontaneously in genes. This change is called mutation. A mutant gene is transmitted in the same way that normal genes are. All the bad genes mentioned (those that cause such diseases are hemophilia and diabetes mellitus) arose from mutations. Radiation from X rays, ultraviolet light, and fallout may also cause mutations. Some mutations are the cause of early miscarriages.

Besides mutations, there are chromosomal abnormalities consisting of too many, too few, or altered chromosomes. Down's syndrome (Mongolism), a form of mental retardation, is characterized by an extra chromosome or an altered chromosome. M.G.

Hernia, or rupture, is an outpouching or pocket of the abdominal cavity which protrudes through a defect in the abdominal wall. An abdominal organ may bulge through this defect, becoming larger when the child cries or strains. The bulge usually becomes smaller or disappears when the child relaxes. It is one of the most common conditions requiring an operation during infancy or childhood. The danger of a hernia is that a loop of intestine gets stuck in the hernia sac, causing an intestinal obstruction. If not reduced either manually or by operation promptly, the intestine can perforate, leading to peritonitis.

Both inguinal (groin) and umbilical (navel) hernias are common. Inguinal hernias are six

Location of inguinal hernia

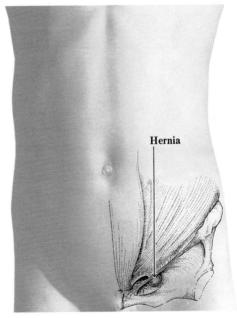

An inguinal hernia allows a loop of intestine to slip through the abdominal wall and into the groin or scrotum.

times as common in boys as girls. They do not correct themselves and are most likely to trap a loop of intestine. They usually appear as an intermittent groin or scrotal mass. Occasionally the intestine may be trapped the first time it is seen as a mass in the groin. An incarcerated hernia (one which contains trapped intestine) requires prompt attention. These hernias can be noted first at any age, but are present most often during infancy. All hernias should be seen by a doctor. Inguinal hernias are frequently present on both sides. An operation is required for correction. This operation can be performed safely at any age in an otherwise healthy baby. Almost all hernia operations in pediatric patients are performed under general anesthesia as an outpatient, and the child can be sent home when fully awake from anesthesia. Convalescence takes only a few days.

If your child has an inguinal hernia for which no immediate operation is planned, watch it carefully. If the child feels pain in the area of the hernia, or if you cannot gently push the intestine back into the abdomen, call your doctor immediately.

Umbilical hernias result from enlargement of the normal defect in the fascia (fibrous tissue which covers muscle) which carries the umbilical cord blood vessels to the baby before birth. These hernias tend to correct themselves by two to four years of age. It is rare for a loop of intestine to get stuck in an umbilical hernia during childhood.

Umbilical hernias do cause problems in adults, and so a school-age child who has this kind of hernia should be seen by a doctor. Repair is generally performed as an outpatient under general anesthesia.

Other hernias are quite uncommon in children, but you should notify your doctor promptly if you notice a bulge in your child's body tissue.

Sometimes, a hernia is confused with a hydrocele (a collection of fluid in the sac surrounding the testicle). Frequently, a boy may have both a hernia and a hydrocele. If he does, the doctor will probably want to repair both in the same operation. T.M.H.

See also **Hydrocele**

Herpes simplex. *See* Fever blisters

Hiccups occur when short, jerky contractions of the diaphragm interrupt the breathing cycle. The diaphragm, a large muscle that divides the chest from the abdomen, normally contracts and relaxes rhythmically to aid breathing. But sometimes the diaphragm contracts suddenly and air is pulled through the larynx (voice box). The air hits the vocal cords and the epiglottis (the cap on top of the larynx) and produces the "hic" sound.

Babies have hiccups frequently—sometimes several times a day. Burping or a drink of warm water may help a baby stop hiccuping. Older children may be helped by drinking water or some other common remedy, such as holding their breath, breathing into a paper bag, or eating a teaspoon of sugar. Usually, however, hiccuping stops by itself after a few minutes. In rare instances, hiccups continue for several hours. If this happens to your child, call your doctor. M.G.

Hip, congenital dislocation. In congenital dislocation of the hip, the ball of the thighbone is not in the socket formed by the pelvic bones. The actual dislocation may occur before, during, or shortly after birth. Although the exact cause is unknown, heredity is believed to be a significant factor. The condition is more common in girls than in boys. It is a serious problem and must be corrected at an early age if a child is to have normal hip function during life.

Congenital dislocation usually affects only one hip. The affected leg is shorter. The skin folds in the upper thigh and buttock are different from the opposite side. A dislocated hip prevents the thigh from bending out as far as normal. Putting diapers on the baby may be difficult. If the dislocation is not discovered before the child walks, a pronounced limp will be noticeable.

If you think your child has a congenitally dislocated hip, consult your doctor. The condition should be treated as early as possible, preferably by 3 months of age. Early treatment may take any of several different approaches. Double diapering or the use of splints is commonly prescribed. In more severe cases, casts and sometimes surgery may be necessary. J.J.G.

Hives are an allergic reaction of the skin. They look like mosquito bites—raised, whitish welts on reddened skin—and they often itch. Hives may last for a short time and suddenly disappear, or they may continue for months. They may occur anywhere on the body. Sometimes, swelling occurs around the eyes or lips. In rare cases, swelling occurs inside the throat or larynx and interferes with breathing. Prompt medical or surgical treatment may be required. Consult your doctor if you suspect that your child has hives. The doctor may recommend that you take the child to an allergist (a doctor specializing in the treatment of allergies).

A child may be allergic to such foods as milk, eggs, fish, nuts, berries, shellfish, or pork. Eating them or inhaling their odors may cause hives. Keeping a record of what your child eats and systematically eliminating certain foods from the diet may help determine which foods cause the allergic reaction.

Certain drugs such as aspirin, antibiotics, and vitamins can also cause hives. A child who is highly sensitive to penicillin may even break out in hives after drinking milk from cows that have received the antibiotic.

The stings of bees, wasps, hornets, or yellow jackets may cause hives and swelling in a susceptible child. The child can be desensitized to the stings over a period of years. The doctor will give the child repeated injections of gradually strengthened insect venom.

Hives may occur after the child has had an infection of the ears, sinuses, teeth, tonsils, or other body parts. Hives can develop when the child comes into contact with cosmetics, wool, or other substances. Hives can result from sensitivity to cold, heat, or light. Food preservatives and other substances may cause hives. Psychological factors may be the cause of hives.

Doctors treat hives by trying to discover and eliminate the cause. They may prescribe antihistamines, tranquilizers, or adrenalin to relieve some of the symptoms.   J.S.H.

See also **Allergy**

Humidifying a child's room is often recommended by a doctor when the child has bronchitis, a cold, croup, laryngitis, whooping cough, or other diseases that make breathing difficult. Humidifying provides moisture that can loosen secretions in the child's bronchial tubes and nasal passages and make breathing easier.

The safest way to add moisture to the air is with a cold-mist humidifier. A hot-steam humidifier is dangerous because a child may get burned by touching it or knocking it over.   M.G.

See also **Croup**

Hydrocele is a collection of fluid in the sac surrounding the testicle. You may first notice it as a swelling of the scrotum (the pouch that contains the testicles). A hydrocele is often confused with a hernia, and it frequently occurs with a hernia. The swelling from a hydrocele alone, however, remains about the same size all the time, and the swelling from a hernia tends to come and go. If your son has a scrotal swelling, have a doctor examine him.

An acute hydrocele, one that appears abruptly, may be caused by an infection around the testicle or by a twisting of the testicle inside its sac that cuts off the blood supply to the testicle. This type of hydrocele causes severe pain and should be examined by the doctor at once.

A hydrocele in a boy less than a year old may disappear without any treatment unless it is acute. If a boy is older, or if he has an acute hydrocele, an operation and a day or two of recuperation in the hospital may be necessary.   T.M.H.

See also **Hernia**

Hydrocephalus. The brain is suspended within the skull in clear and watery cerebrospinal fluid. This fluid also occupies four interconnected cavities (ventricles) within the brain. Cerebrospinal fluid, continually secreted by organs within the brain, flows through the ventricles and into the space around the brain, where it is absorbed into the bloodstream. Normally, the amount of fluid stays the same, because it is absorbed at the same rate it is secreted. Sometimes, however, the amount of cerebrospinal fluid increases abnormally. This condition is called hydrocephalus.

The most common cause of hydrocephalus is an obstruction in the pathway of the cerebrospinal fluid. The obstruction keeps the fluid from being absorbed as fast as it is secreted. As a result, the volume of fluid increases, enlarges the ventricles, and compresses the brain. Brain damage can occur.

Hydrocephalus most frequently occurs in young infants with underdeveloped pathways for the cerebrospinal fluid. The earliest sign is an abnormally rapid rate of growth of the baby's head. The brow enlarges, and the scalp is shiny. The fontanels (soft spots) may bulge. Because the compressed brain does not function normally, the infant may also fail to develop on schedule such skills as sitting, crawling, and standing.

Hydrocephalus is often treated by providing an artificial drainage route for the cerebrospinal fluid from the ventricles into the abdomen. In one method, a small plastic tube is placed in one of the cerebral ventricles. It leads down through the body and drains into the abdomen. In some cases, hydrocephalus may stop by itself.

Early detection of hydrocephalus requires attention to head circumference during the first two years of life. Routine examinations by a doctor during these years usually include measuring the head size of the child.   A.G.S.

See also **Soft spots**

Hysteria (conversion reaction) is a mental illness that may occur suddenly in adolescents or preadolescents. The child may develop what appears to be a physical disability, even though a medical examination shows that there is no physical cause for it. A seeming paralysis of an arm, a leg, or another part of the body is a common symptom of hysteria. Prickling, tingling, or creeping sensations are also common. Other symptoms include blindness or decreased vision, deafness, inability to speak or to speak above a whisper, fainting spells, convulsions, and inability to urinate.

Usually, children with hysteria are unconcerned about their symptoms, and the symptoms may worsen if the child receives extra attention. A child with hysteria may require psychiatric help.

The word "hysterical" is not always connected with the illness hysteria. "Hysterical" usually means a lack of control over laughing, crying, rage, or other emotions. These outbursts can occur in any child.   M.G.

Immunization. The purpose of immunization is to protect a child from disease. Immunization generally starts when a child is 2 months old. A child's first vaccine combines immunization against diphtheria, tetanus (lockjaw), and pertussis (whooping cough). The combined shot is called DPT vaccine. Oral polio vaccine is given separately, usually at the same time as the DPT shots. MMR, a combined vaccine against measles, mumps, and rubella (German measles), may be given when the child is 15 months old. Hemophilus influenzae vaccine may be given at 18 months.

Combined doses. Combined doses of DPT and MMR early in life set up immunity against common childhood diseases. Combined doses save the doctor's time, as well as time and money for parents—and the child undergoes less pain and anxiety.

A combined dose is no harder on a child medically than single ones. Reactions are rarely severe. If your child does react—with swelling or reddening at the site of the injection, or with a fever, unusual sleepiness, or a convulsion—after a dose of triple antigens, tell the doctor before the next dose is given. The doctor may omit the whooping cough vaccine at that time.

Early immunization. Immunization is begun young so that a child will become immune as soon as possible. Inherited immunity from an immune mother cannot be depended upon to protect a child from whooping cough, polio, tetanus, and diphtheria. Immunity to these diseases is not achieved until more than a month after the last of the primary doses, and the doses are given about two months apart. Even with an early start, the child is several months old before becoming immune.

But perhaps the most important reason for early immunization is to prevent whooping cough, which is a most serious and some-

Immunization schedule

Age	Disease	Date given
2 months	Diphtheria, whooping cough, and tetanus; (DPT) polio (OPV)	
4 months	Diphtheria, whooping cough, and tetanus; polio	
6 months	Diphtheria, whooping cough, and tetanus; polio*	
15 months	Measles, mumps, and German measles (MMR)	
18 months	Diphtheria, whooping cough, and tetanus; polio** Hemophilus influenzae, type B (HIB)	
4 to 6 years	Diphtheria, whooping cough, and tetanus booster; polio booster	
14 to 16 years	Diphtheria and tetanus booster (dT)	
Every 10 years thereafter	Diphtheria and tetanus booster (dT)	
Special immunizations (When your doctor advises)	Cholera ——————————— Infectious hepatitis (Hepatitis B) ———— Influenza ——————————— Plague ——————————— Pneumococcal ——————————— Rabies ——————————— Typhoid Fever ——————————— Yellow Fever ———————————	

*The American Academy of Pediatrics considers this third immunization for polio to be optional and generally desirable only in areas where polio is present.
**May be given simultaneously with the MMR vaccine at 15 months.

times fatal disease during the first year of life. Measles is also a dangerous disease, and during an outbreak, 6-month-old babies may be inoculated, with another shot given at 15 months of age.

Booster doses. A periodic booster dose is routine procedure for maintaining immunization against diphtheria, whooping cough, tetanus, and polio. Also, a dose of tetanus toxoid may be given to an immunized child who has been bitten by an animal, has stepped on a nail, or has a burn contaminated by soil.

Special vaccinations. Special immunization is needed by children who are going to travel to places where they may be exposed to diseases other than those for which they have had vaccinations, or where food and water may be contaminated. Immunizations against diphtheria, whooping cough, tetanus, and polio should also be brought up to date. M.G.

See also **Bites and stings; Communicable diseases; Diphtheria; German measles; Measles; Poliomyelitis; Shots; Tetanus; Whooping cough**

Impetigo is a contagious skin infection that most often affects children. It is caused by bacteria (staphylococci or streptococci) that grow on the skin. It may develop from infected insect bites.

Small, blisterlike sores containing pus develop on the skin. These sores usually open and a thick, honey-colored crust devel-

ops over them. The crust drops off in from four to six days.

To lessen chances of spreading infection, a child with impetigo should keep fingers away from infected parts and avoid scratching. Separate washcloth, towels, and toys should be used. Bed linen should be changed daily. The child should not return to school until the condition has improved with treatment prescribed by your doctor.

If your baby shows symptoms of impetigo, consult your doctor. Babies with impetigo should be watched carefully. Rarely, the bacteria may get into the blood and cause blood poisoning. A.M.M.

Infantile paralysis. *See* **Poliomyelitis**

Infectious mononucleosis. *See* **Mononucleosis**

Influenza (flu or grippe) is an infectious disease caused by a virus. There are several

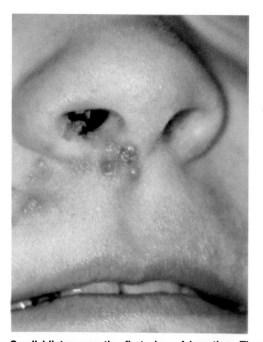
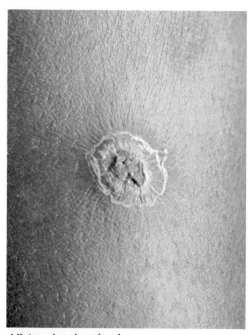

Small blisters are the first sign of impetigo. These blisters break, releasing pus, which forms a crust. The coloring of the crust may vary, depending on the skin coloring. A darker skin produces a darker crust.

types of influenza, caused by different viruses that are present in secretions and other discharges from the nose and mouth of an infected person.

Doctors believe that influenza is spread mainly by coughing and sneezing.

Usually, influenza lasts a relatively short time. Symptoms may include: a chill, aching muscles (especially in the back), and a fever as high as 105° to 106° F. (40.6° to 41° C). The child usually has a hacking cough and may complain of a sore throat. The symptoms of influenza last several days and then gradually fade if no complications develop. Afterward, the child may lack energy for a time.

If you suspect that your child has influenza, call your doctor. Keep the child's diet light—mainly liquids. Do not give the child aspirin, since it is believed that aspirin might induce Reye's syndrome.

The most serious problem with influenza is the complications that may develop. The disease leaves children feeling weak. They are also susceptible to middle-ear infections, pneumonia, and inflammation of the brain.

There is no drug that cures all the various types of influenza; antibiotics may be helpful in the treatment of secondary infections. Antiviral drugs have been found to be effective in the prevention and treatment of influenza A virus strains. They are not, however, normally used except with high-risk patients or with patients suffering from severe influenza A virus illness.

Vaccines for preventing influenza are available, but their protection lasts only a short time, possibly only six months to a year. Also, no one vaccine can immunize against all types of influenza. In rare cases, children react to the vaccine (for example, fever and other symptoms of influenza). Consequently, doctors do not generally recommend the vaccines unless an epidemic of influenza appears to be developing. Children with such diseases as tuberculosis, diabetes, muscular dystrophy, heart disease, and lung disease should receive the vaccine if an epidemic is likely.   H.D.R., Jr.

Inguinal hernia. *See* **Hernia**

Inoculations. *See* **Immunization; Shots**

Itching is a symptom of many diseases and conditions. Cool, moist compresses may help relieve itching, but you must find the cause before you determine the treatment. Here are some causes of itching:
- Allergies including hives and eczema cause severe and, at times, uncontrollable itching. Sometimes, a child who has completely recovered from eczema may continue to scratch when going to bed, when undressed, or when emotionally upset.
- Hay fever may cause itching of the eyes, ears, nose, throat, or the roof of the mouth.
- Pinworms cause intense itching around the anus, usually during the night.
- Athlete's foot (ringworm of the feet) causes itching between the child's toes.
- Mosquito, flea, and bedbug bites can cause itching.
- Chicken pox causes itching when it is forming blisters.
- Scabies causes intense itching in the area of the bites.
- Poison ivy, oak, or sumac causes a burning itch, blistering, and crusting.   J.S.H.

See also **Allergy; Chicken pox; Pinworms; Poison ivy, oak, and sumac; Ringworm**

Jaundice is a yellow discoloring of the skin and eyeballs that results from an excess amount of bile pigment in the bloodstream. It is a symptom of disease rather than a disease itself. If your child appears to have jaundice, call the doctor. The doctor will determine the cause of the jaundice and prescribe proper treatment.

Ordinarily, bile pigment enters the blood as a result of the normal breakdown of red blood cells. The liver converts the bile pigment from a complex to a simple chemical form, so that it can pass through the bile ducts and into the intestinal tract, where it is excreted in the stools.

A number of different conditions may cause jaundice:
- An increased destruction of red blood cells (as may occur in rapidly developing anemia)
- An inability of the liver to excrete bile pigment (as when the liver is damaged)

- An immaturity of the liver that limits its capacity to handle the pigment
- An obstruction of the bile ducts
- An infection of the liver (as in hepatitis)

Jaundice in infants may be completely normal or may indicate a serious disorder. Normal jaundice occurs in the majority of newborn babies, especially premature babies. Such jaundice usually begins when the baby is only 2 or 3 days old and disappears by the 5th or 7th day. It may occur because the immature liver lacks enough enzymes to process the bile pigment. Usually, no treatment is needed for this condition.

Jaundice that appears within the first 24 hours of the baby's life usually is more serious. Incompatibility between the blood types of the mother and the infant is one of its causes. In such cases, the mother is usually Rh-negative and the baby Rh-positive. This cause of jaundice is, however, less common today because of the administration of Rh_o (D) immune globulin to Rh-negative mothers after a delivery or miscarriage. Other blood incompatibilities may also be the cause of jaundice in the newborn. The baby may need one or more exchange transfusions. In an exchange transfusion, the baby's blood, which has a high content of bile pigment, is replaced by blood which has a lower level of bile pigment. High levels of bile pigment in the baby's blood have been associated with brain damage. M.G.

See also **Anemia; Blood type; Hepatitis; Heredity; Rh factor**

Kawasaki disease (mucocutaneous lymph node syndrome) was first described in Japan in the late 1960's. The cause of the disease remains unknown. Although it is most common in Japan, it has been reported throughout the United States.

Kawasaki disease is an inflammatory disease which begins as a sudden illness, after which serious complications can occur. The acute illness usually consists of fever, a rash, red eyes, changes in the lips, swollen glands, and reddening of the palms and soles. Later, heart problems, including heart attacks, can occur. Physicians currently treat children who have Kawasaki disease with gamma globulin and aspirin.

This treatment greatly reduces the chances of cardiac complications. If parents feel that their child has symptoms of Kawasaki disease, they should take the child to the doctor to be examined. s.w.

Keloid is a harmless overgrowth of scar tissue that may develop around cuts, punctures, surgical incisions, or burns. Keloids occur more often in Negroes than in Caucasians. Doctors do not know exactly what causes a keloid.

For the first few months, keloids are usually red or pink. Later they lose this color. They frequently itch and are tender, especially when clothing rubs against them. You can lessen the itching and discomfort:
- Dress the child in loose-fitting clothing of nylon or silk. Avoid wool and cotton.
- Try to keep the child from getting overheated.
- Gently massage the keloid with lanolin every day.
- Your doctor may also recommend the injection of a special cortisone preparation.

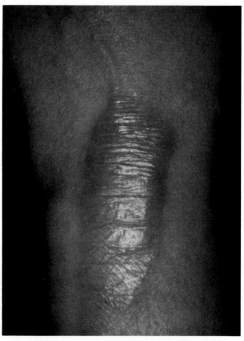

This typical keloid developed around a burn on a boy's wrist.

This may reduce the size and discomfort of the keloid.

In rare cases, a doctor may remove surgically an uncomfortable or disfiguring keloid. Unfortunately, keloids may recur even after they are removed.   т.м.н.

Knock-knee is a condition in which the legs bend inward and the knees come close together. Sometimes, a knock-kneed child also looks pigeon-toed—the toes point together and the heels point outward.

Knock-knee may be positional, or it may be caused by injury or disease affecting the knee growth centers. If positional, knock-knees result from the position in which a child holds the knees and is more common in heavier children. The condition appears to look worse until the child is 5 or 6 years old; it then gradually improves. Positional knock-knees usually correct themselves by the time the child is about 9 years old, and no treatment is necessary. However, if the condition is quite noticeable in a young child, a doctor may recommend shoe corrections and a reduction in the child's weight.

If knock-knee is due to injury to a knee growth center, only one knee is usually affected. If knock-knees is due to disease involving the knee growth centers, both knees are usually involved. Knock-knees caused by injury or disease usually do not correct themselves, and medical treatment is needed. Braces and surgery may be necessary to correct the knock-knee condition.   J.J.G.

See also **Bowlegs; Flat feet; Foot care; Overweight; Rickets**

Laryngitis is an inflammation of the larynx (the organ in the throat that contains the vocal cords). A baby with laryngitis may be hoarse. An older child with this condition will have definite hoarseness.

There are many causes of laryngitis. A common cause at all ages is a brief and severe infection of the respiratory tract. Many of these cases are caused by viruses. Watch babies and young children carefully during such attacks. If the larynx swells, the breathing passages may close. In severe

cases, the doctor may have to establish an airway so that the child can breathe.

If you suspect that your baby or young child has laryngitis, call your doctor immediately. Treatment depends upon the cause. Hoarseness may also be caused by too much talking or shouting. This type of voice abuse responds to rest.

If the child is constantly hoarse, your doctor may suggest that you consult an ear, nose, and throat specialist.   м.G.

See also **Croup; Humidifying; Virus**

Laxative is a medicine, such as mineral oil, that induces bowel movements. Do not give laxatives to your baby except on the advice of a doctor. Never give a laxative to a child who has abdominal pain.

Ordinarily, parents worry unnecessarily about their child "keeping regular." Do not worry if your child misses a day. Some children have bowel movements only every second or third day, but if the stool is soft and normal there is nothing to worry about. Hard, dry stools indicate constipation. They will usually become softer after a minor change in diet, such as increasing the amount of fruit and vegetables, or decreasing the milk intake.

If laxatives are used repeatedly, they may make the problem worse by interfering with the normal muscle tone of the bowel. For this reason, a laxative should not be used unless the child has a special bowel problem. In that case, your doctor will probably recommend a specific mild laxative.   м.G.

Lead poisoning. *See* **Poisonings and poisons**

Leukemia is a form of cancer in which the white blood cells multiply and grow wildly. The first signs include easy bruising, weakness, loss of appetite, anemia, enlargement of the lymph glands, and fever. The disease is diagnosed by examining samples of bone marrow and blood. As yet, the cause of leukemia is unknown.

The several kinds of leukemia are classified according to the type of white blood cell affected. All kinds may be either acute (rapidly developing), or chronic (slowly developing). The acute form is seen most often in children. The chronic form usually occurs in adults.

The kind of leukemia most common in children is acute lymphocytic leukemia. As the name implies, those white blood cells called lymphocytes multiply rapidly in the body's lymph system. Most children with this kind of leukemia respond to drug treatment.

More than half the children treated will stay disease-free for at least five years—and may never have a recurrence. The others will have one or more periods of improvement, called remissions, during which they act and appear normal. But the symptoms may gradually return. As drugs become less effective, the white blood cells multiply rapidly and interfere with the production of red blood cells. The abnormal white cells may also invade vital organs, reducing the body's ability to fight infection and control bleeding.

During periods of remission, the child should be allowed to live as normally as possible, and treated as before the onset of the disease. Any sudden, excessive pampering may be confusing and make the child difficult to handle.

Researchers in the United States and other countries are striving to find the cause of leukemia, to develop new methods of treatment, to extend remissions, and, hopefully, effect a cure.   F.O.

Leukorrhea. *See* **Vaginal discharge.**

Lice are tiny insects which infest the body. The most common type of lice is head lice. Head lice are more common in girls than in boys and occur in any social class. Lice spread from person to person and adhere to hair and fibers. They lay their eggs near hair shafts, and when they hatch, leave nits, which may look like pieces of dandruff. Lice produce substances that irritate the skin and scalp and can cause intense itching.

A child who is suspected of having lice should be examined by a doctor, who will prescribe a lotion or shampoo to eliminate the lice. In some cases, it may be necessary for the doctor to use a microscope to look for nits in order to make the diagnosis. A fine-toothed comb can be used to remove nits from the hair after the hair is soaked with vinegar. It is also important that parents boil the bedding, clothing, hats, combs, and brushes to prevent the lice from recurring. Infrequently, a second application of the shampoo or lotion may be required.

Lip blister. *See* **Blister; Fever blisters**

Lockjaw. *See* **Tetanus**

Lyme disease is named after an area in Connecticut where it was first discovered. It is caused by the germ *Borrelia burgdorferi*, and is spread by tick bites. Certain areas of the country (the Eastern Seaboard and upper Midwest) have more reported cases.

Lyme disease has three phases. Within a few days to a month after the tick bite, a red spot develops at the site of the bite. It expands to a large, red, plaquelike, ring-shaped patch. The diameter varies from an inch to a foot. Flulike symptoms may be present during this initial phase. The rash fades within a month but may recur during the second phase.

The second phase occurs within weeks or months. At this time inflammation of the heart (carditis), nerves (neuritis), and outer brain membrane (meningitis) may develop. Some joint symptoms, such as joint discomfort and swelling, may also be part of this phase, which lasts for a few weeks to three months.

The last phase is the chronic one and is characterized by chronic arthritis and sometimes by chronic neurologic symptoms. A persistent rash may also develop. This third phase has its onset months or even years after the first phase.

Early treatment with antibiotics helps prevent complications of the disease. Consult the child's doctor if you are concerned that your child has possible manifestations of Lyme disease.

Lymph glands. *See* Swollen glands

Malocclusion is the failure of the teeth of the upper and lower jaw to meet properly in biting, or when the mouth is closed. It is caused by irregular placement of the teeth. Malocclusion is also called poor bite.

Malocclusion may occur in both primary (baby) teeth and permanent teeth. It may be inherited; it may be acquired; or a combination of these factors may cause it.

Some children lose their primary teeth too early because of decay or injury. Then, when the permanent teeth come in, they may shift out of position because the guiding channels left by the primary teeth may have changed. Some primary teeth stay in too long and push the permanent teeth out of position. Children who suck their thumbs or fingers excessively after the age of 5 or 6, when the permanent teeth are coming in, may also develop poor bite.

Loss of permanent teeth can leave gaps in the child's jaws and, unless a retainer is inserted, cause the remaining teeth to drift (lean out of position) into the gap.

Children with malocclusions may encounter several problems. They may not be able to chew food properly, or they may have trouble cleaning their teeth. Protruding front teeth or teeth crowded into small jaws may make children feel self-conscious because they look different from other children. Too much space between the teeth may impair children's speech.

All children should start going to the dentist when they are about 3 years old, and they should visit the dentist periodically. The dentist who checks your child's teeth regularly will be able to recognize signs of malocclusion when they occur. The dentist can advise you if the child should see an orthodontist (a dentist who specializes in correcting irregularities of teeth and jaws). Malocclusion can be corrected by braces. M.G.

See also **Braces, dental; Teeth and teething**

Measles (rubeola) is a highly contagious disease caused by a virus. Measles can be prevented by vaccination, and doctors usu-

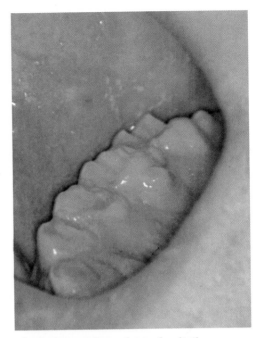

An early symptom of measles is the appearance of tiny white spots on the insides of the cheeks, next to the molars.

ally recommend vaccination because of the complications that can follow measles.

The first symptoms of measles are similar to those of a cold. The child has a hard, dry cough; red and watery eyes; and a fever that may go quite high. The fever appears about 10 days after exposure. Tiny white spots— Koplik's spots—appear on the insides of the cheeks next to the lower molars two to four days after the fever. About two days later, a blotchy red rash begins near the ears and on the neck. It spreads rapidly down the trunk to the feet.

Call the doctor if you suspect that your child has measles. The doctor will probably advise bed care in a partially darkened room if light bothers the child's eyes. The doctor will also prescribe a drug to control the cough. The child will have no appetite while feverish, and so the doctor will probably recommend a liquid diet.

A child who has measles can usually get out of bed in two days after the fever is gone. About a week after the rash begins, if all the cold symptoms are gone, the child can go outdoors and play with other children. The disease is contagious from about

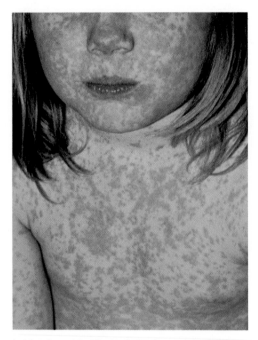

A blotchy red skin rash is the most obvious symptom of measles. It begins at the child's hairline and then spreads.

four to five days before the rash appears until five days after. An attack of measles gives a child permanent immunity.

Some of the complications that may follow measles are pneumonia, middle-ear disease, bronchitis, and encephalitis. Every child who has not had measles should get live measles vaccine at 15 months. In the event of exposure, babies as young as 6 months can be vaccinated, but the child should be revaccinated at 15 months. A child not vaccinated during infancy may be immunized at any time. If an unvaccinated child is exposed to measles, gamma globulin may give temporary protection, or make the disease milder.   H.D.R., Jr.

See also **Communicable diseases; Gamma globulin; Immunization; Virus**

Medicine cabinets have a dangerous fascination for young children. To child-proof your medicine cabinet, follow these safety precautions:

■ Keep all sedatives, pills, or other medicines—including aspirin and all solutions

containing wood alcohol—locked up or out of a child's reach.
■ Keep razors, nail files, and nail scissors on the more inaccessible top shelves of the medicine cabinet. Leave the lower shelves for cotton, bandages, gauze, adhesive tape, and other harmless supplies.
■ Always throw away prescriptions when the illness for which they were ordered is over. Empty all of your leftover medicines into the toilet bowl. Rinse out the empty medicine bottles before throwing them away in the trash containers.
■ Every jar, box, or bottle should be labeled to show what it contains, what the contents are for, and how they are used.
■ Identify anything "for external use only" with a symbol marked in nail polish.
■ Clean out the medicine cabinet at least every three months, discarding anything that is useless or spoiled.

A well-stocked medicine cabinet will enable you to take care of most cuts, aches, and pains. It should contain:

Sterile gauze bandages, 3 inches (7.5 centimeters) square
Sterile bandages, 2 inches (5 centimeters) wide
Sterile bandages, 1 inch (2.5 centimeters) wide
Adhesive tape, 1 inch (2.5 centimeters) wide
Sterile absorbent cotton
Box of small prepared bandages
Petroleum jelly
Acetaminophen
Calamine lotion
Rubbing alcohol (70 per cent)
Syrup (not fluid extract) of ipecac
Rectal thermometer

Other supplies that could be part of a household's medical equipment are an oral thermometer, a medicine dropper, a heating pad, an ice bag, a hot-water bottle, tweezers, and a cold-mist humidifier.   M.G.

See also **Accidents; Drugs; First aid; Poisonings and poisons; Prescriptions**

Meningitis is an infection of the membranes covering the brain and spinal cord. Most cases of meningitis are caused by bacteria that are carried by the blood to the brain from a nose, throat, or lung infection.

In older children, meningitis often begins with a fever, irritability, headache, nausea, and vomiting. A rash of bright red spots may also appear. Gradually, the child's back stiffens, and the child cannot bend the neck forward. The child may have convulsions and may lose consciousness.

In infants and young children, the signs of meningitis are somewhat different. Frequently the child has no fever, and infants rarely have a stiff neck. However, the membrane covering the fontanels (soft spots in the skull) may stretch and become tight.

If you suspect that your child has meningitis, call your doctor. A child with meningitis must be hospitalized in order to receive proper examination and proper treatment. Early treatment with antibiotic drugs is necessary to avoid serious complications or even death.

Recently a vaccine effective against Hemophilus influenzae B, the most common cause of meningitis, has been introduced. It is, at present, recommended that children 18 months through 5 years of age be immunized. H.D.R., JR.

Menstruation. All parents who have a daughter want her to grow up enjoying her femininity. It follows that all girls should learn to accept menstruation as a normal part of growing up, essential to the process of reproduction.

Unfortunately, some girls fear menstrual periods and become emotionally upset when they begin the process. They may have heard their mothers or their friends refer to menstruation as "having the curse" or "being sick." Or they may have been told that menstruation is painful; that they will feel weak; or that they cannot exercise, dance, swim, take baths, or wash their hair.

When a girl becomes about 8 years old—or earlier if she asks questions—her mother should start to tell her about menstruation. Present it to her as the special phenomenon it is—preparation for the wonderful day when she is to be a mother.

Begin by telling your daughter about the two ovaries, one on either side of her uterus (womb), and about the vagina. The ovaries

produce eggs capable of developing into babies if they are fertilized by sperm. The uterus is the special place in the mother's body where the baby will grow until it is ready to be born. It is a pear-shaped organ in the middle of a woman's body. The vagina is the birth canal, through which the baby is born. It is below the uterus.

Menstrual cycle. Once a girl enters puberty, generally by the time she is 11 or 12, the ovaries start to produce one egg a month. This egg is smaller than the head of a pin. About two weeks after menstruation, the egg passes from the ovary through a tube, called the Fallopian tube, to the uterus. The uterus prepares itself in case the egg is fertilized. If a baby is going to grow from this tiny egg, it must receive food. This food is brought to the uterus in the mother's blood. The lining of the uterus becomes thick and spongy to receive the egg and help feed it. If the egg is not going to develop into a baby, this lining is not needed. The lining breaks down, and most of the lining and a little blood pass out of the body through the vagina. This discharge occurs about once a month unless a woman is pregnant. Menstrual periods do not occur during pregnancy and for a month or so afterward.

Some girls associate bleeding with injury and are frightened by the thought of menstrual bleeding. The amount of blood discharged during menstruation varies with the individual. It is usually about 1½ ounces (44.5 milliliters), not enough to make a girl anemic or weaken her. The body quickly replaces this small amount of blood.

Reassure your daughter that an irregular menstrual cycle is not uncommon for the first couple of years. There may even be lapses of two or three months between periods. After that the cycle should recur every 26 to 30 days, each period usually lasting about 5 days.

The cycle, once established, is fairly regular for each girl, but it may occasionally vary. Excitement or nervousness may cause irregularity. Many girls skip menstrual periods when a great change in their normal routine occurs—for example, when they are away at summer camp or during their first year at college. Menstrual periods may also

The menstrual cycle

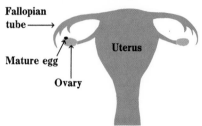

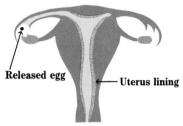

1. Although each ovary may contain thousands of potential eggs, usually only one egg matures during each cycle.

2. The ovary releases the mature egg. The lining of the uterus starts growing to receive and feed the egg if it is fertilized.

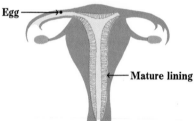

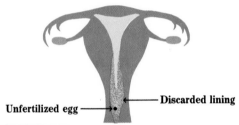

3. The egg slowly moves down the Fallopian tube to the uterus. Fertilization, if it occurs, takes place in the Fallopian tube.

4. If the egg is not fertilized, the lining of the uterus is not needed. The lining breaks down and passes out of the body.

stop in girls who have lost a considerable amount of weight or who engage in constant strenuous activities such as running marathons or seriously studying ballet.

Care during the period. During the menstrual period, some girls use soft, absorbent, gauze pads called sanitary napkins to absorb the menstrual flow. The pads are held in place in the underpants by adhesive strips on the back of the pads. Other girls use tampons—small rolls of compressed, absorbent material that are inserted into the vagina. If tampons are to be used, they should be changed every four to six hours. Hands should be washed before inserting the tampon, and an applicator should be used. Sanitary pads should be worn at night.

Some girls worry about offensive odors that may occur during menstruation. These odors result not from the freshly discharged blood but from changes in the blood as it dries. Frequent changing of sanitary pads or tampons provides greater comfort and less concern about personal hygiene.

Many girls ask if menstruation will hurt. Pain or discomfort does not necessarily ac-

company menstruation. Some girls get cramps, but the cramps usually last only the first few days. Most cramps can be relieved by medication, a hot-water bottle, a heating pad, and warm drinks. But if the pain is too severe, consult a doctor. Tenderness of the breasts, backache, a feeling of heaviness, and a slight gain in weight may also accompany the menstrual period.

A girl usually can continue her normal activities during her menstrual periods. She may dance, skate, and ski; and she may wash her hair and take showers. If tampons are used, a girl may swim at any time during her period.

What to tell boys. Boys, too, ask questions about menstruation. "Do boys menstruate?" "Does it hurt?" These questions should be answered truthfully. Explain to them that menstruation is simply a process of getting rid of material that was ready inside the body with food for a baby. Since men cannot have babies inside of them, men do not menstruate. Tell them also that menstruation does not usually hurt. Some girls are uncomfortable and may be a little cross, but they go right ahead with school or work or whatever they have to do. Reassure them that menstruation is not like bleeding from an injury. M.G.

Moles are commonly found in the older child and adolescent. Large amounts of dark pigment in the cells give moles their color. Moles may be black, brown, gray, purple, or bluish black. Some may also have hair in them, especially the larger moles. Sometimes moles are just small spots or marks, but other times they cover large areas of skin.

Usually, small moles are not harmful and do not change in appearance over the years. In rare instances, however, they can begin to grow and become cancerous, especially larger moles that were present at birth. If a mole enlarges, changes color, bleeds easily, or becomes painful, consult your doctor. Tell your child not to pick or otherwise irritate a mole, for the irritation may cause it to start growing. If a mole is in a place where irrita-

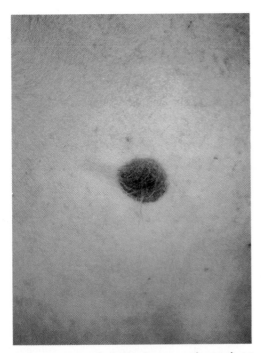

The common soft, hairy, brown mole, such as the one on this child's cheek, is harmless.

tion cannot be avoided, such as at the belt or bra line, the doctor may remove it.

Moles may be removed very easily. Usually, the doctor uses a local anesthesia and simply cuts out the mole and a small portion of the surrounding skin. A.M.M.

See also **Birthmark**

Mononucleosis is a contagious disease that most commonly strikes older children, adolescents, and young adults. It occurs both sporadically and in epidemics. Caused by the Epstein-Barr virus, mononucleosis is also called infectious mononucleosis and glandular fever.

A typical case of mononucleosis begins with chills, fever, headache, dizziness, and sore throat. Lymph glands in the neck or in other parts of the body may swell. The child may feel exhausted and depressed and lose appetite. In some cases, a reddish rash may spread over the trunk and other parts of the body. Call the doctor if you suspect that your child has mononucleosis.

A child who has come down with mononucleosis should rest as needed, but need not be isolated. While symptoms of the disease may last from two to six weeks, it may take months for the child to regain energy. H.D.R., JR.

See also **Communicable diseases; Hepatitis; Jaundice; Virus**

Motion sickness. Some children become nauseated and vomit when they ride in a car, bus, train, ship, or plane. No one knows why one child shows more sensitivity to motion than another.

Some children become sick when riding in almost any type of conveyance, and others are bothered by only one or two. If the motion is very bumpy, as in a small airplane, almost any child will become sick.

Here are a few steps you can take to reduce chances of your child's suffering motion sickness while traveling:

■ Place the child where he or she can easily see out of the vehicle.

■ Avoid seats where motion may be especially bumpy, such as the back of a bus.

■ Do not let the child eat rich or heavy foods before traveling.

- If motion sickness becomes extremely bothersome, consult the doctor. In some cases, drug treatment may help.   M.G.

See also **Vomiting**

Multiple sclerosis (MS) is a disease that affects the brain and spinal cord. The myelin (material coating the nerves) breaks down and becomes spotted with hard scar tissue. The scar tissue hinders the normal functions of the nerves that carry messages from the brain to all parts of the body. Multiple sclerosis may strike children, but it usually affects people between 20 and 40 years old. Doctors do not know what causes it, and they have not yet found a cure.

First symptoms may be blurred vision in one or both eyes; double vision; an unsteady walk; or numbness of an arm, a leg, or a part of the trunk. These symptoms may last only a few days and be followed by a period of complete recovery. Then other attacks may occur—weeks, months, or even years later. Symptoms often differ from one attack to another.

Some people never completely recover from the first attack of multiple sclerosis and become more disabled with each new attack. Others recover almost completely from a series of widely spaced attacks.   A.G.S.

Mumps (infectious parotitis) is a contagious disease caused by a virus. It occurs most often in children.

Mumps begins with a pain below and in front of the ear. Next, the child has difficulty chewing and swallowing. Then, the salivary (parotid) glands just below and in front of the ears swell and become tender. In most cases, one gland swells first and the gland on the other side of the neck swells a few days later. Sometimes only one side swells. Other salivary glands may also be affected, but only the doctor can determine this. In about 30 to 40 percent of all cases, swelling of the glands cannot be seen.

A child with mumps may find it painful to swallow sour or highly seasoned food. Fever and chills may also appear. If you suspect that your child has mumps, consult your doctor.

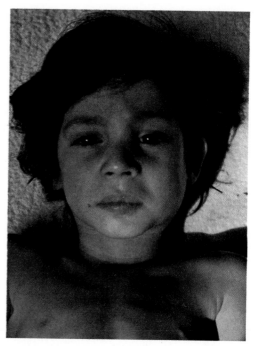

Mumps may cause swelling of the salivary glands on one or both sides of the neck.

When mumps attacks male adults and adolescent boys, the sex glands may be affected. But this complication rarely causes sterility. Another complication of mumps affects the meninges (membranes that surround the brain and the spinal cord). The child may have a high fever and headache and may vomit and become delirious. But this complication (called mumps meningitis) rarely produces serious aftereffects.

In some mild cases of mumps, the doctor may not insist on bed rest. If the case is severe, or if the child is an adolescent boy, the doctor will probably suggest that you keep the child warm and quiet in bed.

Symptoms of mumps usually appear from 14 to 21 days after exposure. Mumps is contagious from about 7 days before symptoms appear until from 7 to 10 days after, or until the swelling disappears. The child may return to school when all swelling has disappeared. A child who has had mumps in either or both parotid glands usually does not get the disease again.

The MMR shot (measles, mumps, rubella), given at 15 months of age, protects against mumps. Mumps vaccine alone may be given to children, particularly boys, who have not had the shot or mumps.   H.D.R., JR.

See also **Communicable diseases**

Muscular dystrophy. The term muscular dystrophy refers to an inherited group of diseases that cause muscles to weaken and waste away. The muscular dystrophies usually attack the muscles that control arm, leg, and face movements. Scientists have not yet found the cause or the cure for this group of diseases.

There are several forms of muscular dystrophy, all varying in degree of seriousness. One form occurs only in newborn babies; another, which is more common, occurs in older children and teen-agers. Some forms spread rapidly and cause severe disability; others spread slowly and cause less disability. Some forms result in early death, while others do not affect life span. A child with the most common form of muscular dystrophy develops unusually large calves, has difficulty going up stairs, has a tendency to fall, and walks with a waddling gait. The child may need to wear braces to stand and walk. As the disease progresses, a wheelchair may be needed.

Physical therapy cannot cure muscular dystrophy, but it can help slow down the crippling effects of the disease and make it possible for children to attend school, which should be encouraged.   J.J.G.

Nail care. A child's nails require regular care to keep them clean. Wash them in warm water and scrub them with a moderately stiff brush. Use either manicure scissors or an emery board to keep them short. Trim and shape fingernails to a rounded point. Toenails should be cut straight across so that they will be less likely to curve into the flesh and become ingrown.

If a toenail becomes ingrown, cut the nail straight across and do not trim the corners. Soak the child's foot in warm water and dry it. Then, use a toothpick to tuck a small piece of cotton under the corner of the ingrown toenail. Each night, for four or six weeks, remove the cotton, soak the foot,

Care of ingrown toenails

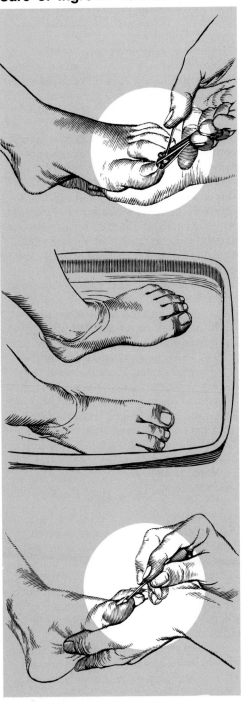

Cut your child's toenail straight across. Do not trim the corners. Soak the foot in warm water and dry it. Then tuck a small piece of cotton under the ingrown corner.

then insert a fresh piece of cotton. If this does not relieve the pain and make the nail grow out, or if there is still an infection, consult your doctor.

To prevent hangnails (pieces of skin hanging by one end at the side or base of a nail), show your child how to push back the cuticle with a towel when drying the hands. M.G.

Navel. The umbilical cord attaches an unborn baby to the placenta (the organ attached to the inside of the uterus) of the mother. Food and oxygen flow from the mother to the unborn baby through blood vessels in the cord. Waste material from the baby flows through the cord to the placenta, where it is picked up by the mother's blood. At birth, the cord is clamped and cut close to the baby's abdomen.

The small piece of cord that remains gradually dries up and turns dark. It falls off in about a week, and the resulting scar is called the navel. Afterward, the navel may look a little red for a few days. Report any redness, swelling, or bleeding around the navel to your doctor. Keep the navel clean and dry until it is healed. Your doctor may recommend cleaning the navel each day with alcohol and giving sponge baths rather than tub baths until the navel heals. The doctor will probably tell you not to cover it with a dressing because the navel heals better if it is exposed to air. M.G.

See also **Hernia**

Near-sightedness (myopia) is a defect in sight. A near-sighted child sees close objects fairly well, but distant objects are blurred. The reason for this is that the eyes are longer from front to back than the normal eye, and light rays from an object are brought into focus too far in front of the retina.

Near-sightedness usually develops in childhood and adolescence. It is rarely present at birth. A near-sighted child may hold things close to see them; but so will a far-sighted child on occasion. Near-sighted children may also keep their eyelids partially closed, making a tiny slit that helps them to see more clearly.

If a child is near-sighted, the world may look like this photograph—near objects are in focus but distant objects are blurred.

When a near-sighted child wears corrective glasses, distant objects are brought into focus.

If you think your child is near-sighted, consult your doctor. An eye examination may be in order and glasses may be prescribed. Near-sighted children should have their eyes checked biannually for the first few years, then annually. A child with near-sighted parents should have an eye examination before entering school, because there is a family tendency toward near-sightedness.

It is recommended that all children have a complete eye examination at 3 years and periodically thereafter. R.O.S.

Nephritis is a general term for several inflammatory diseases that affect the kidneys. It most often follows a streptococcus infection, usually a sore throat. Generally, it does not affect children under 3. Nephritis may be chronic—slow to develop, long lasting, and incurable—or it may be acute—quick to develop, of short duration, and easily cured. Acute nephritis is a more common type found in children.

Acute nephritis varies in severity. Some children become seriously ill, but the outlook is almost always excellent. Generally, acute nephritis begins from one to three weeks after an untreated streptococcal infection. The child's urine often contains blood, giving the urine a smoky color similar to that of a cola drink. The child may also be tired and have a fever, severe headache, and swelling around the eyes. Recovery usually begins in a week or two. M.G.

See also **Urinary disturbances**

Nightmares. A young child—especially between the ages of 2 and 5—may frequently wake from sleep because of a dream, usually a frightening one. After such a dream, your child needs to be comforted. Speak to the child soothingly and encourage the child to tell you about the dream. Listen carefully, even to a garbled account.

Night terrors usually occur 90 to 100 minutes after the child has gone to sleep. The child suddenly sits up, is frightened, and wants to be consoled. Episodes last from seconds to several minutes and usually are not remembered by the child the following morning.

There is no way to prevent bad dreams. But if your child has frequent nightmares, consult your doctor. M.G.

See also **Sleep**

Nose, objects in the. Sometimes by accident, and sometimes just to find out what will happen, a child puts an object into a nostril. If the child's nose bleeds, or if you cannot see the foreign object, call your doctor immediately.

Occasionally, the child may get the object out quite easily by sneezing it out, or may force it out by blowing the nose. Ask a child to blow the nose only if you know the child will not sniff in instead of blowing out.

You may be able to remove a soft object from your child's nose by using a pair of tweezers. Do this only if you can see the object. And be careful not to injure the child's nostril. Warn the child not to move while you are trying to remove the foreign object.

Never try to remove a smooth, hard object from a child's nose. The object may be pushed farther into the nose quite easily and might get into the throat and choke the child. Call your doctor immediately, and let the doctor remove the object. C.F.F.

Nose drops help clear up a stuffy nose, and are often recommended by doctors. Nose drops help clear the nostrils of mucus. A prescription is usually not necessary. You can mix 1 teaspoon of table salt in 2 cups of water and store the solution until needed.

Using a clean dropper, place a few drops of the solution in each nostril until bubbles appear. Then use a small bulb syringe to aspirate the mucus from each nostril. It is helpful to administer the drops before each feeding and before the baby goes to sleep.

In some instances, your child's doctor may order prescription drops. Use the drops only in the specified amount. Young children can suffer from an overdose of the drugs in these solutions. Never continue nose drops indefinitely.

If your baby struggles when you try to administer nose drops, lay the baby in your lap or on a bed, whichever you feel is more convenient and comfortable for you. Put one arm around or over the baby to keep the baby still, and hold the baby's chin with your hand. Leave your other hand free to put in the drops.

Another common method of giving nose drops is to lay the baby on your lap with the baby's head between your knees. In this way, you can confine the head with your knees, hold the baby's hands with one of your hands, and still have one hand free for inserting the drops.   c.f.f.

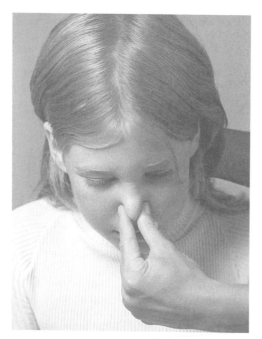

One effective way to stop a nosebleed is to pinch the nostrils shut while the child is sitting up and leaning forward.

Nosebleed may be caused by a punch in the nose or a fall. A child's nose may also bleed if the child picks it, pokes something into it, or blows it too hard. Colds, other infections, and extremely dry air may also rupture tiny blood vessels. Fortunately, most nosebleeds in children occur in the front, central part of the nose, where you can easily apply pressure to stop the bleeding.

If your child has a nosebleed, have the child sit up and lean forward, if possible. Or, place the child in a reclining position with head and shoulders raised. Pinch the nostrils shut for at least 10 minutes as the child breathes through the mouth. If bleeding continues, put a small pad of cotton or gauze in the bleeding nostril and apply pressure.

When the bleeding stops, do not let your child blow the nose for a while. This could disturb the blood clots and start another nosebleed. If bleeding does not stop in 10 to 15 minutes, call a doctor. In severe cases, a doctor may need to pack the nose with gauze, or cauterize the bleeding points.

Nutrition. The nutrients in food can be divided into certain groups—proteins, carbohydrates, fats, vitamins, and minerals. Water is sometimes considered a nutrient.

Proteins are necessary for the growth and repair of cells. Proteins help build blood and form antibodies to fight infection. They also supply energy. The proteins in food are broken down into amino acids by the body's digestive system. Then the body cells use the amino acids like building blocks to put together new and different proteins.

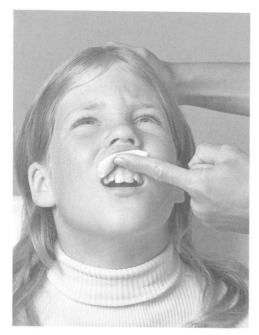

Pressing a wad of cotton under a child's upper lip is another common method of stopping a nosebleed.

For infants, there are 9 essential amino acids. The body can make others if it gets these 9, but it cannot manufacture these 9. Some foods contain all 9 amino acids. These foods, called complete proteins, include meats, poultry, fish, milk, cheese, and eggs. Other foods contain some of the essential 9 amino acids. These foods, called incomplete proteins, include cereals, dried beans, dried peas, and nuts.

Carbohydrates. Starches and sugars, two carbohydrates, supply quick energy. Starches are found in cereals, bread and other baked goods, rice, noodles, macaroni, spaghetti, potatoes, lima beans, and corn. Sources of sugars include candy, fruit, honey, jams, jellies, syrup, and milk.

Other important carbohydrates are celluloses. Celluloses cannot be digested, but they supply roughage. Roughage stimulates muscle contractions in the intestine walls. This helps the body eliminate wastes. The leaves of vegetables and the skin and pulp of fruits are good sources of roughage.

If a child does not eat enough digestible carbohydrates, the body burns protein for energy. A child needs carbohydrates so that the proteins are spared for body-building. Nutritionists recommend meeting the carbohydrate needs of a child mainly through bread, cereals, fruits, green vegetables, milk, and potatoes. If a child takes too much of the carbohydrate requirement in the form of sweets, the child's supply of vitamins, minerals, and proteins from vegetables and fruits may be lowered. Also, a diet high in refined sugar, such as candy, can cause tooth decay.

Excess carbohydrates are converted into fat and stored in the body as fatty tissues. If a child eats more starches and sweets than are needed for daily energy requirements, the child may become overweight.

Fats are highly concentrated sources of energy. They supply more than twice the energy of an equal amount of carbohydrates or proteins. However, fats are digested slower and cannot be used for quick energy. Fats also supply vitamins A and D. Foods containing fats include cream, butter, margarine, cheese, egg yolk, fat in meats, salad oils, peanut butter, nuts, and chocolate.

Basic food groups

The basic seven

Group 1	Meats, poultry, fish, eggs, dried beans and peas, and nuts
Group 2	Leafy, green, and yellow vegetables
Group 3	Citrus fruits, raw cabbage, salad greens, and tomatoes
Group 4	Potatoes and other vegetables, and noncitrus fruits
Group 5	Breads, cereals, and flour
Group 6	Butter and fortified margarine
Group 7	Milk and milk products

The basic four

Meat Group	Meats, fish, poultry, eggs, dried beans and peas, nuts
Vegetable-Fruit Group	Vegetables and fruits that provide vitamin C; dark green, leafy vegetables and deep yellow vegetables and fruits; other fruits and vegetables
Bread-Cereals Group	Bread, muffins, macaroni, spaghetti, rice
Milk Group	Fresh whole milk, skim milk, dried milk, evaporated milk, cheese, ice cream

Nutritionists recommend that a child have at least 2 glasses of milk each day. A teen-ager needs 3 or more glasses. Milk products may also fulfill this need. With the Basic Seven system, nutritionists suggest one daily serving from each of the remaining six groups. With the Basic Four system, they recommend four or more servings from both the vegetable-fruit and bread-cereal groups, and two or more servings from the meat group.

Fat that is not burned up is stored as body fat. Body fat supports and protects vital organs and areas such as the eyeballs, the kidneys, the liver, and the joints. A layer of fat under the skin protects the body from losing an excessive amount of heat. If a child eats too many fats, excess body fat is formed and the child becomes overweight.

Fats can be divided into two types—saturated and unsaturated. Saturated fats are usually solid at room temperature, and unsaturated fats are usually liquid at room temperature. Most doctors recommend reducing the amount of saturated fats in the diet and replacing them with unsaturated fats, because saturated fats are known to raise the level of cholesterol, a fatty chemical found in the bloodstream. A high level of cholesterol in the blood may lead to heart disease.

Foods high in saturated fats include chocolate, fatty beef, fatty dairy products, luncheon meats, and pork. Most margarines, poultry, and veal are lower in saturated fats. Foods high in unsaturated fats include corn oil, fish, mayonnaise, and special margarines. Fried foods are full of the kind of fat they are cooked in.

Minerals. Several minerals are also required by the body. These minerals include calcium, iron, and iodine.

Calcium helps build bones and teeth, helps blood clot, helps muscles and nerves work, and helps the body regulate the use of other minerals. Milk, cheese, ice cream, shellfish, canned sardines, egg yolk, soy beans, and green vegetables supply calcium.

Iron combines with protein to make hemoglobin, the red substance in blood that carries oxygen to cells. Good sources of iron include lean meats, egg yolk, dried beans and peas, green leafy vegetables, prunes, raisins, dried apricots, liver, heart, kidney, liver sausage, shellfish, and enriched or whole grain bread, cereal, and cereal products.

Iodine helps control the rate at which the body uses energy. Seafoods and iodized salt supply iodine.

Vitamins are essential for the utilization of foods for normal growth and for prevention of certain diseases. Some vitamins, such as vitamins A and D, may be stored in the body. Other vitamins must be supplied constantly because the excess is eliminated.

Vitamins can be divided into two general classes. Vitamins A and D and others are called fat-soluble because they dissolve in fat. Vitamin C, B-complex vitamins, and others are called water-soluble because they dissolve in water. For more information on vitamins, see VITAMINS.

Water helps carry nutrients to cells and waste products away from cells. It also helps build tissues and regulate body temperature. Water is obtained from liquids and from foods with a high percentage of water.

Nutrients and diet. A well-balanced diet usually provides all the essential nutrients in sufficient quantity. If your child does not eat exactly the recommended amounts every day, do not be concerned. Through regular physical examinations, a doctor can determine if your child is well nourished.

Conserving nutrients. Store and prepare foods in ways that preserve nutrients:
- Keep meat, fish, and poultry in a refrigerator or freezer, wrapped in plastic wrap or foil.
- Keep frozen food frozen until it is used, and cook it as soon as it is defrosted. Frozen food loses vitamins after thawing and refreezing. Never refreeze frozen foods.
- Wash leafy vegetables and store them in plastic in a refrigerator.
- Cook vegetables for the shortest possible time in as little liquid as possible.   M.G.

Osteomyelitis is a bone infection and should be considered a potentially serious disease. It is usually caused by bacteria that are carried via the bloodstream to the bone, from a source of infection in another part of the body, such as a boil or an infected ear.

Osteomyelitis takes two forms—acute and chronic. The acute form, which is brief and severe, is more common in a growing child than in an adult. The child has a fever, is irritable, and experiences pain and tenderness in the bone. In some children the infection may spread from the bone into a nearby joint. The chronic form, which lasts longer than the acute form, is more common in adults and is characterized by bone pain and draining sinuses (a type of abscess).

If you suspect your child has osteomyelitis, call your doctor promptly. The doctor may give the child intravenous fluids to keep up the child's strength, and antibiotics to combat the infection. Early and vigorous medical attention can cure osteomyelitis in most children. J.J.G.

Otitis media. *See* **Earaches**

Overweight.
Many children who appear to be overweight are not. For example, a child with a stocky build and a large body frame is not necessarily overweight. Nor is the preadolescent girl or boy who gains weight rapidly just before a rapid increase in height. If you think your child is overweight, consult your doctor. By examining the child, the doctor can determine what the child's weight should be for the age and body frame of the child. If your child is overweight, the doctor can determine the cause and prescribe treatment.

Occasionally, children with thyroid disease are overweight. Treatment of the thyroid condition corrects the weight problem. In rare instances, the cause may be a disorder of the pituitary gland or adrenal glands. Usually, however, excessive eating or decreased physical activity (or both) is the cause. The child is consuming more calories than are burned through activity. Sometimes there are underlying emotional problems. Weight problems may start after a family crisis or after the child recovers from an illness or operation. The child may be eating because of anxiety.

In some families, there is a tendency to be overweight. When both parents are overweight, there is a 75 per cent chance that their children will also be overweight.

A little extra weight probably is not harmful. But a child who is quite heavy may significantly increase the workload of the heart, may have trouble performing normal physical actions, or may be ridiculed and rejected by classmates.

A child who is overweight needs help to lose the extra weight. Do not keep tempting foods such as cookies, candy, cakes, soft drinks, ice cream, and potato chips in the house. Discourage between-meal eating. Offer the child fruit, carrot sticks, and other raw vegetables for snacks. Encourage the child to develop an interest in athletics and other activities that will provide physical exercise. If you want to treat the child, do not do it with sweets; instead, take the child to the bowling alley, swimming pool, or skating rink. Praise the child for even the slightest weight loss. When the child loses weight, some new clothes in the child's new size may be an added incentive. M.G.

See also **Anorexia nervosa; Diets**

Pacifiers
commonly are made of a small plastic or rubber nippple attached to a flat disk that keeps the infant from swallowing the nipple. A pacifier offers no nourishment, yet it often soothes a hungry, irritable, or colicky baby. It also gives the infant a chance to satisfy the basic need to suck—a very strong need in infants.

Many parents who object strongly to thumb-sucking are not distressed if the infant sucks a pacifier. They feel that they can offer the pacifier as they wish, whereas the thumb is always at the baby's disposal. One disadvantage of the pacifier is that a baby may become agitated if having trouble keeping the pacifier in or near the mouth. The baby may also become overly attached to the pacifier unless it is discontinued after a few months. Never put a pacifier on a ribbon or string around the baby's neck or wrist in order to keep it handy. The danger of the baby choking is too great. M.G.

See also **Thumb-sucking**

Pimple. *See* **Acne**

Pinkeye. *See* **Conjunctivitis**

Pinworms
are thin white parasites that live in the intestines. They are about ¼ inch (6 millimeters) long. They may be seen in the child's stool, or even protruding from the anus or vagina. Children with pinworms itch about the anus and may scratch the area severely. The itching is worse at night.

after the child goes to bed. Pinworms may cause a vaginal discharge in young girls.

If one child has pinworms, the entire family should be examined by a doctor. The adult pinworm crawls out of the anus or vagina to lay its eggs. The eggs may fall from the infected child onto the bedding or clothing. The child may pick the eggs up under the fingernails, or they may float in the air because they are so light. Other people may pick up the eggs by inhaling them or by touching the child's bedding, clothing, or hands. If the eggs are swallowed, they reach the intestine and become adult pinworms.

Pinworms are harmless unless they occur in large numbers. Doctors usually prescribe drugs to eliminate them. M.G.

Pneumonia is an inflammation of the lungs. It is usually caused by bacteria and viruses. Most children get pneumonia as a complication of a cold, or of influenza. Certain fungi may be inhaled and cause pneumonia. Pneumonia can also develop if a child swallows a chemical substance such as kerosene or furniture polish. Other cases of pneumonia may occur if a child breathes foods, talcum powder, or other foreign materials into the windpipe.

A child with pneumonia usually breathes rapidly, sometimes with a grunting sound, and may develop a cough and a high fever. (Infants usually run a lower fever than older children.) The child usually is listless and, in severe cases, appears desperately ill. An older child may complain of chest or abdominal pain.

If you suspect your child has pneumonia, call the doctor. Pneumonia is usually treatable at home. Occasionally, hospitalization is required in order to treat the child with oxygen and intravenous fluids. M.G.

See also **Colds; Virus**

Poison ivy, oak, and sumac are three common and closely related plants that cause skin rashes. A child who spends a great deal of time in the woods and fields should know what these plants look like so that they can be avoided.

Poison ivy leaves grow in clusters of three, all from the same stem. The edges of the leaves may be lobed or notched.

Poison ivy grows as a vine or shrub. Some forms of poison ivy are called poison oak. Poison ivy always has three smooth leaves on one stem. The leaves are shiny green in summer and turn red or orange in the fall. Bunches of small, green flowers grow on the main stem close to the leaves. In autumn and winter, the plant bears clusters of white, waxy berries.

Poison sumac grows as a shrub or small tree. It has narrow, fernlike leaves and drooping clusters of white berries.

Poison ivy or poison sumac rash is caused by an irritating oil in the leaves, flowers, fruit, stem, bark, and roots. Clothing that has come in contact with poison ivy may irritate the skin just as much as the plants themselves. Wash or clean the clothing before the child wears it again. Dogs and cats that have come in contact with the poison ivy may also cause the rash. Decontaminate your pets by bathing them.

If you think your child has touched poison ivy, immediately wash the child's hands and other exposed skin thoroughly with mild soap. Rinse with plenty of cold water, lather again, and rinse again. Do not rub too hard and do not use brushes, sponges, or other rough or harsh materials. Washing with soap removes or lessens the irritation of the oil.

Poison ivy rash may appear a few hours or a few days after the child touches the plant. At first the child's skin itches or burns. Then the skin becomes inflamed, and it usually develops blisters. Scratching may cause an infection. Cut the child's fingernails short. To reduce itching, soak the rash-covered skin in plain or salt water for 20 to 30 minutes, four or five times daily. Use one level teaspoon of table salt in one pint (0.5 liter) of water. Apply calamine lotion every two or three hours. Your doctor may prescribe medicine such as Benadryl® to reduce itching.   A.M.M.

Poisonings and poisons. According to the National Capital Poison Center, approximately 1,500,000 poisoning cases occur each year. Of all reported accidental exposures to poisonous substances, 65 per cent involve children under 6. In addition, an unknown number of poisoning cases are not reported to poison control centers.

Cases that are reported to poison control centers include exposure to a wide variety of chemical substances such as cosmetics, plants, cleaning substances, analgesics, and cold and congestant medications. Approximately 65 per cent of the incidents are non-toxic, rather than cases of actual poisoning. Approximately 35 per cent are considered *toxic exposures*, or actual poisonings that involve symptoms, hospitalization, or death.

Factors that affect poisonings. Many factors determine the eventual outcome for a potentially poisoned child or adult:
- The inherent toxicity of the material itself; for example, household bleach as compared to cyanide.
- The concentration of the substance ingested (taken in); for example, bleach drunk straight from the bottle as opposed to a cupful diluted in a bucket of water.
- The sensitivity of the child to the substance in question.
- The route of the exposure; for example, gasoline spilled on the skin as opposed to gasoline swallowed during siphoning.

- The volume or amount ingested.
- The time interval since the exposure.
- The presence or absence of symptoms.
- The number of substances ingested.
- The ability to follow instructions from a poison control center or doctor. Often an appropriate and timely reaction to an incident can mean the difference between taking care of the problem at home and going to the emergency room of a hospital.

How and with what children are poisoned. Cosmetics are the leading poisonous substance ingested by children under 6. Other leading poisonous substances, in order, are plants, soaps and detergents, cold medications (antihistamines or decongestants), analgesics, and vitamins and minerals.

Aspirin was once a major poison problem with children. However, since 1972, the number of aspirin-related poisoning incidents has declined steadily. One factor is the Poison Prevention Packaging Act of 1972, which requires child-resistant packaging. However, other common household analgesics that are provided in child-resistant packaging show a slow but steady increase in frequency of ingestions. Unfortunately, no packaging is absolutely childproof.

Therefore, a number of factors other than child-resistant packaging are believed to account for the reduction in the number of aspirin poisonings. The most significant factor is thought to be increased public awareness of the danger of aspirin. Evidently, parents recognize the potential danger of aspirin and use and store it properly—out of sight of curious little minds and out of reach of curious little hands. The same need for safety precautions applies to all potential poisons in the home, including acetaminophen, which has replaced aspirin in the treatment of fever.

Poison prevention. Normal children are inquistive, resourceful, and almost tireless. They learn by touching, smelling, and tasting the elements of their environment, and by imitating their parents and other family members. If an item is attractive in appearance or packaging, is brightly colored, resembles a food item, or has been consumed by other family members in the child's presence, it is a potential poison. Observing some safety rules, and checking or cleaning out a few areas of your house, can help protect your child from poisoning and perhaps help prevent needless pain to both your child and you.

Safety rules. By following a few simple safety rules, you can "poison-proof" your home:

- Keep hazardous products out of your child's sight and reach. Periodically check the entire house and all storage areas for hazardous materials. Discard any potential poisons that are of little or no use. Some items commonly involved in poisonings are furniture polish, lighter fluid, bleach, boric acid, turpentine, pesticides, antifreeze, drain cleaners, and medicines. Store all colognes, perfumes, and aftershave lotions (which are all high in alcohol content) and all "super" glues out of reach.
- Take extra care during times of family stress or any disturbance of normal routine (for example, when moving or going on vacation, during illness, or during holidays).
- Never refer to medication as candy.
- Purchase only those medications and household products that are available with child-resistant closures. Use these packages as directed.
- Never leave alcoholic beverages within your child's reach. Before retiring, always discard any alcoholic beverages left in glasses or cans and empty all ashtrays.
- Always read the warning labels on hazardous products.
- Keep all products in their original containers.
- Never put nonedible or hazardous products in cups, pop bottles, or other containers that would normally be used for food or beverages.
- Avoid taking medication in the presence of your child.
- Promptly dispose of any leftover medication used to treat an acute illness.
- Teach your preschoolers not to eat or drink anything unless given to them by an adult they know.
- Do not depend on close adult supervision. A child moves quickly, and with purpose.
- Be alert for repeat occurrences. For some unknown reason, a child involved in an improper exposure or poisoning is likely to attempt a second ingestion within one year.

- Know the names of all your house plants. Keep potentially toxic plants out of your child's reach.
- Maintain your furnace in good working order. This will help prevent both natural gas and carbon monoxide poisoning.
- Keep the telephone number of your physician, hospital emergency room, and poison control center near your telephone.
- Seek professional help if your child swallows any nonfood substance.
- Keep a one-ounce bottle of syrup of ipecac in your home medicine chest. This is used to induce vomiting in *some* poisoning situations. But do not use syrup of ipecac without professional advice. In 95 per cent of all cases, syrup of ipecac will cause vomiting within 30 minutes.
- Do not use outdated, ineffective, and potentially toxic methods of inducing vomiting, such as mustard, salt water, or copper sulfate. In some circumstances, inducing vomiting can have a harmful effect and may actually create a serious situation from what would have been a benign ingestion.
- Do not attempt self-directed home treatment of a poisoned child. Call the local poison control center.

Guidelines for parents. If a child swallows a nonfood item or is exposed to toxic fumes, a few basic rules may help to minimize both physical and emotional trauma to the child and family:

- Remain calm.
- When possible, estimate the amount ingested or duration of exposure to the solvent or fumes.
- Observe the child for symptoms or unusual behavior.
- Try to estimate the elapsed time since the ingestion or exposure.
- Bring the container to the telephone in case there are questions about the substance.
- Call the poison control center.
- If the child vomits spontaneously, do not discard the vomit.
- If a significant time lapse occurs between ingestion and your realization of the exposure, save approximately two ounces of each urine specimen produced. Both vomit and urine may be analyzed if an emergency room examination is necessary.

Outdoor plants that are poisonous when eaten

Lily of the valley

German iris

Field buttercup

Mistletoe

Poinsettia

A partial list of toxic plants
(All or some of the parts of these plants are poisonous.)

Aconite (Monkshood)	Deadly Nightshade	Jimson Weed	Poinciana (Bird of Paradise)
African Violet	Delphinium	Jonquil	Poinsettia
Amaryllis	Devil's Ivy	Lantana (Red Sage or Wild Sage)	Poison Hemlock
Azalea	Dieffenbachia* (Dumbcane)	Lily of the Valley	Poison Ivy
Begonia	Elderberry	Lobelia	Poison Oak
Black Locust	Elephant's Ear	Marijuana	Poison Sumac
Black Nightshade	English Ivy	Marsh Marigold	Pokeweed
Bleeding Heart (Dutchman's-breeches)	Flax	Milkbush	Pothos Plant
Buckeye	Four-O'Clock	Mistletoe	Privet (berries and leaves)
Buttercup	Foxglove	Moonseed	Rhododendron
Caladium	Golden Chain (Laburnum)	Morning Glory	Scotch Broom
Calla	Holly	Mother-in-Law	Shamrock
Christmas Cherry	Horse Chestnut	Mountain Laurel	Star of Bethlehem
Christmas Rose	Hyacinth	Mushrooms (various wild types)	Tobacco
Chrysanthemum	Hydrangea	Narcissus	Tulip
Crocus, Autumn (Meadow Crocus)	Iris	Oak	Virginia Creeper
Crown of Thorns	Jack-in-the-pulpit	Oleander	Water Hemlock (Cowbane)
Daffodil	Jequirity Bean (Rosary Pea)	Pansy (seeds)	Wisteria
Daphne	Jerusalem Cherry	Pencil Tree	Woody Nightshade
	Jessamine, Yellow	Peony (common)	Yew
		Philodendron*	

*These are the most poisonous house plants.

Cautions. Do not attempt home assessment or home treatment of a poisoned patient. Do not rely upon a poison antidote/treatment chart. Call upon the professional experience of personnel who routinely treat poisoned patients. Inducing vomiting can worsen the patient's condition in certain situations.

For example, you might cause unnecessary injury by inducing vomiting if the child has ingested certain stimulants, strychnine, an acid or an alkali, or certain petroleum products (depending upon the nature and volume ingested), or if the child is unconscious or having a seizure.

Eye contamination. The one situation in which it would be advisable to begin treatment before seeking professional assistance is in the case of eye contamination. If damage occurs to the cornea (clear portion of the eye), it may cause a partial or complete loss of vision. An eye that has been exposed to

an irritant should be flushed with lukewarm water for 15 minutes. If more than one adult is present at the time of the exposure, one can flush the eye while the other contacts a physician, emergency room, or poison control center.

Several methods of eye washing are possible. The quickest method is to use a soft stream of lukewarm water from a kitchen faucet. Check the water temperature several times during the washing, because the temperature may increase or decrease. Remember to use a gentle stream of lukewarm water so as not to cause further injury to the contaminated eye.

The second option is to fill a pitcher with lukewarm water and slowly pour the water over the eye for 15 minutes. You may need several pitchers of water to complete a 15-minute flush of the eye.

Any form of eye washing is difficult. If the child is particularly uncooperative as a result of pain or fear, the parent has two options. The first would be to step into the shower with the child, using the shower spray to decontaminate the eye. Do not waste time removing either the child's clothes or your own. Using the shower, however, can be difficult because the force of the water may contribute to the irritation of the eye.

Second, the parent who is alone and dealing with a combative child may wish to ask a neighbor for help. But, if you have to work on your own, wrap the child in a large towel, sheet, blanket, or pillowcase. Keep the child's arms inside the wrap. Using a chair to prop your knee up, you can hold the child on your knee with one hand and, after adjusting the water temperature, hold the eyelids open with the other hand.

Skin contamination. Another area in which you can do something before calling for professional assistance is in treating the skin following exposure to acids, alkalis, petroleum products, or insecticides. Remove the child's clothing and bathe the child thoroughly. Areas that children often wash inadequately include the fingernails, behind the ears, the groin area, and the scalp. Failure to wash these areas thoroughly can provide sites for the continued absorption of the contaminant. Be careful not to splash soap or contaminated water into the child's eyes during the bathing process.

Articles made from porous material such as leather cannot be decontaminated after exposure to most liquid organic substances. Shoes, belts, watchbands, or other articles made from leather must therefore be discarded once contaminated.

Warning. Remember, all substances are poisons. There are none that are not poisons. Only the right dose, administered under the appropriate circumstances, constitutes a remedy for a poison.

See also **Accidents; Bites and stings; Coma; Convulsions; CPR; Emetics; Food poisoning; Medicine cabinets; Poison ivy, oak, and sumac; Prescriptions; Vomiting**

Poliomyelitis (infantile paralysis or polio) is a serious contagious disease that is characterized by inflammation of the brain and spinal cord. It is caused by a virus.

Symptoms of polio may at first resemble those of a common cold. The child may have fever, chills, sore throat, headache, severe intestinal upset, stiff back, muscle spasms in the neck or thighs, or pains and stiffness in the legs, back, and neck. Some children become paralyzed, but most do not remain paralyzed permanently. All children with polio should be under a doctor's care.

Vaccine has almost eliminated polio in the United States and Canada. The first vaccine perfected was the inactivated Salk vaccine, in which the virus is dead but still able to cause production of antibodies. Later, a live oral vaccine was developed by Albert Sabin. This vaccine contains the living poliovirus, but the virus has been weakened so that the child does not catch the disease. Live vaccine provides longer-lasting immunity, and so children who have been immunized with the Salk vaccine should also receive oral vaccine.

Giving the oral vaccine is simple. Two drops of the vaccine are dropped directly into the child's mouth or onto a small lump of sugar, which is then fed to the child.

Three types of viruses cause polio, and so a child must be protected against all three. Type I is the most frequent cause of polio. Type III is the next most frequent cause, and Type II is the least frequent cause.

There is an oral vaccine for each of these three types. The doses can be given separately. These vaccines, called MOPV (monovalent oral poliovirus vaccine), are most helpful to doctors during an epidemic caused by a single type of polio.

For routine immunization, most doctors prefer TOPV (trivalent oral poliovirus vaccine). This vaccine protects against all three types of polio. It is usually given at 2 and 4 months of age, with a third dose a year later. If a child is at risk for exposure to polio, an extra dose of TOPV may be given at 6 months. Many doctors also recommend a fourth dose of TOPV at 4 to 6 years, or when children enter kindergarten or first grade. H.D.R., Jr.

Posture is the way children hold the body as they stand, sit, and move. Good posture is important for good appearance and good health.

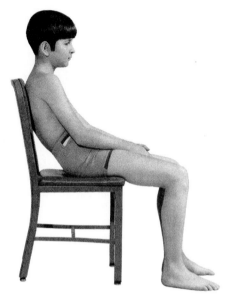
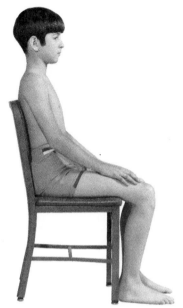

Poor sitting posture (*above left*) can cause swayback, backache, round shoulders, spinal curvature, muscle strain, and can hinder normal functioning of body organs. In a good sitting position (*above right*), a child should sit well back on the chair, with both feet squarely on the floor. The head should be over the shoulders, and the back should be straight.

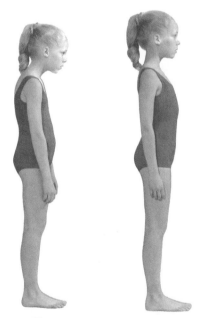

Poor standing posture is shown above left. In a good standing position (*above right*), the head should be balanced over the shoulders, the chest held high, the shoulders back, and the abdomen drawn in.

When a child with good posture stands, the child holds the head up, balanced over the shoulders. The chest is held high, the shoulders are back, and the abdomen is drawn in. Weight rests equally on both feet. When a child with good posture walks, feet point nearly straight ahead and the child leads with thighs and knees.

If a child has poor standing posture, the head falls forward, the shoulders are rounded, the back curves, the chest slopes, and the abdomen sags.

When a child with good posture sits, hips are against the back of the chair and feet are flat on the floor. Body weight rests on both thighs to evenly distribute the weight. When leaning forward to write, the child bends from the hips instead of curving the back.

When a child with good posture lifts heavy objects, leg muscles, not back muscles, are used. The child stands close to the object, bends the knees, keeps the back straight, and lifts the object.

Poor posture can cause swayback, spinal curvature, round shoulders, and backaches. Body weight is abnormally distributed and can strain leg muscles. Lifting heavy objects with the body in poor posture can strain back muscles.

Nagging a child to "Stand up straight!" and "Square your shoulders!" does not help the child acquire good posture. A child with the double problem of bad posture and nagging parents is likely to sag and slump all the more. A child more readily listens to a doctor and takes part in good-posture campaigns at school. Bicycling, walking, basketball, and other sports may also help improve a child's posture. M.G.

See also **Scoliosis**

Prescriptions are usually written directions provided by a doctor to prevent or treat an illness. Most prescriptions are for medicines, but prescriptions may also be given for diet, physical therapy, eyeglasses, and exercises. At the top of the prescription form you may notice an ℞, which stands for the Latin word *recipe*, meaning "take."

Have all prescriptions filled by a qualified pharmacist. Follow exactly the doctor's instructions for giving the medicine. Remember that almost all medicines are harmful if taken in larger amounts than prescribed.

And a last word of caution: never give medicine prescribed for one member of the family to another whose symptoms seem to be similar. The cause and treatment of the second illness may be entirely different from the illness for which the medicine had been prescribed. M.G.

See also **Drugs; Medicine cabinets**

Prickly heat is a skin rash caused by excessive heat or humidity. The rash is made up of raised, red, pinpoint spots. The surrounding skin also becomes red. Prickly heat occurs especially in areas of the body where perspiration accumulates. In fat babies and young children, it may be found in the groin folds, neck, face, and over the shoulders.

Prickly heat may cause itching and scratching. The skin may become raw, irritated, and infected. Try to clear the condition promptly. Sponge the child's skin frequently with cool tap water, or give the

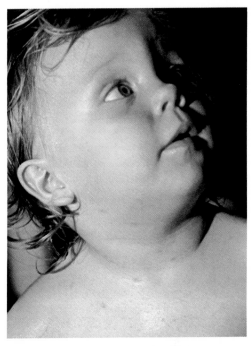

Prickly heat rash consists of raised, red, pinpoint spots.

child a cool bath. Avoid clothing that may irritate the affected areas. Leaving the skin exposed to the air can help keep it dry. The child's room should be well ventilated with a fan, and the room temperature should be cool (72° to 76° F.; 22° to 24° C). Medicines usually are not necessary if the child can be kept cool. Do not apply petroleum jelly! A powder made of cornstarch or talcum may be helpful. Apply the powder three or four times daily after a cool bath. If prickly heat does not clear up, call your doctor. A.M.M.

Rash. Since it is difficult to tell a mild, relatively harmless rash from a serious one, consult a doctor if your child develops a rash which persists and continues to spread, especially if the child is not feeling well. Skin color can affect the appearance of a rash. A severe rash on dark skin may appear milder than it really is. The following are some common causes of rashes:

• Measles—blotchy red rash, cough, conjunctivitis, fever

- German measles—rosy rash, low fever, swollen glands in neck and behind ears
- Roseola infantum—flat pink rash on the chest, abdomen, and neck after high fever
- Scarlet fever—a rash that looks like a sunburn with goose pimples, usually associated with a sore throat and fever
- Chicken pox—separate, raised pimples, some of which blister, then break and crust
- Eczema—patches of itchy, rough red skin
- Hives—itchy white welts on red skin
- Ringworm—circular, rough patches
- Impetigo—blisterlike sores that crust
- Prickly heat—raised, red, pinpoint spots, usually in the groin and neck folds
- Diaper rash—red, chafed-looking skin
- Poison ivy—blisters and inflammation accompanied by much itching
- Rocky Mountain spotted fever—purple spots on palms and soles, with headache and fever following a tick bite. Take your child to the doctor at once if you suspect Rocky Mountain spotted fever. A.M.M.

Reye's syndrome is an uncommon disease that occurs in children from a few years of age to adolescence. It involves the liver and brain and often follows an attack of chicken pox or influenza.

A child may be recovering from a mild respiratory infection when suddenly there is persistent vomiting. This is followed by behavioral changes consisting of lethargy alternating with irritability, hyperactivity, and hallucinations. Should your child show such symptoms, call your doctor immediately. If the diagnosis is Reye's syndrome, the patient needs emergency treatment and should be taken to a hospital equipped to give all the help necessary.

This disease is named for Dr. R. D. K. Reye, who, with Australian colleagues, first described cases of it in 1963. Its cause is still uncertain and proper treatment is unclear. The general aim is to reduce the brain swelling and restore normal liver metabolism. Most patients also have a high blood ammonia level which must be lowered. S.L.K.

Rh factor is a chemical substance that most people have in their blood. It gets its name from rhesus monkeys, in whose red blood cells it was first discovered. The Rh factor is inherited. If the factor is present in a child's blood, the blood is Rh-positive. If the factor is absent, the blood is Rh-negative. Both types of blood are normal and healthy, but they do not always mix safely.

For example, if a child with Rh-negative blood receives a transfusion of Rh-positive blood, the Rh-positive blood may cause production of antibodies that attack the child's normal red blood cells. The child may become seriously ill or even die. Hospital technicians test a child's blood to determine the Rh factor before transfusions are given.

It is also important to know the Rh factor when a woman is pregnant, or when a husband and wife are planning to have a baby. The baby of an Rh-negative mother and an Rh-positive father may be Rh-positive or Rh-negative. If the baby is Rh-negative, there is no problem. But if the baby is Rh-positive, the blood may cause the mother's Rh-negative blood to produce antibodies against the Rh factor. These antibodies may then return to the baby's blood and destroy the red blood cells. The infant—commonly called an "Rh baby"—may die before birth or may be born with mild to severe jaundice and anemia. The opposite condition— an Rh-positive mother and an Rh-negative baby—does not cause trouble.

Once the blood of an Rh-negative woman starts to produce antibodies, the level of antibodies becomes progressively stronger with each Rh-positive pregnancy. Generally, an Rh-negative woman with an Rh-positive husband can have two or three healthy Rh-positive babies because her antibody production may be slow enough that these first babies escape its effects. But if an Rh-negative woman has ever had a transfusion of Rh-positive blood, her blood may already contain antibodies that can react dangerously with her baby's Rh-positive blood.

With correct and immediate treatment, a seriously affected Rh baby can usually make a good recovery and be normal. Doctors can detect Rh incompatibilities by simple blood tests that measure the level of antibodies. If the level rises threateningly, the doctor may induce early labor so that the baby can be delivered before the level of antibodies is dangerously high. Sometimes, exchange transfusions must be given to the baby immediately after birth. These transfusions replace the baby's blood with fresh blood. In rare cases, transfusions of blood have been given to unborn infants. Transfused blood must be Rh-negative, because Rh-positive blood would be destroyed by the antibodies in the baby's system.

For protection in future pregnancies, a vaccine is available to prevent the production of antibodies in the mother's blood. It may be given to a mother with Rh-negative blood within 72 hours after delivery or miscarriage of an Rh-positive baby.

The best protection against the heartbreak of an Rh baby is competent prenatal care. A doctor can take proper measures to have on hand the equipment, typed blood, and other materials for treating the Rh condition.   F.O.

See also **Anemia; Blood type; Jaundice**

Rheumatic fever is a disease that follows an untreated infection by group A beta hemolytic streptococcal bacteria. The infection is usually a strep throat. Rheumatic fever, now an uncommon disease, usually first strikes between the ages of 5 and 15.

Symptoms of rheumatic fever generally appear within two to five weeks after the strep infection has cleared up. Chorea (St. Vitus's Dance), with uncontrollable twitching of muscles, may be one of the first symptoms. Or, the child may have vague pains in the muscles. (However, the great majority of children with muscle pains in their legs at night do not have rheumatic fever.) These pains may become intense. The joints in the child's legs and arms may become red, painful, and swollen. The child may also have a fever and a skin rash. At the same time, the heart and the heart valves usually become inflamed. This inflammation causes a heart murmur.

Rheumatic fever can cause permanent damage to the child's heart, but not always. When permanent damage does occur, it usually results from inflammation of either or both of the valves on the left side of the heart. As the inflammation lessens, a scar forms on the valve. This scar prevents the valve from opening and closing properly.

The damaged valve may allow blood to leak back when the heart contracts. Or, the valve may become so puckered and shrunken that the child's heart can scarcely force blood through it.

If you suspect that your child has rheumatic fever, consult your doctor. The doctor will likely advise hospitalization of the child. Bed rest during the severe phase of the disease is essential for a child with rheumatic fever. Convalescence at home may be necessary for a time. The doctor will probably prescribe a gradual increase of physical activity as well as acetaminophen, and, in special cases, steroid medications to relieve the symptoms.

A child who has had rheumatic fever is not immune to it. The child is susceptible to recurring attacks. Each additional attack may damage the heart valves. Eventually, the valves may become so scarred that an operation is necessary. Strep infections are a greater threat to a child who has already had rheumatic fever. To protect the child, the doctor will prescribe a long-term program to prevent a strep infection. The child may receive a daily oral dose of a sulfa drug or an antibiotic such as penicillin, or may have an injection in the buttocks of a long-acting antibiotic once a month. This protective treatment may be continued until the child is about 21 or even older.

The best way to fight rheumatic fever is to prevent it. Call your doctor if your child has a sore throat with a fever, a persistent sore throat, or an extremely sore throat. The doctor may want to take a throat culture, because this is the only way to identify the beta hemolytic streptococcus. If the doctor finds this streptococcus, antibiotics will be prescribed immediately. This treatment will continue until another throat culture shows that the infection has cleared up. Fortunately, most sore throats are not strep throats.   M.G.

See also **Arthritis; Chorea; Cramps; Growing pains; Heart murmur; Strep throat**

Rickets is a bone disease caused by a metabolic disturbance in the body. Some children with rickets do not get enough vitamin D in their diets. Others have an inherited disability that prevents absorption of vitamin D from food. Rickets is extremely rare in the United States and Canada.

In most cases rickets occurs before the child is 3 years old. The bones of the child do not calcify (harden) adequately. They are so soft that they can bend out of shape. Bumps can also develop on the bones. Severe rickets causes bowed legs, short stature, and deformed skull, rib, backbone, and pelvic bones. Bone damage can be corrected if it is not too severe. If rickets is not corrected, the bones may eventually harden and leave the child misshapen. M.G.

Ringworm is a contagious skin disease caused by fungus. It may be itchy. Ringworm of the body usually appears as scaly, circular, pinkish patches. As a patch grows larger, the center clears and the eruption looks like a ring. Ringworm of the scalp is characterized by round, red, scaly patches in which hairs break off close to the scalp. Ringworm infection of the feet, commonly called athlete's foot, usually appears in the webs of skin between the toes. It usually produces cracked, itchy, tender skin. Blisters and scaly skin may appear on the soles and sides of the feet. If you think your child has ringworm, call your doctor. Antifungal drugs can clear up the disease.

Ringworm may be spread by contact with infected people, infected dogs or cats, or infected brushes, combs, and furniture. Children who have ringworm should use their own combs, brushes, washcloths, towels, and other personal articles. They should be cautioned against scratching the infected areas, because if they scratch, they may spread ringworm to other parts of the body. A.M.M.

Roseola infantum is a disease characterized by a rash and a fever. Doctors believe that it is probably caused by a virus. Roseola infantum usually affects children between 6 months and 3 years of age.

Roseola infantum usually begins with a fever of 103° to 105° F. (39.4° C to 40.6° C). After three to five days, the child's temperature suddenly drops to normal or below.

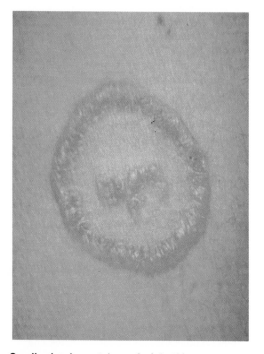

Small, circular patches of pink skin are characteristic of ringworm of the body.

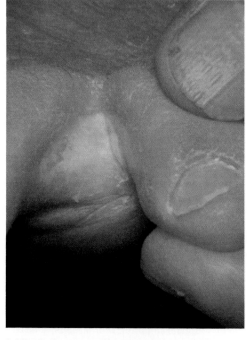

Athlete's foot usually produces cracked, itchy, tender skin between the toes.

Then a rash of small, pink, flat spots appears on the chest, abdomen, and neck. Only rarely does it spread to the child's face, arms, and legs. The rash may last a few hours or one or two days. One attack usually provides permanent immunity.

Call the doctor if you suspect that your child has roseola infantum. The doctor will probably tell you to give the child acetaminophen to bring down the fever and liquids to prevent dehydration. You do not have to isolate a child with roseola infantum. H.D.R., Jr.

Rubella. *See* **German measles**

Saint Vitus's dance. *See* **Chorea; Rheumatic fever**

Scald. *See* **Burns**

Scarlet fever is a contagious disease that is caused by the same streptococcus bacteria that produces sore throats, swollen glands, tonsillitis, ear abscesses, and other infections. A person with a streptococcal infection can spread scarlet fever even though the person does not have scarlet fever. For example, a child may develop scarlet fever after picking up the bacteria from someone in whom the streptococcus produced only a sore throat.

First symptoms of the disease come on suddenly—high fever, sore throat, chills, vomiting, and headache. Early treatment prevents spreading the disease to others, so call your doctor whenever your child has a sore throat and a fever.

Two to three days after the first symptoms appear, the child breaks out in a deep red rash. The rash resembles a sunburn with goose pimples and may feel like sandpaper. It consists of pinhead-sized, raised spots that are close together. The rash begins on the child's neck and in the groin and armpits. Then it gradually spreads over the rest of the body and the sides of the face. The area around the mouth is pale. The throat is inflamed, and the tongue becomes red and pitted looking. After the rash fades,

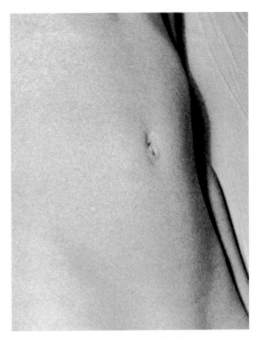

The deep red rash that a child develops with a case of scarlet fever looks like a sunburn with goose pimples.

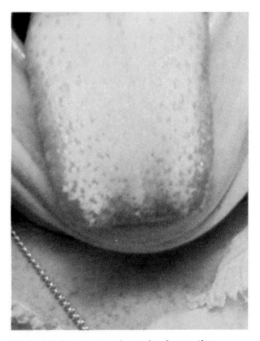

In the early stages of scarlet fever, the tongue is coated. Then it becomes red and pitted looking (strawberry tongue).

the child's skin usually peels or flakes off for three to eight weeks. If the rash is widespread, peeling will be extensive. Scarlet fever usually affects children between 3 and 12 years old.

Doctors usually prescribe penicillin or other antibiotics to treat scarlet fever. Isolate the child for about seven days—or longer if the doctor so advises. Remind the child to cover the mouth and nose when sneezing or coughing. Provide tissues for this and burn the used tissues in a safe place. Scarlet fever is contagious for two to five days before symptoms appear and for about 24 to 48 hours after treatment with antibiotics starts.

Scarlet fever was once considered a very serious disease. Prompt use of antibiotics in treating streptococcal throat infections has currently reduced its threat and incidence. The virulence or strength of the bacteria can, however, change over the course of time.   H.D.R., Jr.

See also **Sore throat; Strep throat**

Scoliosis (curvature of the spine) is a condition in which the spine curves from one side to the other. Scoliosis occurs in about 3 per cent of the young population. It is more common in girls than in boys, and causes the child to appear to stand with a crooked posture. School screening programs for early detection of scoliosis are now common and very effective. Consult your doctor if you suspect your child has scoliosis. Your doctor may suggest that you take the child to an orthopedist (physician specializing in deformities and diseases of bones and joints).

There are two types of scoliosis—functional and structural. Functional scoliosis may be caused by poor posture, a short leg, or muscle spasms around the hip or back. It is not considered serious and does not result in any bone changes. Functional spinal curves are flexible and disappear when the child lies down. Functional scoliosis can be treated by correcting poor posture with exercises, fitting the child with special correction devices such as a built-up shoe, or prescribing drugs to relax muscle spasms.

Structural scoliosis is a spinal deformity that begins in childhood and usually results in permanent bone changes. In some children scoliosis may be caused by a spinal deformity that was present at birth. In others, it may be caused by a disease that deforms the bones of the spine during growth. Doctors do not know what causes scoliosis in about 80 per cent of the affected children.

Although structural scoliosis is rarely painful, it causes deformity because compensatory curves develop above and below the affected portion of the spine. Unlike a functional curve, a structural curve does not disappear when the child lies down. Frequently, one hip and the opposite shoulder appear higher than on the opposite side. The chest appears off-center in relation to the pelvis. The backs of the ribs bend out, pushing out the shoulder blade. When the child bends forward, a hump appears on one side of the upper back. Although the deformity caused by structural scoliosis frequently worsens as the child grows, this is not always the case. Early diagnosis, advice, and treatment are important.

Treatment of structural scoliosis depends on the severity of the curve. Mild curves are simply followed and watched by the doctor. A child with a moderate curve is usually fitted with a Milwaukee brace, a straightening device that may have to be worn for several years. Severe curves, or curves that progressively worsen, should be corrected surgically. Structural scoliosis can rarely be completely cured, but early treatment can lessen its deforming effects.   J.J.G.

Shock is one of the body's reactions to physical or infectious stress. The normal flow of blood is upset and normal functions of the body are weakened. A child suffering from shock may be weak or faint; may become pale; may have cold, clammy skin; and may have a weak, irregular, or "fluttering" pulse. Nausea and vomiting are also common in shock.

Bleeding, major burns, severe pain, infection, and severe injury such as a broken bone may cause shock. Fear or other strong emotions may cause a different kind of shock.

A child in shock should be placed on a flat surface. If blood has been lost, legs should

First aid for shock

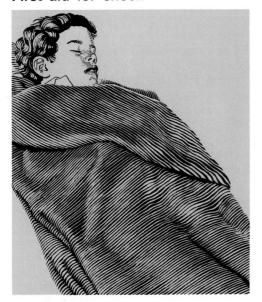

A child in shock should be placed on a flat surface. Wrap the child in a blanket. This will help keep the body temperature normal.

be elevated. To prevent loss of normal body heat, the child should be wrapped in a blanket. A hot-water bottle or other artificial heat should not be used, since too much heat draws blood to the skin and away from more vital organs where it is needed.

If your child is in shock, call the doctor promptly or take the child to a hospital. Most forms of shock need immediate, specific treatment. M.G.

Shots that children usually receive may be divided into three categories: (1) preventive, to avoid a disease; (2) curative, to rid one of a disease; and (3) desensitizing, to decrease allergic reactions.

Children are injected with their first preventive shots early in life. Doctors usually give a diphtheria-whooping cough-tetanus shot (DPT) when a child is around 2 months of age. Polio vaccine is given orally at the same time. Later, shots are given to prevent measles, German measles, mumps, and hemophilus influenzae infections.

Curative shots, such as antibiotic drugs, not only cure a disease, but also often pre-

vent serious complications from a disease. Although curative drugs may be given orally, doctors may decide to give them by injection for several reasons. The drug more quickly enters the blood stream to fight the disease; the drug is not tasted (regardless of how well the taste of oral drugs is disguised, some children refuse to take a second dose, or they vomit it); and the doctor is certain that the drug has been taken.

Doctors give desensitizing shots to many children who are allergic to substances from which they cannot constantly be protected. These shots are injected into the child in small, but increasing, doses. As a result of the repeated shots, the child's body manufactures antibodies and effects cellular changes that lessen the allergic reaction.

If your child is allergic, or has had a previous reaction to a drug, and your doctor does not already know about the condition, be sure to tell the doctor. Penicillin and other drugs may cause undesirable reactions.

Your attitude and that of the doctor and nurse can influence the child who is fearful of getting shots. Be truthful when a child

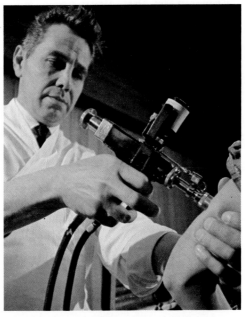

Hypospray is a painless way of giving shots. Air pressure forces the liquid drug or vaccine through pores of the child's skin and into the child's body.

asks, "Will it hurt?" You might tell a toddler that it will hurt a tiny bit, but not much, and that the doctor is a friend and wants to keep him or her well. You can minimize your infant's crying and comfort him or her if you lean over the baby's face so that he or she can see you when the doctor gives the shot. M.G.

See also **Allergy; Immunization**

Sinusitis is an inflammation of one or more sinuses. The sinuses are cavities in the skull. They are lined with mucous membranes that are the same as, and join with, the mucous membranes of the nose. When a child has a cold or other infection in the nose, the infection often spreads to these membranes.

Normally, mucus drains from the sinuses into the nose through tiny openings. When the membranes of the sinuses become infected, they swell and block drainage. Pressure then builds up, and a child may have severe, throbbing pain over one or both cheeks. Or, the child may have a severe, general headache. Also the face may swell. If the sinusitis is chronic (constant), the symptoms may not be so severe, but the child may have a nasal discharge (sometimes with a foul odor).

If you think your child has sinusitis, consult your doctor. The doctor may recommend nose drops, an oral decongestant, or antibiotics. Home treatment also should include humidifying the child's room and applying hot compresses to the child's nose. C.F.F.

Sleep. To avoid needless concern about your child's sleeping habits, remember: (1) the length of time a child sleeps decreases as the child grows older, and (2) two children of the same age do not necessarily need the same amount of sleep. Each child develops an individual sleep pattern. This sleep pattern may be affected by several factors.

For example, a preschooler may be so busy learning new things that the child is

Location of the sinuses

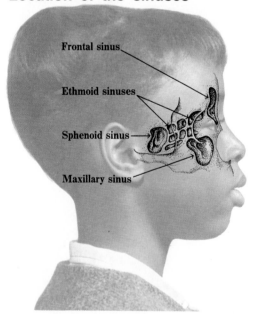
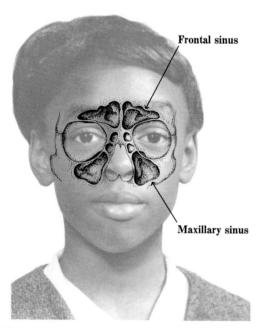

The frontal sinuses are above the eyes. The maxillary sinuses are in the cheek bones, below the eyes. The ethmoid sinuses are above the nasal cavity. The sphenoid sinuses are behind the ethmoid sinuses.

Most children enjoy having stories read to them at bedtime.

stimulated to a point where both the amount and the quality of sleep suffer. A child who becomes overtired may resist going to bed and may have difficulty going to sleep.

Children may use sleep to escape from situations that disturb them. Dread of school, fear of failure, childhood depression, and fear of neighborhood bullies can cause a child to resist getting up in the morning. However, these same fears may make another child sleepless.

Amount of sleep. Newborns need more sleep and spend more time sleeping than they ever will again. In the first few days after birth, babies may sleep as much as 23 hours a day. But many newborns sleep much less. New babies' sleep is often restless and broken up into short and long periods. They are aroused mainly by hunger or other discomfort. After the first few days, they spend more time awake or half awake—being fed, bathed, or diapered.

As babies grow older, they stay awake during the day for longer periods of time. When they are about 3 months old, they may start sleeping 12 hours through the night and taking several naps during the day. Gradually, as they require less sleep, they take fewer naps during the day. When they are a year old, they may sleep 14 to 15 hours a day, including two naps. When babies are 2 years old, they may sleep 13 to 14 hours a day, including one nap. When they are 4 years old, they may sleep 11 to 12 hours a day, including a nap.

After children enter school, bedtime is affected by homework and the family pattern of living. Some children feel tired enough to go to bed as early as 8:30 P.M. Children between the ages of 6 and 10 years may need only 10 or 11 hours of sleep. When children reach junior high school, homework and extracurricular activities may keep them up later. Their sleep requirements may decrease to about nine hours.

Sleeping arrangements. Proper sleeping arrangements can help children fall asleep and sleep peacefully. Infants should sleep in cribs with sides to keep them from rolling over and falling onto the floor. Until they are about 3 years old, they should have smooth, flat, moderately hard mattresses. Pillows are unnecessary.

Do not expect a young baby or toddler to lie under bedcovers all night long, or even throughout a nap. Keep the child warm and snug in sleepers or a sleeping bag that suits the season. Even preschoolers continue to appreciate one-piece pajamas with feet in them for winter wear. Too much clothing and cover is almost as bad as too little, because a child who is too warm will be just as restless as one who is too cold. In warm weather, a baby requires nothing more than a diaper and a lightweight shirt.

Do not make a child who is afraid of the dark sleep without some kind of night light. Some children have trouble falling asleep after daylight-saving time goes into effect because it is still light outside at bedtime. They usually adjust in a week or two.

Sleeping in parents' bedroom. If possible, it is best for children to have their own bedrooms and not sleep in the same room with their parents. Even during illness or periods of fearfulness, children should be comforted in their own beds in their own rooms.

Movement and positions. Babies and older children move frequently in their sleep. Healthy young babies make trembling and sucking movements with their lips, their eyelids flutter, and their hands and feet twitch. They whimper as if talking in their dreams. Their breathing is normally fast and irregular. Older babies and toddlers sleep restlessly at night, moving from one part of the crib to another. They also assume positions that seem most uncomfortable—neck turned sharply to one side, arms and legs bent acutely on the chest and abdomen, legs extended beyond cribside, or on the stomach with head turned to one side, knees brought up close to the chest. These positions are healthy for most infants and young children. Lying on the stomach is safe.

Sleep resistance. Many babies resist going to sleep when they are between 6 and 9 months old. These children, even though they are tired, cry when they are put into bed. They get quiet when they are picked up, held, and rocked, but they start to cry again as soon as they are put back to bed. This routine may be repeated over and over, night after night.

To interrupt this cycle, parents have to be firm and be prepared to withstand about ten to twenty minutes of crying for a few nights. At bedtime, put the baby to bed and leave the room. Try not to look in on the crying baby. At least, do not let the baby see you looking. Usually, the length of the baby's crying period decreases each night, and the crying may disappear by the end of three nights.

Sleep resistance usually crops up again toward the end of the second year, when the child has learned to climb over the side of the crib. If this occurs, put the toddler back to bed promptly and firmly and leave the room.

Dreaming. If your child is restless, talks, or cries out while sleeping, you can be fairly sure that the child is dreaming. Sometimes the dreams are pleasant. Sometimes they are nightmares, in which case the child will look to you for comfort. The child may want to be cuddled or rocked, or may settle for a few reassuring words and a drink of water. The child may want a light left on close to the bedroom for the rest of the night.

Let the child talk about the dream, especially if the dream was upsetting. Usually the preschool child cannot remember dreams. A school-age child may not only remember dreams, but may also spontaneously tell you about them.

Rituals and routines. Everybody goes through some kind of ritual in preparing to go to sleep. For an adult or older child, it may simply involve undressing, taking a bath, brushing teeth, and getting into a comfortable sleeping garment at a certain time each night. A young child may want you to read a story out loud, or may get a favorite stuffed animal ready for bed, kiss everybody good night, recite prayers, or wait to be tucked in.

The child who is accustomed to a certain routine continues to expect it. Routine provides a sense of security and makes the child happier than a series of irregular and unpredictable performances. Routine should not be rigid or punishing or threatening, and certainly there should be no implication that going to bed is unpleasant. Going to bed can become a game in which your child enjoys an opportunity to learn new skills—to undress, arrange clothes, and take a bath. But

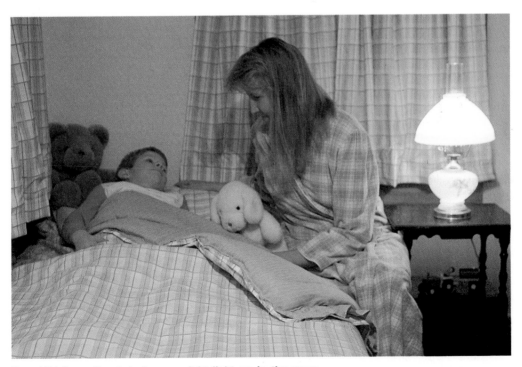

If a child fears the dark, keep a night light on in the room.

any bedtime routine should not be too long, too exciting, or too complex.

If your child is uncooperative at times, the child may have had too long a nap in the afternoon. In this case, postpone bedtime or prolong the routine. Some children regularly fight going to bed. They want a drink of water. They have to go to the toilet. They want to hear another story. They want still another drink of water. Anger is useless. If you can be firm and limit the ritual, yet keep it flexible, your child will probably respond to the limitations set, argue less, and be more willing to part from you and go to sleep.

Many toddlers go to bed with a toy, a favorite blanket, or some object that represents security to them. To other children, thumbsucking offers bedtime security. Sometimes parents, feeling that their child is now a "big boy" or a "big girl," attempt to stop these bedtime habits. There really is no need to worry, because a child assumes increasing responsibility for going to bed after about the age of 4 and relies less and less on rituals and routines. M.G.

See also **Nightmares; Thumb-sucking**

Smallpox was one of the most feared of contagious diseases. Throughout history, it brought death, blindness, or disfiguring facial scars to hundreds of millions of people. But it became the first disease to be conquered by medical science. The last known case of smallpox in the United States occurred in 1949, and the last known naturally occurring case in the world was in Africa in 1977. In 1980, the World Health Organization announced that smallpox had been wiped out.

Smallpox was spread by a virus through direct contact with the coughing or sneezing of a patient, or the pus from a patient's sores, or from articles the patient had used. The disease began with chills, fever, vomiting, headaches, and backaches. Red spots appeared on the patient's skin about three or four days after the onset of the disease. Later, these spots changed to blisters filled with pus.

As the patient recovered, the blisters dried up and formed scabs that fell off, leav-

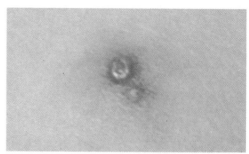

About three days after a smallpox vaccination, a small, red, itchy pimple appears.

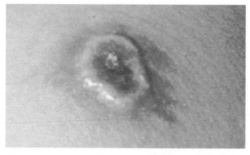

About nine days after vaccination, the pimple develops a white-colored blister.

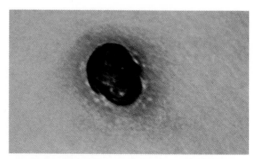

About 14 days after vaccination, the blister dries up and forms a scab.

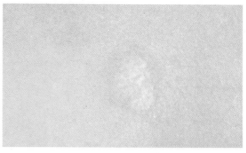

About 21 days after vaccination, the scab falls off and leaves a scar.

ing scars. About 20 per cent of all those contracting smallpox died. Survivors were permanently scarred, and many were blinded.

The war against this dreadful disease began in the year 1796, when an English doctor, Edward Jenner, developed a vaccine that prevented smallpox. (It was also the *first* vaccine to be developed.) Use of the vaccine soon spread to other nations.

While the disease was still widespread, the federal and local governments in the United States instituted regulations making smallpox vaccinations routine for all persons. Usually, vaccinations were given to children between 1 and 2. Vaccinations were also required for anyone traveling to and from countries where smallpox was known to occur regularly. In 1971, the program of routine vaccinations for children was terminated, and smallpox vaccinations are no longer required for foreign travel.

Smothering. *See* **Suffocation**

Sneezing. Most babies sneeze occasionally, even when they do not have a cold. Sneezing is how a baby cleans dirt, lint, or mucus from the nose. Tiny hairs that line the nose move the mucus and other material down the nose. This material usually collects in a ball on the large hairs near the opening at the front of the nose. This collection tickles and makes the baby sneeze the material out.

Usually, you can tell when your baby is getting a cold because there will be more than the normal drop or two of mucus in the sneeze. Also, a baby with a cold is more apt to be irritable, may have trouble eating because of nasal congestion, may lose normal appetite, and may show other signs of illness such as fever.

Lint frequently irritates a baby's nose and causes sneezing. You can eliminate some of the lint in new blankets and baby clothes if you wash them before using.   M.G.

See also **Colds**

Soft spots (fontanels) are areas of a baby's skull where the bones have not yet

joined and hardened. In place of bone, a very tough membrane covers the area.

A baby may have as many as six soft spots at birth. Generally, you can feel only two of them. Gradually, through the months, the soft spots disappear as the skull bones grow and harden. By the time a baby is a year old, it is usually hard to find the soft spots.

The largest soft spot is shaped like a diamond and is about 1 to 1½ inches (2.5 to 4 centimeters) on a side. It is just in front of the top of the child's skull. Another large spot is at the back of the skull. The fontanels vary in size in different babies.

Although the brain may seem unprotected in these softer areas, the tough membrane is actually very strong. Mild shampoos and ordinary handling of the head and scalp will do no harm. In fact, shampooing the baby's scalp, including the soft spots, is necessary to prevent cradle cap, a scalp condition that causes whitish scales.   M.G.

See also **Cradle cap**

Sore throat usually results from an infection. It may range from a mild soreness to a painful condition in which the child has difficulty in swallowing.

Children often have sore throats. The infection can accompany colds, tonsillitis, and other illnesses. Call your doctor if your child has a fever along with the sore throat, if the throat is more than mildly sore, or if the sore throat persists.

Because most sore throats are caused by viruses, they cannot be cured with antibiotics. Your doctor will probably prescribe acetaminophen (aspirin substitute) or other drugs to control fever. Doctors generally do not recommend gargling for children, but throat lozenges for children may help relieve minor irritations. The doctor may take a culture from the child's throat to check for streptococcic infection (strep throat). If your child does have strep throat, your doctor will prescribe antibiotics.   M.G.

See also **Colds; Communicable diseases; Strep throat; Tonsillitis; Virus**

Spine, curvature of. *See* **Scoliosis**

First aid for sprains

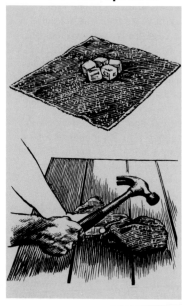
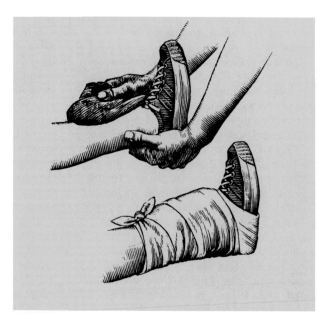

Wrap some ice in a cloth and crush the ice with a hammer. Elevate the sprained limb and apply the ice pack. Then wrap the cloth around the ankle to hold the ice pack in place. Leave the child's shoe on to prevent swelling.

Splinters usually penetrate the upper layer of the skin only and lie embedded there. But they can be very painful and annoying because they press on nerves underneath.

A splinter is usually easy to remove. First, wash the area around the splinter with warm water and soap. This cleanses and softens the skin and makes the splinter easier to remove. Sterilize a sharp needle or a pair of tweezers either with alcohol or by passing the needle or tweezers through a flame. Then, pick out the splinter. The tweezers will probably be less upsetting to the child, but sometimes they are not effective in catching hold of the splinter. You may have to ease the splinter up with a needle and then pull it out with the tweezers. A school-age child may be able to remove the splinter without help.

After the splinter is removed, swab the area with alcohol and apply a sterile dressing. If inflammation begins, if the splinter has not been completely removed, or if the splinter is deeply embedded, consult the child's doctor. T.M.H.

Sprain and strain. The term sprain refers to a joint injury; the term strain refers to a tendon or muscle injury.

A sprain is the stretching of ligaments (the tough bands of fiber that connect joints) or the stretching of the tissue around a joint (the capsule). Sprains may occur with or without fracture of the bone.

Sprains may occur in any joint, but are most common in the ankle, wrist, knee, and fingers. They may result from a strong, sudden wrench or from jumping or falling. They occur frequently from basketball, hockey, and other athletic competition.

A sprain usually causes a rather rapid swelling because fluid (and sometimes blood) accumulates in the tissues around the injured joint. The area may also appear bruised. There is pain, especially when the child tries to use the injured part.

Immediate first-aid measures for a sprain include splinting the injured part if possible, elevating and resting the injured limb, and applying cold water or, if available, ice. This treatment reduces swelling. If the sprain involves the ankle, leave the child's shoe on. Call a doctor and take the child to the hospital for X rays to find out whether or not a bone has been broken and to get proper treatment for the sprain. Your doctor may wrap the joint with an elastic bandage to provide support or may apply a plaster splint or cast. Heat, massage, and hydrotherapy (specialized treatment using water) may be necessary following some sprains.

Strain refers to a stretching injury of a tendon or a stretching and tearing injury of a muscle. When a muscle or tendon has undergone unusual stress, there may be soreness and tenderness to the touch, but without the damage to tissues that may occur in sprains or fractures. As a rule, all that a mild strain requires is rest of the muscles or tendons involved and, perhaps, the application of heat or warmth for comfort. If pain is intense and persistent, consult the child's doctor. J.J.G.

See also **Broken bones; Charley horse; Dislocation of joint**

Stammering. *See* **Stuttering**

Steaming. *See* **Humidifying**

Sterilizing means destroying all germs. Disinfecting means destroying only disease germs or other harmful microorganisms.

Sterilizing baby's formula. Most sterilizing begins with the baby's formula or with bottles and nipples for baby's juice. Formula equipment and formula can be sterilized in two ways. In the first method, the equipment—bottles, nipples, caps, measuring utensils—and the formula ingredients are sterilized separately. Then, the formula is mixed and poured into the bottles. This method is also used to sterilize the water babies drink. Water is boiled for three minutes and then poured into bottles that have been boiled previously.

In the second method of sterilizing formula, the formula and the bottles, caps, and nipples are sterilized together. The formula is mixed and poured into the bottles, the nipples placed on, and the caps screwed on

loosely. Then the bottles are boiled, formula and all.

Other needs for destroying germs. In every home, there occasionally will be other reasons to kill germs by sterilizing or disinfecting. Different methods are used. You can use heat, chemical germicides, or soap and water:

- You can sterilize a needle that will be used to probe for a splinter by putting the point of the needle directly into a flame.
- You can sterilize some liquids, including water and milk, by boiling them for 5 to 10 minutes.
- You can disinfect diapers by hanging them out to dry in the sun or by ironing them.
- You can disinfect cloth or gauze for bandaging by ironing it.
- Hands can be disinfected by cleansing with soap for 3 to 10 minutes, or by being dipped in germicidal solutions.
- You can usually disinfect a thermometer by washing it with soap and cool water.
- Wounds can be disinfected with soap and water or with medicines made for this purpose, and can be safeguarded by having sterile dressings applied by a person with freshly washed hands. M.G.

Stings. *See* **Bites and stings**

Stomachache is a common complaint of children, but discovering the exact cause of the stomachache is often not simple. Many times, a stomachache is a passing complaint of little consequence. In other cases, it indicates a serious disorder.

If your child has a severe, persistent, or recurrent stomachache, call your doctor. Never give food, drink, laxatives, or cathartics to a child with a sudden attack of abdominal pain.

The following are some of the causes of stomachache:

- Appendicitis may cause a stomachache that is first felt throughout the child's abdomen. In a few hours, the pain moves to the right lower abdomen. The child may also become nauseated and vomit.
- Influenza (flu) may cause a stomachache with vomiting and diarrhea.

- Colds, sore throats, and earaches are sometimes accompanied by abdominal pain that is caused by swollen lymph glands in the abdomen.
- Food poisoning usually causes nausea, vomiting, and stomachache.
- Constipation can cause cramping abdominal pain.
- Eating too much food or eating an irritating food may cause stomachaches.
- Emotional disturbances or stresses are common causes of recurrent abdominal pain. This is most common in children who are 9 or 10. The child may be concerned about such problems as a parent's illness, a recent death, or school difficulties. M.G.

See also **Appendicitis; Colds; Colic; Colitis; Constipation; Earaches; Food poisoning; Influenza; Sore throat; Swollen glands**

Strabismus. *See* **Cross-eye**

Strain. *See* **Sprain and strain**

Strawberry mark. *See* **Birthmark**

Strep throat is an inflammation caused by a bacterium called the streptococcus. A child with strep throat usually has a fever, lacks energy, and has a sore throat—especially when swallowing. The lymph glands in the neck are also swollen; and yellow, gray, or white patches may appear on the tonsils.

If untreated, strep throat may lead to rheumatic fever, nephritis, and other illnesses. For this reason, call your doctor if your child has a sore throat and a fever, if the throat is more than mildly sore, or if the sore throat persists.

Symptoms of strep throat are often the same as those for a sore throat that is caused by a virus. To determine whether your child's sore throat is strep throat or virus-caused, your doctor may do a throat culture. Usually, the doctor will treat strep throat with antibiotics. M.G.

See also **Communicable diseases; Nephritis; Rheumatic fever; Sore throat; Swollen glands; Virus**

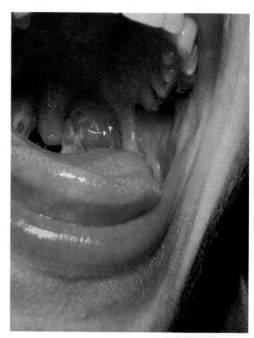

A child who has contracted strep throat may develop yellow, gray, or white patches of membranous material on the tonsils.

Stuttering is an interruption in the flow of speech caused by repetition of certain sounds, prolongation of others, or hesitancy in talking. A child who stutters in normal speech may not stutter when singing, repeating memorized material, or acting in a play. Stuttering occurs in about 1 child in 125. It is much more common in boys than in girls, but no one knows why.

Primary stuttering. Between 2 and 5 years, most children pass through a normal period called "primary stuttering," or "transient stammering." The problem ordinarily disappears after six months or a year.

Parents who are not aware that primary stuttering is normal may make a child feel that there is a serious speech problem. They may show their concern by facial expressions, by completing what the child is trying to say, or by constantly telling the child to "take your time" or "start over." The best thing to do is nothing at all. Do not ask the child to repeat what was said. Do not ask the child to slow down. Do not scold. Accept this temporary period of stuttering as a normal part of development.

If stuttering persists longer than usual or becomes severe, you may want to discuss the problem with the child's doctor.

Secondary stuttering. Secondary, or true, stuttering begins when the child is aware of the difficulty and attempts to prevent it. As the child tries harder to get the words out without hesitating, the muscles involved in speech may move even less smoothly, and the child develops a stuttering block. A stuttering child may attempt to break this block by stamping the foot, jerking the head, or other maneuvers. The child may use similar actions in anticipating difficulty with certain words or may eventually avoid these words. The child may be reluctant to answer questions at school or to speak on the telephone.

Children with secondary stuttering should go to a speech clinic. Your doctor can tell you the location of the nearest clinic. M.G.

Sty. *See* **Eyelids**

Suffocation is a state of unconsciousness that occurs when the body does not get enough oxygen. Suffocation can cause death very quickly.

If your child is suffocating, the first thing to do is to give the child air. The best method of getting air back into the lungs of children is to administer CPR. (See **CPR**.) One person should begin this while someone else calls the paramedics or, if not available, a physician. Continue CPR until the child resumes normal breathing or until professional help arrives.

A person whose air supply is cut off will suffocate. For example, a child who stays underwater too long will drown. Also, a child may be accidentally shut inside an airtight container such as a refrigerator or buried under a pile of dirt. A child who puts a plastic bag over the head may also suffocate. Some children have been strangled by poorly designed harnesses intended to keep them in chairs. A baby may be smothered under a thin sheet of plastic. On rare occasions a baby has been accidentally smothered by an adult sleeping in the same bed.

Suffocation may also occur when there is not enough oxygen in the air. This may oc-

cur when open-flame heating units—such as coal stoves, oil stoves, or gas stoves—are operated in close, unventilated spaces such as trailers or small cottages. These conditions produce excess carbon monoxide, which prevents the hemoglobin in the blood from carrying oxygen throughout the body. All open-flame heaters should be properly vented to the open air. If a child is suffocating because of lack of oxygen in the air, carry the child into fresh air before giving artificial respiration.

Many infant deaths once attributed to smothering have been found to be due to sudden infant death. M.G.

See also **Accidents; Artificial respiration; Choking; Crib death; Poisonings and poisons**

Sugar diabetes. *See* **Diabetes mellitus**

Sunburn is the skin's reaction to ultraviolet rays of the sun or to artificially created rays from a sun lamp. Mild sunburn reddens the skin. More severe sunburn may blister the skin or cause a fever.

For mild sunburn, apply cold cream. For severe sunburn, give fluids and analgesics for pain and to reduce fever. Apply cold tap water compresses to relieve pain. If the condition does not improve within a few hours, call a doctor.

The safest way to avoid severe sunburn is to allow the skin's protective responses to develop by exposing the skin for a short time once daily at first (perhaps 15 minutes), and then regularly increasing the length of time. Suntan creams or lotions used before exposure are recommended for protection.

Children with fair skin, and especially those with red hair, are prone to sunburn. A number 15 sunscreen should be applied several times daily. However, any skin—even if tanned—will burn if exposed too long. Do not let your child stay too long in the sunshine, especially on the beach. Reflected rays from the water intensify the effect of the sun. Burning can also occur on hazy days. Recent studies have shown a greater chance of developing skin cancer in people overexposed or repeatedly (chronically) exposed to ultraviolet rays. A.M.M.

Suppositories are medical preparations that are usually inserted into the rectum. Most are cylinders about 1 inch (2.5 centimeters) long and 1/4 inch (6 millimeters) wide.

There are two kinds of suppositories. The more common one is made of soap or glycerin and used to induce a bowel movement. Suppositories should be used only when a doctor prescribes them. Their routine use interferes with normal bowel function.

The other type of suppositories contains medicine for use in the rare instance when certain types of medication are needed and cannot be taken by mouth, such as medicines for constant vomiting.

Insert a suppository gently above the muscle ring at the rectum opening. Hold the child's buttocks together for a few moments, so that the suppository will not be pushed out. If the suppository is pushed out, wait a few minutes before trying again.   M.G.

Swallowed objects. Children have a natural tendency to put things into their mouths. Obviously, this tendency can be dangerous because a child may swallow something

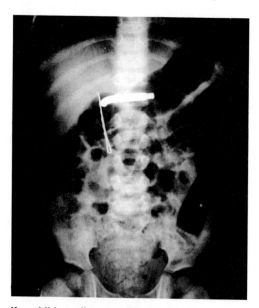

If a child swallows an iron or steel object, the doctor may have the child swallow a small magnet attached to a string. Using X rays, the doctor maneuvers the magnet until it attracts the object, and then pulls the object out.

harmful. If your child swallows an inedible object, keep calm so that you do not alarm the child. Since almost any inedible object may prove harmful if swallowed, call the doctor. If the object is a sharp one, such as a tack or an open safety pin, the doctor may want to X-ray the child to determine whether surgery is needed to remove it.

Small, smooth objects such as fruit pits, coins, beads, and buttons will usually pass through a child's body without harm in a few days. Do not give a laxative to the child. It will not help, and it may be harmful. Instead, keep the child on a normal diet. If the child has abdominal pain or vomits, call a doctor immediately. If you cannot reach a doctor, take the child to a hospital.

Protect your child by keeping small objects out of reach. A string of beads, for example, may be dangerous if the string breaks and the beads come loose. Keep your button box well out of reach.

When you are changing diapers, close each safety pin as you remove it. A closed safety pin will probably pass harmlessly if swallowed. An open safety pin may not.

Do not give a young child toys with detachable small parts, especially glass eyes, buttons, or bells. Do not give the child a toy that might break into fragments that can be swallowed or breathed into the windpipe and lungs. The small cadmium batteries used in calculators, cameras, and watches are extremely dangerous if swallowed. Keep these stored out of reach and discard them as soon as they are no longer being used.

As soon as your child is old enough to understand, encourage the child to give you dangerous objects that he or she finds. You can then thank the child and substitute a safe plaything. Remember, too, that children are great imitators of their parents. Children who observe parents holding open safety pins in the mouth, or nails or pins between the lips, will probably duplicate the deed at the first opportunity.   M.G.

Swollen glands. Lymph glands (nodes) are one of the body's means of fighting infection. They are located throughout the body but are especially concentrated in the neck, armpits, elbows, groin, abdomen, and chest.

Location of the lymph glands

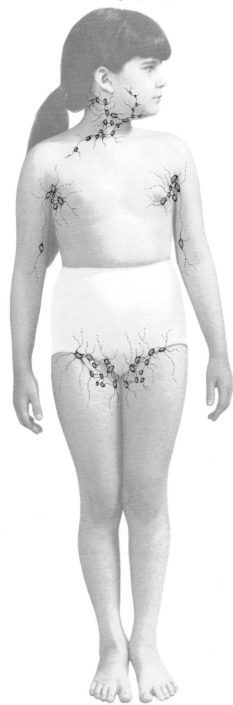

Lymph glands are located throughout the body. They swell to fight off infection. Those in the neck, armpits, and groin can be felt when they swell.

When an infection invades the body, the lymph glands collect and destroy bacteria that drain from the infected area. Normally, the lymph glands range in size from as small as a pea to as large as a plum. However, when they are fighting an infection, they become enlarged and are known as "swollen glands."

- When the throat, tonsils, or gums are infected, lymph glands of the neck swell. Mumps may cause lymph glands in the neck to swell.
- When an infection occurs on the hands or arms, lymph glands in the elbows and armpits swell.
- When an infection occurs on the leg or foot, lymph glands in the groin swell.
- When vaccinations are given, lymph glands in the area of the shot usually swell.
- When measles, scarlet fever, or some other infection affects the entire body, the lymph glands of the entire body may swell. In some infectious diseases, like German measles and mononucleosis, the lymph glands may remain quite large for some time.

Leukemia, Hodgkin's disease, and other malignant diseases of the lymphatic system may also cause swollen glands. However, in most cases, the child will have additional symptoms.

You can usually feel the lymph glands in the neck, armpits, and groin when they are swollen. They may be inflamed and tender to the touch. If your child has swollen glands, consult your doctor. Since the swelling is most often caused by an infection, antibiotics are usually prescribed to eliminate the infection. Sometimes, a lymph gland that is fighting an infection forms an abscess. In such a case, hot packs on the swollen gland may help to get rid of the abscess. Or, your doctor may have to lance the abscess to release the pus. M.G.

See also **Abscess; Adenoids; Communicable diseases; Fever; Immunization; Leukemia; Mononucleosis; Sore throat; Tonsillitis**

Tearing eyes. It is not unusual for a baby's eyes to water during the first few weeks of life. The doctor puts silver nitrate, or antibiotic drops or ointment, into the baby's eyes at birth to prevent infection. This often causes many tears. The watering usually disappears in a few days, and no treatment is necessary.

However, persistent watering may occur if a tear duct becomes blocked by mucus. The tear duct is a small tube leading from the tear sac (which is inside the lower eyelid next to the nose) to the inside of the nose. Normally, the duct carries away the tears that lubricate the eye. But if the duct becomes blocked, the eye waters.

Treat tearing eyes by wiping away the excess fluid with a small piece of sterile cotton that has been moistened in cool boiled water. If the condition continues after the baby is about 2 months old, if it is severe, or if it is accompanied by irritation and reddening of the eye, or by a discharge of pus, consult the baby's doctor. M.G.

See also **Conjunctivitis**

Teeth and teething. The first primary, or "baby," teeth begin to form within a baby's jaws about two months after conception. At birth, the crowns of all 20 primary teeth, and even part of the first permanent molars, are forming in the jaws. By the time a child is 3 years old, all the primary teeth have come in. By this time, too, parts of more than 20 of the permanent teeth are developing within the jawbones.

Your baby will probably get a first tooth at about 6 months. Generally, the teeth in the lower jaw appear first. At 1 year, your child will probably have the four upper and four lower front teeth, which are called the incisors.

The first molars appear when the child is about 15 months old. Then, at about 18 months, the canines come through between the incisors and the first molars. The second molars, or "back teeth," usually appear when the child is about 2 years old.

Teething. As a tooth comes through, your baby will drool, bite, chew, and gnaw on anything that can go into the mouth. The baby may also thrust the lower jaw forward and move it from side to side to rub the gums together and help the teeth push through the overlying tissue. Firm teething

Teething

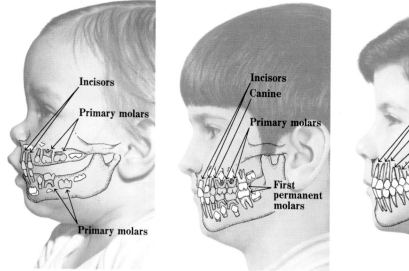
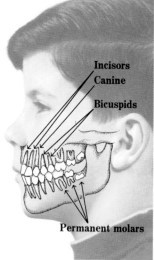

When a child is about a year old (left), primary incisors have pushed through the gums and primary molars are beginning to appear. By about 8 (center), a child has some permanent teeth—incisors and first permanent molars—and some primary teeth—canines and primary molars. At about 12 (right), a child has all the permanent teeth except for the third permanent molars (wisdom teeth).

How to brush teeth

1. The hand should be twisted so that the brush moves over the gums and teeth toward the chewing surfaces. The upper teeth should be brushed downward; the lower teeth upward.
2. Be sure the surfaces next to the cheeks are brushed.
3. And be sure the surfaces next to the tongue are brushed.
4. Teach your child to use a scrubbing motion when brushing so that the chewing surfaces of the teeth are cleaned.

rings may satisfy the urge to bite. Chewing hard foods like toasted bread may help teething and jaw development. Babies may be fussy while teething, and this irritability may be confused with signs of illness.

Usually, a child has more difficulty getting the primary teeth than getting the permanent teeth. The primary teeth have to make their own path through the gums, but 20 of the permanent teeth follow the paths already made by the primary teeth they replace. The 12 molars in the set of 32 permanent teeth have no channel set up for them by preceding primary teeth. Fortunately, they do not come in until the child is older. The first permanent molars usually appear when the child is about 6 years old, the second molars when the child is about 12, and the third molars (wisdom teeth) after the child is 17 years old.

Dental care. Foods that are good for general health—milk, fruits, vegetables, meat, poultry, fish, eggs, and butter—are also good for teeth and gums. Fibrous vegetables and fruits that require chewing have the added value of acting as tooth-cleansing agents. Some foods can harm teeth. Sugars and starches actually encourage tooth decay.

Tooth decay usually begins in the pits and grooves on the chewing surfaces of the teeth, between the teeth, and along the gum margin on the cheek sides. Bacteria act upon food particles, producing acids and other substances that can dissolve tooth enamel and eat away the underlying dentine. Sugars are the most harmful foods because they more readily produce acids.

Many children eat far more sugar than they need for good nutrition. To reduce tooth decay, substitute fruit, nuts, popcorn, cheese, and other sugarless snacks for sweets. Try to satisfy your child's appetite for sugar by supplying sweets at one meal a day.

Teach your child to use the toothbrush at about 2 years. To encourage your child, let him or her pick out a toothbrush. Supply an attractive tumbler for rinsing the mouth, a small size of toothpaste or powder, and a sturdy stool to stand on so that your child can reach the washbasin. For best results, encourage brushing after every meal.

Regular dental examinations are the surest way for your child to have healthy teeth and to keep the teeth for a lifetime. Your child's first visit to the dentist should be made at 3 years, soon after all the primary teeth are in. Before the first visit, take the child with you on one of your routine visits to your dentist. Arrange this beforehand with your dentist so that your child may sit in the dental chair, examine some of the instruments, and get acquainted with both the dentist and the surroundings. Then the first real visit will not be strange and alarming.

If your child has a tooth knocked out, save the tooth and call your dentist immediately. It may be possible to reinsert and retain the tooth.   M.G.

See also **Braces, dental; Malocclusion**

Tetanus (lockjaw) is an acute infectious disease that causes muscle spasms and convulsions. The spasms of the jaw muscles make it difficult to open the mouth, which is why this disease is called "lockjaw." Spasms may also occur in other muscles. If you suspect that your child has tetanus, call your doctor at once.

Tetanus is caused by bacteria that produce a powerful poison as they grow. Because the tetanus bacilli cannot grow if they are exposed to oxygen, they settle in deep tissue pockets where there is no oxygen. Tetanus most often develops in puncture wounds, or in children with great tissue destruction.

Tetanus bacilli live in the intestines of domestic animals and infect the soil touched by the animal droppings. A child may step on the droppings and pick up the bacilli, but the bacilli remain harmless until they are carried deep into the tissues, usually by way of a puncture wound. For this reason, if your child has a puncture wound, or a cut that does not bleed readily, consult your doctor. In the meantime, clean the wound and cover it.

The best protection against tetanus is tetanus toxoid, a vaccine. It is usually given to babies in a DPT shot (combined diphtheria and tetanus toxoids, and pertussis vaccine). Children 6 years old or less are given two shots about two months apart, and a

third shot a year after the second. Ideally, these shots are given during infancy. A booster, usually as a DPT shot, is given when the child enters school. If a serious injury occurs before the DPT shots are completed, a tetanus booster is given.

A nonimmunized school-age child should get two Td shots (combined tetanus and diphtheria toxoids) two months apart, with a third shot six months to a year later, and a Td booster every 10 years thereafter.

Tetanus toxoid is almost 100 per cent effective in preventing tetanus. Tetanus immune globulin (human) should be used to treat tetanus.   H.D.R., Jr.

See also **Bites and stings; Cuts and scratches; Immunization; Shots**

Thermometer. *See* **Fever**

Thrush is a mild fungus infection of the mouth. White patches that look somewhat like milk curd form on the inside of the cheeks, the roof of the mouth, and the

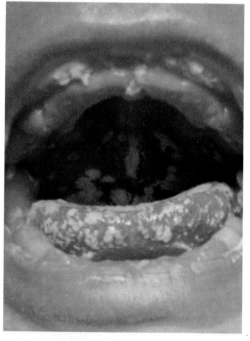

A thrush infection produces white patches on the inside of a baby's mouth.

tongue. But unlike milk curd, these patches do not wash away with a drink of water. Do not rub the patches, because the skin will bleed. The baby's mouth is usually sore, and the baby may be uncomfortable when eating. Diarrhea may accompany thrush.

Thrush is not uncommon during a baby's first few weeks of life. It is often contracted during delivery from a fungus infection in the mother's vagina.

If you suspect that your baby has thrush, consult your doctor for diagnosis and proper treatment. The doctor will probably prescribe medication that can be swabbed on the patches in the baby's mouth after the baby has been fed. Until you can reach the doctor, give the baby cooled boiled water after the baby drinks milk. The water will wash the milk out of the baby's mouth, giving the thrush fungus less to live on.   H.D.R., Jr.

See also **Diarrhea**

Thumb-sucking, for an infant, is almost as natural as eating. Sucking is itself a drive, a basic need. Babies can receive food only by sucking. But some babies have a greater tendency to suck their thumbs than others do. Even though satisfied at the breast or bottle, they seem determined to get further gratification by sucking fingers or thumbs. Persistent thumb-sucking is normal in babies. However, parents still often worry. If they are worried, they may ask themselves a few simple questions.

Is my baby being cuddled enough? Most babies want to be held at times, rocked and snuggled and sung to now and then.

Is the baby bored? Perhaps the baby spends too much time alone in the crib or playpen and has too few objects to handle and explore. Boredom is as real to a crawler as it is to an adult.

After a child is a year or so old, the sucking need becomes less powerful. Thumb-sucking may be a carry-over response to hunger or a way for the child to get to sleep. Often thumb-sucking stops as sleep habits change. If the thumb-sucking persists after the age of 2, it is evidently satisfying some further, unexplained need. Perhaps a new baby in the family has made the child want to be a baby again. Perhaps the child

is shy when pressured too much by adults or when confronted with new playmates. Perhaps thumb-sucking is a way to feel less lonely, or perhaps only a request to be hugged.

Do not be upset if others point out that they did not let their children become thumb-suckers. Let your child alone. Do not talk about the child's thumb-sucking, and certainly do not nag, punish, or humiliate the child because of it.

Do not put distasteful substances on the thumb to discourage thumb-sucking, and do not use mechanical restraints. Unless there are problems that cause a child undue tensions, the child will generally discontinue thumb-sucking.

One of your biggest worries about thumb-sucking may be the effect it will have on your child's teeth and jaw formation. In some cases, prolonged thumb-sucking past the age of 5 can interfere with normal dental development. If you have any concerns, you should consult your dentist.   M.G.

Tick bites. *See* **Bites and stings**

Tics are uncontrollable spasms of certain muscles. A child with a tic may repeatedly blink the eyes or shrug the shoulders. The child may cough, sniffle, or mumble words (verbal tic). Cheek muscles may twitch; the neck may jerk to one side or the other, or, in unusual instances, the child's entire body may jerk. Both motor and verbal tics occur in Tourette's syndrome. Tics usually occur more frequently and are more noticeable when the child is tense or emotionally upset.

If your child has a tic, consult a doctor. Do not try to force the child to stop the movements. The child does not have voluntary control over the muscle spasms causing the tic, and pressure only tends to make the tics worse.   M.G.

See also **Chorea**

Tonsillitis is an inflammation of the tonsils. The tonsils are composed of lymphatic tissue and are located in small pockets on both sides of the throat, behind the mouth.

Location of the tonsils

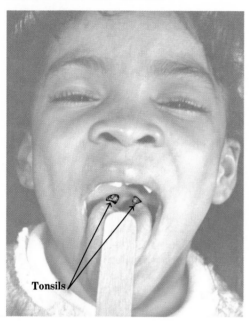

Tonsils

Tonsils grow on each side of the throat, in the back of the mouth. Healthy tonsils help the body to fight infection.

Healthy tonsils help protect the body against infection.

During early childhood, most children have an average of four infections of the upper respiratory tract each year. Each time, tonsillitis occurs. Just how severe the tonsillitis is usually depends upon the kind of virus or bacteria that causes it. Some cases of tonsillitis are so mild that the child is bothered very little.

Most often, a child with tonsillitis complains of a sore throat and has trouble swallowing. In severe attacks, the tonsils become quite swollen and red. Patches of yellowish or grayish membrane may form on them. Usually, the child has a fever and the lymph glands at the angles of the jaws swell. Other signs of severe tonsillitis are headache and vomiting.

If the tonsillitis is caused by a bacteria sensitive to antibiotics, a doctor may prescribe drugs. For example, the doctor may prescribe penicillin for "strep tonsillitis," to shorten the attack and to reduce the possibility of complications such as nephritis or rheumatic fever.

Rarely, in severe attacks of tonsillitis, an abscess may develop in the tissue around the tonsils. Or the tonsils may remain inflamed after several attacks of tonsillitis, and the child may have a constant low fever and constant swelling of the lymph glands in the neck. In such extreme cases, the doctor may recommend a tonsillectomy. If the adenoids are also constantly infected the doctor may remove them in the same operation. Tonsillectomy is performed less often than it was many years ago because the tonsils can be treated, and the indications for this surgical procedure, which carries some risk, have become more conservative. M.G.

See also **Adenoids; Nephritis; Rheumatic fever; Swollen glands**

Tourniquet. *See* **Bites and stings; Bleeding**

Tuberculosis is a serious contagious disease caused by tiny, rod-shaped bacteria called tubercle bacilli. It usually develops in the lungs, but it may appear in almost any part of the body.

The two main types of tuberculosis are commonly called primary infection tuberculosis (when a person gets the disease for the first time) and reinfection tuberculosis (when a person is infected a second, third, or fourth time).

When a child develops a primary infection, the invading tubercle bacilli are killed by white blood cells or walled up by cells and fibers that prevent their spreading through the body. Usually, the child does not feel ill or show any symptoms of the disease.

Reinfection tuberculosis may occur if the body's resistance is low because of illness, poor diet, or other causes. Then the tubercle bacilli that have been walled up break out and multiply. They may spread faster than they can be killed or walled up. A reinfected child usually has a fever, loses weight, has a cough, and is weak. Primary infection tuberculosis is more common among children who have not yet reached adolescence. An adolescent is more likely to develop reinfection tuberculosis.

If you suspect that your child has tuberculosis, or if you know that the child has been

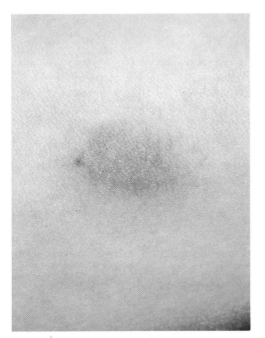

If the site of a tuberculin test shows significant redness and swelling after two days, the test is positive.

exposed to it, contact your doctor immediately. With a doctor's care, a child with tuberculosis may be cured in a year or two.

A child with tuberculosis usually begins treatment in a hospital. Eventually, the child may be treated at home. Doctors rely primarily on drugs to cure tuberculosis, but surgery is sometimes called for.

The tuberculin test is a simple method of learning if a child is infected with tubercle bacilli. The test may be made at 12 months, or at 15 months when the measles-mumps-rubella shot is given. A drop of harmless tuberculin (liquid prepared from dead tubercle bacilli) is injected, scratched, or rubbed into the child's skin. If after two days the spot becomes red and swollen, the test is considered positive. A positive reaction means the child has been infected by tubercle bacilli at some time. A test resulting in no reaction indicates that the child has never been infected by tubercle bacilli. A child who has a positive reaction should have a chest X ray to determine if the disease is active. The doctor may also order other tests and X rays of other parts of the body.

Adults who have been in contact with the child also should have chest X rays to determine who infected the child. Almost all cases of tuberculosis in infants and young children are contracted from someone in the child's household. Other people in the household should have tuberculin tests to determine if they have been infected, too.

Some children who live in areas where tuberculosis is prevalent, and children in a family with an active case, may be immunized against primary infection by drugs or shots of BCG (Bacillus Calmette-Guérin) vaccine.   H.D.R., Jr.

Tumor. *See* **Cancer**

Twitch. *See* **Chorea; Tic**

Umbilical Hernia. *See* **Hernia**

Underweight. Before you worry about an underweight child, make sure that the child really is underweight. Children have individual growth patterns, so that the "normal" weight for age and height varies. Let your doctor decide whether your child is underweight. The doctor can also look into the cause of the child's weight problem.

Most underweight children do not eat enough. Sometimes underweight may be caused by a chronic illness or emotional upsets. Anorexia nervosa and bulimia are important though infrequent causes of weight loss in adolescent girls.

Perhaps your youngster is eating enough food, but the food lacks nutritive value. A nutritionally balanced diet may be all that the child needs to gain weight. Rarely, the child may be eating nutritious foods, but a chronic disease, such as chronic diarrhea, regional enteritis, or a metabolic disorder, may prevent the body from absorbing or using food properly.

In rare cases, a young body uses food too rapidly. An overactive thyroid gland can cause such a condition.

Some children lose interest in food because their parents worry too much about eating habits. Too often, parents coax the child to eat.

An infant, unless physically sick, usually eats enough to keep gaining a reasonable amount of weight. Children may briefly lose interest in food during their second year, as they begin to walk and explore the environment. Also at this time, they lose the chubbiness of infancy. This loss makes many parents mistakenly believe that children are not eating as well as they should. This is not the time to coax a child to eat, because you may cause a chronic eating problem. The child usually starts eating properly again.

An illness may make a child lack appetite for a while. Again, do not coax. The child usually regains appetite with recovery. Jealousy of a new baby, depression, or unhappiness may also make a child stop eating as much as usual.

If your doctor tells you there is no cause for concern, stop talking about weight. Constant reminders can make a normally thin child feel uneasy. M.G.

See also **Anorexia nervosa**

Undescended testicles. Normally, a boy's testicles descend from the abdomen into the scrotum (the pouch of skin that hangs under the boy's penis) shortly before birth. However, one or both testicles may still be in the abdomen or groin when a boy is born, particularly if he is born prematurely. In most cases, the testicles descend shortly after birth. If you think your son has undescended testicles, consult the pediatrician.

Many boys have highly sensitive testicles that retract into the groin or abdomen whenever the testicles become chilled, or whenever the boy's thighs or scrotum are touched. These are not true undescended testicles. They are mobile undescended testicles. Most undescended testicles are mobile.

A doctor may have to examine a boy many times to determine whether a testicle is truly undescended. Parents can check to see if the testicle descends when the boy sits in a tub of warm water. If the testicle has been seen in the scrotum, or if the testicle can be moved into the scrotum by the doctor, the testicle is mobile. No treatment is

needed. The testicle will descend normally before adolescence.

Surgery and hormone treatment are used to correct true undescended testicles. Some doctors recommend hormone treatment to see if the testicle will descend without surgery. Surgeons are now frequently advising that an operation be performed to place the testicle in the scrotum before the boy's second birthday, if hormonal therapy fails. If surgery is planned, the parents and the doctor should explain to the boy the reason, reassuring him that he will be completely normal after the operation. M.G.

Upset stomach. *See* **Colic; Communicable diseases; Food poisoning; Motion sickness; Stomachache; Vomiting**

Urinary disturbances. Children can develop several types of urinary disturbances, including unusual frequency of urination, decreased urination, blood in the urine, and enuresis (persistent, involuntary wetting after the child is about 4 years old). Consult your doctor if you suspect that your child has a urinary disturbance.

Unusual frequency of urination is a common disturbance. It often signals an infection of the urinary tract. Pain or a burning sensation when urinating is often part of a urinary tract infection. An infant obviously cannot use words to describe the discomfort, but such a child is often feverish and may be irritable and cry excessively. A doctor can determine whether infection is present by examining the urine.

Most urinary infections are cleared up with antibiotics. If an infection does not clear up, its cause may be an abnormality in the formation of the kidneys, the bladder, or the ureters (the tubes that connect each kidney to the bladder). Or, an abnormality of the urethra (the passage through which urine flows from the bladder to outside the body) may be responsible for poor urine flow and infection. When infection of the urinary passages occurs, the doctor may examine the urinary tract by indirect means, such as by ultrasound or a pyelogram (an X ray of the kidneys and ureters), or by direct means, such as with a cystoscope (an instrument to examine the inside of the bladder).

Unusual frequency of urination may also be a symptom of anxiety in children. Frequent urination and a large increase in the amount of urine produced may also be a symptom of diabetes.

Decreased urination may result if the child's bladder retains the urine because of an obstruction. Decreased urination may also result from a decrease in the production of urine. This decrease may be caused by nephritis (a kidney disease), poisoning by certain drugs or metals, obstruction in the urinary tract, or dehydration.

Blood in the urine should be reported to the doctor. Remember, however, that a child's urine may sometimes appear red after the child has eaten beets. Slight bleeding may result if ammonia, which forms from urine, causes ulceration of the urinary opening of a baby boy's penis. The blood is bright red and appears in only the first few drops of urine passed. Blood in the urine may also occur because of nephritis, infection, certain types of anemia, poisoning, or some abnormality of the urinary tract.

Enuresis usually occurs during the night but may also happen during the day. Enuresis may be developmentally normal or may be caused by many things—a defect in the urinary tract, a urinary infection, or emotional disturbances. Enuresis may also be simply a family pattern. Or it may just be that the child is a sound sleeper and is not awakened by the feeling of a full bladder. M.G.

See also **Dehydration; Diabetes mellitus; Hysteria; Nephritis; Wetting**

Vaccination. *See* **Communicable diseases; Immunization; Shots; Virus**

Vaginal discharge may result from an infection that causes the external genital area of a girl to become inflamed. It may also develop if the girl's underpants are too tight and rub against the genital region. In either of these instances, the vaginal discharge causes whitish stains in the girl's underpants. Vaginal discharge may also occur if a foreign object has been inserted into the vagina. The discharge is then usually bloody and may be foul smelling.

In all these cases, consult a doctor. The doctor may prescribe antibiotics and will probably also suggest bathing the external genital area by having the girl sit in a tub partly filled with comfortably warm water.

A slight discharge from the vagina is common and normal for girls who are reaching adolescence and beginning to undergo sexual growth and development. You should explain these changes to your daughter and tell her about menstruation. M.G.

See also **Menstruation; Pinworms**

Vaporizer. *See* **Humidifying**

Virus is a living organism that is so tiny that it cannot be seen under an ordinary microscope. Smaller even than bacteria, viruses enter the body in various ways—through eating or drinking, inhalation, injection, or through breaks in the skin. Once in the body, they grow inside cells and form more viruses, which invade more cells.

Viruses can cause infectious diseases such as poliomyelitis, influenza, measles, chicken pox, smallpox, mumps, and the common cold. Viruses can also produce specific infections in certain cells. The liver cells are affected in hepatitis; the brain cells, in sleeping sickness; the skin cells, in fever blisters.

Doctors do not know of any cure for diseases caused by viruses, but once a person has had a virus disease, the person often becomes immune to that virus. Also, vaccines can be made from certain viruses and used to immunize a child against the diseases they cause. If your child has a virus disease, your doctor will probably tell you how to make the child more comfortable and how to avoid complications of the disease. H.D.R., Jr.

Vitamins are necessary for good health and proper growth. You can supply all the vitamins your child needs—with the exception of vitamin D in infants not drinking

Important vitamins

Vitamin	Functions in the body	Food sources
A	Helps develop teeth and maintain skin, tissues lining body cavities, glands that produce digestive juices, and night vision.	Whole milk, cream, butter, egg yolks, liver, kidneys, fats, fish liver oils, green and yellow vegetables, cantaloupe, peaches, and apricots.
B_1 (Thiamine)	Gives body energy. Helps maintain appetite, a healthy mental attitude.	Lean pork, organ meats, dried beans and peas, nuts, eggs, milk, whole grain cereals, and enriched cereals and breads.
B_2 (Riboflavin)	Helps carbohydrates release heat and energy in the body and keeps skin healthy.	Liver, heart, kidneys, turkey, beef, whole grain and enriched cereals, milk, cheese, eggs, and leafy green vegetables.
C (Ascorbic acid)	Increases resistance to infection. Helps form sound teeth and bones. Necessary for healthy gums and body tissues.	Citrus fruits, tomatoes, cantaloupe, strawberries, green and chili peppers, pineapple, cabbage, broccoli, asparagus, and greens of all kinds.
D	Helps body absorb calcium and phosphorus for bone growth.	Saltwater fish, vitamin D-fortified milk, and fish liver oils.
Niacin	Helps maintain healthy skin and other body tissues.	Meat, poultry, fish, and enriched and whole grain bread.

fortified milk—by providing an adequate daily diet of properly prepared foods.

Millions of dollars are spent each year on self-prescribed vitamin pills. Dispensing vitamin pills may make a mother feel that each child's nutritive needs are being met. But the vitamins are unlikely to be needed.

Vitamins work in subtle relationships with each other and with other nutrients. The amount of a certain vitamin needed depends on the amount of other vitamins and food elements in the body.

The contents of a vitamin pill are limited to those vitamins that have been discovered and that can be manufactured. Food may contain undiscovered but essential food substances.

It is best to rely on a good, balanced diet to supply your child with adequate vitamins, unless, of course, the doctor prescribes vitamin supplements.

Most milk today is commercially fortified with vitamin D. One quart (1 liter) contains the required daily amount. Sunlight can also provide the body with vitamin D. The ultraviolet rays of the sun, or a sun lamp, act on a substance in the skin and produce vitamin D. Because sunlight produces vitamin D in the human body, this vitamin is sometimes called the "sunshine vitamin."

The accompanying table shows the sources of six vitamins and how the body uses the vitamins.   M.G.

Vomiting is a common symptom among infants and children. Its cause may be physical or emotional.

■ Infants may vomit if they swallow too much air during feeding, or if they have an allergic reaction to a certain food, such as cow's milk.

- Any illness that is accompanied by a high fever may cause vomiting.
- Abnormalities in the formation or position of the esophagus, stomach, or intestines may cause vomiting.
- Disorders of organs other than the stomach, such as the kidneys, the ears, or a brain tumor, may cause vomiting.
- A child who swallows a poisonous substance may vomit. If you suspect poisoning, save some of the vomit for analysis. It may help a doctor decide how to treat the child. (For ways to induce vomiting, see POISONINGS AND POISONS.)
- Appendicitis may cause vomiting that is accompanied by pain in the lower right abdomen.
- Some children vomit when they ride in cars, trains, planes, or ships.
- Vomiting may be a sign of an emotional problem. For instance, a child who is apprehensive about going to school or who wants attention may vomit every morning. Such a child may need psychological help.

Because of its many possible causes, and because early treatment is important in many instances, never take vomiting lightly. Three instances, in particular, call for a doctor's attention: vomiting accompanied by pain in the lower right abdomen or severe abdominal pain (which may indicate appendicitis), persistent vomiting (which may cause dehydration), and vomiting green material (which may mean that some obstruction in the intestine has caused bile to back up from the intestine into the stomach). For simple vomiting, or until you can reach a doctor, keep the child quiet and give nothing to eat. Offer a little water, ginger ale, or weak tea. If the child continues to vomit, do not give any more liquids—not even water. M.G.

See also **Appendicitis; Communicable diseases; Dehydration; Emetics; Food poisoning; Influenza; Motion sickness; Poisonings and poisons; Stomachache; Swallowed objects**

Warts are small, hard growths on the skin. They tend to appear in groups of three or four, but they may appear singly or in large numbers. Most warts grow on the backs of the hands and on the soles of the feet. Warts on the soles of the feet are called

plantar warts. Warts are caused by a papilloma virus. Caution children against "picking" at warts. This may spread the virus and increase the number of warts.

There are several effective and painless methods for removing warts. These methods include blistering agents, liquid nitrogen, salicylic acid plasters, special solutions, or electrosurgery. Your doctor should be consulted.

Some doctors prescribe suggestion therapy, a safe method that you can try at home. The power of suggestion therapy performed by the child under a doctor's direction will often "cure" warts in a few months. Most warts disappear without treatment of any type within two years. Plantar warts, however, rarely disappear without treatment. A.M.M.

Wetting. Persistent wetting after a child is 4 to 5 years old is called enuresis. Most incidents of enuresis occur at night, and are accompanied by occasional wetting in the

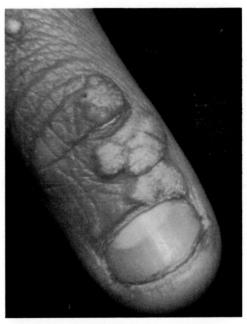

Aside from the discomfort caused if they grow at the base of a fingernail or toenail, warts do not seem to have any harmful effect on a child's general health.

daytime. If your child has enuresis, consult your doctor.

Some cases of enuresis are caused by a defect in the urinary tract or a chronic urinary infection. Your child may complain of painful urination, difficulty in starting or stopping urination, discolored urine, or increased frequency of urination.

Sometimes the problem is emotional, particularly if wetting occurs after the child has been toilet-trained for several months or years. Usually, some difficulty in relations with others is involved—especially with parents, but also with teachers, brothers, sisters, or playmates. One of the most common causes for a child's bedwetting is the arrival of a new baby.

Do not threaten, punish, ridicule, or plead with a child to stop wetting. These actions may increase the child's anxiety and make wetting more persistent. The child is not doing it deliberately and usually feels bad about it already. You can help most by discovering what is distressing the child. Is the child in too high a grade level at school? Is the child trying too hard to compete? The child may feel like a failure in social and school relationships. Build up a feeling of self-confidence. The child may need more of your time and attention. When anxiety and tensions are reduced, wetting may stop.

Most enuretic children have no urinary tract defect and are not emotionally disturbed. Frequently, the child is a deep sleeper and may not be awakened by the feeling of bladder fullness. Bedwetting may also be a family pattern. During the day, these children urinate often.

Drug therapy has been used in treating enuresis, with varying success. Conditioning devices (a pad attached to an alarm which rings as soon as the child begins to wet the bed) have also been successful. But they should be used only in selected instances with children who are old enough to understand what is being attempted and who are willing to cooperate. M.G.

See also **Urinary disturbances**

Whooping cough (pertussis) is a contagious disease that is caused by bacteria. It begins like an ordinary cold. The child has a runny nose, a slight fever, and a dry cough. After a few days, long spells of coughing occur that are usually worse at night. The child may begin to whoop—a long drawing in of breath that sounds like crowing—after a spell of coughing. The coughing spells may also cause vomiting.

If you suspect that your child has whooping cough, call your doctor. Also, be sure to call your doctor if your child has been exposed to whooping cough and has not been immunized against it.

Whooping cough is spread by a spray of droplets from the child's mouth or nose. A child who has whooping cough should use tissues to cover the mouth and nose when sneezing and coughing. The used tissues should be burned or disposed of in a safe place. The child should be isolated from other family members.

Whooping cough is communicable from about seven days after exposure to three weeks after coughing begins. If your child has been exposed to whooping cough and is not immune, your doctor will probably recommend that the child be quarantined for 14 days after exposure. One attack usually provides immunity. There is also a whooping cough vaccine.

Whooping cough vaccine is usually given along with diphtheria and tetanus vaccines in a single shot, commonly called a DPT shot. Children 6 years old or less are given two shots about two months apart, and a third shot about a year after the second. Ideally, these shots are given during infancy. A booster, usually as a DPT shot, is given when the child enters school. There are certain contraindications to the use of pertussis vaccine, and it is not given to some children. (*See* DIPHTHERIA for guidelines about immunization with DPT.)

All infants, except those with contraindications, should be immunized against whooping cough. The disease can be fatal to any child. The death rate is, however, far higher for infants less than a year old who have not been immunized. Immunization is so effective and widespread that the disease is less common, but it is still potentially serious for the unimmunized child. H.D.R., Jr.

See also **Communicable diseases; Diphtheria; Immunization; Shots**

Getting to know *Childcraft*

The best kind of learning is fun. Children have a natural curiosity about themselves and their world, and they enjoy satisfying that curiosity. *Childcraft* helps children find answers to their questions and encourages them to explore further and find more questions to answer. It is an exciting companion for an inquisitive child. In addition, *Childcraft* is an ideal assistant for the parent or teacher of any child, because it provides accurate information on a wide range of topics in language that children themselves can understand.

Objectives of *Childcraft*

Childcraft is for children. These four words represent the purpose for creating *Childcraft*. The goal of *Childcraft* is to explain ideas clearly and interestingly to children, so as to challenge, stimulate, and create an appetite for more.

The creators of *Childcraft* worked with both children and adults to choose topics of high interest to children from preschool through elementary school years. They chose stories and poems from folk literature, the classics, and the best of today's literature for children. They researched and reported on topics in nature, the sciences, the arts, and social studies—topics that large numbers of children consider significant. Then they organized the material in volumes centered around children's interests and filled with simple, direct writing and informative, exciting photography and art.

Childcraft and children's interests

Childcraft is designed to satisfy both young children's need to know and their need to explore and understand the world of imagination and feelings. Volumes 1, 2, and 3 nourish a child's

imagination with the best of children's stories and poems—
selections that help children become more aware and understanding of themselves and others. Volumes 4-14 explore the
outside world, developing basic concepts with enough supporting information for children to understand and enjoy. Each
volume presents its particular topic in a way that builds on the
child's knowledge and interests and points toward further
learning.

In Volumes 4-14, the writers of *Childcraft* have used a style
that lets children enjoy the language while learning the facts.
The writing is conversational and direct, with a natural
rhythm. Unfamiliar words are introduced where they are
needed, and they are explained either in the selection itself or
in a glossary at the end of the volume.

The illustrations for both literature and factual material are
colorful and appealing. Children will find charts and diagrams
that clarify and add to the text, as well as illustrations and
photographs that stimulate emotional responses to the stories
and poems.

Childcraft and developmental needs

Childcraft is designed both to satisfy the interests and needs
of children and to meet the needs of parents, teachers, and
other responsible and caring adults in a child's life. Adults who
use *Childcraft* will find a wealth of information, literature, and
activities for a range of ages. This section of *Guide to Childcraft* provides an overview of content, together with suggestions for introducing and using specific volumes at home and in
the classroom. Two articles that follow, "Introducing *Childcraft*
to Children" and "Curriculum Enrichment Guides," together
with the tables of contents and indexes of the individual volumes, will help you guide children to the books and pages that
are right for them.

The people behind *Childcraft*

Since its inception in 1934, the editors of *Childcraft* have
sought the assistance of distinguished educators and experts in
child growth and development. An Editorial Advisory Board
evaluates existing content and considers new material to meet
the changing interests and needs of children. This board is
assisted by a Library Consultant Committee, experienced professional librarians who are qualified authorities on children's
reading needs. Both groups meet regularly with the editorial
staff, and programs are implemented by a close working relationship between individual advisers and editors.

In addition, these special consultants provided technical assistance and advice in the preparation of particular volumes:

Volume 5, About Animals
Paul Bigelow Sears, Ph.D.
Professor Emeritus of
  Conservation,
Yale University

Loren D. Potter, Ph.D.
Professor of Biology,
University of New Mexico

**Volume 6, The Green
  Kingdom**
Paul Bigelow Sears, Ph.D.
Professor Emeritus of
  Conservation,
Yale University

Volume 8, About Us
Fred R. Eggan, Ph.D.
Professor of Anthropology,
University of Chicago

Nancy Modiano, Ph.D.
Associate Professor of
  Education,
The Catholic University of
  America

**Volume 12, How Things
  Work**
Larry Small
Science Consultant,
Schaumburg (Illinois) Public
  Schools

Volume 13, Mathemagic
Lola J. May, B.S., M.A.,
  Ph.D.
Mathematics Consultant,
Winnetka (Illinois) Public
  Schools

Volume 14, About Me
Paul L. Doerring, Ph.D.
Psychological Institute of
  Hilton Head Island

Virginia Samter
Member, Association of
  Medical Illustrators

Award-Winning Authors and Illustrators in *Childcraft*

Included in *Childcraft* are works of many award-winning authors and illustrators of children's books. Eight major awards are described, with names of winners who are in *Childcraft*. Listed below are winners of these and other awards and where in *Childcraft* to find examples of their work.

The **Newbery Medal** is given by the Association for Library Service to Children (ALSC) of the American Library Association for the most distinguished contribution to American literature for children. It is named for John Newbery (1713–1767), a London bookseller who first had the idea of publishing books for children. Seven winners are represented in *Childcraft:* Beverly Cleary, Elizabeth Coatsworth, Rachel Field, Jean Craighead George, William H. Armstrong, Scott O'Dell, and Elizabeth George Speare— the last three by excerpts from their winning books: *Sounder* (Armstrong), *Island of the Blue Dolphins* (O'Dell), and *The Witch of Blackbird Pond* (Speare).

The **Caldecott Medal** for the most distinguished American picture book for children is also given by the ALSC. It is named for Randolph Caldecott (1846–1886), an English illustrator of children's books. Winners in

Childcraft are Ezra Jack Keats, Arnold Lobel, Robert McCloskey, Uri Shulevitz, Louis Slobodkin, and Lynd Ward.

The **Canadian Library Association Book of the Year for Children** is given for a book by a Canadian citizen or resident. Winners in *Childcraft* are Kay Hill, James Houston, and Dennis Lee.

The **Vicky Metcalf Award for Children** is given by the Canadian Authors Association for the body of work of a Canadian author. Winners in *Childcraft* are Kay Hill, James Houston, and Farley Mowat.

The **Carnegie Medal** is given by the Library Association (British). It is the English equivalent of the Newbery Medal. Winners in *Childcraft* are Eleanor Farjeon and Ivan Southall.

The **Kate Greenaway Medal** is given by the Library Association (British) for distinguished work in the illustration of children's books first published in the United Kingdom. It is named for Kate Greenaway (1846–1901), an English illustrator. A winner in *Childcraft* is Helen Oxenbury.

The **Australian Children's Book Awards** are given by the Children's Book Council of Australia. Winners of the Book of the Year award in *Childcraft* are Ivan Southall and K. Langloh Parker. The latter is represented by a selection from her winning book. Ron Brooks, who won the Picture Book of the Year award, is represented by his winning pictures.

The **Hans Christian Andersen International Children's Book Medals** are given by the International Board on Books for Young People to a living author and illustrator whose complete works have made a distinguished contribution to international literature for young people. Winners in *Childcraft* are Eleanor Farjeon of the United Kingdom, Astrid Lindgren of Sweden, and Scott O'Dell of the United States.

Verna Aardema (author & illustrator) 1/110
Dorothy Aldis (author) 1/169, 179, 291; 2/28
William H. Armstrong (author) 3/188
Harry Behn (author) 3/298
Claire Huchet Bishop (author) 1/95
Judy Blume (author) 2/124
N. M. Bodecker (author & illustrator) 1/17, 52; 2/295
Gwendolyn Brooks (author) 1/289; 2/99, 253
Ron Brooks (illustrator) 1/211
Natalie Savage Carlson (author) 1/127
Bliss Carman (author) 3/230
Marchette Chute (author) 1/162, 170; 2/151
John Ciardi (author) 2/72, 73, 274
Beverly Cleary (author) 2/188
Elizabeth Coatsworth (author) 1/188, 234, 247; 2/152; 3/245
T. S. Eliot (author) 3/196
Eleanor Farjeon (author) 1/62, 210, 246; 2/166, 234
Rachel Field (author) 1/290; 2/233, 292
Aileen Fisher (author) 1/163, 171; 2/291
Louise Fitzhugh (author) 3/42
Robert Frost (author) 2/294
Wanda Gág (author) 1/238
Hamlin Garland (author) 3/152
Jean Craighead George (author) 3/131
Kay Hill (author) 3/143

Russell Hoban (author) 2/29, 187
James Houston (author) 2/28, 151, 153, 235, 297
Langston Hughes (author) 1/290; 2/295; 3/299
Norton Juster (author) 13/94
Ezra Jack Keats (author & illustrator) 1/165–168
Carol Kendall (author) 3/93
X. J. Kennedy (author) 2/41, 42, 168, 232; 3/194
Rudyard Kipling (author) 1/248
Karla Kuskin (author) 2/14, 26, 166, 168, 187; 3/23
Dennis Lee (author) 2/101, 139, 251; 3/175
Ursula K. Le Guin (author) 3/176
Lois Lenski (author) 2/252
Joan M. Lexau (author) 2/16
Astrid Lindgren (author) 2/254
Vachel Lindsay (author) 1/178; 2/169
Myra Cohn Livingston (author) 2/54, 291
Arnold Lobel (author & illustrator) 2/44–53
Robert McCloskey (author & illustrator) 2/212–231
David McCord (author) 1/309; 2/253; 3/296
Phyllis McGinley (author) 2/251, 293
Eve Merriam (author) 2/236, 252; 3/66
Edna St. Vincent Millay (author) 3/296
Farley Mowat (author) 3/24
Ogden Nash (author) 1/252
Evaline Ness (author & illustrator) 2/154

Scott O'Dell (author) 3/164
Mary O'Neill (author) 2/74
Helen Oxenbury (illustrator) 2/14
Peggy Parish (author) 2/102
K. Langloh Parker (author) 3/83
Laura E. Richards (author) 1/178; 3/87
Carl Sandburg (author) 3/245
Lew Sarett (author) 3/153
Ernest H. Shepard (illustrator) 1/181
Uri Shulevitz (illustrator) 1/23
William Jay Smith (author) 2/169
Zilpha Keatley Snyder (author) 3/299
Donald J. Sobol (author) 2/170
Ivan Southall (author) 3/218
Elizabeth G. Speare (author) 3/232
Sara Teasdale (author) 2/235
Louis Untermeyer (author) 2/234
Judith Viorst (author) 2/55, 98
Jill Paton Walsh (author) 3/154
Lynd K. Ward (illustrator) 3/198, 201
Richard Wilbur (author) 2/54
Laura Ingalls Wilder (author) 2/276
Garth Williams (illustrator) 2/276
Laurence Yep (author) 3/267
Charlotte Zolotow (author) 2/55

Organization of *Childcraft*

The first three volumes of *Childcraft* introduce children to literature from all ages and from around the world. In Volumes 4 through 14, children learn about living things, about machines and numbers, about the world and its peoples, and about themselves. Volume 15, for parents and teachers, contains information about child growth and development.

The first three volumes present children's literature in collections designed for specific age levels, as indicated in the following descriptions. Each of these collections includes author, title, and first-line indexes.

In Volumes 4 through 14, most material is presented as two-page articles that are grouped in units on particular topics. Each of these volumes includes a subject index.

Description of Contents

Volume 1 **Once Upon a Time**

This volume contains selections to read aloud and share with young children—stories, nursery rhymes, and poems, including classics such as Mother Goose rhymes and *The Tale of Peter Rabbit* by Beatrix Potter, and modern favorites such as *Why Mosquitoes Buzz in People's Ears* by Verna Aardema.

The selections are arranged in five sections—"Nursery Rhymes," "Folk & Fairy Tales," "Favorite Fables," "Stories & Poems," and "Things to Know," which introduces the alphabet, counting rhymes, and poems about other concepts.

Volume 2 **Time to Read**

The second volume features selections for children who are beginning to read—read-aloud and easy-to-read stories, poems, and riddle rhymes, including tales about such memorable characters as Paddington Bear, Ramona Quimby, Encyclopedia Brown, and Amelia Bedelia. Authors and illustrators include

Arnold Lobel, Laura Ingalls Wilder, Astrid Lindgren, Eve Merriam, and John Ciardi.

Selections on related topics are grouped together, and the groups are arranged by reading level.

Volume 3 **Stories and Poems**

The third volume contains selections for more mature readers—a sampling of myths, legends, folk tales, modern fantasy, classic and contemporary fiction, lyric poetry, and narrative poetry. Among the 118 selections are poems by Jack Prelutsky and Lillian Morrison, tales by Yoshika Uchida and Hans Christian Andersen, and excerpts from novels by William H. Armstrong, Scott O'Dell, and Elizabeth George Speare.

Selections on related themes are grouped together.

Volume 4 **World and Space**

The volume explores earth—what it is, how it came to be, how it makes life possible; weather; planets, stars, galaxies; maps, globes, compasses; and the work of people who study the world and space.

Volume 5 **About Animals**

Mammals, birds, fish, reptiles, amphibians, and other animals are featured, along with what makes each group special, how different animals fit into the web of life, and how animals and people affect each other.

Volume 6 **The Green Kingdom**

In this book, readers learn about flowers, trees, and odd plants; plants of long ago; how plants live and grow; gardens; how plants and people affect each other; tales and true stories about plants.

Volume 7 **Story of the Sea**

The mysterious world of the sea is explored with photographs, poetry, and scientific facts about the oceans; animals of the sea, from starfish through shark; and legends, historic adventures, and modern exploration of the sea.

Volume 8 **About Us**

This volume explores the many likenesses and differences in people and cultures of more than 50 nations, from Afghanistan to Zaire—ways of life, beliefs and customs, foods, houses, games, and arts.

Volume 9 **Holidays and Birthdays**

This book offers explanations of over 100 special days in 40 countries—national holidays, religious holy days, birthdays of famous people, and other birthdays and anniversaries; stories behind the names of days and months; and stories, poems, and projects for holidays.

Volume 10 **Places to Know**

This volume introduces children to famous places around the world, from sites of historical importance, such as the Pyramids, to scenes of great natural beauty, including Niagara Falls, to modern attractions, such as Disneyland.

Volume 11 **Make and Do**

This book provides instructions, with pictures, for more than 300 how-to-do-it projects and activities, including games, stunts, tricks, making costumes and gifts, and such crafts as painting, weaving, and working with clay.

Volume 12 **How Things Work**

Here are explanations and experiments concerning forces and machines; sound, light, heat, motion, and electricity; the six simple machines; and such everyday machines as clocks, cameras, and engines.

Volume 13 **Mathemagic**

This book entertains and challenges young readers with stories, puzzles, games, tricks, and facts about numbers and shapes; how we can play and work with numbers; what numbers can do for us; careers involving numbers.

Volume 14 **About Me**

This book answers questions of special interest to a young child—questions about how people are alike; being born into a family; growing; learning about the world; understanding feelings; what makes each individual unique.

Volume 15 **Guide to Childcraft**

This volume for parents and teachers outlines a child's growth and development from birth through the preteen years and explores issues of special concern. The volume includes articles about child development, a Medical Guide, these suggestions for introducing and using *Childcraft*, and the General Index for the series.

Introducing *Childcraft* in the home

Sharing pictures and stories from *Childcraft* is an easy and natural way to introduce a young child to each volume of the set. These pages offer you a choice of activities for exploring each volume of *Childcraft* with your child.

Volume 1 *Once Upon a Time*

Preschool

ACTIVITY 1: *Once Upon a Time,* the first volume of children's literature in *Childcraft,* is intended especially for the young listener. Pages 7 through 9 discuss reading aloud to children, from birth through the primary grades. You may find it helpful to read these pages, not only to put the stories and poems in *Childcraft* to the best possible use, but also to take advantage of other books for children to which *Childcraft* will naturally lead you and your child.

ACTIVITY 2: Introduce Volume 1 to your child by reading one or two nursery rhymes (pages 11-65). Put your finger under the words as you read them to help your child make an association between spoken and written words. Repeat each rhyme so that your child can learn part or all of it and recite it with you. If there are pictures illustrating the rhyme, point them out and talk about them with your child. In later sessions, as your child's attention span increases, go on to the other sections of poetry and to the shorter tales and stories.

School Age

ACTIVITY 1: After your child has begun reading, help him or her begin using Volume 1 independently, even while you continue reading aloud. For example, read to your child one of the long story poems. (Examples include "Wynken and Blynken and Nod," by Eugene Field, on pages 298-299; "The Duel," also by Field, on pages 210-211; "The Owl and the Pussycat," by Edward Lear, on pages 264-265; and "The Tale of Custard the

Dragon," by Ogden Nash, on pages 272-275.) Then point out that most of the poems in Volume 1 are much shorter than the one you read, and that your child may be able to read some of them. Turn to the "Things to Know" section on pages 66-85. Point out that almost all the words in these poems are easy-to-read words. Encourage your child to turn to this section first to begin reading Volume 1.

ACTIVITY 2: If your child is developing strong reading skills, take time to look through Volume 1 with him or her. Note where the nursery rhymes and other poems are found, as well as the easy-to-read "Things to Know" section (pages 66-85). Point out the easiest story, "The Little Red Hen" on pages 98 and 99. Ask your child to choose a short poem and to read it to you as independently as possible. (If encouragement is needed, you and your child can take turns reading it.) Encourage the child to read other poems and "The Little Red Hen" alone.

(Note: Although the fables are short, the vocabulary in them is difficult. Read and discuss these with your child, rather than encourage the child to attempt them independently.)

Volume 2 *Time to Read*

Preschool

ACTIVITY 1: *Time to Read*, the second of three literature volumes in *Childcraft*, has a higher percentage of stories than Volume 1 but still includes many poems. Among these are several folk songs and poems with repeated stanzas or lines. Have a "say-along" in which you read and your child joins in on the repeated lines. If the poem is enjoyable to both you and your child, a second (and even third) reading of the same poem will add to the pleasure. Two folk songs to consider are "The Fox Went Out on a Chilly Night," pages 118-123, and "I Know an Old Lady Who Swallowed a Fly," pages 206-211. (If you have not already read Volume 1, pages 7-9, do so now.)

ACTIVITY 2: Preschoolers also will particularly enjoy hearing any of these stories from Volume 2:

Mother, Mother, I Want Another (pages 6-13)
Abu Ali: Three Tales of the Middle East (pages 30-39)
Frog and Toad (pages 44-53)
The Riddles (pages 82-91)
Harry the Dirty Dog (pages 92-97)

School Age

ACTIVITY 1: Volume 2 features a special format for the early reader. The stories range from a very low beginner's level to third-grade and above. Browse through the stories in *Time to Read* with your child and have him or her predict from the pictures what each story is about. Ask which stories look most interesting and why. Help your child identify which stories are comfortable reading for him or her and choose one of these stories to read. Have your child read the first paragraph or so aloud to you and finish reading the story independently. Encourage your child to go on to others.

ACTIVITY 2: Read some of the short, humorous poems to your child, such as "The Ostrich Is a Silly Bird" (page 73), and let your child find others to read to you. You can also sample riddles in "A Riddle! A Riddle!" (pages 82-91) with your child. Encourage your child to find other poems to read alone or to a younger child.

Volume 3 *Stories and Poems*

ACTIVITY 1: *Stories and Poems,* the third volume of children's literature in *Childcraft,* is intended for the upper-elementary child. There are a few stories and poems, however, that your preschooler will enjoy hearing you read:

Preschool

> Limericks (pages 38-41)
> The Bremen Town Musicians (pages 88-92)
> Anansi and the Plantains (pages 108-113)
> Baba Yaga's Geese (pages 114-118)

ACTIVITY 2: From your knowledge of your child's interests and attention span, you may find that your child enjoys some of the other poems throughout the book and some of the stories listed for children in Kindergarten to Grade 2. (If you have not already read Volume 1, pages 7-9, do so now.)

ACTIVITY 1: The Volume 3 stories and excerpts listed below are of interest to children in kindergarten and primary grades, but above their reading level. Your child will appreciate hearing you read one or more of these stories aloud.

School Age

> Toad's Escape (pages 6-21)
> The Cow-Tail Switch (pages 32-37)
> The Old Man with the Bump (pages 58-65)
> Why the Kangaroo Hops on Two Legs (pages 83-86)
> The Living Kuan-yin (pages 93-99)
> The Emperor's New Clothes (pages 100-106)
> Clever Manka (pages 120-127)
> Macavity: The Mystery Cat (pages 196-197)
> How It Snowed Fur and Rained Fry Cakes in
>   Western Virginia (pages 199-200)

ACTIVITY 2: Whenever you read a story, you can point out to your child any short poems with simple words that follow the story. Encourage your child to try reading the poems independently, or with your help.

Volume 4 *World and Space*

Preschool

ACTIVITY 1: Although some of the topics in *World and Space*, Volume 4, are difficult for a preschooler to understand, many address questions in every child's mind very early in life—"What makes the wind blow?" "Where does the sun go at night?" "Why is the sky blue?" Let the child know that Volume 4 has answers to some of these questions.

Introduce *World and Space* to a preschool child in several very short sessions. You may be able to take advantage of your child's own questions. If so, use the index to find pages that answer those questions. If not, let your child find a two-page article with a high-interest picture. (Pages 21 through 57 are good for this activity.) Read the title, and ask the child to look at the picture and try to figure out what it shows. Meanwhile, skim the article and decide whether you should read it aloud or explain it in simpler terms. Encourage your child to talk about the picture, and discuss what it means. Then read or talk about other interesting facts the text presents. Limit this activity to no more than 10 minutes.

ACTIVITY 2: Let your child examine other pictures in the book independently whenever he or she feels like it and bring questions about the pictures to you for explanations.

School Age

ACTIVITY 1: If your child is beginning to read, he or she may be ready to read picture labels and captions in Volume 4 with some independence. Turn to a page with an easy-to-read caption. (Any of these pages are possibilities: 57, 103, 107, 113, 124, 125, 139, 156-157, 171, 195, 197.) First talk with your child about the illustration(s). Then read the label or caption aloud. Ask your child to use what he or she has learned from the pictures to read the caption(s). Compliment your child for correct or approximate readings. Let your child try reading other captions, and even short paragraphs, independently.

ACTIVITY 2: As reading skills improve, encourage independent reading by working one of these experiments with your child: "Is air something?" (experiment directions on pages 148-149); "Air can push!" (pages 154-155); "Why the moon 'changes' shape" (pages 230-233).

Begin by showing the illustrations to your child. Invite your child to explain what is happening in the pictures. Read the text aloud, and have your child listen for information that is given in the text and not the pictures. Then work the experiment together. When the experiment is finished, point out some other experiments and projects and encourage your child to look at the pictures and directions. At a later time, your child can try another activity with you or independently.

Volume 5 *About Animals*

ACTIVITY 1: After reading the title of Volume 5, *About Animals*, to your child, explain that the book shows how animals belong in groups. Turn to the table of contents and read the six chapter titles from "It's a Mammal" to "Many-Legged Creatures." Invite your child to choose one of those chapters to find out what the title means. Then turn to the first two pages of the chapter selected. Read them and talk about the illustration with your child. Each of these six chapter openers is followed by a "looking page" featuring pictures with a wealth of detail. After reading the introduction, you can turn the page to the "looking page" and encourage your child to talk about what he or she sees in the picture on that page. Read the article, which points out some of the details, and help your child find details in pictures.

Conclude by pointing out the many other colorful and informative pictures throughout this volume. Encourage your child to look at the pictures just for fun and to find out about animals of all types.

ACTIVITY 2: Introduce the volume by reading one of the picture stories, "The life of a black bear" (pages 47-49) or "The life of a Canada goose" (pages 64-67), and looking at the photographs with your child. Encourage him or her to look at the other pictures in the volume independently.

ACTIVITY 1: Explain that people who study animals put animals that are alike into groups, because this makes it easier to talk about where the animals live, what they eat, and how they grow. Explain that several chapters in *About Animals* tell about different animal groups. Turn to any of the chapter openers on pages 28, 50, 68, 82, 98, 110 and read the title and, if possible, the introduction to your child. Point out the animal group that is named in the title. Encourage your child to choose one chapter and to browse through the articles and pictures independently.

ACTIVITY 2: Ask your child to name one or two favorite animals. Use the index to find pages of Volume 5 that discuss or illustrate the animal(s) that your child names. If there is a picture, help your child read the caption. As reading ability increases, your child's interest may lead him or her to read some of the text on the page as well as the caption.

Invite your child to name several other favorite animals. Look them up in the index and mark the pages with scraps of paper. Encourage your child to turn to those pages later, to look at the pictures and to read what he or she can of the captions and text.

Volume 6 *The Green Kingdom*

Preschool

ACTIVITY 1: Read the title of Volume 6, *The Green Kingdom*, and let your child guess what is inside. Explain that the book is about plants. Turn to the chapter entitled "Weeds and Wild Flowers," beginning on page 110. Choose a plant that your child is familiar with, and have your child look at the picture as you read the text, which may include a poem about the plant or a description of how it is useful. Encourage your child to browse through the book independently to enjoy the pictures of all kinds of plants.

ACTIVITY 2: Introduce Volume 6 as a reference source. Explain that the book tells about all kinds of plants, beautiful and plain, helpful and harmful. Look through the book and point out some of the most interesting plants. Then turn to pages 132 to 135 and explain that this section warns about dangerous plants. Point out any that your child might come in contact with, and talk about what they look like. Then point out that not many pages in the book are about dangerous plants, and that most plants are helpful instead. Encourage your child to look at the rest of the book for fun, and to show you any plants that look interesting. If your child has questions about the pictures, read some of the text to find answers.

School Age

ACTIVITY 1: Explain the title of Volume 6. Then turn to one of the four-page articles in the chapter titled "Nature's Neighbors" on pages 48-85. Encourage your child to read the title. Read the first two pages with your child and look at and talk about the picture. Continue with the remaining two pages. First talk about the photographs of plants with your child. Then read the text in the box at the far right and discuss the small illustrations as well. Encourage your child to look through the rest of this chapter, and other chapters, independently, and to use the pictures, picture captions, and titles to preview the content.

ACTIVITY 2: If you have a globe or map of the world (or of the United States), you can make use of it as you and your child look through Volume 6. Turn to the chapter "Famous Gardens," which begins on page 161. Have your child choose favorites among the gardens pictured. Then find on the globe or map the area of each favorite garden. Point out where you live, and the areas of land and water between you and the place your child picked. Discuss how your family would travel to visit the garden.

You can also introduce "The tree-path game" on pages 172 to 186. Read the directions on page 172 to your child. Work through the first two pages (pages 172-173) with your child, using the chart at the bottom of the page often. Turn the page to make sure that you have chosen the correct path so far. Continue with the remaining pages or let your child continue the game independently and find the correct path to the end.

Volume 7 *Story of the Sea*

Preschool

ACTIVITY 1: The element of Volume 7, *Story of the Sea*, that most preschoolers will find fascinating is its illustration of animal life in and about the sea. Introduce the book by turning to "Animals of the Sea," pages 103-253. Look through this section with your child, pointing out things of interest to you and encouraging your child to comment on the pictures. Then point out that every section of the book includes colorful and exciting pictures to look at later.

ACTIVITY 2: Take time to point out that many photographs and drawings show how people of long ago traveled on the sea and how people work on it today. (Note: Explain that in "Strange stories of the sea," on pages 255-263, there are several illustrations of imaginary people and animals of the sea; point out those pages and let your child know that pictures there are of make-believe things. Then look at the photos and illustrations in "people who work on the sea" with your child. Compare the pictures in both sections and talk about which things are real and which are make-believe.)

School Age

ACTIVITY 1: Beginning readers will enjoy figuring out chapter titles and illustration captions, even though much of the text of Volume 7 will be hard for them. Direct your child's attention to "Animals of the Sea" on pages 103-253. Explain that this section shows how sea animals belong in different groups. Turn to page 108; point out the title *Fish* and the fact that it is printed in color. Explain that the title of each of the nine groups will be printed in a different color. Read page 108 and talk about how fish are alike and about the differences between fish and other animals. Briefly look through pages 108-151, reminding your child that all the pictures in this section show fish.

On page 152, point out the word in colored letters and read it. Explain that *crustaceans* are another group of animals, different from fish, and that the animals shown on the next few pages are crustaceans. Now or later, turn to each of the pages listed below and read the name of each of the other animal groups introduced there:

166 (mollusks)	220 (reptiles)	242 (sponges, sea squirts,
198 (coelenterates)	226 (mammals)	and worms)
208 (echinoderms)	248 (birds)	

Encourage your child to browse, both to enjoy the pictures and to learn about each of these groups of animals.

ACTIVITY 2: Take some time to read to your child one of the stories about people and the sea, such as the Vikings (pages 58-59), pirates (pages 70-73), the *Titanic* (pages 78-83), or exploration under the sea (pages 94-97). Then encourage your child to look at other parts of the book independently, including the final section about people and the sea.

Volume 8 *About Us*

Preschool

ACTIVITY 1: Volume 8, *About Us*, is packed with colorful pictures that a preschooler can enjoy on his or her own, but a first session with you will make your child's browsing much more informative. Open the book to pages 4 and 5. Read page 5 aloud or reword the text in simpler language, stressing the fact that although there are many differences among people, we all have common needs and desires. Briefly discuss the pictures on page 4 with your child. Then read the text and talk about the pictures on the following pages, through page 15. Explain that the rest of the book tells more about how people around the world do the things that are told about on pages 6 through 15. Encourage your child to look through the book to see how people dress, work, eat, play, and enjoy life.

ACTIVITY 2: Pick a section with pictures of activities that are easily identified, such as "Time for Fun." Talk about what the children in the pictures are doing, and let your child guess what the section is about. Read the captions of pictures that interest your child. Repeat the activity with one or two more sections, and then let your child browse through the book.

School Age

ACTIVITY 1: Each of the twelve chapters on pages 47 through 251 discusses a particular need—food, clothing, communication, and so on—and shows how different peoples around the world respond to that need. Choose one of the chapters that interests you and your child, and read it with him or her, taking time to talk about the pictures. Often children look down on or laugh at any unfamiliar way of life, simply because they don't know how to react to strange things. Your acceptance of other people's right to be different will be a good model for your child and will help give your child the confidence to learn about other people. When your child has had some time to become comfortable with the idea of many different cultures, encourage him or her to look at more of Volume 8 and read some of the titles and, if possible, captions and text.

ACTIVITY 2: If you have a globe or world map, you can use it when you introduce *About Us*. Browse through the book with your child, talking about the pictures and pointing out the name of the country in each caption. Make sure your child understands that the pictures were taken in that country. Then turn to the globe or map and point out where several of those countries are. Help your child to see that some countries are close to the North or South Pole, and that pictures from these countries often show cold weather, strongly built houses, and people dressed in heavy clothes. Point out that pictures of countries close to the equator often show warm weather, houses of lighter materials, and people with light or little clothing. Help your child understand that people who live in different kinds of places do things in different ways. Encourage your child to look at or read the book independently, and to use a globe or map to try to find the different countries pictured.

Volume 9 *Holidays and Birthdays*

ACTIVITY 1: Have a calendar for the year, or the page for the month, handy when you introduce Volume 9, *Holidays and Birthdays.* Explain that this book tells about the days of the year and what makes each one special. Point out today's date on your home calendar, and turn to the chapter about the month. Briefly compare your own calendar with the first two pages of the chapter, and explain that the calendar in the book shows birthdays of famous people. Find today's date and read the name(s) listed. Then turn to the book page with the calendar that lists your child's birthday and read the names listed on that date. Explain that the rest of each chapter tells about things that really happened in that month or tells stories about days of the month. Then read one of the articles or stories.

ACTIVITY 2: When your family observes a holiday, find the appropriate selection, look at the pictures with your child, and read or explain the text. For family birthdays, use the calendar to learn which famous people share the same birthday. Using the book regularly is an easy way to help your child become acquainted with it.

Preschool

ACTIVITY 1: Introduce *Holidays and Birthdays* by explaining its organization according to the months of the year. Then choose one month—perhaps the present one, or the one with your child's birthday, or another month with special significance for the two of you—and read one or more of the short articles, beginning with the birthday list on the first two pages of the chapter. Encourage your child to look at the book each month to find out about some special days.

ACTIVITY 2: You can show a child who is reading fairly independently how to use *Holidays and Birthdays* for reference as

School Age

well as entertainment. After looking at the month-by-month organization and the variety of topics for each month, turn to the index at the end of the volume. Read through some of the topics there, and turn to the pages listed. Help your child see that he or she can use both the table of contents at the front of the book and the index at the back of the book to find information about a special date, ceremony, or event.

Volume 10 *Places to Know*

Preschool

ACTIVITY 1: Volume 10, *Places to Know*, introduces both places of historic significance and scenes of natural beauty, in and out of the United States. Since young children have very little sense of the past or awareness of faraway places, it is best to introduce the book with scenes or buildings that exist now, and not to emphasize their location. Begin with some "Oh! and Ah! Places" (pages 19-38) or other places of interest to you. Read or explain the text, and talk about the picture(s) with your child.

ACTIVITY 2: You can make a place real to your child by bringing out likenesses and differences between the place in the book and a place or thing that is familiar to your child. For example, if the picture is of a geyser, compare it to steam coming out of a teakettle; if it is of a snow-covered building or mountain, remind your child of the last time he or she went out in snowy winter weather. If you have read your child other stories set in places mentioned in the text, remind your child of those stories, and look at the picture together to find things the other stories mentioned.

School Age

ACTIVITY 1: Explain that the book is organized by themes. Read several titles from the table of contents (the page after the title page) and invite your child to choose a part in which he or she is interested. Look through the pages together, reading the titles and captions. Encourage your child to look at other parts of the book independently.

ACTIVITY 2: Show your child the index of Volume 10 and explain the purpose of an index. Ask your child to name different kinds of places—such as *river*, *castle*, or *market*—and look for the term in the index. If articles are listed, read them or encourage your child to read them later.

Volume 11 *Make and Do*

Preschool

ACTIVITY 1: Prepare to introduce Volume 11, *Make and Do*, by previewing "Toys, Crafts, and Make-Believe" (pages 7-33) to discover what types of materials are needed for the easy projects and activities in this chapter. Then, with your child, look through the pages and choose one of the projects. Help your child with the directions if necessary. Then talk about what odds and ends to collect for other projects, where to store them, where to work on the projects, and how to clean up afterward. Encourage your child to try some of the other easy activities.

ACTIVITY 2: Help your child make a puppet, following the directions on pages 266-267. Encourage your child to use the puppet to act out familiar situations, an original story, or a story he or she has heard.

School Age

ACTIVITY 1: Page through *Make and Do* with your child to determine what sorts of materials and crafts he or she would like to work with. Discuss where and how your child can get materials, where to store the materials and work, and how to take care of the materials and workspace. Let your child work as independently as possible, but offer to read directions as necessary.

ACTIVITY 2: If your child is reading fairly independently, point out the section with directions for indoor and outdoor games, pages 273-297. Let your child find an unfamiliar game, read the directions, and teach it to friends. Encourage your child to look for other projects to do alone or with friends. (See the preceding activity for suggestions about materials, workspace, and cleaning up.)

Volume 12 *How Things Work*

Preschool

ACTIVITY 1: Choose one of the easy projects listed here and collect any materials needed:

> page 11—helicopter
> page 15—magnetizing a needle, magnet boat
> page 19—rocket balloon
> page 40—wind-skipper
> page 42—snake-dancer

Read the title of Volume 12, *How Things Work*, to your child and briefly look through the book to point out the variety of things discussed. Look at the pages that explain the project you have chosen, read the directions, and do the project with your child. Talk about just as much of the basic principle involved—for example, wind power, magnetism, or heat—as you think your child will understand.

ACTIVITY 2: Just for pleasure, read one of the stories included in Volume 12: "Windwagon Smith," pages 46-52; or "The Fire Bringer," pages 158-165.

School Age

ACTIVITY 1: Introduce *How Things Work* by having your child try some experiments with sound. Read "Hear All About It," pages 240-253. When your child understands that different materials conduct sound, point out the experiments on pages 254-259 and the make-it-yourself instruments on pages 268-271. Let your child look at the pictures, read as much of the captions and text as possible, and choose a project to do or a musical instrument to make, alone or with your help.

ACTIVITY 2: If your child reads well enough to understand the text without help, introduce *How Things Work* with a challenge. Without explaining what makes it work, make either the wind-skipper (page 40) or the snake-dancer (page 42) with your child. Then show where in the book to look for the directions you followed. Let your child read as much of the chapter as needed and then explain his or her ideas about why the wind-skipper or snake-dancer works.

Volume 13 *Mathemagic*

Preschool

ACTIVITY 1: Have three different colors of paper on hand. Open Volume 13, *Mathemagic*, to "Triangle tricks," pages 226-229. Talk about the illustrations with your child and read or explain the article. Be sure to explain the terms *triangle* and *legs*, and, if your child likes long words, introduce *isosceles*. Together cut the paper as shown, making two or three sets of triangles. Help your child copy one of the patterns in the book, and encourage him or her to make original patterns.

ACTIVITY 2: Some children enjoy learning to count in more than one language. If you think your child may be among them, turn to pages 80 through 83 of Volume 13 and point out the pictures of children from various lands. Read the names of languages on the chart and let your child pick one of the languages. Read the number words for the language and repeat them with your child until you can count from one to five or from one to ten together.

School Age

ACTIVITY 1: Together with your child, work out the answers to your choice of these puzzlers in Chapter 1 of *Mathemagic:* "Rebus riddles" (pages 8-9); "Toothpick teasers" (pages 10-11); "Rescue Ribidip" (pages 16-17); "The mysterious Möbius strip" (pages 18-19).

ACTIVITY 2: Explain that *Mathemagic* is all about numbers and ways to think about and work with numbers. Read through the table of contents; then turn to one or more of these lessons to explore some math concepts in simple terms: "The biggest number" (pages 136-137); "The smallest number" (pages 138-139); "Pie puzzles" (pages 142-143). Depending on your child's reading ability, read the text yourself or help him or her to read.

Volume 14 *About Me*

ACTIVITY 1: Explain that Volume 14, *About Me*, is all about growing. Turn to "The Many Me's" on pages 233 through 253. Look at and talk about the photographs that show children's activities, moods, emotions, relationships with friends and family members, and curiosity about the future.

ACTIVITY 2: "Becoming Me" (pages 95-107) is a useful reference for answering the typical child's question, "Where did I come from?" The pictures illustrate the development of a baby and the life of a newborn infant, and the text gives a child solid information to satisfy his or her curiosity. Read and talk about this section with your child when you feel the time is right.

ACTIVITY 1: After explaining that *About Me* tells about many experiences in growing up, read and talk about one of these high-interest chapters with your child: "Watch Me Grow," pages 153-181, which tells about changes in height, bones, shape, and so on; or "Me and My Family," pages 109-127, which discusses the many forms a family can take.

ACTIVITY 2: If your child is interested in learning about parts of the body and the internal organs, give him or her a preview of the contents of Volume 14. Point out sections that talk about and show pictures of muscles, bones, the respiratory system, the heart and the blood system, the digestive system, the brain and the nervous system, the sensory organs, and so on. Look at some of the pictures together, and encourage your child to look at others. Read together and talk about any text that especially interests your child.

Curriculum enrichment guides

The following sections relate *Childcraft* to typical preschool, primary, and lower intermediate-grade curriculum objectives in six subject areas: (1) Language Arts and Literature; (2) Critical Thinking Skills; (3) Mathematics; (4) Science; (5) Social Studies; (6) Creative Arts; (7) Self-Understanding, Health, and Safety. Each section includes suggested introductory activities and a list of selections that can be used to extend and supplement classroom work.

The Curriculum Enrichment Guides for each section are arranged by topic of study. The entries used in the guides describe the content of the articles, and so do not always follow exactly the wording of the actual article titles.

The numbers following the entry indicate the volume and page where a selection or picture is found. For example, the entry Stonehenge, **10/114** refers to Volume 10, page 114.

Some entries refer only to an illustration, painting, photograph, or sculpture. This is because the illustration, painting, photograph, or sculpture is relevant to the topic even though the accompanying text may not be. An abbreviation or word in parentheses (illus., photo) indicates such an entry.

Language arts and literature

Listening

For information: (2–4) Read a short factual article about an animal or animal behavior (Volume 5), plant life (Volume 6), sea life (Volume 7), or a holiday (Volume 9). Then ask several questions that require children to recall details in the article.

For pleasure: (Preschool) Read stories in Volumes 1 and 2 and have students draw, color, or paint illustrations of the characters or events in the story.

Speaking

In discussions: (1–2, 2–4) Read a selection from Volume 8 that discusses a custom or way of life of a different country. Ask the children to tell how this behavior is like or different from what is done in the students' native culture.

Making presentations: (2–4) Challenge an individual student to read one of the math puzzles in Volume 13, Chapter 1, and work out (or read) the answer. Invite the student to present the puzzle to the rest of the class and, if the other students cannot figure it out, to explain the answer.

Poetry and choral reading: (Preschool) Teach one or more poems in Volumes 1 and 2 to the children until they can say the poem(s) in unison. Encourage good pronunciation and appropriate expression.

(1–2, 2–4) Invite the children to choose favorite poems from Volumes 1 to 3 and read them to the class. As needed, help individual students select poems at their reading level or prepare the poem for presentation.

Dramatics: (Preschool) Have the children make stick puppets as suggested in Volume 11, page 263. Call on pairs of children to have their puppets introduce themselves to each other.

(2–4) After the children have read a story in their reader or heard one of the stories in Volume 1 or 2, have them make paper-bag puppets of the characters in the story, following the directions in Volume 11, page 28. Then call on small groups of children to act out the story with their puppets.

Vocabulary

Recognizing context clues: (2–4) When reading a passage that explains a new term in context or with the help of an illustration, as in Volume 4 or Volume 7, point out the new term. Reread the passage and have the children raise their hands when they hear its meaning explained.

Using the glossary: (2–4) Distribute Volumes 4, 5, 6, 7, 8, 12, 13, and 14 to students. Have them turn to the glossaries of their volumes. Explain that a glossary is like a dictionary for that one book, and have students compare words listed in different volumes.

Identifying word origins: (1–2, 2–4) Read to the class Volume 14, pages 200–201, concerning words from different languages, or have students read the passage. Ask the students to name additional words from other languages that have become part of English. If necessary, tell them to think of names of foods from other countries.

Writing

Mechanics (prose vs. poetry): (1–2) Ask students to compare the selections in the "Nursery Rhymes" section (pages 11–65) and in the "Folk & Fairy Tales" section (pages 87–157) of Volume 1. Point out the use of lines in poetry and paragraphs in stories, the differences in the use of capital letters, and the difference in length.

Spelling: (2–4) Read "The Secret Word" (Volume 13, pages 14–15) to the class. (If appropriate, have the children work out the problem together.) Then set up a code for numerals 0–9, using letters in spelling words the class is studying. Challenge the students to create math problems whose answers, when coded, will translate into spelling words.

Uses of writing: (Preschool) Read to the class "Rosa-Too-Little" (Volume 1, pages 300–305) and discuss the story. Or, read the two short articles on writing party invitations (Volume 11, pages 302–303) and write a class invitation to an upcoming party to send to parents, school staff, or another class.

Original (creative) writing: (2–4) Read stories to the class from "Strange stories of the sea" (Volume 7, pages 255–265). Ask students to write stories of their own.

(1–2, 2–4) Point out, or read to the class, the student writing in Volume 14, pages 216–230. Make sure the children understand that this writing is by other children. Use one or more selections as a springboard for creative writing sessions with your class.

Report writing (research, outlining, verifying, revising): (2–4) Use articles in Volumes 4–14 as models of nonfiction writing. Read, for example, "How the Longest Rivers Got Their Names" (Volume 10, pages 118–119) and ask such questions as "What does the first paragraph tell you?" "How do the next paragraphs help you understand the first paragraph?" and "Is there any other information you need to understand this?" Or read "Paper-plate mask" (Volume 11, page 56) and ask "Are you told all you need to know?" and "What things help you follow the directions?"

Reading

Reading readiness: (Preschool) Reinforce your teaching of rhyming sounds by reading some rhymes in Volumes 1 and 2. Read each poem up to the concluding rhyme, and let the students provide the last word.

Reading in content areas: (2–4) Encourage students to read selections in Volumes 4 through 14 for information and to use their findings in oral or written reports, posters, or art projects.

Reading techniques—using illustrations: (Preschool, 1–2) Encourage students to read Volumes 4–14 for the information they can glean from pictures. Suggest that they use "Show and Tell" time to tell about the pictures they have examined.

Reading techniques—using graphic devices such as captions and illustrations: (1–2, 2–4) Ask questions about a selection whose answers can be found in the title or picture caption(s). Allow students a short time to find the answers, and let them tell what led them to a particular answer.

Literature appreciation

Awareness of style and word choice in poetry or prose: (1–2, 2–4) Use poems in Volumes 1, 2, and 3 to compare and contrast two types of writing or writing styles. For example, read Rossetti's "Who Has Seen the Wind?" and Stevenson's "The Wind" and "Windy Nights." (All three poems are in Volume 2, pages 296–297.) Ask about the different ways the poets show how we "see" the wind. Encourage the children to create original descriptions.

(2–4) After students have read or heard a selection from *Childcraft*, discuss the words the author uses and their special connotations. For example, in "Why the Bear Has a Stumpy Tail" (Volume 1, pages 96–97), the fox is described as "slinking along." Ask students whether they think "slinking" is a good descriptive word, and what reaction it causes in the listener. Ask students to think of other words that might be used in place of "slinking."

Childcraft selections in prose and poetry
(for independent reading)

(2–4) In addition to the activities listed above, your students may wish to read about the following topics in language arts:

Masks and Costumes
Paper-plate Mask, **11**/56
Costumes, **11**/246–259

Puppets and Marionettes
Puppets, **11**/28, 98, 144,
 262–270

About Speaking and Sound
Causes of Sound, **12**/240
Echoes, **12**/252–253
Singing and Speaking,
 12/272–273
My Voice Box, **12**/272–273;
 14/198–199

**Words—Meanings, Origins,
 Word Play**
American and British English,
 14/200–201

Body Language, **14**/210
English Words from Other
 Languages, **14**/200–201
Limericks, **3**/38–41
Onomatopoeia, **14**/202–203
Playing with Sounds and Words,
 14/202–203

About Listening
Learning to Listen, **14**/204
My Ears, **14**/80, 85, 150
"Seeing" with Your Ears, **12**/276
Stereophonic Sound,
 12/276–277
Using Your Eyes to "Listen,"
 14/208

Listening with Instruments
Hearing Aids, **14**/82
Listening in Special Ways,
 14/206

Stories
Birth of Christ (Saint Luke),
 9/307
Creation stories from different
 cultures, **8**/17–41
Eep's Valentine, **9**/79–83
The Fire Bringer, **12**/148–155
Independence Day (from *Farmer
 Boy*), **9**/216–225
Milo in Digitopolis (from *The
 Phantom Tollbooth*), **13**/94–113
My Mother Is the Most Beautiful
 Woman in the World,
 9/174–183

Poems

Nonfiction—Biographical Sketches

Critical thinking skills

Classification

(2–4) Ask students to look at the Tables of Contents and/or specific chapters of Volume 4, 5, 6, 7, or 12 and discuss how the topics are grouped.

Drawing comparisons and contrasts

(1–2, 2–4) Help students use various articles about animals and plants in Volumes 5, 6, and 7 to discover characteristics of specific types and differences between types. Read the articles to the class, or have students read them, and then discuss the information. Have small groups of students collect magazine and newspaper photographs illustrating some characteristics of a certain group of animals or plants, or have them make charts showing differences between groups.

Separating fact from opinion

(2–4) Read your choice of articles in "Strange stories of the sea" (Volume 7, pages 255–265), and ask students to listen for both the facts and the theories that have been suggested to explain the facts. Have students list the facts and theories on the chalkboard in two separate columns.

Logical reasoning

(2–4) Challenge students to work out the brain teasers in Volume 13, pages 5–21.
See also Science: *Scientific Method.*

Mathematics

Numbers and numerals

Counting: (Preschool) Use the rhymes in Volume 1, pages 76–78, to enliven learning to count.

(Preschool, 1–2) For enrichment, teach the students to count from one to ten in different languages, as shown in the chart in Volume 13, pages 80–83.

Place value: (2–4) As a small-group or independent project, use "Make your own abacus," Volume 13, pages 62–67.

Solid shapes: (2–4) Have individual students make and display some of the solid shapes for which directions and patterns are given in Volume 13, pages 252–261.

Measurements, ratio

Length: (2–4) Have students make a theodolite for class or individual use, following the directions in Volume 13, pages 211–213, and use a theodolite to measure the school building, flagpole, or another tall structure.

Childcraft readings in mathematics or related topics

(2–4) In addition to doing the activities listed above, your students may wish to read some of Volume 13, *Mathemagic,* on their own. See the Table of Contents and Index of Volume 13 for complete information about topics from counting through geometry through probability, all slanted toward interests of young readers.

In other volumes of *Childcraft,* the following passages discuss or relate to topics in mathematics:

Nature's Clock
The Four Seasons, **4**/220–223
High Tide, Low Tide, **4**/119
Moving into Daytime, **4**/217
Shadow Clock, **12**/182
The Sun's Boundary Lines, **4**/302
Why the Moon Changes Shapes,
  4/231–233

**Poems and Stories about
  Nature's Clock**
The Clock, **1**/85
Daylight-Saving Time, **2**/293

The Star, **1**/237
Star-Light, Star-Bright, **1**/62

Our Calendar
The Changing Calendar, **9**/24–26
Different Calendars, **9**/27–29
Seven Days Make a Week, **9**/17
Names of Days, Origins of,
  9/18–19
Names of Months, Origins of,
  9/33, 65, 101, 135, 177, 195,
  211, 235, 249, 269, 283, 299

Twelve Months Make a Year,
  9/20–21
When Does a Year Begin? **9**/22

Stories with Numbers
The Five Chinese Brothers,
  1/115–121
The Gingerbread Boy, **1**/89–91
Millions of Cats, **1**/258–263
The Three Bears, **1**/92–95
The Three Billy Goats Gruff,
  1/87–88
The Three Little Pigs, **1**/102–106

Science

Awareness of scientific concerns

(Preschool) Teach poems about the weather. (See list.)

Scientific method

Experimenting, observing: (1–2, 2–4) Have younger children do selected experiments in Volume 4 under your direction; have older students choose experiments to work on in small groups. With younger students, record the children's observations on the chalkboard or an experience chart. Older students can record their own observations.

Testing hypotheses: (2–4) Read your choice of articles in "Strange stories of the sea" in Volume 7 and have students listen for the objections raised to various theories that have been proposed. If the selection tells how a theory was tested, have students identify the process. If not, have students suggest possible tests.

(See also *Critical Thinking Skills*.)

Childcraft Readings on Topics in Science

(2–4) Five separate volumes of the *Childcraft* series are devoted to topics in science: Volumes 4, 5, 6, 7, and 12. Volume 14 also includes a wealth of scientific information about the human body. In addition, the literature volumes include numerous poems and stories about scientific topics, such as the weather; other volumes show scientific principles at work, as in articles in Volume 10 about famous buildings that make use of simple machines.

The list below is only a suggestion of the topics covered. For more complete information, see the Table of Contents and Index for Volumes 4, *World and Space;* 5, *About Animals;*

6, *The Green Kingdom;* 7, *The Story of the Sea;* 12, *How Things Work.*

Light

Activities:
Experiments with Light,
12/166–169
Shadow Clock, 12/172
Water-Drop Lens, 12/179

Understanding light:
The Colors in Sunlight, 4/192;
12/186–191
Electric Eye, 12/194
Electric Light, 12/196
Holograms, 12/204
Infrared Light, 12/190
Lasers, 12/202
Reflection, 12/164, 169, 174, 181
Refraction, 12/168, 176, 179,
180, 182, 192
Speed of Light, 4/212; 12/166
The Sun, 4/206–209; 12/163
Ultraviolet Light, 12/190

Sound

Understanding sound:
Acoustics, 10/70
Cause of Sound, 12/240
Conduction, 12/244
Echoes, 12/252
How We Hear, 14/80
Making a Tin-Can Telephone,
12/246
Pitch, 12/264–266
Speed of Sound, 12/244
A Stethoscope Amplifies Sound,
14/260
Voice Pictures, 14/260
Volume, 12/242

Sounds in nature:
Animal Hearing, 5/182

Bats, 12/278
Dog Whistle, 5/183
Earthquake, 4/36–37, 314
Fish Noise, 5/80
Geyser, 4/142; 10/25
Insect Noise, 5/124; 12/248
Meanings of Animal Sounds,
5/164
Thunder, 4/190
Tornado, 4/166
Volcanoes, 4/32–35, 314
Waterfalls, 4/131; 10/22, 28, 118

Stories and poems:
Cynthia in the Snow, 1/309
Hurricane, 4/168
Ice, 1/311
The Little Whistler, 1/189
I Speak, I Say, I Talk, 1/228
Soft Noises (poem), 14/254
Thaw, 1/308
Whistle for Willie, 1/185
Whistles, 1/189

Magnetism and electricity

Activities:
How to Make a Battery, 12/235
How to Make a Compass,
4/298–299
How to Make a Conduction
Tester, 12/218
How to Make an Electromagnet,
12/230
How to Make a Magnet, 12/15
How to Make Static Electricity,
12/215

Magnetism:
Compass Needle, 4/298–299
Magnetic Force, 12/14

Electromagnets:
Generator, 12/221
How Electromagnets Work,
12/228, 230
Phonograph, 12/284–285
Telephone, 12/236–237

Electricity in nature:
Static Electricity, 12/214

Understanding electricity:
Conductive, 12/232
Current Electricity, 12/216
Fuses and Circuit Breaker,
12/232
How a Battery Works, 12/234
How a Switch Works, 12/222
How Electricity Moves Through
Wires, 12/212–217
What Makes Light in a Light
Bulb? 12/224

Household electric appliances:
Hair Dryer, 12/227
Phonograph, 12/284–285
Radio, 12/237
Telephone, 12/236
Television, 12/208–209
Toaster, 12/227
Vacuum Cleaner, 12/54

The six simple machines:
Inclined Plane, 12/64
Lever, 12/60–63, 92–93
Pulley, 12/76
Screw, 12/68–69
Wedge, 12/66–67, 92
Wheel and Axle, 12/70–75,
92–93; 10/273

Social Studies

The Family: (Preschool) From Volumes 1, 2, and 3, choose poems about family life and family members. Read them to the children and have the children pick one to three favorites. As a class project, create a bulletin board display on "The Family," featuring the poems and illustrations drawn by the children.

The Community: (1–2, 2–4) Supplement a unit of study about ways the community meets such challenges as housing, transportation, and communication by reading or having students read from Volume 8 about how other communities meet these needs. Have students make collages on themes such as food, housing, and clothing, using photographs and original illustrations of examples from around the world.

Maps and globes, geography: (2–4) Use material about world geography in Volume 4 to develop an awareness of the areas of the world and to build a foundation for understanding map symbols. When students have a basic understanding of what a world map or globe represents, display a large world map or globe and post on it little flags at the places discussed in a volume you are using with the class—for example, in Volume 8, countries whose ways of life are illustrated; in Volume 9, places where events occurred or are commemorated by holidays; in Volume 10, famous places.

Community helpers, farm and town life, etc.: (1–2) Choose art activities from Volume 11 to enrich the study of these primary-grade social studies themes. For example, you could ask students to make clay models of farm animals, mobiles showing various means of transportation, puppets of community helpers, and paintings of events in local history.

Childcraft readings on topics in social studies

(2–4) The relationship of the individual to the community, and of the community to the physical world, is a major theme throughout the entire *Childcraft* series. Volumes 8 and 10 are dedicated exclusively to this theme. In addition, Volumes 4 and 10 discuss geographical concerns; Volumes 5, 6, and 7 consider people's responsibilities to preserve the environment; Volumes 9 and 10 present holidays and monuments that reflect national and cultural values; and the literature of Volumes 1, 2, and 3 touches on issues of importance to individuals and groups. Therefore, the list below only suggests the topics covered.

American heritage: Symbols
Eagle (adopted June 1782), **5**/50 (illus.)
Flag (adopted June 14, 1777), **9**/204–205
Liberty Bell (1753), **10**/88–89
Star-Spangled Banner, Story of (written Sept. 13–14, 1814; adopted by Congress March 1931), **10**/92–93
Statue of Liberty (1884), **10**/180

American heritage: Historic events, places, and holidays
Early exploration:
Leif Ericson Day (about A.D. 1000), **9**/271
Columbus Day (Oct. 12, 1492), **9**/274–275

Colonial days:
Mayflower (1620), **10**/197
Plymouth Rock (Dec. 21, 1620), **10**/197
First New England Thanksgiving Day (1621), **9**/292-293
Williamsburg (founded 1699), **10**/227–228
Mount Vernon (built 1743), **10**/241

George Washington's Birthday (Feb. 11/22, 1732–Dec. 14, 1799), **9**/88–89

Revolutionary War:
Independence Hall (built 1735; photo), **10**/89
Fourth of July (1776), **9**/214–215

The new nation:
White House (1800), **10**/40–41
U.S. Capitol (1800; photo), **10**/40
U.S.S. *Constitution* (built 1797; saved 1833), **10**/233–234
The Battle of the Alamo (Feb. 23–Mar. 6, 1836), **10**/209
Donner Pass (1846–1847), **10**/247

Creative arts

Music—Rhythm band: (Preschool) Have the children create their own rhythm band instruments as described in Volume 11, pages 12–15. Have them use the instruments to accompany themselves in singing or singing along with a record.

Art–Sculpture: (1–2) Have students create a clay menagerie, as suggested in Volume 11, pages 116–117.

Art—Drawing: (2–4) Ask students to draw plants, animals, or scenes with both, using illustrations in Volumes 5, 6, and 7 for reference.

Art—Painting: (2–4) Read from Volume 1, 2, or 3 several poems with strong moods. Ask the students to paint a picture or an abstract design that expresses the mood of one of them.

Childcraft readings in the creative arts

(2–4) Volume 11 contains directions for all sorts of creative activities. See the Table of Contents and Index for a clear idea of what it offers for group and class projects. In addition, other volumes give directions for making such things as musical instruments and contain many photographs of examples of natural and artistically created beauty, which contribute to art appreciation. Here is a partial list of activities children can enjoy, working under supervision or independently.

Self-understanding, health, and safety

Games: (Preschool, 1–2, 2–4) Volume 11 contains a variety of games that provide whole-body movement and exercise.

Behavior, manners, and attitudes: (1–2) Read and talk about poems and stories in Volumes 1, 2, and 3 that concern feelings and values. For example, "The Sheep with the Wooden Collar" develops the difference between entertaining with an imaginary story and fibbing. (See list.)

Understanding the body: (2–4) Encourage students to use Volume 14 as a reference book to help them understand how their bodies function and grow.

Careers: (2–4) Over several weeks or months, read to the class the job descriptions found in Volumes 4 ("People Who Study the World and Space"), 5 ("People and Animals"), 6 ("People and Plants"), 7 ("People Who Work on the Sea"), 8 ("People Watchers"), and 13 ("People Who Work with Numbers and Shapes"). Have students find magazine pictures to make posters of careers that interest them. Also, encourage them to find and share books in the school library or local library that tell about careers.

Childcraft readings in self-understanding, health, and safety

(2–4) Volume 14 answers children's questions about their physical, intellectual, emotional, and social growth. See the Table of Contents and Index of Volume 14 for a complete listing of topics. Related material throughout the other volumes can be used to help build a good self-image as well as good health and safety habits. Much of the literature of Volumes 1, 2, and 3, for example, contributes to self-understanding, while discussing the effects of weather (Volume 4) can lead to better health practices.

Air and water pollution
Air Pollution, **5**/285
Is Air Something?, **4**/148
Radiation Safety Check, **12**/294
Water Pollution, **5**/285
Waves from Space, **4**/282
A Wrapper of Air, **4**/146

Behavior, manners, and attitudes
Animal Instinct, **14**/192
Do I Have To?, **14**/112
What's Right and Wrong?, **14**/188

Games and sports
Card Games, **11**/286
Indoor and Outdoor Games, **11**/274–285
National Professional Football Hall of Fame, **10**/100
Roll and Toss Games, **11**/32–33

Safety devices
Radar, **12**/298–299
Seat Belts, **12**/8

Stories and poems about self-understanding, health, and safety

Accidents:
Doctor Foster, **1**/57
The Flight of Icarus, **3**/208
Freddy, **2**/251
Humpty Dumpty, **1**/20
Jack and Jill, **1**/34
J's the Jumping Jay-Walker, **2**/251
Pooh Goes Visiting, **1**/201
Spring Rain, **2**/151

How to use the general index

This General Index is a key to all of the material in volumes 1 through 15 of *Childcraft*—with the exception of the titles of the poems in volumes 1, 2, and 3, which can be found using the title indexes in those volumes.

The thousands of pages in *Childcraft* are filled with information on many subjects, in both text and pictures. Frequently, different aspects of a subject are covered in more than one volume. Although each volume has its own index, this General Index is the only place to learn where in *Childcraft* you can find *all* the information on a subject.

The illustration on the opposite page shows the special features used in the General Index and in the individual volume indexes. To make the best use of any of the indexes, you should be aware of these various features.

The entries in dark type are of two kinds: specific and general. A specific entry is one that is the name of a person (**Aardema, Verna**), a place (**Acropolis**), or a thing (**Achernar**). A general entry is one that covers a broad area or field of interest (**accidents, adult, Afghanistan**). All general entries, and many specific entries, are subdivided to help you locate quickly the exact information you are looking for. One feature especially helpful for children is the use of an identifier in parentheses after many of the entries, as **Achernar** (star).

Cross-references guide you to additional headings and preferred headings. For example, if you are looking for information about adults, the cross-reference, *see also* **parents**, tells you to look under that heading also. If you are looking for information about agriculture, the cross-reference, **agriculture**, *see* **farming**, tells you where to look for the information.

The entries are arranged in alphabetical order, letter by letter, regardless of the number of words. Some entries are inverted (**Aborigines, Australian**), so that the key word in each entry is alphabetized.

The numbers following an entry or subentry (**15**/262) give the volume number in dark type and the page number or numbers in light type. When there are references to more than one volume, the volumes are listed in numerical order.

If there is information in both words and pictures, the words *(with pictures)* appear after the page number or numbers. If the reference is to a picture only, the word *(picture)* appears after the volume and page number or numbers.

Author entry ——————→ **Aardema, Verna** (author)

Title subhead —————→ *Why Mosquitoes Buzz in*
(in italics) *People's Ears,* **1**/130–137

Aborigines, Australian (people)

cave painting, **10**/139 —————→ Volume number
(in boldface) and
measuring temperature, **13**/208 ←— page number
Reference to text *only*

origin of, **7**/49

riddle, **8**/224

story from
Why the Kangaroo Hops on
Two Legs, **3**/83–86

Title entry —————→ ***Abu Ali: Three Tales of the*** —————— Work identified by type
(in italics) ***Middle East*** (story), **2**/30–39

accidents, 15/170–177

baby's, **15**/29, **15**/170–173

eyes, **15**/236 —————— Volume 15 references
are for parents and
poisoning, **15**/277–281 teachers

preschooler's, **15**/61–62,
15/170–175

self-care by child, **15**/139–140

toddler's, **15**/41–42 *(with* —————— Identifier
picture), **15**/170–174

Specific subject entry —→ **Achernar** (star), **4**/273 *(picture)*

Acropolis (Athens, Greece),
10/105, *with picture*

Addams, Jane (social reformer),
10/244

adoption of child, 14/110,
15/102–105

General subject entry ——→ **adult** —————— References listed
in volume order
learning from, **14**/142–143 *(with*
pictures)

preteen attitude to, **15**/90–92

Cross-reference to —————→ *see also* **parents**
additional heading

Afghanistan (Asia)

handmade goods, **8**/118 *(with* ←— Reference to *both*
text and picture(s)
picture)

housing, **8**/94 *(picture)*

prayer, **8**/176 *(picture)*

road sign, **8**/191 *(picture)* ←—————— Reference to picture(s) *only*

Cross-reference to —————→ **agriculture,** *see* **farming**
preferred heading

amphibian (animal group), **5**/26
(with picture), **5**/98–109 *(with*
pictures)

biggest, **5**/201 *(with picture)*

prehistoric, **5**/226 *(with picture)*

smallest, **5**/201 *(with picture)*

amphibians, names of

caecilian, **5**/103 *(with picture)*

frog, *see* **frog**

newt, **5**/103 *(with pictur*

salamander, *see* **sal**

toad, *see* **t**

anemone, *see* **sea anemone**
anesthetics (medication), **15/**182
Angel, Jimmy (aviator), **10/**123
angel costume, 11/248–249 *(with picture)*
Angel Falls (Venezuela), **10/**123 *(with pictures)*
angelfish, 7/120–121, **7/**122 *(picture)*
anger, 14/240 *(with picture)*
  and divorce, **15/**122–123
anglaspis (prehistoric fish), **5/**224 *(picture)*
angle (shape), **13/**220–221 *(with pictures)*
  in triangles, **13/**222–223 *(with pictures)*
  measuring height with, **13/**211–213 *(with pictures)*
angler fish, 7/132–133 *(with picture)*
  deep-sea, **7/**139–140 *(with picture)*
animal
  and energy, **12/**25
  biggest, **5/**142–143 *(with picture)*, **5/**200–201 *(with pictures)*
  bites, *see* **bites and stings**
  extinct, **6/**259
  in desert, **6/**77 *(with picture)*
  in evergreen forest, **6/**69 *(with picture)*
  in grasslands, **6/**57 *(with picture)*
  in national parks (Africa), **10/**153 *(with pictures)*
  in ponds, **6/**61 *(with picture)*
  in rain forest, **6/**73 *(with picture)*
  instinct and training, **14/**192–193 *(with pictures)*
  in tundra, **6/**81 *(with picture)*
  in woodland, **6/**53 *(with picture)*
  in zoos, *see* **zoo**
  movement, **5/**8 *(with pictures)*
  playing with, **8/**138–139 *(with pictures)*
  size of, **14/**29 *(with picture)*
  smallest, **5/**200–201 *(with pictures)*
  survival strategies, **5/**146–156 *(with pictures)*
  unusual, **5/**194–197

animal *(continued)*
  see also names of, such as **ant; snake;** *and* names of groups, such as **mammal; reptile**
animal costume, 11/21 *(with picture)*, **11/**250–251 *(with pictures)*, **14/**225 *(picture)*
animal figure
  clay, **11/**112–113 *(with pictures)*, **11/**116–117 *(with pictures)*
  jewelry, **11/**228 *(with picture)*
  paper, **11/**28–29 *(with pictures)*
  pine-cone, **11/**146 *(picture)*
  shell, **11/**149 *(with picture)*, **11/**150 *(pictures)*
  stone, **11/**142–143 *(with pictures)*
  stuffed, **11/**235 *(with picture)*
  wood, **11/**217 *(picture)*
animals, poems about, 1/39, **1/**51, **1/**66, **1/**198–199, **1/**227–228, **3/**152–153, **3/**245, **14/**224
animals, stories about
  Ant and the Dove, The, **1/**164
  Baba Yaga's Geese, **3/**114–118
  Bear Called Paddington, A, **2/**237–250
  Bremen Town Musicians, The, **3/**88–92
  Bunyip of Berkeley's Creek, The, **1/**231–235
  Cat on the Dovrefell, The, **1/**100–101
  Crow and the Pitcher, The, **1/**160
  Dog and the Bone, The, **1/**165
  Fire Bringer, The, **12/**148–155
  Foolish, Timid Rabbit, The, **1/**166–168
  Frog and Toad, **2/**44–53
  Hare and the Tortoise, The, **1/**161, **8/**218
  Harry the Dirty Dog, **2/**92–97
  Homecoming, The, **3/**188–195
  How the Camel Got His Hump, **1/**268–271
  How the Turtle Saved His Own Life, **1/**172–173
  Hunter in the Darkness, **12/**278–279
  I Find Wol, **3/**24–31
  Lion and the Mouse, The, **1/**159

animals, stories about *(continued)*
  Little Red Hen, The, **1/**98–99
  Millions of Cats, **1/**258–263
  Monkey and the Crocodile, The, **1/**169–171
  Mother, Mother, I Want Another, **2/**6–13
  Nina Terrance, **3/**131–142
  Riddles, The, **2/**76–81
  Sheep with the Wooden Collar, The, **1/**147–156
  Shepherd Boy and the Wolf, The, **1/**162–163
  Tale of Peter Rabbit, The, **1/**192–196
  Three Bears, The, **1/**92–95
  Three Billy Goats Gruff, The, **1/**87–88
  Three Little Pigs, The, **1/**102–106
  Toad's Escape, **3/**6–21
  Whistle for Willie, **1/**185–188
  Why Mosquitoes Buzz in People's Ears, **1/**130–136
  Why the Bear Has a Stumpy Tail, **1/**96–97
  Why the Kangaroo Hops on Two Legs, **3/**83–86
anklebone, 14/37 *(pictures)*
  splint for broken, **15/**196–197 *(with picture)*
anniversary
  wedding, **9/**16
Anniversary of the Revolution (Soviet Union), **9/**287 *(with picture)*
Anniversary of the Throne (Morocco), **9/**10 *(with picture)*
annual plants, 6/150–151 *(with pictures)*
Annunciation, Feast of the (Greece), **9/**128–129
anorexia nervosa (disorder), **15/**182
ant, 5/174 *(with picture)*
  fable about
    Ant and the Dove, The, **1/**164
  harvester, **5/**129 *(with picture)*, **5/**160 *(picture)*
  wood ant, **5/**174 *(with picture)*
Ant and the Dove, The (story), **1/**164

B

C

F

f (letter)
rhyme about, **1/**68
fable (story), *see* **Aesop**
face, 14/18–19 *(with picture)*
decoration of, **8/**247 *(picture),*
8/248 *(with pictures)*
individual differences, **14/**256
parts of, **14/**20–21 *(with pictures)*
two sides of, **14/**264–265 *(with pictures)*
factory work, 8/116–117 *(with pictures)*
Fahrenheit scale (temperature measurement), **13/**209 *(with picture)*
fainting, 15/237 *(with picture)*
fairy tales, *see* **elves and fairies** (stories about)
faith, religious, *see* **religion**
fall, *see* **autumn**
falling star, 4/259, **4/**260–262 *(with pictures)*
Fallopian tube in menstruation, 15/265 *(with pictures)*
False Cross (star group), **4/**273 *(picture)*
family, 14/110 *(with pictures)*
around the world
Ashanti, **8/**56–57 *(with pictures)*
Bushmen, **8/**14–15, **8/**182–183, **8/**204–205 *(with pictures)*
Dyak, **8/**52 *(with pictures)*
Eskimo, **8/**48–49 *(with pictures)*
Israeli kibbutz, **8/**50–51 *(with pictures)*
Japanese, **8/**54–55
Norwegian, **8/**54 *(with pictures)*
United States, **8/**14–15
customs
becoming an adult, **8/**60 *(with pictures)*
birth ceremonies, **8/**58–59 *(with pictures)*
death, **8/**64–65 *(with pictures)*
wedding, **8/**62 *(with pictures)*
heredity, **14/**106–107 *(with pictures)*

family *(continued)*
life together, **14/**116–117 *(with pictures)*
adopted child, **15/**102–105
divorce, **15/**122–123
emotionally disturbed child, **15/**106–109
home, **14/**130–131 *(with pictures)*
mentally retarded child, **15/**145
recreation, **14/**121, **14/**126–127 *(with pictures)*
religion, **14/**122 *(with picture)*
remarriage, **15/**123
responsibilities, **14/**113
rules, **8/**152 *(with pictures)*
travel, **15/**153
vacation trips, **14/**140–141 *(with pictures)*
work, **14/**118–119 *(with pictures)*
working mother, **15/**154–156
poems about, **1/**16, **1/**38–39
relatives, **14/**114 *(with picture)*
stories about
Come Away! Come Away!, **1/**276–295
Rosa-Too-Little, **1/**300–307
Tale of Peter Rabbit, The, **1/**192–196
see also **parents**
Family Dog, The (story), **2/**124–138
family name, 8/66–67
family tree, 14/114–115 *(picture)*
fan, 11/41 *(with pictures)*
Farjeon, Eleanor (poet)
Bedtime, **2/**166
Kitten, A, **1/**266
Moon-Come-Out, **1/**62
Mrs. Peck-Pigeon, **1/**230
Night Will Never Stay, The, **2/**234
Farmer Boy (story from), **9/**216–225
Farmer in the Dell (game), **11/**283
farming, 6/228 *(with pictures),* **8/**112 *(with pictures)*
growing peanuts, **10/**143 *(with picture)*
step farming, **10/**140 *(with pictures)*

farsightedness, 14/78, **15/**237–238
fasting (religious practice)
Lent, **9/**96–97
Ramadan, **9/**202–203
Yom Kippur, **9/**259
father
and working mother, **15/**156
poems about, **1/**227, **2/**236, **2/**274–275
story about
Cow-Tail Switch, The, **3/**32–37
see also **parents**
Father's Day (United States), **9/**172
fats (nutrition), **15/**273–274
Faubion, Dorothy (poet)
Hump, the Escalator, **12/**94–95 *(with picture)*
fear, 14/241 *(with picture)*
day care, **15/**117
of death, **15/**127–128
preschooler's, **15/**57–58
Feast of the . . ., *see* name of the feast, such as **Weeks, Feast of**
feathers, bird, 5/50, **5/**52 *(with pictures)*
February, 9/62–65 *(with pictures)*
feeding the baby, 15/18–21
feeler (antenna) **of insect, 5/**112–113, **5/**185 *(with pictures)*
feeling, *see* **touch**
feelings, *see* **emotion**
feet, *see* **foot**
Felt, Sue (author)
Rosa-Too-Little, **1/**300–307
fern (plant), **6/**24–25 *(with pictures)*
ostrich plume, **6/**147 *(picture)*
staghorn, **6/**98 *(with picture)*
whisk, **6/**199 *(picture)*
Ferris wheel (Vienna), **10/**273 *(with picture)*
fertilizer, leaves as, 6/263
festival
costumes, **8/**143 *(pictures),* **8/**269
Festival of Lanterns (Japan), **9/**226 *(with picture)*
fetus (unborn child), **14/**96–99 *(with picture),* **15/**132

G

g (letter)
rhyme about, 1/68
gadget printing, 11/78 (with
picture)
Gág, Wanda (author)
Millions of Cats, 1/258–263
gagging, 15/243
Galapagos Islands (Pacific
Ocean), 10/154–155 (with
pictures)
galaxy, 4/280 (with pictures)
Milky Way, 4/278–279 (with
pictures)
gale (weather), 4/161 (with
pictures)
Galileo (scientist), 10/281
gall, insect, 6/42 (with pictures)
gall bladder, 14/67 (picture)
galleon (warship), 7/67–69 (with
picture)
gallon (unit of measurement),
13/180–181
game board, 11/61 (picture),
11/237 (with pictures)
games
blindfold, 8/131 (with pictures)
boards for, 11/236–237 (with
pictures)
card, 11/288–290
cat's cradle, 8/128 (with picture)
guessing, 11/294–295 (with
pictures)
Hanukkah, 9/318 (with picture)
indoor or outdoor, 11/26 (with
picture), 11/32–33 (with
pictures), 11/279–283 (with
picture)
jacks, 8/128 (with picture)
marbles, 8/128 (with picture)
outdoor, 11/274–275 (with
pictures), 11/278 (with picture)
party, 11/308–309 (with pictures)
pencil and paper, 11/237 (with
pictures), 11/291–293 (with
picture)
poems about, 1/60–61
prizes, 11/310 (with picture)
riddles, 8/224–225

games (continued)
tree-path, 6/172–186 (with
pictures)
see also pretend play; puzzle;
sports
game warden, work of, 5/256
(with picture), 5/286 (with
picture)
gamma globulin (part of blood),
15/244
infectious hepatitis, 15/250
gamma ray, 4/282
Gandhi, Mohandas (Father of
India), 9/242 (with picture)
gang, preteen, 15/90–94
Ganges River (India), 10/64 (with
picture)
gannet (bird), 7/251
Ganymede (moon of Jupiter),
4/252–253
garden, 10/13 (with picture),
10/278 (with picture)
poem about, 6/144
poems about, 1/35, 1/80–81
tips, 6/156–159 (with pictures)
see also gardens, kinds of
gardener, work of, 6/232 (with
picture)
gardens, famous, 6/161–169
(with pictures), 10/266 (with
picture)
gardens, kinds of
aquarium, 6/142
flower, 6/150–153 (with pictures)
formal, 6/164 (with pictures)
fun, 6/154 (with pictures)
indoor, 6/138–141, 6/162 (with
pictures)
natural, 6/166 (with pictures)
outdoor, 6/144 (with pictures)
rock, 6/147 (with pictures)
terrarium, 6/142 (with pictures)
vegetable, 6/148–149 (with
pictures)
Gardner, John (poet)
Lizard, The, 3/119
gargoyles (statues), 10/76 (with
picture)
Garland, Hamlin (poet)
Do You Fear the Wind?, 3/152
gas, 12/109, 12/111, 12/142
changing to liquid, 12/114–115
(with picture)

gas (continued)
freezing with, 12/300
from burning wood, 12/116–117
fuel, 12/29
hydrogen, 12/105
in air, 4/148–149 (with pictures)
in nebula, 4/276 (with picture)
in refrigerator, 12/147
in solar system, 4/13–15 (with
pictures)
in sun, 4/207–208 (with pictures),
4/211 (with pictures)
jet plane, 12/292
nitrogen, 4/148, 4/153
oxygen, 4/148–149, 4/153,
12/105
water vapor, 12/112
gasoline
energy from, 12/24–25
engine, 12/118–119 (with
picture)
gastropod (animal group)
abalone, 7/180 (with picture)
snails, 7/178–180 (with pictures)
gazelle, 5/146 (picture), 5/157,
5/206
gears, 12/89 (with picture)
project, 12/90–91 (with pictures)
gecko (lizard), 5/87
shedding skin, 5/91 (picture)
West Indian, 5/200 (picture)
Geiger counter (instrument),
4/76
gemstone, 4/83–85 (with
pictures)
crown jewels, 10/87 (with
pictures)
diamond, 10/134 (with pictures)
generator, electrical, 12/34,
12/221, 12/295
genes (heredity), 14/106–107,
15/251–253
gentian, mountain (plant), 6/84
(picture)
geologist, work of, 4/307 (with
picture), 7/272 (picture)
George, Jean Craighead (author)
Nina Terrance, 3/131–142
George, Saint, 9/156–157 (with
picture)
Georgia
Stone Mountain, 10/184–185
(with pictures)

i (letter)
rhyme about, **1**/69
Icarus, legend about, 3/208–211
ice
and heat energy, **12**/134–135
experiment, **12**/114–115 *(with picture)*
glaciers, **4**/52–55 *(with pictures)*
hail and sleet, **4**/194 *(with pictures)*
icicles, **4**/200 *(with picture)*
in polar regions, **4**/50–51 *(with picture)*
melting, **12**/110–111 *(with picture)*
trick with, **12**/138–139 *(with picture)*
iceberg, 4/122–123 *(with pictures)*
Titanic, **7**/79–80
Iceland, 7/59
geysers, **10**/25 *(with picture)*
Mount Hekla, **4**/33 *(picture)*
personal names, **8**/67, **8**/69
Surtsey Island, **4**/48–49 *(pictures)*
ichthyostega (prehistoric amphibian), **5**/227 *(picture)*
icicle, 4/200 *(with picture)*
icosahedron (solid shape), **13**/258 *(with pictures)*
Id al-Fitr (Islamic holy day), **9**/203
identical twins, 14/107 *(picture),* **15**/251 *(picture)*
identification bracelet, hospital, 14/103, **14**/177 *(with pictures)*
I Doubt It (card game), **11**/288
I Find Wol (story), **3**/24–31
igloo (house), **8**/94
igneous rock, 4/61–62 *(with picture)*
iguana (lizard), **10**/155 *(with picture)*
I Leave the Island (story), **3**/164–173
Illinois
Bahá'í House of Worship, **10**/72 *(with picture)*

Illinois *(continued)*
statue of Lincoln (Quincy), **10**/186 *(with picture)*
see also **Chicago**
illness, *see* **sickness**
imagination, 14/214–215 *(with pictures)*
of preschooler, **15**/54
poems about, **14**/226
immigrant, 8/262–263 *(pictures)*
immunization, 15/256–258
baby's, **15**/28
day-care centers, **15**/120
diphtheria, **15**/227
for communicable diseases, **15**/211
poliomyelitis, **15**/281
schedule for, **15**/257
shots, **15**/289–290 *(with picture)*
smallpox, **15**/294 *(with pictures)*
tetanus, **15**/304
vaccines, **15**/228
whooping cough, **15**/312
Imperial Palace (Tokyo), **10**/54 *(with picture)*
impetigo (disorder), **15**/258 *(with pictures)*
diaper rash, **15**/226
symptoms, **15**/76
Inca Indians
Machu Picchu (ruins), **10**/103 *(with pictures)*
inch (unit of length), **13**/178–179
incisors (teeth), **15**/302 *(with pictures)*
inclined plane, 12/64–65, **12**/69, **12**/88, **12**/94–95 *(with pictures)*
incubation period, 15/210
Independence Day
Brazil, **9**/255
Ghana, **9**/11
Greece, **9**/128–129 *(with picture)*
India, **9**/242
Indonesia, **9**/243 *(with picture)*
Mexico, **9**/260–261 *(with picture)*
United States, **9**/214–215 *(with pictures)*
story about
Independence Day, **9**/216–225
see also **Bastille Day; National Day**
Independence Day (story), **9**/216–225

Independence Hall (Philadelphia), **10**/89 *(with picture)*
India (Asia)
Botanic Garden (Calcutta), **6**/169 *(picture)*
Buddhism, **8**/172–173
food, **8**/78, **8**/81
guttak (game), **8**/128 *(with picture)*
Hinduism, **8**/166–167 *(with pictures)*
Hindu numbers, **13**/73, **13**/76–77 *(with pictures)*
holidays and festivals
Divali, **9**/276–277 *(with pictures)*
Independence Day, **9**/242
New Year, **9**/39
Republic Day, **9**/58–59 *(with picture)*
house, **8**/240 *(picture)*
jewelry, **8**/247 *(picture)*
pedicab, **8**/236 *(picture)*
physical fitness, **14**/124 *(picture)*
riddle, **8**/224
stories from, **1**/268–271
Foolish, Timid Rabbit, The, **1**/166–168
How the Turtle Saved His Own Life, **1**/172–173
Monkey and the Crocodile, The, **1**/169–171
Toda (people), **8**/251 *(picture)*
Varanasi, **10**/64 *(with picture)*
Indian, American
All American Indian Days, **9**/253
American Indian Day, **9**/252
American Indian Exposition, **9**/252–253
arrowheads, **8**/259 *(picture)*
Battle of Little Big Horn, **10**/216 *(with pictures)*
dancing, **8**/268 *(picture)*
folk tales, **8**/218
houses and shelters
cliff dwelling, **8**/92 *(with picture),* **10**/110–111 *(with picture)*
hogan, **8**/95 *(picture)*
pueblo, **8**/101 *(with picture)*
wickiup, **10**/237 *(with picture)*
Indian City, U.S.A. (Oklahoma), **10**/237 *(with pictures)*

J

N

n (letter)
rhyme about, **1**/71
nail (part of body), **14**/49 *(with pictures)*
care of, **15**/269–270 *(with pictures)*
of baby, **15**/16
nail (tool), **12**/66
kinds of, **11**/199 *(picture)*
name
family, **8**/66–67
given, **8**/68–69
Namibia (Africa)
toy, **8**/144 *(picture)*
nanosecond (unit of time), **13**/205
nap for toddler, 15/37
narwhal (whale), **7**/237 *(with picture)*
nasal cavity, 14/57 *(picture),* **14**/86 *(with pictures)*
adenoids, **15**/177–178 *(with picture)*
breathing, **14**/38 *(with pictures)*
see also **nose**
Nash, Ogden (poet)
Tale of Custard the Dragon, The, **1**/272
National Botanic Garden (South Africa), **6**/166–167 *(picture)*
National Day (Nigeria), **9**/270 *(with picture)*
national park, *see* **park, national**
naturalist, work of, 5/252 *(with picture)*
nature
poems about, **2**/233, **3**/296–297
nature crafts
helpful hints, **11**/134–136 *(with pictures)*
projects, **11**/132 *(picture),* **11**/137 *(with pictures),* **11**/138–139 *(pictures),* **11**/140 *(with picture),* **11**/141 *(picture)*
nature window (craft), **11**/138–139 *(picture)*

nautilus (mollusk)
chambered, **7**/174–175 *(with pictures),* **7**/194 *(with pictures)*
paper, **7**/193 *(picture)*
Nautilus (submarine), **7**/86–87 *(with picture)*
Navajo Indian, 8/7 *(picture)*
hogan, **8**/95 *(picture)*
jewelry, **8**/246
names, **8**/69
Navajo Nation Fair (Arizona), **9**/251–252 *(with picture)*
navel (part of body), **14**/25 *(with picture),* **15**/270
baby's, **15**/15–16
umbilical hernia, **15**/253–254
navigation, 7/64–65 *(with pictures),* **7**/268 *(picture)*
by stars, **4**/268
Navy, 7/270–271 *(pictures)*
Ndebele (African people)
house, **8**/241 *(picture)*
wall painting, **8**/233 *(with picture)*
nearsightedness, 14/78 *(with pictures),* **15**/270–271 *(with pictures)*
Nebuchadnezzar (king of Babylon), **10**/13 *(with picture)*
nebula, 4/276 *(with pictures)*
neck (part of body)
injury to, **15**/197
lymph glands in, **15**/301 *(with picture)*
nectar, 6/39, **6**/210
needle (plant part)
identifying tree by, **6**/172–187 *(pictures),* **6**/191 *(picture)*
on desert plant, **6**/75
on evergreen tree, **6**/36–37 *(with pictures)*
needle, phonograph, 12/285
needle, sewing, 11/154 *(with pictures),* **12**/66
how to thread, **11**/155
weaving, **11**/178 *(with pictures)*
negative number, 13/152–153 *(with pictures)*
neighborhood, 14/134
stores in, **14**/136–137 *(with picture)*
Nelson, Horatio (admiral), **10**/171 *(with pictures)*

nephritis (disease), **15**/271
Neptune (god), **7**/262
Neptune (planet), **4**/242 *(picture),* **4**/257 *(with picture)*
nerves, 14/46 *(with pictures)*
brain and, **14**/70, **14**/73 *(with pictures)*
feeling pain, **14**/166
work of
in ear, **14**/80, **14**/84 *(with pictures)*
in elbow, **14**/186
in eye, **12**/180, **14**/76 *(with pictures)*
in mouth, **14**/89
in nose, **14**/87 *(with picture)*
in skin, **14**/91 *(with picture)*
nervous system
ataxia, **15**/186
epilepsy (disorder), **15**/234–235
Saint Vitus's dance (chorea), **15**/203
Ness, Evaline (author)
Sam, Bangs & Moonshine, **2**/154–165
nest
alligator, **5**/88 *(with picture)*
bird, **5**/56–57 *(pictures),* **5**/62–63 *(with pictures),* **5**/64–65 *(pictures)*
wood-ant, **5**/174 *(with picture)*
Netherlands, The (Europe)
barge families, **8**/208–209 *(with picture)*
children, **8**/189 *(pictures)*
dikes and windmills, **10**/136 *(with picture)*
holidays and festivals
Feast of Saint Nicholas, **9**/302–303 *(with picture)*
Madurodam (miniature city), **10**/274 *(with picture)*
nursery rhyme, **1**/37
tulips, **6**/233 *(picture),* **6**/248 *(with picture)*
nettle (plant), **6**/133 *(picture)*
Nevada
Hoover Dam, **10**/147 *(with picture)*
New Jersey
Duke Gardens, **6**/163 *(picture)*

O

Paris *(continued)*
Statue of Liberty, **10**/180 *(with picture)*
see also **France**
Parish, Peggy (author)
Teach Us, Amelia Bedelia, **2**/102–117
park, amusement
Disney World (Florida), **10**/270 *(with pictures)*
Prater (Vienna), **10**/273 *(with picture)*
Tivoli (Copenhagen), **10**/269 *(with pictures)*
park, national
Ayers Rock—Mount Olga (Australia), **10**/139 *(with picture)*
Crater Lake (Oregon), **10**/201 *(with picture)*
Gettysburg (Pennsylvania), **10**/220 *(with picture)*
in Africa, **10**/153 *(with pictures)*
Mesa Verde (Colorado), **10**/110–111 *(with picture)*
Yellowstone (Wyoming), **10**/25
Parker, K. Langloh (author)
Why the Kangaroo Hops on Two Legs, **3**/83–86
parliament (government)
Australia, **10**/52–53 *(with picture)*
Canada, **10**/42 *(with pictures)*
Great Britain, **10**/45 *(with pictures)*
Japan, **10**/54 *(with picture)*
Sweden, **10**/50 *(with picture)*
parrot (bird), **5**/60 *(with picture)*
parrot fish, **5**/76
Parthenon (temple), **10**/105 *(with picture)*
party, **11**/298–311
activities, **11**/306–307 *(with picture)*
check list, **11**/311
decoration, **11**/302–303 *(with pictures)*
favors, **11**/303 *(with pictures)*
food, **11**/304–305 *(with picture)*
punch, **9**/39 *(with picture)*
games, **11**/308–309 *(with pictures)*
inviting guests, **11**/300–301 *(with pictures)*

party *(continued)*
prizes, **11**/310 *(with picture)*
when to give, **11**/299
passenger liner, **7**/88
Titanic, **7**/78–82 *(with pictures)*
work on, **7**/268 *(picture)*
passionflower, **6**/72 *(picture)*
Passover (Jewish holy days), **9**/140–141 *(with picture)*
Pass the Orange (game), **11**/308 *(with picture)*
paste, papier-mâché, **11**/89 *(with picture)*
patch test for allergy, **15**/180 *(with pictures)*
Patrick, Saint, **9**/108–109 *(with picture)*
Patriots' Day (Massachusetts), **9**/153–154
Patterson, Penny (psychologist), **5**/254 *(picture)*
Pavo (star group), **4**/272 *(with picture)*
pea (plant), **6**/208 *(with picture)*
peanut, **6**/213 *(with picture)*
pea, sweet (plant), **6**/151 *(picture)*
Peace Memorial Park (Hiroshima), **10**/235 *(with picture)*
peach (fruit), **6**/209 *(with picture)*
peacock, **5**/50 *(picture)*
peanut (plant), **6**/213 *(with picture)*
study of, **10**/143 *(with pictures)*
pearl (gem), **7**/189 *(picture)*
formation of, **7**/184
peat, **4**/91
pecan (nut), **6**/213 *(picture)*
Peddler of Ballaghaderreen (story), **9**/110–123
peer group
of preteen, **15**/90–93
social problems in, **15**/82
pelican, **5**/20 *(picture)*, **7**/251
pencil holder, **11**/131 *(picture)*
pencil sharpener, **12**/73 *(with picture)*
pendulum clock, **13**/205
penguin, **5**/8, **5**/58, **7**/252 *(with picture)*, **12**/128 *(with picture)*
emperor, **5**/12 *(picture)*, **5**/163
king, **5**/252 *(picture)*

penguin costume, **11**/251 *(with picture)*
penicillin (medicine), **6**/216
penis (part of body), **14**/45 *(with picture)*, **14**/69
circumcision, **15**/16
secondary sex development, **15**/98
Pennsylvania
Liberty Bell (Philadelphia), **10**/89 *(with picture)*
Longwood Gardens (Kennett Square), **6**/163 *(picture)*
pen pal letters, **8**/200 *(with pictures)*
pentagon (shape), **13**/242–243 *(with pictures)*
dodecahedron made from, **13**/261 *(with pictures)*
pentagram (shape), **13**/242–243 *(with pictures)*
people
evolution of, **8**/45
study of, **8**/254–261 *(with pictures)*
pepper (spice), **6**/210 *(with picture)*
peppermint (plant), **6**/212 *(with picture)*
perceptual handicap, **15**/229
perch (fish), **5**/68 *(picture)*
percussion instrument (music), **12**/256–259, **12**/268–269 *(with pictures)*
perennial plants, **6**/152–153 *(with pictures)*
perfect number, **13**/37
perfume from plants, **6**/218
period (menstruation), **15**/265–266 *(with pictures)*
perpetual motion, **12**/12–13
Perrault, Charles (author)
Cinderella, **1**/122–129
Perseus (star group), **4**/271 *(picture)*, **4**/272
Persia (ancient kingdom)
Battle of Salamis, **7**/52–55 *(with picture)*
persimmon (tree), **6**/182 *(pictures)*
personality changes of preteen, **15**/86–89

Q

R

S

T

t (letter)
rhyme about, **1**/73
tadpoles, **5**/108 *(picture)*
Tahiti (Asia)
creation story, **8**/33–35 *(with pictures)*
Tai-Chi (Chinese exercise), **8**/271 *(with picture)*
Taiwan (Asia)
holidays and festivals
Dragon Boat Festival, **9**/196–197 *(with picture)*
school, **14**/125 *(picture)*
tsoo, tsoo (game), **8**/130 *(picture)*
woodcarving, **8**/245 *(picture)*
see also **China**
tale, *see* **stories**
Tale of Peter Rabbit, The (story), **1**/192–196
Tales of a Fourth Grade Nothing (story from), **2**/124–138
talking, *see* **speech**
tamarack (tree), **6**/185 *(pictures)*
tambourine (musical instrument), **11**/15 *(with picture)*
tampon, 15/266
Tanabata Matsuri (festival, Japan), **9**/240–241
tanker (ship), **7**/88 *(with picture)*
Tanzania (Africa)
Serengeti Plain, **4**/43 *(picture)*
tapestry, *see* **wallhanging**
tapestry needle, 11/154 *(picture)*
tarpon (fish), **5**/76
taste, sense of, 14/89
tattoo (skin decoration)
Berber (people), **8**/248 *(with picture)*
Toda (people), **8**/251 *(picture)*
tawny frogmouth (bird), **5**/146 *(picture),* **5**/152–153
Taxco (Mexico), **10**/239 *(with pictures)*
Taylor, Jane (poet)
Little Pussy, **1**/266

Taylor, Jane *(continued)*
Star, The, **1**/237
Td (shot)
tetanus, **15**/304
tea (food), **8**/91
Teach, Edward (pirate), **7**/71–72, **10**/191 *(with picture)*
teacher
poem about, **2**/74
Teach Us, Amelia Bedelia (story), **2**/102–117
tears, 15/301–302
cleaning eyes, **14**/75, **15**/235
eye health, **15**/235–236
see also **crying**
Teasdale, Sara (poet)
Falling Star, The, **2**/235
Night, **2**/235, **6**/264
teeth, *see* **tooth**
teething, 15/23, **15**/302–303
telephone, 12/236–237 *(with pictures)*
and laser, **12**/203
Telephone (game), **11**/308
telephone, string, 11/16 *(with picture)*
project, **12**/246–247
telephone booths, 8/197 *(pictures)*
telephone switchboard (toy), **11**/20 *(with picture)*
telescope, 12/178 *(with picture)*
radio, **4**/283 *(picture),* **4**/320
spyglass, **7**/65 *(picture)*
use of, **4**/320 *(with picture)*
television, 8/199 *(with pictures)*
and children, **15**/110–113
and laser, **12**/203
and light, **12**/208–209 *(with picture)*
Tell, William (Swiss hero), **10**/178 *(with pictures)*
tempera paint, 11/66 *(with picture)*
temperature, 13/153, **13**/208–209 *(with pictures)*
highest recorded, **4**/47
lowest recorded, **4**/51
of sun, **4**/208
temperature, body
amphibians, **5**/106–107 *(with pictures)*

temperature, body *(continued)*
human, **14**/24
fever, **15**/238–240 *(with picture)*
mammals, **5**/28
reptiles, **5**/96–97 *(with pictures)*
sensing, **5**/186–187
temper tantrums, 15/45–46
temple
Abu Simbel (Egypt), **10**/195 *(with pictures)*
Bahá'í House of Worship (Illinois), **10**/72 *(with picture)*
Borobudur (Indonesia), **10**/107 *(with pictures)*
Buddhist, **8**/173 *(with pictures)*
Hindu (India), **10**/64
Horyu-ji (Japan), **10**/97 *(with picture)*
Indian (Mexico), **8**/164 *(picture)*
in Jerusalem, **10**/68 *(with picture)*
Jewish, **8**/169 *with picture*
of Artemis (Turkey), **10**/8 *(with picture)*
Pantheon (Rome), **10**/228 *(with pictures)*
Parthenon (Greece), **10**/105 *(with picture)*
see also **church; mosque; shrine**
ten (number), **13**/45 *(with picture),* **13**/52–54 *(with pictures)*
ancient Egyptian, **13**/70 *(with pictures)*
ancient numerals, **13**/72–73 *(pictures)*
in base two, **13**/85
in other languages, **13**/80–83
Roman numeral, **13**/75 *(with pictures)*
tendon (part of body), **14**/34 *(with picture),* **14**/54 *(with pictures)*
strain, **15**/297
tendril (plant part), **6**/44, **6**/101
tennis racket cover, 11/226 *(with picture)*
Tennyson, Alfred (poet)
Follow the Gleam, **3**/297
In Memoriam, **9**/34
tent, 11/20 *(with picture)*
Bedouin, **8**/104–105 *with picture*
Mongolian yurt, **8**/106 *with pictures*

X

Z